NetPolicy.Com

NetPolicy.Com

Public Agenda for a Digital World

Leslie David Simon

W *Published by The Woodrow Wilson Center Press*
Distributed by The Johns Hopkins University Press

EDITORIAL OFFICES

The Woodrow Wilson Center Press
One Woodrow Wilson Plaza
1300 Pennsylvania Avenue, N.W.
Washington, D.C. 20004-3027
Telephone 202-691-4010
www.wilsoncenter.org

ORDER FROM

The Johns Hopkins University Press
P.O. Box 50370
Baltimore, Maryland 21211
Telephone 1-800-537-5487
www.press.jhu.edu

2 4 6 8 9 7 5 3 1

Library of Congress Cataloging-in-Publication Data applied for

ISBN 1-930365-02-0 hardcover; 1-930365-03-9 paperback

ABOUT THE CENTER

The Center is the living memorial of the United States of America to the nation's twenty-eighth president, Woodrow Wilson. Congress established the Woodrow Wilson Center in 1968 as an international institute for advanced study, "symbolizing and strengthening the fruitful relationship between the world of learning and the world of public affairs." The Center opened in 1970 under its own board of trustees.

In all its activities the Woodrow Wilson Center is a nonprofit, nonpartisan organization, supported financially by annual appropriations from the Congress, and by the contributions of foundations, corporations, and individuals. Conclusions or opinions expressed in Center publications and programs are those of the authors and speakers and do not necessarily reflect the views of the Center staff, fellows, trustees, advisory groups, or any individuals or organizations that provide financial support to the Center.

*For Ruth, and for our grandchildren,
Rachel, Rebecca, and Benjamin, and all the
children of the next generation*

Contents

For I had dipped into the future, far as human eye could see,
Saw the vision of the world, and all the wonders that would be.

—Alfred Lord Tennyson, "Locksley Hall"

Between the idea and the reality,
Between the notion and the act
Falls the shadow.

—T. S. Eliot, "The Hollow Men"

Preface

This book is a survey of public policy issues in the digital age. It defines the broad phenomenon of the "Net," describes its properties, examines its impact on our social and economic institutions, and discusses the public policy issues that all of these items raise in the United States and around the world. It is intended not only to provide a comprehensive overview for the general reader, but also to offer suggestions for the government and private-sector officials around the world who are wrestling with this profound revolution in trying to create public policies.

For me, the story began in 1966. That year, the Federal Communications Commission (FCC) started an obscure proceeding that came to be called "Computer Inquiry I." A few years earlier, computer users had begun to connect their mainframes to the telephone network so that data could be transmitted from one computer to another. Since the telephone system was regulated and the computer industry was not, the FCC wanted to understand the physical and therefore the legal boundaries between the two, which were connected literally by a twisted pair of copper wires and a plug in the wall. From this humble technological and regulatory beginning a third of a century ago arose the powerful phenomenon of convergence, the explosion of the Internet and electronic commerce, and an international storm of regulatory and government policy debates. These phenomena have created a hurricane that blows across the Atlantic and the Pacific like a technological El Niño, threatening years of economic, social, and technology policies in both industrial and developing countries, challenging established institutions and industries, but also offering a bounty of new jobs, social services, and economic opportunities to those willing to make the necessary changes.

In that same year, 1966, I left the American Telephone and Telegraph Company (AT&T) to join the International Business Machines Corporation (IBM). I had been working on FCC matters at AT&T headquarters in New York and had just written a book for the managers of what was then the Bell System. The book was called *Business Information Systems* and dealt with the new uses of computers in business organizations and their centrality to Bell operations. An opportunity had come along at IBM's headquarters in Armonk, New York, and I soon found myself working on some of the same issues I had been working on at AT&T, but from the unregulated side of the looking glass. Telecommunications policy, privacy and data security, research and development policy, and matters such as intellectual property rights, international trade, and investment were just a few of the issues I found myself working on over the next thirty years, at IBM headquarters, in Washington, D.C., as IBM's lobbyist on these issues, and in Paris, France, as vice president for government affairs at IBM's headquarters for Europe, the Middle East, and Africa.

By 1998, these issues had stormed the walls of governments around the world and were crowding out more traditional concerns. Terms like "cyberspace" and "convergence" appeared in the press every day, electronic commerce was exploding throughout the economy, Internet stocks were the hottest things on Wall Street, and governments felt compelled to devote more time than ever to the issues related to these new technologies. I had personally spent much of my time from 1992 to 1998 visiting governments around the world, from Beijing to Pretoria and from Brazil to Brussels. My task was to explain the significance of these phenomena for these countries' industries, their educational and health care systems, and their government services. I urged them to examine the public policies that would need to be changed if they were to exploit the best and avoid the worst in this cyberspace revolution. I was also busy lobbying the executive branch in Washington and members of Congress on their public policy concerns—telecommunications deregulation, copyright law, federal funding for advanced computer and communications research, and electronic commerce policy in general.

Two things struck me about government reactions almost everywhere: First, the overwhelming majority of high-level elected officials and civil servants accepted the economic significance of the powerful new information revolution and the potential benefits it offered to their countries. They recognized the adverse affects their nations might suffer if they did not fully participate. Second, most were all but overwhelmed by the complexity of the subject and the speed with which the information hurricane was moving. Although they reached broad agreement on basic principles, governments seemed unable to keep pace with specific policies. Organized around late-nineteenth and early-twentieth-century concerns ranging from cumbersome systems for regulating monopolies to notions of property based on the physical world, governments were slow to act.

This observation was the original catalyst for this book. I submitted my plan to write a survey of the field to the Woodrow Wilson International Center for Scholars in Washington, D.C. The center is a place where academicians, government officials, and others come together to think and write about critical international subjects. My proposal aligned well with the Wilson Center's determination to look ahead to the twenty-first century and the new issues it would present. I became a Public Policy Scholar at the center in June 1998.

One of the first questions I dealt with was the difficulty of making policy for the "wired" age. Was this process more difficult than that for previous technological developments or shifts in major institutions? How did it compare, for example, to the new policies that accompanied the petroleum age? Was the difficulty due just to the speed with which cyberspace was developing, or were there other factors that made policy making more difficult now? For example, did the global nature of cyberspace hinder policy development? Or did the fact that the digital world lacked physical forms such as land or minerals or manufactured items make its policy framework more complex?

A second question dealt with the economics of cyberspace. Governments seemed to accept the assertion that electronic commerce offered a harvest of economic benefits, including economic growth, improved competitiveness, and good new jobs. This outlook was a turnaround from the views that held sway from the 1960s to the 1980s in many countries: that information technology would cause massive unemployment. By the 1990s most policy makers had forgotten that President John F. Kennedy had once said that automation and unemployment would be the greatest challenges facing the United States. Now, with the exception of a few affected groups such as unionized telecommunications workers, little or no protest was left. And yet annoying questions remained. In a major policy speech in 1996, even the chairman of the Federal Reserve Board, Alan Greenspan, expressed great concern that the new computing and communications technologies were not contributing to productivity improvements. Research since then by the government and a number of scholars has helped to resolve this issue, but not yet definitively.

Even more difficult to ascertain has been the social impact of the cyberspace revolution. Despite the raging debate about information "haves" and "have-nots," not enough is known about the effect of the differences in access to the Internet that now exist worldwide. Nor is there a great deal of understanding about the social impact of the global availability of content, some of which conflicts with national norms. The issues raised in this arena range from almost universal concerns about pornography to narrower national fears of cultural invasion by the English language, to anger over racism or hate speech. Are there standards by which we can measure the social impact of cyberspace?

Another area that raised my curiosity was the concept of "convergence." Initially used to refer to the apparent merging of computing with telecommunications, the term had been broadened to refer to the merging of much of our computer, software, consumer electronics, telephone, cellular, broadcasting, and even content industries (an example of the latter being films and recording). The more I examined the issue, however, the more I became convinced that the notion of convergence had much wider implications. Fields from banking to insurance, and from utilities to transportation were being sucked into the black hole of cyberspace. As more and more of the fundamental activities of the banking industry, for example, became digitized, the more banking became part of cyberspace. As the vice chairman of one of the nation's largest banks told me, the competitor he was most worried about was no longer another large bank or other financial institution—it was Microsoft.

The borderless nature of cyberspace also raised intriguing questions. With the transparency of political and economic borders within and between countries raised almost to infinity by the Internet, could the policy questions related to it be resolved satisfactorily by nation-states or their subdivisions, or would digital policy questions all demand international solutions? If so are existing bodies, such as the World Trade Organization, the Organization for Economic Cooperation and Development, or the United Nations, competent to tackle such issues, and are the existing rules of the road sufficient? Or will the world community have to invent new organizations and rules, much as it did for the advent of telegraphy and telephony with the International Telecommunications Union?

A related and even more complex question was the ultimate impact of cyberspace on the power and role of the nation-state itself, as well as of its subdivisions. Already under fire from local and regional ethnic movements, as outlined in Senator Daniel Patrick Moynihan's book *Pandaemonium*,[1] and under economic pressure from globalization, the nation-state in the early twenty-first century would also have to deal with cyberspace and its ability to empower marginal groups. Groups ranging from the Chiapatistas in Mexico to the Chinese community in Indonesia to militia groups in the United States had used the reach of the Internet to proclaim their once-obscure causes. One week before the tenth anniversary of its military crackdown in Tiananmen Square, the Chinese government in June 1999 shut down one of the country's most popular Web sites, out of fear that people would read antigovernment messages there.

Yet another key issue was the respective roles of government and the private sector in regulating cyberspace. Like two aging sumo wrestlers circling the ring warily, government and the private sector seemed unwilling to assume roles that were different from past experience. The American government, and other national governments to some extent, granted that the lead in cyberspace belonged to industry, recognizing that the old regulatory concepts were doomed in the face of the technology juggernaut. Thus, the U.S. government turned to the private sector to protect privacy and to exercise restraint over content. Industry, on the other hand, needed government to establish predictable rules in areas such as taxation and intellectual property. Although governments made some progress in those arenas, the regulatory forces in areas like telecommunications fought back, slowing progress. The old boundaries were fading, but they were not all dead.

Finally, although nations (and individual states in the United States) were moving quickly to "wire" themselves, few yardsticks were available to benchmark their progress or lack thereof. How did a country know where it stood on the cyberspace scale, or if it and its citizens and institutions were ready to enter the age of electronic commerce? These variables depended not only on the physical infrastructure in the country, as important as that was, but also on the educational system, from primary levels to continuing technical training, and also on many other factors, such as use by the government itself of electronic commerce.

My research yielded another important result: it convinced me that these questions were all critical and would have defining importance for our future social, political, and economic structures. It was a book I had not read in many years that convinced me of this—Daniel Bell's 1973 work, *The Coming of Post-Industrial Society.*[2] Bell had written, "If capital and labor are the major structural features of industrial society, information and knowledge are those of the post-industrial society." These words had been sharply attacked at the time by Soviet theorists, who greatly feared that the idea of an information society would make Marxism irrelevant. Unfortunately for them, they were right. Their society crumbled less than two decades later, and the pieces have still not been put back together. With their example freshly in view, we have more than ample warning that we need to discard nineteenth- and even twentieth-century notions and replace them with new policies and new institutions, some building on the old, some radically different.

As I reviewed the literature, I also realized that it would be useful to introduce readers of the book to the "cyber-gurus" and technical experts who had already produced an extensive literature about the impact of the Internet. Esther Dyson, Regis McKenna, Michael Dertouzos, Don Tapscott, and Nicholas Negroponte all taught me a great deal about the overall topic. Writers such as Alan Westin, Michael Godwin, and David Osborne also contributed to my understanding of specific issues such as privacy, free speech, and the role of the Net in government services.

Thus, this book became a survey of the field for all those who want an understanding of how our society and our institutions will be increasingly shaped by the global digital revolution, and how we can use public policy to guide this metamorphosis in benign directions. It is organized into three parts, divided into fourteen chapters.

The chapters of Part I explain the topics and technologies of the Net. Chapter 1 provides some definitions needed to understand the digital age, along with a brief history of the Internet and the relevant information technologies. It also provides some quantification of the current size and scope of cyberspace, as well as the speed with which it is developing. Chapter 2 deals with the properties of the Net and its broad underlying themes and issues. Among these are the separation of the digital world from the physical world; the hurricane force of the Internet's growth; the implications of the borderless nature of electronic commerce; and the shift in power between the private and public sectors. This chapter also discusses the current economic underpinnings of cyberspace, the empowerment of fringe cultures, new measures of competitive advantage, and the phenomenon of megaconvergence, or the melding of many institutions into cyberspace.

Chapter 3 details the impact of megaconvergence on our public-sector activities and looks at the social services, including government; elementary, secondary, and higher education; health care; and criminal justice. Chapter 4 looks at megaconvergence in the worlds of finance and commerce. It deals with financial services including banking, securities, and insurance and other industries including retail, distribution, travel, manufacturing, communications, and utilities.

Part II introduces the public policy issues that governments are facing and will have to face in the years ahead. Chapter 5 covers the essentials of digital democracy—individual privacy, free speech and content regulation, and universal access, or assuring everyone's ability to use electronic commerce. Chapter 6 covers digital economics and the issues of economic growth, productivity and employment, the taxation of digital transactions, international trade and investment matters, and antitrust and competition policy. Chapter 7 discusses the technical regulatory issues that will govern the physical growth of the "global information infrastructure," including telecommunications deregulation and privatization, Internet security, and especially cryptography and standards. Chapter 8 deals with the legal issues of cyberspace, particularly the legal framework around digital contracts and signatures, consumer protection laws, and intellectual property rights. Chapter 9 discusses research and development policies and the national interest as they relate to the Net.

Part III brings us to the critical issue of governance—that is, how governments and other organizations are managing the issues raised in Part II. Chapter 10 serves as a guide to government activities in the United States on this subject, including the federal government and its agencies, Congress, and state governments. Chapter 11 does the same for governments around the world, focusing on the European Union and its member nations, Canada, Finland, India, Japan, Korea, Singapore, Malaysia, China, Brazil, and certain countries in Africa and the Middle East. Chapter 12 examines the various international organizations that are active in the field of electronic commerce, including the World Trade Organization, the Organization for Economic Cooperation and Development, the World Intellectual Property Organization, the United Nations Conference on International Trade Law, the Asia-Pacific Economic Cooperation group, and the International Telecommunications Union. And Chapter 13 focuses on organizations in the private sector that are involved in the field, including those in the business community and in academe. Business groups include trade associations such as the International Information Industry Congress; the Information Technology Industry Council, the Computer Systems Policy Project, the U.S. Council on International Business, the Online Privacy Alliance, and others. On the academic side, groups include the Harvard University Program on Information Infrastructure, the Progress and Freedom Foundation, and the Global Information Infrastructure Commission.

The conclusion looks to the future. It sets out a plan for determining which are the most critical issues and how they should be dealt with. It asks if our current governmental and especially our international organizations can deal with the issues, and if not, how they need to be fixed. Finally, it asks how we will know how well or poorly we are doing and what guideposts and measurements we might use for measuring our progress.

I want to offer a great deal of thanks to the many institutions and people who helped me prepare this book. First, and foremost, my best helper by far was the Net itself. Of course, researchers all over the world are using cyberspace resources, but my subject particularly lent itself to Web research. Many of the sites I used are cited in the endnotes; the Web sites on this subject set up by governments, especially the U.S. government and the European Union, were especially helpful, as were the Net-related news sites of Internet portals and search engines such as Excite. A number of key university sites, such as that of Harvard's Information Infrastructure Project, with their links to other sources, were particularly helpful.

I would also like to thank the Woodrow Wilson Center and its staff, including such fine scholars and professionals as Dean Anderson, Rob Litwak, Kent Hughes, Joe Brinley, and others who have encouraged me and made my stay so productive, including my three researchers, Lisa Flanagan, Ezana Woldegeorgise, and Flor Barajas, and my copy editor, Traci Nagle. I especially want to thank the IBM Corporation for a challenging career that allowed me to be both an observer and a participant in this marvelous digital revolution. Among the many IBM people to whom I am indebted are Bill Ewald, Chuck Francis, Jane Cahill Pfeiffer, Chuck McKittrick, Lew Branscomb, David Grove, and Terry Lautenbach. Other individuals in Washington who played a role in the ideas for this book were Ken Kay at the Computer Systems Policy Project, Rhett Dawson at the Information Technology Industry Council, key government officials such as Tom Kalil and Mike Nelson at the White House and Don Abelson at the office of the U.S. Trade Representative, and my friend, public affairs consultant Norman Gelman.

Most of all, I want to thank my wife, Ruth, who patiently listened to hours and hours of the material in this book before it ever hit the keyboard. Her sense of the world always brings me back down to earth. She is my ultimate reality check. Our three wonderful sons, Bruce, Josh and Gregg, also endured years of discussions on these subjects and deserve my thanks.

One final thought: Eventually the impact of the digital age will be measured by its social impact, by how it affects the way all of us live, every day. In the midst of my research, at the end of 1998, I noted that we were celebrating the fiftieth anniversary of the Universal Declaration of Human Rights. As I read through the document, with its thirty articles drawn heavily from the French Declaration of Human Rights and the American Declaration of Independence and Bill of Rights, I was struck by how many of the articles were directly relevant to the issues of cyberspace: privacy, security, property ownership, freedom of expression, equal access to government services, protection of intellectual property, and freedom to "seek, receive and impart information and ideas through any media and regardless of frontiers." The global leadership of the United States in securing and expanding these rights is certainly a key reason for U.S. dominance in the development of a digital world. Nations that fail to embrace these democratic principles will fall further behind not only in the digital revolution, but in virtually every other field as well.

My hope is that this comprehensive view of the worldwide policy implications of the digital revolution will help not only the policy makers but also those whose businesses and professional lives are being radically changed by the new information storm. As citizens, as workers, as parents and students, and as participants in the worlds of culture and society, all of us have an obligation to understand these changes and our role in harnessing them for the common good.

I

The Net and Its Impact

1

The Net Defined

There will be no book left unprinted and no man who will not learn.
—From a Korean book printed in 1437 after the invention of movable type.

Although it had existed unnoticed for two decades as a kind of underground network for scientists and defense researchers, ordinary citizens took little notice of it until 1995. Almost as if an enervating signal had been sent from somewhere, signs of it began to appear everywhere. Cryptic codes were spotted, first in one place, then in another, until they seemed to be everywhere: on a television commercial, http://kodak.com; in a university catalog, http://www.yale.edu; at the end of a government document, www.whitehouse.gov.

In a society attuned to conspiracy theories and devoted to television series like *The X-Files,* it might easily have been viewed as something sinister, like gang signs or the marks that spies might leave on a building or other public spot. But it wasn't. It entered the popular culture in the most benign ways, and the population seemed to have been lulled into compliance. Companies that embraced it had trendy names like Yahoo, Amazon, Excite, DoubleClick, and eBay. The *New Yorker* ran cartoons about it. One showed two dogs at a computer screen, one telling the other, "On the Internet, no one knows you're a dog." Another showed a group of elderly farmers lazing in front of an old country store with the name "Countrystore.com" painted across the window. It even engendered romance: A third cartoon showed two lovers in a café, looking blissfully at each other, as the young man says, "Ellen, we were made for each other. I'm a software developer and you're a content provider."

Almost overnight, ordinary people began to alter the habits of a lifetime in going about their normal business. Planning a vacation, a family might no longer go to a travel agent or even call an airline. Instead, the parents would consult their computer screen, looking at hilton.com, usair.com, and arizona.gov or one of thousands of other sites to make hotel or plane reservations or learn about tourist destinations. Or instead of consulting their stockbroker or banker, they might use schwab.com or e*trade.com to make a securities trade or mortgage.com to find a home loan.

Automobile sales techniques were quickly altered. With a click of a mouse button, a prospective buyer, consulting edmunds.com or carprices. com could look at every new feature of every new car model, retrieve not only retail prices but also the dealer's cost and any special incentives to dealers from the factory. With a few more clicks, the sales prospect could also look at the retail and wholesale prices for his or her used car and get comparative rates for both auto loans and insurance policies from different banks, finance companies, and insurers. If that weren't enough, the buyer could also look at a state Web site like florida.gov to see registration, inspection, and sales tax requirements. If the buyer decided to purchase a particular vehicle, another click would bring him or her price offers from three or more nearby dealers, much like an old-time auction.

At the same time, huge changes were creeping into people's professional and business lives. Although many people had been communicating within their companies with E-mail for a decade, suddenly they could also communicate with outsiders—customers, suppliers, dealers, government regulators and others. Businesses began to do their purchasing online, offering suppliers the chance to bid on contracts in cyberspace.

Health care workers began to retrieve patient information and clinical data from community networks using the Internet. Even patients could look at sites like jama.org or neurosurgery.com for health information ranging from the latest studies on different prostate treatments to mortality statistics on open-heart surgery. As a result, physicians soon found themselves facing patients armed with the latest article from the *New England Journal of Medicine* or with detailed information on mitral-valve surgery from the National Library of Medicine or the Mayo Clinic.

Government administrators explored how to provide government benefits, such as food stamps and welfare payments, electronically, a great potential benefit to the poor, who formerly had lacked access to all banking services and typically cashed welfare checks at exorbitantly expensive storefront check-cashing services. Governments at all levels also scrambled to make information and services available over the World Wide Web. Some states, such as California, experimented with multilingual electronic kiosks. Placed in public spaces, these kiosks provided services in the areas of public education and employment. States' elaborate and competitive economic development agencies learned that the Internet was a wonderful way to sell their cities and towns as potential locations to investors and businesses around the world.

Similarly, education, which was in great need of comprehensive and even revolutionary reform, began to change. Universities, whose research departments had pioneered the technologies underlying the Internet, moved most quickly. Within a few years, term papers and projects began to be submitted on-line. College applicants could look at sites like stanford.edu or michigan.edu and increasingly even apply for admission on-line. Parents and even grandparents could keep in touch with their far-away children and grandchildren through E-mail. Students could photograph new roommates and friends with digital cameras and send pictures to parents instantly. Experiments that began in elementary and secondary schools across the country had the potential to revolutionize school practices dating back hundreds of years and based on the needs of pre-industrial societies. Teams of students began to do assignments around locally networked computers, replacing the old, rigid, hierarchical system where the teacher stood at the front of the room. Other experiments permitted parents access to student records and work on the Internet, or provided much-needed teacher-training materials in the same way. Mathematics teachers in Chicago could and did compare teaching methods and student work with teachers in Frankfurt, Germany, or Lyon, France.

As if this weren't enough, the Internet cornucopia overflowed when it came to Wall Street. Technology stocks soared, plunged, and soared again. Firms like America Online, Cisco Systems, Dell, Microsoft, Yahoo, and the thousands of other semiconductor, hardware, software, telecommunications, and other companies that supported the Internet delivered astounding financial returns to their investors. Technology fueled the general Wall Street boom, which in turn sparked consumer spending, government surpluses, burgeoning retirement plans, and a new national pastime of following business and stock-market news that heretofore had been buried in the back of most newspapers. Few people didn't know how many billions of dollars had been earned by Bill Gates or Steve Case (the chairmen of Microsoft and America Online, respectively) or didn't check often—on the Internet—the values of their own retirement investments.

As this quiet revolution got under way in 1995 and 1996, there were few sounds of discontent. In the business community, the greatest concerns focused on which companies and industries were threatened by the new technology. Talk arose of "disintermediation," or the ability of electronic commerce to do away with some traditional businesses or parts of the central activities of others. Among the early worriers were travel agents fearful of losing their franchises to Internet travel sites, brokerage houses worried about losing large commissions, and realtors who nervously recognized that searching for a new home in the calm privacy of one's living room might be preferable to using the services of a real estate broker. Suddenly a couple nearing retirement could sit in their kitchen in Rochester or Cincinnati on a snowy January day and browse full-color displays of homes for sale in Boca Raton or Tucson. The displays they saw were replete with floor plans, photos of every room and feature, and all the pertinent information, from property taxes to square footage.

More important, the strategic thinkers at every business and organization were beginning to realize that the digital revolution would soon change virtually every institution in modern life and that they would have to keep ahead of this curve. The alternatives were either to be buried by the competition or, in the case of government officials, to be voted out of office for providing outdated services. Who, for example, would want to buy insurance from a company whose office they would have to visit during working hours to fill out forms when they could buy from a company that offered the same service on the Internet twenty-four hours a day, seven days a week ("24/7" in Web parlance) and accessible anywhere? Why should a citizen ever again have to stand in a long line in a crowded motor-vehicle bureau office ten miles from her home or office during work hours to register a car when she could complete the same task over the Internet from home? Who would choose to attend a university that was not equipped with up-to-the-minute technology?

At the same time, governments were beginning to see the digital phenomenon as two sides of a coin. On the one hand, the Internet and its applications could bring new jobs, economic growth, and a toughened national competitiveness. Politicians and government officials alike wanted to create public policy that would pave the way for the new technologies to take hold. They began to talk about new laws to legalize electronic contracts and signatures and to update copyright laws to protect works on the Internet. They passed new laws intended to deregulate telecommunications and stimulate innovation in the new advanced communications technologies.

Yet politicians were also beginning to hear early but loud grumbles of discontent from constituents. Parents and teachers were expressing concern about the amount of pornography easily available to children on the Internet. Cases of electronic stalking by child molesters were highly publicized, and the Oklahoma City bombing in 1996 put the spotlight on the use of the Internet by militias and hate groups. Even worse, the killings at Columbine High School in Colorado in the spring of 1999 made many people aware of the violent content available to anyone on the Internet. In more authoritarian countries around the world, governments attempted to regulate the content that they viewed as objectionable, such as political or religious material. Some actually criminalized unauthorized use of the Internet. Others, like France and Canada, fretted about the apparent dominance of the English language in cyberspace.

Meanwhile, the issue of privacy took on a growing urgency as a number of cases involving invasion of privacy either by government or by the private sector hit the country's newspapers and television shows. In one case, a corporation's Web site offered children the opportunity to play games on the Internet—after the children responded to various questions about their parent's spending habits. In another, a government agency placed individuals' financial information on the Internet—but without adequate privacy safeguards. People also worried about the security of credit card or other information sent on the Internet, and law-enforcement officials worried about sophisticated criminals and terrorists able to use these new advanced technologies to conceal their activities.

Some were also growing increasingly concerned about whether every citizen—rich or poor—would be able to share in the benefits of the new technologies. It was reported that of Microsoft's 30,000 employees, 10,000 had become millionaires thanks to stock options. Towns like Palo Alto, California, were awash in money. At the same time, rural and remote regions and states such as Alaska began to worry about the costs of connecting to the Internet. School boards and hospital managements wrestling with tight budgets asked how they would pay for the new technologies. The government published a report called "The Digital Divide" that showed racial fissures along a digital fault line. Congress skirmished with the administration and the Federal Communications Commission about the use of federal money to support Internet connections for schools.

In the world's developing countries, governments pondered falling further behind in the development race as they watched richer neighbors make large investments in telecommunications and computing infrastructures. Thabo Mbeki, then the deputy president of South Africa, came to the meeting of ministers of the group of seven advanced industrialized nations (G-7) on the global information infrastructure in Brussels in February 1995 to point out that countries like his, which provided even ordinary voice telephone service to only a tiny fraction of their populations, wondered if and how they could afford investments in high-speed Internet services. Other countries, such as Brazil, feared that their own national telecommunications systems would be gobbled up by the more advanced and richer systems and companies of the United States, Europe, or Japan. An official of the Brazilian Ministry of Science and Technology told a group of American, European, and Japanese high-technology executives that to him, telecommunication liberalization meant "Hello, we're here to buy your national telephone company."

Thus, the specter of this new revolution—the digital revolution—began to enter the political and social consciousness of people and political systems around the world. Although governments generally viewed its effects as economically positive and socially benign, they also began to face its potentially dark side. What frightened them the most was the dramatic speed with which it was expanding into every aspect of daily life, casting a fast-moving shadow over many traditional institutions. They feared that governments could not make laws quickly or wisely enough to keep up. The immediate dilemma faced by most people and governments was trying to understand what they were dealing with. What exactly was meant by "information infrastructure" or "Internet" or "electronic commerce"? Where had these phrases come from? And where was it all headed?

A HISTORY OF THE INFORMATION AGE

The Beginnings

The story of the Internet is usually begun with the development of packet switching and the formation of the Advanced Research Projects Agency Network (ARPANET) at the Department of Defense in the 1960s. But to fully comprehend the digital revolution, it is necessary to go back even further, and much farther east, to China in the second century, where the information revolution had its earliest stirrings.[1] It was here that the art of making paper was developed and perfected. Paper was substantially less expensive than the materials it replaced—principally parchment (and the even earlier papyrus)—thus making it possible for many more people to have access to information and for knowledge to be transmitted both geographically and for years into the future. The invention of paper started a centuries-long process of reducing the cost of processing, storing, and transmitting information, eventually making information ubiquitous and knowledge a commodity.

The diffusion of paper manufacturing technology was incredibly slow by today's standards, when a technology such as cable television takes less than a decade to become widely available. In fact, it took roughly a thousand years for paper to be manufactured in Europe, brought there from the Far East by the technologically gifted Arabs after their conquest of the Iberian Peninsula. Paper was also the necessary precursor for the next innovation—the invention of movable type. Once again, a significant breakthrough occurred in China.

Movable type was invented in China in the eleventh century, a few hundred years before Johannes Gutenberg was born in Mainz. Originally produced from clay, movable type slowly improved; the Koreans were using type cast from metal by the fifteenth century. But despite the invention of both paper and movable type, China and Korea did not experience the revolutionary effects that were to be seen later in Europe beginning with Gutenberg. Although it appears those earlier societies did recognize how the new inventions could greatly improve the dissemination of knowledge, they were nevertheless not broadly used. Some believe that the technology was just not good enough. Others think that those old and static societies had neither the will nor the means to harness change. Still others think that the mandarin classes did not want to see knowledge available to large numbers of people, since the effect would simply be to undercut their own authority and encourage revolution. If the mandarins did believe this, they were right.

Much has already been written about the impact on Western civilization of Gutenberg's "invention," or more properly, his introduction of movable type around 1450. Certainly the democratization of knowledge—its spread throughout Europe regardless of geography or class—set in motion events that changed the world:

1. The rise of capitalism and a modern banking system, which depended on laws, accounting systems, and means of communications made possible by printing. One outgrowth was the development of printed money, which would itself be challenged later by electronics.
2. The Reformation, as printed Bibles and religious literature drained the Church's monopoly on knowledge and undercut its authority, making religion less mysterious and more accessible to ordinary people.
3. The acceleration of scientific inquiry and technological development, as educated people across Europe gained access to the latest scientific discoveries and information.
4. The development of national languages and literatures, since the cost of publishing materials in local languages was greatly reduced.

5. The modern notion of education, or the idea that children should be educated in institutions and learn reading and writing, as well as be taught domestic skills and trades in the home or on the farm.
6. The notion of copyright and the understanding that an author's works were valuable in the same way that a silversmith's or blacksmith's creations were in providing them a living.

As these cataclysmic changes took place, the boost that printing gave to new ideas did not go unnoticed by those most placed in jeopardy. The Church in Rome and royal families in a number of countries, including England and France, moved to control the spread of new technologies by censorship and licensing of the right to print. Those who attempted to print materials without a license were severely punished. The "Royal Stationer," a seemingly quaint name conjuring images of a bespectacled Benjamin Franklin–like printer producing personal greeting cards, was originally not merely a monopoly on printing but also the chief censor, with broad police powers. Sixteenth-century Europe was not twelfth-century China, however, but a fertile ground for the vast social and economic changes that the invention and use of printing helped unleash. The earliest phase of the information revolution was well under way.

Industrialization and Information

If the printing press was a key stimulus for the growth of capitalism and the rise of scientific research, it also set in motion the seeds of the Industrial Revolution. In its turn, the Industrial Revolution would set the stage for the digital revolution that would usher in the twenty-first century.

Just as cheap paper and the printing press had greatly reduced the cost of knowledge dissemination, the demand for even faster ways of manipulating data and transmitting information grew rapidly with the advent of industry in the eighteenth and nineteenth centuries. Larger trading and manufacturing companies spread across national boundaries. They needed to keep timely accounts and communicate information over large distances. The national post offices developing in Europe and in the United States relied first on horse-drawn coaches and sailing ships, and later on steamships and railroads to receive and deliver messages.

By 1830, the U.S. postal system was especially well developed, employing more than three-quarters of all federal employees and delivering in that year almost fourteen million letters and sixteen million copies of newspapers. As Richard John documents in his book *Spreading the*

News: The American Postal System from Franklin to Morse, the U.S. postal system played a key role in the development of the vast new nation, while Europe's systems lagged behind.[2] For the large new banking houses and for governments, however, the postal system was too slow and too insecure for many tasks. They developed their own communications systems, often involving secret codes and ciphers, another advance that would have significant implications for the digital age.

In a parallel development, by the eighteenth century, early devices for manipulating data and making calculations, also necessary to the new growing industries, had been developed. The 5,000-year-old abacus, used by the Chinese and the Romans, consisted of stones or pieces of ivory mounted on rods to represent numbers. By the mid-seventeenth century, its principles had been converted into early mechanical calculators by mathematicians such as Blaise Pascal and Gottfried von Leibniz. In the 1830s, Charles Babbage conceived his Analytical Engine, a steam-powered device with more than 50,000 components. Using perforated cards for both processing and memory, the engine's design foreshadowed the modern computer.

Another major breakthrough occurred in 1889 when a U.S. Census Bureau employee named Herman Hollerith took the concept a step further by using punched cards to store data, like those the French weaver Joseph-Marie Jacquard had used to control his mechanical looms in the earlier part of the century. Hollerith patented his invention and founded the Tabulating Machine Company, which later evolved into the International Business Machines (IBM) Corporation. When used together with printing devices, these card-reading and sorting machines could keep track of numerous complex banking or business transactions or make difficult scientific calculations.

In parallel, advances in such technologies as metallurgy, hydrodynamics, and fuels led to the developments of the steam engine, the railroad, and the steamship, and industrial machinery such as the engine lathe, the milling machine, mining tools, and powered agricultural tools. These new technologies would culminate in the internal combustion engine, which fundamentally changed the modern world. The invention of the internal combustion engine led to the rapid development of the petroleum industry, which has become one of the world's most important and strategic industries—and has posed difficult public-policy problems with broad international overtones.

Distance continued to be the major problem for the dissemination of information into the nineteenth century, however, and although the new canals, toll roads, and steamships of the early part of the century had sped communications somewhat, information still traveled slowly—generally at less than twenty miles per hour. Without some way to free information from its physical form, the speed of its transmission would always be limited.

The answer came initially from Samuel Morse in 1844 in the form of the telegraph, a device that used a code made of electrical pulses to send information virtually at the speed of light over a copper wire. Now, business information, and perhaps more important for the time, government messages, could be sent almost instantaneously. Among the telegraph's drawbacks, however, were the high cost of stringing copper wires across entire countries and the need to rely on a cadre of trained telegraphers to transmit and receive messages.

At least one of these disadvantages was eliminated shortly thereafter by Alexander Graham Bell's invention of the telephone in 1876. With the telephone, Morse code and telegraph clerks could be bypassed and the sound of one's voice could travel at the speed of light using analog signals, or sound waves converted into electrical signals. In 1877, Bell established the Bell Telephone Company and within a few decades, coast-to-coast telephone calls were possible in the United States. By 1927, the first transatlantic radio telephone service from New York to London was operational. Later, in 1956, cable was laid under the Atlantic Ocean and Europeans and Americans were able to speak to each other clearly and relatively inexpensively. The first communications satellite, Telstar, followed in 1962. Before long, the entire world was wired for telephony, but communication was still tethered for the most part by fragile and expensive wires.

Just as significant for the coming digital age, the telephone industry spawned a global regulatory web involving thousands of jurisdictions. Treated as a monopoly service, telephony in the United States became essentially a single corporate entity by 1913: the Bell Telephone System, regulated by both federal and state governments and in some instances, by city governments. Around the world, most countries treated the telephone and telegraph system as an extension of their postal monopolies, with national "PTTs" holding monopoly ownership of telephone and telegraph services. Thus, in most countries, a shared culture was nurtured and grew between the regulators and the political systems, on the one hand, and the managers and employees of the private and public telephone systems, on the other. This culture linked the national interest with the telephony institutions under the comforting umbrella of government ownership or regulation.

In the United States, the Bell Telephone System eventually grew to more than a million employees, all immersed in the doctrine of public service until the Bell system's breakup in a consent decree with the U.S. Department of Justice announced in 1982. As early as 1865, this culture had also begun to become international when the International Telegraph Union was founded to facilitate a global telegraph system. Later, as the International Telecommunications Union (ITU), this organization expanded its activities into telephony and eventually into wireless services as well. Whether it should exercise any control over the Internet would become an issue in the late 1990s.

It was left to Guglielmo Marconi in 1897 to round out the telecommunications portion of the Industrial Revolution with the invention of wireless telegraphy. Marconi helped usher in the twentieth century with a wireless transatlantic telegraph connection in 1901; the next few decades saw the rapid development of the new technology of electronics, which quickly spawned the broadcast radio and television industries. Over the course of the next century, modern telephony, radio and television broadcasting, and other advances such as radar, satellite and microwave transmission, cable television, and cellular telephony came rapidly into use. In each case, information took on the form of energy to move at the speed of light from its source to its destination, where it reconstituted itself in a form comprehensible to the receiver. With the maturing of electronics after World War II, the stage was set for the flowering of the information revolution in the 1970s.

The Information Revolution

If capital and labor are the major structural features of industrial society, information and knowledge are those of the post-industrial society.
        —Daniel Bell, *The Coming of Post-Industrial Society*[3]

Perhaps the best and one of the earliest chroniclers of what would be called the information revolution was Daniel Bell, a professor of social science at Harvard University. His 1973 book, *The Coming of Post-Industrial Society,* foresaw many of the changes that would later be greatly accelerated by the Internet and electronic commerce. Bell recognized that the nonphysical phenomenon of information was taking center stage in the world's economy. His forecast that information and knowledge would be the central components of the new postindustrial society, replacing labor and capital and therefore ending the age-old conflict between them, was derided by the

Soviets, then at their peak. After all, where would Marxism be without class warfare? In a sense, the Marxists were right. Communism would be doomed if capital and labor lost their preeminent position. They did, and it was. Less than twenty years after Bell's book was published, the Soviet empire collapsed. One of the main reasons was glasnost, the former Soviet president Mikhail Gorbachev's policy of dissemination of truthful information. But Russia, which had ignored the information revolution for years except within its military, was decades behind the Western countries and would find it very difficult to catch up.

Others were also noticing the growing importance of information to both the economy and society in general. A decade before Bell, the economist Fritz Machlup had written his book *The Production and Distribution of Knowledge in the United States*.[4] Machlup recognized the growing importance of information and knowledge to the health of the economy and set about measuring the knowledge industry—including such areas as print and broadcast media, telephony, postal services, and the new "information machines," or computers. A few years after Bell published his work, a Stanford economist named Marc Porat released his Commerce Department study, "The Information Economy: Definition and Measurement."[5] Porat took Machlup's work a step further by showing not only that the "information industry" was becoming a major sector of the economy, but that this industry required workers with higher skills and more education. By Porat's definition, by 1980, almost half of the American workforce would be involved in information work, as compared to 20 percent in manufacturing and only 3 percent in agriculture.

Porat's work became central not only to how the U.S. government would measure "the information society" in the future, but also to how the Organization for Economic Cooperation and Development (OECD, the organization of 29 industrially advanced nations that promotes market economics and democracy) would define it, a development that would later have particularly important implications for policy in countries such as Japan, France, Canada, and Germany. These countries and others slowly began to notice that their futures would increasingly depend upon how successfully their industries, government agencies, and other institutions entered the information age. To a large extent, their success would depend on the physical development of information infrastructure in those countries.

In his book, Bell categorized the infrastructural developments of the Industrial Revolution into four types:

1. transport, including the construction of roads, canals, railroads, and later, airlines;

2. energy, including the exploitation of coal, oil, gas, and eventually electricity;
3. telecommunications, including the use of telephony, radio, and television; and
4. information, which in 1973 encompassed computers and their peripheral equipment, such as printers and cathode-ray displays.

This last segment, information infrastructure, had developed rapidly after World War II because of the swift evolution of computing and electronics. During the war, the U.S. Navy had used early stored program concepts to build devices that could calculate shell trajectories. The Germans had developed an early computer in 1941 to design aircraft. The war also saw the development of special-purpose computers in England, Germany, and the United States for encrypting and decrypting messages—capabilities that were kept secret for many years.

Computers Arrive

Events moved swiftly in the United States. A Harvard engineer and physicist named Howard Aiken worked with IBM to create an electronic calculator called the Mark I by 1944. At about the same time, the Electronic Numerical Integrator and Computer (ENIAC) was developed in a joint effort by the University of Pennsylvania and the federal government, in a precursor of the government-university-business partnerships that would later create the Internet. The ENIAC used 19,000 vacuum tubes, generating great amounts of heat and using stupendous amounts of electrical energy. The ENIAC was turned into a real computer by Princeton mathematician John von Neumann's concept of "stored memory," whereby a computer's memory would store not only data but also the instructions that told the machine what to do. By 1951, the first commercial computer, the Universal Automatic Computer (UNIVAC I), was built by the Remington Rand Corporation, and soon a number of companies, including Remington Rand, Sperry Gyroscope, IBM, and the Radio Corporation of America (RCA), were making commercial computing devices for business and government. Using sorting machines based on Hollerith punched cards, and hand-wired boards for programming algorithms, these early machines used cumbersome machine language— lengthy strings of zeroes and ones—for entering instructions. (To save space on punched cards limited to 80 columns, years were represented by only two digits, dropping the initial "19"—the origin of what would later become the "Y2K" problem.)

Vacuum tubes, however, not only generated great quantities of heat and used large amounts of electricity, but they were also unreliable and frequently broke down. The invention of the transistor at Bell Laboratories in 1948 changed that, and by the late 1950s, transistors became the main element in computers. The IBM 1401 computer became a standard, along with its tape storage system, printers, and other peripheral gear. Within a decade, other enormous advances took place: more sophisticated and easier to use programming languages such as COBOL and FORTRAN were developed, making programming easier to learn and programmers more productive. Soon, the first simple integrated circuit boards containing as many as three or four transistors were produced, starting a dramatic trend of reducing computing costs while increasing computing speed—the shorter the distance between components, the less distance for electrical impulses to travel, and the faster those impulses can be received.

By the mid-1960s, most government agencies and large businesses had installed mainframe computers to handle their recordkeeping chores—invoicing, accounts receivable, purchasing records, inventory control, and personnel transactions such as payroll, benefits processing, and expense accounts. Computers were also used for special tasks in various industries, such as for check payment and settlements by banks, or for recording billing information by the telephone industry. New specialized applications such as these also stimulated technological advances such as optical character reading for processing checks or the use of bar codes for retail transactions. Large new supercomputers for applications in fields such as nuclear physics were designed, built, and used by such research facilities as the Lawrence Radiation Laboratory in Livermore, California.

With the Cold War in full swing, the government also began to make more use of computers in defense. Perhaps the most significant application, in terms of what it portended for the future, was the SAGE (Semi-Automatic Ground Environment) early-warning system to detect Soviet aircraft in the late 1950s. This system, deployed in Alaska, was developed by the Lincoln Laboratories at the Massachusetts Institute of Technology (MIT), together with IBM and Western Electric (now Lucent Technologies). Consisting of banks of vacuum-tube-powered computers connected to radars, the system provided information on incoming aircraft in real time. This was the first use of computers to process information in real time as the information was received. The technology soon led to its first commercial application, the American Airline's SABRE system that processed airline reservations.

But all this information-handling equipment was still just that—very fast recording and calculating devices that could improve productivity but that had little strategic impact on organizations. Although the use of computers was growing, they were still operated by a relatively small group of highly skilled programmers and systems analysts who tended the "glass house" mainframes. Government and corporate budgets for information processing were still a small percentage of overall budgets. Most important, few individuals had any direct contact with computers, although some mystery, tinged with a bit of fear, had begun to surround them. When Mario Savio, the leader of the Free Speech Movement at the University of California at Berkeley in 1964, used the slogan "Don't Fold, Spindle, or Mutilate Us!" (playing on the usage warning on IBM punched cards) he touched a nerve on campuses that would tingle for many years, raising early fears of invasion of privacy.

While Californians at Berkeley were worried about computers, other Californians a few dozen miles to the south were about to invent the next phase of the information revolution and make their state one of its biggest economic beneficiaries. A group of mostly Stanford University–trained electrical engineers developed and exploited the microchip, and in so doing created Silicon Valley. Originally invented by an engineer at Texas Instruments, the integrated circuit combined a number of components on a single silicon chip. Whereas the earliest integrated circuits had just a handful of transistors per chip, within a few years thousands of transistors per chip were the norm. By the late 1970s, the sixteen-thousand-bit memory chip was an industry standard, and in the early 1980s, the first million-bit, or megabit, chips were introduced. Gordon Moore, one of the original inventors of the microchip and a founder of the Intel Corporation, expressed this progression as Moore's Law: microprocessing power, he said, would double every eighteen months. If anything, his forecast was too conservative. Along with these rapid increases in speed and power came comparable declines in price. Cheaper, smaller chips led to cheaper and smaller computers, and thus the second phase of the computing revolution came about—the age of the personal computer.

For the first time, computers could be used by everyone—at small businesses or in the home. First used by hobbyists and students, personal computers were made popular at the outset by Steven Jobs and Stephen Wozniak, the founders of Apple Computer, who exploited a simpler way for people to interact with their computers—a graphical user interface (or GUI, pronounced "gooey") that used icons or symbols to represent commands such as "print," "file," or "delete." Apple's Macintosh computer quickly became a favorite of students and "nerds." Meanwhile in Albuquerque, N.M., and later in Seattle, Bill Gates developed his operating system (called the Disk Operating System, or DOS) and licensed it (as MS-DOS 1.0) to IBM, who introduced their Personal Computer (PC) in 1981. The PC became a sensation and was chosen by *Time* magazine as "Man of the Year" in 1982. By that year, 5.5 million PCs were in use. Ten years later, the number had increased to 65 million. Unfortunately for IBM and Apple, nimble companies such as Compaq, Hewlett-Packard, Dell, and Gateway exploited PC technology and manufacturing logistics and reaped many of the benefits.

Personal computers quickly joined mainframes in large organizations, and work began to be "distributed" on them from the mainframe to many individuals. Soon, tens and hundreds of thousands of people were learning to use word-processing programs, spreadsheets, and other "software" applications. Within corporations and other institutions, PCs were connected in local-area networks, or LANs. No longer was knowledge of computers limited to a few expert programmers; workers, students, professionals, physicians—virtually everyone—was learning to use software packages and manipulate a desktop, laptop, workstation, or "palmtop."

Children were often the most avid users, stimulated in part by early computer games such as Pong and Tetris, as well as by new educational software that was beginning to infiltrate the schools. But the use of personal computers was still limited by their "stand-alone" quality (or the inability to link to other networks outside of a LAN) and a belief that the growth of the home market might be limited by only a few applications. Connecting personal computers together over telephone lines was made difficult because the many different types of computers and software could not "talk" to each other. Fortunately for the industry, advances in computer networking that were begun at the Defense Department's Advanced Research Projects Agency (ARPA) were about to end the era of the stand-alone desktop personal computer.

Up to this point, the computer industry, unlike its older sibling the telephone industry, and despite the early involvement of the government during World War II, was evolving with little or no government regulation. Although the government had a continuing interest in helping fund leading-edge research, principally because of Cold War pressures, it made few moves to regulate the new industry. With the major exception of the IBM antitrust case that nearly destroyed the company because of the lengthy trial's impact on the company's conduct and culture, and some peripheral involvement in matters such as tariff and nontariff barriers and specialized tax policy, the government maintained a hands-off policy. Thus, in contrast to the telecommunications industry, which had grown comfortable with and even dependent on regulation, the computer and semicon-

ductor industries developed a mirror culture rejecting any government involvement. Many of these companies did not even have Washington offices until the mid-1970s. Later, in the age of convergence, these two cultures would clash loudly.

The Coming of the Internet

In the mid-1960s at the height of the Cold War, the Pentagon wanted to
be able to connect supercomputers doing advanced defense research at a
number of government and university laboratories scattered around the
country. A new project, ARPANET, was begun, and by the end of the
decade it connected four different host computers around the country.
Soon, E-mail, both technical and social, became a favorite application of
the researchers on the "net." Coincidentally, ARPANET had developed
a system that improved the resistance of the defense communications system to a nuclear attack. Previously, if a single trunk line in the nation's
defense communications system were destroyed, the entire network could
be jeopardized. An unintentional benefit of ARPANET was to improve
that situation.

By the 1970s, more than twenty institutions played host to the new
network, including two overseas in England and Norway.[6] A new company, called Bolt, Beranek, and Newman, after its three founders, used
the new network technology to create the first commercial network,
known as TELENET. By the 1980s, there were hundreds of ARPANET
hosts. What made all this possible was the development of new transmission methods and protocols for those transmissions. Earlier work at
MIT, the Rand Corporation, and ARPA abandoned the old hierarchical
switching systems that sent entire telephone messages over a single dedicated switched circuit created just for that message, and substituted
"packet switching." In this system, messages are broken up into smaller
digital packages, or "packets." Instead of traveling over a single dedicated line, each packet is given an address and routed to that address by
a specialized switch or computer called a router that sends it through the
network in the most efficient way available. Each packet is also given a
number so that when the various packets in a message reach their destination, they can be reassembled in the correct order.

The method used to reconcile the technical differences between many
different networks and computers, since they all had to work together to
send and receive packets, was also standardized in a technical protocol
known as Transmission Control Protocol/Internet Protocol (TCP/IP). De-

veloped by Bob Kahn at Bolt, Beranak, and Newman, and Vint Cerf of the University of California, Los Angeles, both of whom were working on ARPANET, TCP/IP made possible a vast open network that allowed messages to be sent from and received by all different types of computer hardware and software. In 1982, this loose, open network was first referred to as the "Internet." It spread rapidly: by 1987 there were more than ten thousand host computers; five years later, the number had grown to over a million.

The first use of this new tool was to build ARPANET for the use of the military and defense researchers. But the word soon spread throughout the nation's research community. The National Science Foundation realized the general benefits such a network could hold for academic researchers. Supported by Congress, it funded the development and construction of the NSFNET, a packet-switched network that connected physicists, chemists, astronomers, and other researchers from universities across the country. By 1985, corporations were also beginning to use the new Internet, and business use exploded in 1992, when the National Science Foundation lifted its ban on commercial use. Yet this was just the beginning.

The network's complexity still deterred nontechnical people from using the new technology. In 1991, however, Timothy Berners-Lee, a researcher at CERN, the high-energy physics laboratory in Geneva, Switzerland, developed the World Wide Web, a new GUI tool that greatly simplified the task of retrieving and viewing all kinds of information on the Internet. Two years later, a University of Illinois student named Marc Andriessen released a new type of software program called a "browser." With this program, named Mosiac, anyone who could point and click a computer mouse could use the World Wide Web and access any host computer linked to it, no matter where in the world it was or what kind of hardware or software it used.

These last few developments caused the center of gravity of the new Internet to shift rapidly from researchers and defense officials to corporations and consumers. Overnight, commercial and private use of the Internet exploded, much of it on the World Wide Web. By 1996, 40 million people were on the network, with access to 10 million hosts. People in more than 150 countries connected to transact $1 billion in business over the Internet. This shift would create the most important public policy implications for the future of the Internet and its broader manifestations.

Since the Internet is a kind of digital glue consisting of tools such as the World Wide Web, E-mail, and others, and serves to link thousands of separate but interwoven private and public networks, writers and analysts have struggled to find a simple term to define the entire phenomenon. I believe Esther Dyson, the personal computer guru and author, and Nicholas Negroponte, the director of the Media Laboratory at the Massachusetts Institute of Technology, have found the best solution by referring to it simply as the "Net." That is the term this book will use.

In just a few decades, an infrastructure and a technology had been developed and deployed with major government involvement and funding. Numerous members of Congress and government officials therefore felt they had a strong stake in the system. This colored their views not only of how the future system would be paid for and deployed, but also of how regulated—or unregulated—the new system should be. As interested in the progress of the system were foreign governments, many of whom saw the system as a creation of the United States government, with whatever economic and political consequences that might have for them.

A FEW DEFINITIONS

So many terms are used to discuss and debate this topic that it is important to define them before entering into policy discussions. As we shall see, defining the scope of the physical and nonphysical building blocks of the digital age helps to suggest the policy questions themselves. It is easiest to begin with the Internet itself, the heart of the digital age. It is easy because the Internet was officially defined by the Federal Networking Council (FNC) in 1995:

> The Federal Networking Council (FNC) agrees that the following language reflects our definition of the term "Internet". "Internet" refers to the global information system that (i) is logically linked together by a globally unique address space based on the Internet Protocol (IP) or its subsequent extensions/follow-ons; (ii) is able to support communications using the Transmission Control Protocol/Internet Protocol (TCP/IP) suite or its subsequent extensions/follow-ons, and/or other IP-compatible protocols; and (iii) provides, uses or makes accessible, either publicly or privately, high level services layered on the communications and related infrastructures described herein.[7]

In other words, the Internet is a vast global network of networks, all made interoperable through the use of the common TCP/IP protocols, and able to offer many services such as the World Wide Web, E-mail, user groups, chat rooms, and so forth. The Internet is not owned by anyone, nor run by the government, but is governed by a loose collection of private technical institutions. Among the most important are the following:

The *Internet Society (ISOC)* is a group of professionals and experts representing more than 150 different organizations and 6,000 individuals who oversee Internet policies and practices in such areas as standards. It is the organizational home for the Internet Engineering Task Force and the Internet Architecture Board.

The *Internet Engineering Task Force (IETF)* is responsible for the technical development of the Internet, including such critical areas as routing, transport, and security.

The *Internet Architecture Board (IAB)* provides oversight for the architecture of technical protocols and procedures used by the Internet.

The *Internet Corporation for Assigned Names and Numbers (ICANN)* is a relatively new, nonprofit corporation that has responsibility for allocating Internet space, managing the allocation of address names (i.e., the choice of "dot-coms" vs. "dot-orgs"), and managing the system through which information traverses the Net. ICANN was formed in 1998, when it took over these functions from the U.S. government and entities funded by the government.

There are other, more specialized organizations as well, and continual discussions of how the Internet should be governed; what the proper roles of the private and public sectors should be; and how big a role should be assigned to countries outside the United States, the country where most of these organizations reside. The Internet itself, as important as it is, is only the tip of the digital-age iceberg.

The broader terms that have been used to characterize the digital phenomenon has been "national information infrastructure" (NII) or "global information infrastructure" (GII). These terms were popularized by Vice President Al Gore, who has also used the phrase "information superhighway." During his years in Congress, Gore championed advanced research in new information and communications technologies and personally played a key role in the development of the digital age. In spite of critics who chided him early in 1998 for his remark that he "took the initiative in creating the Internet," the vice president's claims were not totally off the mark. He had foreseen the importance of the new technology long before any other national politician. He especially liked to remind people that his father, as a senator from Tennessee, had played a key role in the construction of the interstate highway system during the 1950s and 1960s—an infrastructure that transformed the American economic and physical landscape, creating millions of jobs in road and housing construction, shopping malls, and countless other enterprises. The vice president would go on to say that now the government needed to create an infrastructure for the next century—an "information superhighway." In a speech to the ITU in Buenos Aires in March 1994, Gore extrapolated his concept from the United States to the world and called for the creation of a "global information infrastructure."[8]

The Global Information Infrastructure, or the "Net"

What is meant by the terms "national" or "global information infrastructure," and of what do they consist? For simplicity's sake, and to stress the global nature of the digital phenomenon, this book will use the term GII as shorthand for both the national and global entities, and as a synonym for "the Net." In the broadest sense of the term, the GII, or the Net, is a vast, interconnected, worldwide network of networks made up of four key elements: communications, computing, content, and human resources. These four combine synergistically into a living and evolving system in which the sum is far greater than the parts.

The Communications Nets

The communications networks at the heart of the Net are changing rapidly. They include first the public switched telephone network, operated by private or public telephone companies and open to everyone. These networks, around the world, consist of central offices with electromechanical or electronic switches to route calls; transmission media, which include twisted copper wires, optical fibers, submarine cables, cellular, microwave and satellite transmission systems; and the telephone devices themselves, which are becoming more versatile and complex. For some public applications such as the ship-to-shore system and in some countries, radio broadcasting is also used.

These public networks are subject to government regulation or ownership, and in virtually every country the system is heavily cross-subsidized to provide universal service. Thus, more cost-effective urban users, for example, typically subsidize rural users, who are more expensive to connect to the system. Other subsidies, such as special low rates and services for the elderly or disabled people, are also part of many systems, and add an important public-interest component.

The advent of the new technologies has also created new networks that are sometimes totally private and sometimes also connected to the public switched network. The number of private networks used by corporations, universities, and other institutions has also grown rapidly. Typically, these networks do not own their own physical facilities but lease them, often from the public telephone system. In addition, Internet service providers (ISPs) now provide not only access to the Internet and its various domains and services but also offer their own proprietary network services, such as home shopping or chat rooms. America Online is by far the most popular of such ISPs; the Microsoft Network and Prodigy are among its numerous competitors. Governments set the conditions under which these private networks and ISPs connect to the public switched network, setting the stage for conflict between the two sides as Internet connections are built and operated.

All of these networks subscribe to certain technical standards to make them available to all users everywhere and can provide a wide variety of services, transmitting voice, images (i.e., faxes), or large amounts of data. Using the Internet protocols together with powerful computer switches called "routers," their facilities can be and are the transmission medium for Internet communications for most people.

In addition to the telecommunications networks, both public and private, other communications networks also play a role in the Net. Cable television networks, while not originally designed for two-way communications, have a large advantage over traditional telephone networks. Wired with coaxial cable rather than twisted-pair copper, they can transmit larger volumes of information at much higher rates of speed; i.e., they have more "bandwidth." With some engineering changes, they are also becoming a key part of the Net. The largest cable company in the nation, TCI, was acquired by AT&T, whose aim is to offer a single comprehensive communications and media service, including Internet access, to its customers. Not to be left behind, the telephone companies are speeding up their connectivity with new techniques such as digital subscriber line (DSL) technology, which competes with cable in terms of speed. Traditional radio and television broadcasting systems and the new direct satellite transmission systems are finding roles for themselves to play, as with the Philips Corporation's WebTV system, which merges television with Internet service. These systems also have varying degrees of government regulation.

Computing and Software. The computers that comprise part of the Net range from the increasingly small to the staggeringly large. At the high end of the scale are the giant supercomputers (for whom the Internet was originally created as a research tool) residing in the large research universities, government laboratories, and a few private corporations, including those used by Wall Street firms to model securities markets. The Department of Energy's national laboratories and companies such as IBM and Intel are working on powerful new supercomputers, "teraflop" and "petaflop" machines, and quantum computing. Such supercomputers are beginning to work on simulations that may accomplish such tasks as earthquake and weather prediction, or answer the question of how the universe began.

Below these are the powerful servers and workstations that provide the switching and hosting capabilities that make the Internet work, that operate Web pages and store and process the information on them, as well as perform much of the rest of the mundane work that makes our business and government agencies run. At the bottom are the personal computers, laptops, and "palmtops" that respond to many types of human interactions, delivered via keyboard and mouse or through handwritten or spoken commands. Increasingly, these devices are merging with other devices, such as telephones, fax machines, and television sets, to become the "information appliances" of the digital age. Attached to all of them are numerous peripheral devices, including many types of printers; keyboards; displays of all types, sizes, and resolutions; storage devices; scanners; modems; and smart faxes. The storage device, in particular, is growing in importance; networked petabyte storage assets are proving to be amazingly powerful tools for determining the most subtle and complex relationships among trillions of bits of data. (A petabyte is roughly one thousand trillion bytes of storage.)

None of this computer hardware would run without software, and operating-system software is the invisible mechanism that makes all computers run. Operating systems range from those that run tiny "palmtop" computers (also known as personal digital assistants, such as the Palm Pilot line of products), to the ubiquitous Microsoft Windows and new challengers such as Linux, to the complex operating systems that run large servers and supercomputers. "Middleware" is software that invisibly runs various functions on computers, such as management of the network itself, of transactions such as a banking deposit or an airline reservation, and of large databases.

The software equivalent of the information appliance is the application software package that runs a specific task, such as word processing, graphics creation, or spreadsheet calculation. Thousands of such application packages are available, and many of them can be obtained by simply downloading them over the Net, often at no charge. Other specialized types of software also exist and support the Net, such as software tools that make software engineers more productive as they develop new products, or security software that automatically scans files for viruses. The line between hardware and software is also increasingly difficult to discern, as some types of software become embedded in hardware, and some hardware tasks are taken over by software.

The hardware and software industries also differ significantly from the telecommunications industries in that the former are fundamentally unregulated, if such isolated actions as the government's antitrust suit against Microsoft is not considered a form of regulation. Thus, for example, there is no government subsidization for "universal service"— that is, the provision of service to all who wish it, even those in difficult geographical locations. As we shall see, however, the diffusion of hardware and software has been extremely rapid nonetheless, because of competition, the rapid rate of innovation, and the corresponding dramatic decreases in prices.

Content: From Mickey Mouse to Dow Jones. Content, or information, is the third vital component of the Net. Content can include material from public and private libraries and databases worldwide—material stored in any form, whether data, image, voice, video, or combinations of these forms. Thus, films, sound recordings, books, newspapers, magazines, periodicals, paintings, musical scores, museum collections, architectural drawings, maps, government documents, financial tables, and more are included. Content must be digitized in order to become part of the Net, and every form of content from books to paintings is in the process of being scanned and fed into cyberspace, whether by individual institutions such as businesses and governments or by public libraries.

Key to content is information retrieval, and so also included in this category are the search engines, such as AltaVista, Yahoo, or Lycos; directories and locators, such as Switchboard; and tools for uploading or downloading information. In 1998, search engines were the most frequently visited sites on the World Wide Web, as people searched for virtual stores, museums, medical advice, or airline schedules. Not just Time Warner, Disney, and Dow Jones, but every individual Web site and every E-mail user is a content provider for the GII.

Unlike the telecommunications and computer segments, which represent the poles of regulation, the world of content is more complex from a regulatory standpoint. Although content in many countries is protected by free speech doctrines, in others it is subject to stringent regulation.

Moreover, even those countries that espouse free speech regulate content in many ways, ranging from copyright and libel laws to controls on pornography, racism, or other types of "objectionable" speech. Speech is also regulated in some media, such as broadcast television, more heavily than in others, such as telephone conversations or mail. Thus, we can see the beginnings of yet another difficult public policy issue for the GII.

Human Resources: Education and More Education. The fourth and perhaps most important component of the Net is people—both those who use the infrastructure and those who work to create it. Millions of people around the world have already seen their working lives changed dramatically by the digital age. Factory workers, for example, who once operated machine tools or assembled parts by hand, now find themselves operating complex automated systems that require extensive training. Office workers who once relied on secretaries to type memoranda and documents now themselves send E-mail and master word-processing programs. Physicians use voice recognition software to record patient data and lawyers search Lexis for precedents. A small-business worker might use a hand-held device combining the features of a cellular telephone and a small computer to transmit directly to his or her office sales, inventory, or service data as a sale or service is performed. From this, the office computer may automatically produce an inventory report, order materials, and mail invoices.

On the other hand, there are also untold numbers of factory workers who did not or could not receive training to operate new equipment and lost their jobs as their companies modernized. Office workers, small-business workers, and others who have not refreshed their technical skills may also find themselves out of work as employers seek more technically capable people, or as customers turn to more technically savvy businesses that can lower prices or provide better service. In some areas, this has affected entire communities, as plants have evolved, moved, and shifted production in various ways.

These changes have created a new dichotomy in the workforce. By 1997, the U.S. government reported that almost five million American workers were employed in the information technology–producing industries alone, with average annual wages in 1997 of just under $53,000.[9] This number did not count all those working with technology in the rest of the economy, in fields ranging from financial services to manufacturing to retailing. In 1998, the Information Technology Association of America (ITAA) reported that 346,000 jobs were going unfilled in the

United States because companies could not find trained talent.[10] By April 2000, the ITAA reported that that number had grown to 843,000 jobs.[11]

The clear message was that countries that expected to compete in the new digital age would have to dramatically overhaul their educational systems. In the United States and other industrial countries, that would require a special focus on elementary and secondary education, as well as on technical training and lifelong learning. It would also trigger a variety of public policy debates in Congress, ranging from immigration policy to the federal role in education. For developing countries, the stakes were even higher and the challenges even more daunting. The GII—the Net—would only grow as quickly as there were skilled and motivated people to use it.

Other Terms and Definitions

While the term "global information infrastructure" had come into wide use among policy makers concerned with the subject by 1994, other terms are also commonly used. The term "cyberspace" was coined by the novelist William Gibson in his 1984 science fiction novel, *Neuromancer*.[12] He used it to refer to the nonphysical realm of content and software created by the new digital technologies. Although it is still used to refer broadly to the world of content residing within the Net, the term still retains some of its science-fiction and perhaps ominous overtones, thereby raising the specter of policy issues such as loss of privacy.

The term "information society" or "global information society," as it is used more formally in Europe, has existed since the earlier work of Bell and Porat, who looked at how the new information technologies were changing the world's economies. But the term has taken on a more precise meaning in Europe, where the Commission of the European Union has taken an activist role in dealing with the impact of the GII on many aspects of society. For example, the commission's 1994 report, *Europe's Way to the Information Society: An Action Plan*, deals with issues ranging from the free movement of information within the European Union to matters involving linguistics and culture. The term has not caught on widely elsewhere, however. The Japanese government tends to refer to the GII or the "digital economy," perhaps reflecting its emphasis on economic matters whereas Canada tends to use the term "information highway" along with all the others. In most other countries, the "GII" is most commonly used. However, as the volume of commerce has grown on the GII, a new and powerful term has come into use—"electronic commerce."

Electronic Commerce. Electronic commerce encompasses the marketing, ordering, delivery, and fulfillment of products and services over the Net. It involves before-market activities, such as market research, advertising, and "shopping"; the physical delivery of a product or service, either electronically or physically; and after-market activities such as billing and inventory control. It can involve commercial products and services, ranging from books, food products, and clothing to software and architectural services, and noncommercial products such as education, health care, or government services. It can include transactions where merchandise is actually shipped physically, by public mail or private delivery, or those that are entirely electronic, such as securities trading, the ordering of insurance, or the downloading of software.

Today, the bulk of electronic commerce takes place between businesses ("B2B," as Wall Street has named such commerce), with many firms conducting their purchasing and other activities over the Internet and private intranets. For example, Cisco Systems, a provider of advanced equipment for Internet and telecommunications companies, was already booking more than $3 billion in sales by 1997 over the Internet in the "B2B" sector.[13] But many other types of activities are already under way, including on-line home shopping; financial-services transactions, including home banking and securities trading; and electronic delivery of government services such as automobile registration or income-tax filing. For example, AutobyTel, a Web site that markets automobiles, automotive parts, auto insurance, financing, and other automobile-related services was handling 100,000 purchase requests per month by the end of 1997, generating more than $500 million per month in auto sales, according to the U.S. Department of Commerce. Dell Computers, a personal computer manufacturer and distributor, was booking more than $18 million in retail sales per day in 1999 over the Internet.[14] In 1998, it was estimated that the value of goods and services sold on-line to consumers in the United States and Europe surpassed $5.1 billion—doubling the 1997 amount.[15] Overall, it is estimated by the Commerce Department that the total value of electronic commerce, including B2B and retail transactions, will be close to $1.4 trillion by 2003.[16]

Thus, the sheer volume of electronic commerce is forcing more policy focus on this subject and causing more widespread use of the term. In fact, Michael Dertouzos, head of MIT's Laboratory for Computer Science, sees electronic commerce as the defining activity for the Net and envisions the worldwide network of computers as an electronic European flea market.[17] In describing this electronic structure as the ultimate market, with buyers and sellers having access to up-to-date information, Dertouzos uses the term "information marketplace," which may yet become the term of choice.

With this shift in Net focus from communications to business transactions, the public debate broadens from the regulatory debates over telecommunications policy to involve such issues as consumer protection, privacy, the security of financial data, the licensing of professionals, and jurisdictional disputes over taxation. This leads to our last definitional discussion—of the term "convergence."

Convergence: Narrow and Mega. A great deal has been written about the phenomenon of convergence. The term as commonly used refers to the fact that as all information is digitized, i.e., reduced to a series of bits, the traditional distinctions between different information appliances such as telephones, radios, television sets, and personal computers fade away. Thus, it is thought, the traditional technical barriers between the computer, telecommunications, and broadcast and cable industries begin to disappear, opening the possibility for competition and indeed a convergence of all four industries. Since, as we have seen, the computer and telecommunications industries occupy the opposite ends of the regulatory spectrum, the policy aspects of convergence become exceedingly important.

A number of important implications arise from this fundamental view of convergence:

1. Convergence opens the way for many new products and categories of products. For example, a television set may be combined with a personal computer to allow interactive on-line home shopping. A telephone may be combined with a computer and become a roving Web browser. A television set, telephone, and personal computer may be combined to allow videoconferencing with on-line graphics capability.
2. Convergence may destabilize companies and entire industries, bringing great new opportunities for winners and oblivion for losers. For example, the recent battle at the Federal Communications Commission over standards for high definition television came down to a fight between the manufacturers of television receivers and the computer industry over who would dominate the future market for converged television sets and personal computers.
3. Convergence will stimulate new technological competition and innovation, creating many benefits for consumers, including sharply

lower prices and radically new products and services. Prices have not declined as much in the regulated telecommunications markets as they have in the unregulated computer sector, and new competition would force telecommunications prices down faster.

4. Convergence poses new challenges to regulators who must choose between the telecommunications half of the converged world, which is regulated and the computer half, which is not, knowing that both sides will fight to the death to maintain their privileges and market advantages. Numerous special-interest groups, including users, investors, and employees, will play an important role in this process. This battleground will become particularly important in countries where the telecommunications carriers are owned by governments and employ thousands of people.

5. Convergence will set off global policy and trade battles, as nations seek to maintain their own industries and competitive advantages and protect their most important industries. Thus, countries with powerful public telecommunications companies and weak computer industries will tend to choose a more regulatory path, whereas those with interests in the more rapid development of computer hardware and software will choose the path of competition and free markets.

As significant as the form of convergence we have so far discussed is, it represents a narrow view of the real convergence that digitization is creating. For while digitization is clearly causing product convergence in the telecommunications, computing, and broadcast industries, it is beginning to cause a much more profound form of convergence in products and services in a wide range of industries and even public institutions. This "megaconvergence" will have the same destabilizing effects on many industries and other sectors that the narrower form of convergence is having on the high-tech industry. Not only will new forms of competition spring up, but for those sectors that are regulated in some way by government, the regulatory and even legal underpinnings of those sectors will be threatened.

Consider the following example: The consulting firm Booz Allen and Hamilton estimates that the cost per transaction performed by a teller at a bank branch is $1.08. The same transaction performed over the Internet costs $0.13. That kind of cost efficiency, with its benefits to both the bank and the consumer, is irresistible. Moreover, the consumer can perform the Internet transaction 24 hours a day, from home, from the office, or from anywhere he or she wishes to be.

For the bank, however, the implications are even more significant, because its value chain is now dramatically altered. The economics of the teller transaction are based on a banking model built on physical assets—real estate and physical space—on the one hand, and a human resource—the teller—on the other. The Internet transaction is based principally on software and computer-service fees for outsourced information services—services such as developing and operating the bank's information system—that is performed for the bank by an information services company like IBM or EDS (the computer services company founded by Ross Perot). Unlike the physical asset that is owned by the bank, the software must be licensed from a software developer such as Microsoft or Intuit. In fact, so much of the value provided to the consumer is embedded in the software that the software companies themselves could become bankers, or at least could capture so much of the bank's revenues that the software companies become the de facto bankers.

This new form of competition has not gone unnoticed by bankers, of course, who now fear becoming "money morgues," or institutions whose sole function is to warehouse money in safe deposit boxes or long-term savings accounts that require few if any transactions. Many bankers now believe their main competitor is no longer the bank on Main Street or Wall Street, but the Microsofts and Intuits of the world, who, traditional bankers worry, will increasingly define the services that banks offer and collect the tolls on the transactions that take place. But with 60 percent of the U.S. public soon to own a personal computer, the banks have little choice but to move quickly into the digital world.

This convergence of banking with the Net also has tremendous public policy implications for the banking industry. Although the same rules that apply to payments and transactions in physical space should also generally apply to transactions in cyberspace, the ability to perform virtual transactions raises numerous questions. Since the Internet provides such easy integration of so many types of financial services, the traditional barriers between banks and so-called nonbanks, or credit providers, as well as between banks and other types of financial-services organizations such as insurance companies, financial planners, or stockbrokers, become even more porous than they already are.

Banks, for example, must set up financial reserves to back their liabilities, whereas other institutions are not required to do so. Although the U.S. Treasury and virtually all governments now have a monopoly on issuing currency, could funds downloaded over the Internet onto a smart card be considered a form of private currency? Would financial institutions offering services on the Internet across state lines be liable to state regulation? Even more complicated is the question of how to regulate cyberspace banks internationally: What country has jurisdiction when a banking transaction is conducted electronically with a Swiss bank whose server is located in Ireland and whose customer is an American living in Japan? Are the banking-privacy laws adequate to protect financial transactions conducted on the Internet?

These are just of a few of the policy questions that are raised by the issue of megaconvergence in the banking industry. The same types of public policy questions can be raised about most sectors.

1. *Insurance:* With insurance companies and their agents able to open Web sites and do business on the Internet, can the current system of state regulation of insurance endure, or will we need a new, national system? If so, how easily will states yield their powers to the federal government—or the member states of the European Union (EU) give up their sovereignty to the European Commission in Brussels? Since insurance policies are complex and important legal documents, will electronic policies hold up in court? How are disclosure requirements for policies to be translated for virtual policies?

2. *Retailing:* How do consumers know if the retail Web site with which they are dealing is reliable or fraudulent? If a dispute arises between a consumer and a retailer, where do they go to court? Whose consumer protection laws apply? If retailers use Web sites as advertising, with whose advertising laws must they comply? If an EU citizen living in Canada purchases clothing from an American retailer whose supplier is in Thailand, what kind of taxes are due from which parties and to which jurisdictions?

3. *Education:* Can a technical training institute accredited in one state or country offer courses to students in another state or country? Where do its teachers have to be licensed? How can a graduate of an international "virtual university" get credit in his or her home country? How can public education be maintained in a digital world when many students and even school systems will not be able to afford the necessary equipment and services? How can teachers be retrained to exploit the new technologies?

4. *Health care:* Can medical institutions offer "telemedicine" across state or national boundaries? What rules apply to the privacy and security of patient records? In malpractice cases involving a number of jurisdictions, whose rules apply? Will we need new rules for

the licensing and accreditation of physicians and other health care
professionals? Can medical records be legally kept in digital form?
Is it legal or ethical to diagnose illness online?

5. *Government services:* If government information and transactions
   become digital and therefore are made more convenient or more valuable for citizens, can the government charge for the service? If commercial firms wish to exploit government data in some fashion, will
   they need to pay royalties to the government? If services such as welfare payments or food stamps become digitized, how will the poor
   access them, and how can the benefits be maximized for the beneficiaries? If welfare checks become debit cards, will the same rules
   regarding liability for commercial cards be applied to them?

These are just a few of the policy questions in a few fields that arise from
megaconvergence. They and others can easily be applied to numerous
other fields, including travel and transportation, libraries and cultural institutions, industrial processes and manufacturing, and small businesses.
All will have to be dealt with, and the rate of growth of the information
infrastructure and electronic commerce makes the problem an immediate one.

THE EXPLODING NET

The stupendous rate of growth of the Net causes policy makers a special
problem since it is difficult, if not impossible, to keep up with. Since the
period from 1991 to 1993, when the National Science Foundation lifted
its ban on commercial Internet traffic and when Berners-Lee and Andriessen made possible the point-and-click browsing of the World Wide
Web, the Internet itself and electronic commerce have exploded. In 1992,
there were about one million "hosts," or computers attached to the Internet with a unique Internet address, according to the Internet Society.
By mid-1997, the number of hosts had grown higher than 19.5 million
and by 1999 was growing at 55 percent per year. Similarly, the number
of "domain names" (system addresses used to locate a site on the Net; a
hypothetical example might be "shoestore.com.uk," for a shoe retailer
located in the United Kingdom) jumped from about 26,000 in 1993 to
more than 1.3 million in 1997.

In terms of people using the Internet, estimates vary, but there is general
agreement that over 300 million people worldwide were using the Internet
by mid-2000, with almost half of them in the United States and Canada.

According to the Intelliquest Information Group of Austin, Texas, about one-fourth of the 62 million North American users in 1997 were newcomers to the Internet that year—further evidence of increasingly rapid growth. Moreover, the penetration of the Internet into households is growing rapidly. The Department of Commerce estimates that on-line usage reached into 37 percent of U.S. homes in 1998, up from 17 percent in 1997. That compared to almost 100 percent of U.S. homes with television sets and telephones and about two-thirds with cable television. The total number of people projected to use the Internet by 2001 worldwide is more than half a billion.

The speed with which this occurred can be seen best by comparing the diffusion of Internet use with other technologies. According to the Department of Commerce, it took 38 years for radio broadcasting to reach 50 million people, and 13 years for television to do the same.[18] Once opened to commercial use, the Internet took 4 years.

Another way to look at the size of the Internet is by the amount of information accessed. Creative Networks, Inc., estimates that over 625 terabytes (one terabyte equals a trillion bytes) of information was accessed over the Internet each month in 1998. That is the equivalent of three million sets of encyclopedias—and the traffic is increasing by 30 percent per month.[19] The U.S. Commerce Department reported that by January 2000, the World Wide Web contained more than one billion unique pages.

Although the majority of Internet users are Americans (in large part because the Internet has its principal roots in the United States), the most rapid growth is now taking place in other countries, as the price of personal computers, storage, and Internet access falls. In fact, Finland is currently the world's most wired country, with an Internet link for every 25 people, compared to a link for every 50 Americans. Australia, Canada, the Netherlands, Singapore, Britain, Germany, and Israel are among the other most heavily wired countries; China and India, with their enormous populations, rank at the bottom. This growth is not escaping the notice of businesses in many countries overseas. For example, two out of three major European companies now use the Internet for business.

Business Week estimates that electronic commerce could boost the U.S. gross domestic product by $10–20 billion by 2002. A 1998 OECD report on Internet economics looked further into the future and echoed the Commerce Department report referenced earlier by projecting a $1 trillion economic commerce market by 2005. Of the more than one-third of U.S. households on-line in 1998, about one-third made purchases on-line in the first six months of 1998. And although most electronic commerce has been business-to-business in the past, sales to consumers are soaring. Among the top sectors and their 1999 revenues are travel services at $7.1 billion, projected to grow to $14.6 billion in 2000; computer hardware/software at $6.6 billion, growing to $9.2 billion; financial brokerage at $6.4 billion, growing to $11.1 billion; collectibles (auctions) at $3.1 billion, growing to $6.0 billion; automotive at $1.9 billion, growing to $3.4 billion, and books and music at $2.5 billion, growing to $4.6 billion.[20]

All of this activity will amount to substantial portions of sales for each of these industries. By 2002, it is expected that 35 percent of all travel-industry sales will be on-line. Book sales and software will total 10 percent of that industry's revenues, insurance 9 percent, music 8 percent, and clothing 7 percent. Not surprising, this is attracting substantial advertising and marketing resources as firms shift advertising and merchandising budgets to the World Wide Web. In 1997, U.S. industry spent more than $480 million on on-line advertising, with the computer and software industries spending the lion's share—$275.3 million. Other key industries included financial services, telecommunications, media, automotive, retail, and travel.

All of this Internet and electronic commerce activity, based on the underlying information and advanced communications technologies, is becoming a significant part of the total U.S. economy. The information technology sector's share of the U.S. economy grew from 4.9 percent in 1985 to more than 8 percent in 1998. Equally important, the information technology industry contributed 35 percent of U.S. economic growth in the years 1995–98.[21] Declining information technology prices also lowered overall inflation in the U.S. economy by almost one percentage point.

These figures benefited both companies and workers. By 1998, U.S. business spending on information technology equipment had risen to $233 billion, or one-third of total business capital investment, with business seeing important payoffs from these investments. By 1999, 4.3 million people were employed in an information technology occupation. They earned an average of $53,000 per year, compared to an average of $28,000 in the private sector as a whole.[22] Worldwide, the OECD said that in 1998 600,000 information technology jobs were unfilled, with more than half of them in the United States alone.

There is no end to the growth in sight. Computer and software technology continues to evolve rapidly, with personal computers now available for just a few hundred dollars. A few vendors are even giving personal computers away free when customers agree to purchase other services such as Internet access. Communications technology is also beginning to catch up, with faster and more sophisticated Internet connections on the way. One such technology, asynchronous digital subscriber lines (ASDLs), is lowering the time necessary to download a 3.5-minute video on the Internet from 46 minutes to 10 seconds. Cable modems are even faster. When Internet II (an advanced version of the Internet being developed by a consortium of companies and universities) comes on-line, its speed will be a hundred or more times faster than today's Internet—making possible live two-way video, for example.

The pace of change in storage technology is also speeding up. In recent years, the progress in storage has been dramatic. Since 1991, according to data from IBM, storage density has grown by 60 percent annually. The density of data expressed as the number of millions of bits of information that can be stored in a square inch has increased from 62.5 in 1989 to 3,090 in 1997. In fact, the per-megabyte cost of storage dropped from $11.52 in 1988 to 10 cents in 1997 and reached 2 cents in 2000. The implications for the storage and use of all types of content on the information infrastructure are staggering.

CLOUDS AND SHADOWS

By the mid-1990s, as the Net began to reach into every business, government institution, and home, politicians also began to discover it. The phenomenon had already been not only noticed but nurtured in the United States, but in the middle of the decade the pace of this nurturing began to pick up, as President Bill Clinton appointed his National Information Infrastructure Advisory Committee and also set up an interagency working group under the late commerce secretary Ron Brown in 1993. The European Union and its member states, Canada, Singapore, and Japan followed with studies, commissions, and reports by different government ministries, often coordinated at the highest level within the government. International organizations also began to join the fray, as the United Nations, the World Trade Organization, and the OECD all began to act on parts of the digital policy agenda.

Many of their actions were aimed at enabling the new infrastructure and lifting some of the policy clouds that hung over it, but some were also targeted at lengthening shadows that appeared to be darkening some aspects of the digital age. Since, for the most part, governments sought to encourage the growth of the new information infrastructures and the economic activities they made possible, the first actions of governments were aimed at clearing away policy debris from earlier regulatory and legal eras. Among their key activities in this arena were

1. Attempting to deregulate telecommunications and to create a more competitive and innovative environment for the new technologies. In some countries this meant dismantling regulatory agencies that had existed for a century and untangling thousands of pages of complex regulations. In others, it meant privatizing the national telecommunications company and turning it and its politically powerful employees over to private hands. In at least one country, Brazil, it actually meant amending the national constitution.

2. Trying to modernize their commercial laws to legitimize electronic signatures and documents and to spell out consumer protections in the on-line world. This often requires numerous international negotiations and agreements.

3. Changing their tariff systems and customs duties to permit duty-free entry of the key information and communications technology products that their institutions would need to build the new information infrastructure. This involves significant international negotiations at the World Trade Organization.

4. Debating the role of public funds to be used in research and development for the new infrastructure, including national funding for key applications in the areas of government, education, and medicine, as well as in areas such as emergency management, space research, and national defense. Particularly difficult in this arena is determining the role of public funds when foreign companies or other institutions are involved.

5. Bringing national and local income and sales tax systems up to date so that electronic commerce could be taxed in a fair and unbiased way. Countries would also have to agree on issues of jurisdiction, with much electronic commerce taking place across international boundaries.

6. Providing a reasonable legal basis for the use of cryptography, so that sensitive business or personal data sent over the network could be encrypted and protected from prying eyes. Since some countries, such as the United States, have considered cryptography a kind of "munition," this is a particularly nettlesome issue.

7. Finally, bringing the world's system of intellectual property rights up to date, so that authors and creators of content, whether books, business data, films, software, or motion pictures, would continue to produce their material. With record worldwide piracy of intel-

lectual property juxtaposed with the ease of access and copying via the Net, this was a critical issue.

If the debates over clearing away policy underbrush were difficult, those that dealt with the newly darkening shadows cast by the Internet and its offspring were even more so. Among the key issues were

1. Protecting the privacy of citizens who sensed the growing intrusiveness of the new information infrastructure, particularly as they began to use electronic commerce. Internet users began to learn from vivid newspaper accounts how government agencies, businesses, and others could collect and use vast amounts of personal data, ranging from medications used to taxes paid. With dramatically differing views of privacy around the world, the international implications were particularly difficult.

2. Guarding the security of information and systems as government agencies and businesses began to confront the reality of hackers, vandals, disgruntled employees, criminals, and terrorists. Law-enforcement agencies began to warn against many types of computer crime, and individual cases began to appear in the press.

3. Assuring access to the new information infrastructure for everyone, not only for those who could afford the still relatively expensive equipment or those in countries or regions where service was already available. In most countries, this issue was enmeshed with the reform of telecommunications laws that usually required "universal service." But more important, it also required new forms of access, such as through kiosks in public places, including libraries, schools, post offices, or community centers.

4. Preserving free speech rights while also preventing the Net from becoming a "red light" district or a communications media for criminals, hate-mongers, or terrorists. With free speech rights differing significantly from country to country, and even within countries for different types of media, this is proving to be an extremely difficult issue to resolve.

5. Safeguarding children in particular against pornography and criminals of all types. With a number of Internet stalking cases already logged by police in a number of countries, this issue ranked high on the lists of governments everywhere.

6. Finally, and by no means the least significant, dealing with the hundreds of sectoral issues raised by megaconvergence in areas such as banking, retailing, health care, and education.

By the end of 1998, governments in the United States and around the world were grappling with all of these questions and more. Their progress was uneven, at best. In many areas, such as telecommunications deregulation or privacy regulation, each step forward seemed to bring a step backward. Although governments did appear to agree on a number of basic principles, such as the role of the private sector in developing the new information infrastructure, the agreements were tenuous, and subject to the vagaries of politics and public opinion.

For example, for years governments had fretted about the apparent loss of jobs caused by the diffusion of information technology throughout the economy. But the explosion of demand generated by the Internet had changed that, and by the time of the G-7 ministerial meeting on the GII in Brussels in February 1995, the attendees were able to agree that the new technologies would create more and better jobs than they would eliminate. By 1999, the U.S. government noted that employment in the information-technology-producing industries alone was growing at 2.4 percent annually, compared to 1.7 percent for all private industry.[23] Nevertheless, some economists and policy makers in practically all countries argued that the digital age would damage not only employment, but economic growth and productivity as well. Although their numbers have dwindled, a serious economic downturn might give their ideas new life.

Not only were the fundamental concepts of the brand new digital age difficult to understand and often obscure, but there were other reasons why policy-making was so difficult. To see why, we need to examine some of the underlying themes.

2

Properties of the Digital World

Imagine a world in which time seems to vanish and space seems completely malleable. When the gap between need or desire and fulfillment collapses to zero. When distance equals a microsecond in lapsed connection time. A virtual world connected at your command.

—Regis McKenna, *Real Time*[1]

If it is true that our present economic and social institutions are mainly the consequences of choices made in the past, then the future of the Net will also depend principally on the informed choices we make today. But choosing the best policies for cyberspace may be more difficult than was policy-making in the past. Unlike earlier institutions that were created by the choices of government interacting with those of the private and civic sectors, the digital world is virtually unbounded by the physical laws, legal jurisdictions, and international borders that limited previous examples.

Furthermore, the development of the Net and its diffusion throughout the world's institutions has been far more rapid than earlier innovations. Its impact on those institutions is far more profound, as well, both in the number of institutions it changes and in the radical nature of the changes themselves. The economics of the digital world are also largely unsettled; neither its market and pricing mechanisms nor its impact on national economies and the global economy have been determined. Although all the signs are positive, the ultimate impact of the Net on employment and productivity is still being debated.

Additionally, the future impact of the Net on such issues as ecology and quality of life or on the balance between established cultures and smaller fringe groups is yet to be determined. Nor do we know how it will affect the balance of power between large institutions and smaller groups and subgroups. In the economic and financial sphere, electronic commerce will change money and the way we view it and will alter how nations view their comparative advantages and competitiveness.

As political leaders ponder how to make public policy in the digital age, they will need to understand these difficult conundrums, as well as the immediate effects of the policies they wish to enact, nationally or internationally.

THE BEARABLE LIGHTNESS OF THE DIGITAL AGE

As author Diane Coyle has pointed out in her book, *The Weightless World,* as modern economies continue to grow, their economic output (as measured in tons) has been flat.[2] The digital age is light because of the collapse of the physical world into the many forms of cyberspace. Thus, policy makers who deal with the Net must deal not with tangible and easily measurable artifacts such as land, buildings, or industrial products, but with abstract concepts and ideas. In making policy for the settlement of the American West, for example, policy makers could grasp the significance to a farmer of forty acres of land. In a more recent and more complicated example, the formulators of the Clean Air Act, a complex and lengthy piece of legislation, could at least understand the chemistry of auto emissions or noxious factory pollutants in terms of specific amounts of different gases or particulates. Dealing with cyberspace is more like making policy for intellectual property, where the basic notion of copyright is ownership of the *expression* of an idea, rather than the idea itself—a difficult and abstract notion to grasp and one that is endlessly interpretable. Indeed the issue of intellectual property in cyberspace is one of the most troublesome for policy makers.

Consider, for example, the creation of the modern American oil industry. Today's industry and the governmental framework in which it operates grew out of the aggressive entrepreneurship of industry titans like John D. Rockefeller and the powers of governments driven by concerns about monopoly and national security. A radically different oil industry, either monopolistic and unfettered by government, or heavily regulated and even owned by government, would have resulted in a very different modern world. For example, scarcities or chronically high prices for gasoline in an unregulated market might have produced an America today in which the majority of the population lived in urban centers without suburbs, interstate highways, Holiday Inns, shopping malls, or drive-through McDonald's windows. Whether that world would have been better or worse is debatable; that it would have been different is certain.

Yet the power of industrialists and politicians to create the future of the oil industry was limited by physical facts: petroleum deposits exist only in certain geographical areas and in certain quantities. The derivation of gasoline and other useful substances from crude oil is dependent on chemical processes that obey physical laws. The methods of transporting and distributing gasoline are limited by both physical laws and economic realities. Physics, chemistry, metallurgy, and the environment played a major role, for example, in the construction of the Alaska pipeline.

Other examples abound. The distribution of electrical power is limited by the distances electricity can flow unimpeded; different transmission methods are required for long distances than for short ones. The air transportation system is defined by the need for airports and runways requiring large tracts of real estate, and increasingly by the amount of air traffic that can fit in a city's and even a nation's airspace. Even the educational system, perhaps the most intellectual of government undertakings, has been limited, at least until now, by the need for physical classrooms and by the number of qualified teachers available.

But in creating the Net, the infinite world of virtual content, the physical limitations are far fewer. Cyberspace is almost entirely a creation of the human mind, and its links to the physical world are becoming even less important as technology advances. It is certainly true that the processing, transmission, and display of digital content is dependent on hardware such as personal computers, telephone lines, workstations, displays, routers, and servers. In the end, one must still view the data, graphics, or video produced by the information infrastructure on a flat-panel or cathode ray tube display; type on a keyboard or wield a mouse; and make contact with others through webs of copper wire, optical fiber, coaxial cable, satellite dishes, and electronic switches.

These physical artifacts, however, although they make the digital world possible, do not define it and, increasingly, do not limit its potential. Crude oil can produce only hydrocarbon fuels that power vehicles or chemicals that perform other discrete functions; it cannot produce nuclear or other forms of power. But the hardware that makes cyberspace possible can produce a possibly infinite number of content forms and uses. The Internet can function as a post office, telephone, retail store, broadcast studio, soapbox, auction house, sound recording, movie theater, or used-car showroom. It can also be an examining room for a physician, an office for an insurance agent, a distributor's warehouse, a studio for a fashion designer, or a university classroom. It can be used to design a home, to learn how to repair an automobile, to run a political campaign, or to evaluate antique furniture. The forms that each of these examples can take is also almost infinite: consider the potential varieties of school curricula or medical diagnostic systems.

The tie to physical objects is receding even further as market-driven innovations in the computer hardware, software, and communications industries make information appliances remarkably easier to use. Voice-recognition systems already in use eliminate virtually any physical contact between the user and the equipment. Some include translation systems, whereby an English speaker can be understood by a Spanish-speaking listener. New systems that use techniques such as hand signals are also on the way. In fact, experiments with simple commands dictated by thoughts alone are also in development.

The virtual (nonphysical) nature of the digital age poses special problems for policy makers by virtue of its very complexity and abstractness. In this sense, it poses a policy challenge more like that encountered in the creation of the educational and banking systems, or the original establishment of real property rights, than in the evolution of other industries and institutions grounded in the physical world. The Net is orders of magnitude more complex than these earlier examples, however, because it also poses other unique challenges, not the least of which is its borderless nature.

BORDERLESS DOMAIN

If the Net has already broken the bounds of physical laws, it has also broken free of the constraints of national boundaries. At the European Ministerial Conference on Global Information Networks in July 1997 in Bonn, the ministers declared that although they saw the emergence of global information networks as highly positive and critical for Europe's future, they also stressed the "special characteristics and fundamentally transnational nature of the Internet . . . which set it apart in almost every way from traditional means of communications."[3]

This "transnational nature" has several characteristics. The first is that, by design, the Net is truly and uniquely worldwide. Content created in one country can be viewed in any other country or number of countries at any time or as many times as users wish. With the click of a mouse button, the geographical and political obstacles that created different languages, literatures, music, art, cuisines—in short, cultures—can be wiped away. This is not a prospect that most governments—or most cultural institutions—view with ambivalence.

Second, services based on this transnational content can also be performed across national boundaries, whether they involve education, banking, the arts, or shopping. Already, universities are establishing transnational virtual campuses, often in alliances that cross national boundaries.

Shoppers buy goods from Web sites with little notice of where the site originates. Patients even make use of medical services, such as the wireless monitoring of blood-sugar levels, across borders when similar services are not locally available. Oddly, the services that are not transnational—at least not yet—are government services. Although a Brazilian may purchase goods from a virtual French shop or take an education class from a Canadian or Japanese school, he or she cannot apply for and receive German social welfare benefits. Obviously, cross-border shopping for benefits is also not a prospect that governments welcome. In the future, different government entities might actually be competing for clients in other countries. The legal and fiscal issues arising from such a scenario, not to mention the social and political ones, would pose enormous problems.

Third, the physical communications web that delivers this content is, also by design, amorphous and ever changing, aligning itself not with national borders but according to the traffic patterns that packet-switched networks are designed to optimize. Thus, unlike a steel gas pipeline that traverses different countries, states, or provinces in a fixed, physical manner, the packet-switched pathways of the Net are fluid, crossing three or four national borders one second and two or three others the next. It is as if the heavy August automobile traffic between Paris and Lyon could be automatically rerouted via Warsaw one minute and Hong Kong the next—at no additional cost and with no loss of time. In fact, the dynamic routing of the Net is economically efficient. These virtual and ever-changing connections are proving too sublime for orthodox forms of government regulation, frustrating regulators in telecommunications, content, banking, and other fields. As packet switching makes further inroads into traditional switched networks, governments will find this issue growing more serious.

Once again, the digital-age policy maker faces a daunting task. Even if a national consensus can be reached on an issue, the issue cannot be completely resolved until some international understanding can be reached. With greatly differing national norms on issues such as privacy or free speech, and differing national economic interests on matters of taxation or telecommunications regulation, such agreements will come slowly and with difficulty. Moreover, the framework for reaching international agreements is fractured, either along regional geographic lines, as with organizations such as the European Union (EU), the Asia-Pacific Economic Cooperation group, and the Organization of American States, or according to issues, as in the World Trade Organization, the United Nations Commission on International Trade Law, and the International Telecommunications Union.

Some have suggested an alternative based on the recognition that the digital world is a domain of its own, a unique "place."[4] Supporters of this view draw an analogy to maritime law, in which nations recognize that the sea and the sky are jurisdictions unto themselves, and that those who use them agree to be bound by special rules pertaining to those domains. The law of the sea does provide a relatively sound legal framework for maritime commerce, for example, but it took centuries for this body of law to be developed. Even the development and acceptance of the Law of the Sea Treaty adopted in 1982 took a decade. Airline treaties today involve tortuous negotiations that go on for years, prompting a recent British ambassador to the United States to note that Roosevelt and Churchill set the entire tone for postwar Europe in a few days on a ship at sea. In contrast, he said, the United States and the United Kingdom now take years to agree on an airline treaty.

Moreover, unlike the sea or the sky, which are generally marked by clear and recognized boundaries, the digital world is amorphous, changing, and heterogeneous. In some places, its boundaries may be marked by passwords or technical standards; in others it may be bounded by different operating systems. In still others, cyberspace domains may be limited to groups of individuals such as employees, or subscribers who sign online agreements, such as those used to permit entry to certain Web sites that require user acceptance of contractual obligations.

Nonetheless, aspects of the developing legal framework for electronic signatures, writings, and documents do resemble a separate international legal code for cyberspace, and it can be useful to view this effort as similar to the making of maritime or aviation law. Although the analogy is not exact, we can learn from some important parallels.

If lawmakers can deal with both the virtual and the borderless characteristics of the Net, they will still have to deal with yet another factor—the unending rush of innovation that is changing the digital world faster than even the innovators can keep up with.

FAST LANE, SLOW LANE

We have already seen how rapidly the Net has developed over the past decade. We have also seen how it has been quickly adopted for a wide variety of uses by millions of people and institutions around the world—growing from about three million users in 1994 to a projected one billion users by 2005.[5] Similarly, the economic impact of the Internet, as measured by the explosion of electronic commerce, is expanding dramatically. This is the fast lane of the information superhighway—innovation, technology, and declining prices are driving superheated growth. The slow lane is the political lane.

Democracies, as Winston Churchill once said, are the worst form of government except for every other one. One of the reasons that democracies do well is their deliberative pace. Issues are carefully weighed, hearings are held, witnesses called, and all interest groups heard from before legislatures take action. After legislation is passed, regulations must be developed and vetted with the public and enforcement must begin. Often legal challenges must slowly make their way through the judicial maze. These feedback mechanisms build a constructive inertia into policy making and act like a great political flywheel, helping to smooth the ups and downs of national life. Thus, rash or foolish laws are generally (but not always) avoided and unintended consequences kept to a minimum. Authoritarian regimes, lacking such useful checks and balances, tend to make serious mistakes and, over time, crash and fail.

The problem for the world's democracies—which constitute the vanguard of the digital age—is that technology is developing and being practiced so rapidly by the private sector that the world of the Net is being created de facto, in ways that may be difficult or impossible to change once they are established. On the whole, this may be a good thing; so far most agree that the private sector should lead the development of electronic commerce. But the failure to articulate clear policy obstacles in a timely manner or to use policy to open up new opportunities could cause delays and distortions in the constructive development of cyberspace. The effects of those delays and distortions could be felt for years. For example, failure to deal with the issue of universal access could restrict market growth, either because of resulting restrictive regulation or because millions of people will be unable to participate in electronic commerce. Meanwhile, political debate over the future shape of many aspects of the Net drags on.

In the United States, laws often take years to pass both houses of Congress and be signed by the president. The same is true for the directives of the European Commission in Brussels and the laws and administrative guidance of the Japanese government. In Europe, each of the member states must also implement any new directive. In Japan, where consensus must be reached among agencies that often compete with each other, the process can take even longer. Because of their extreme complexity, as we have seen, laws affecting cyberspace may take still longer.

The effects of this time constraint can already be seen in a number of areas. In the United States, Congress debated telecommunications reform for a decade before passing the Telecommunications Act of 1996. That law, which is hundreds of pages long, takes dozens of pages just to summarize. Unfortunately, the implementation of its provisions have been slowed to a crawl by numerous Federal Communications Commission (FCC) hearings and proceedings and by court challenges brought by affected parties. All this was made possible by the many compromises and ambiguities purposely inserted into the law by different interest groups, and by issues such as universal service that Congress simply couldn't solve and so left to the FCC and other bodies to tackle. Thus the advent of competition in local telephone service has been delayed significantly, slowing innovation and retarding the growth of home Internet services that depend on fast, inexpensive, broadband connections. Perhaps even more significant, the act barely mentions the Internet and even then made a serious misstep on the issue of content regulation.

Another example is the export-control laws that affect not only the export of computer and telecommunications hardware but also the export of software, cryptography, and technical data. These laws, designed during the Cold War to deny advanced technology to the Soviet Union and its allies, have been consistently leapfrogged by technology. As Moore's Law drove computer processing power, for example, the export-control laws have had to be updated every few years to keep up. Perhaps the best illustration of the government's inability to keep up with technological change is the 1999–2000 change in the regulations regarding export of supercomputers. In July 1999, to keep up with the increasing power and availability of supercomputers, the government raised the export-control threshold for computers from 2,000 MTOPS (million theoretical operations per second, a benchmark used only by the government to define a supercomputer) to 6,500 MTOPS. Barley seven months later, on February 1, 2000, the government was forced to raise that threshold again, to 12,300 MTOPS. From a commercial standpoint, these governmental restrictions have never quite caught up with the global marketplace.

The heated debate over the export of strong encryption products has also continued for years; meanwhile, both widespread foreign availability and the worldwide ability to download encryption algorithms via the Internet has stymied policy makers. Although the Clinton administration moved to end controls on cryptography products at the end of 1999, the debate over details continues.

At the state level, progress is even slower. Some states have still not passed laws to deal with electronic signatures and contracts. Those that did so early, such as Utah, have seen their legislation become obsolete.

The commission that oversees uniform commercial law for the states worked for more than four years on its draft legislation. Finally accepted by the commission, it had been passed by only one state—Virginia—by spring 2000.

Overseas, the story is much the same. The EU took many years to develop its directive on privacy. Although this directive went into effect in October 1998, few countries within the EU were prepared to meet all of its enforcement terms, and little was resolved with regard to its impact on Europe's trading partners. Although in some areas movement has been more rapid, as with duties on information-technology products and intellectual property, a slower pace is the story throughout much of the world.

MEGACONVERGENCE AND THE SECTORAL INTERLOCK

One of the most difficult problems facing policy makers generally is the danger that laws passed to resolve one situation will create new problems in other, unanticipated areas. The enclosure laws of Tudor England, for example, helped set the stage for Elizabethan prosperity and benefited many farmers. But they also created an underclass of landless wanderers who went on to cause social unrest. In modern times, banking deregulation in the late 1970s, designed to create more competition among various types of banks, succeeded in that goal but also contributed to the savings and loan debacle of the 1980s by permitting and even encouraging some bankers to make more risky loans. Passage of a luxury tax in the early 1980s resulted in massive layoffs in the recreational boat industry, seriously damaging the economies of some coastal towns. In the case of policies affecting the Net, this problem is magnified by the potential impact of the digital age on so many interrelated fields.

For example, the U.S. Congress and state legislatures have generally viewed the privacy issue within the context of a specific sector. Privacy laws have been drafted specifically for such areas as banking, health care, education, government, credit, and even videotape rentals. As records become digitized and more readily accessible on the Internet, a new question arises: are these sectoral rules still the best approach, or would an omnibus approach covering all kinds of data and administered by a single, powerful agency make more sense? Omnibus rules, of course, would impinge on sectors already covered by existing laws.

Another area that would be greatly affected by Internet policies is professional licensing. Presently in the United States, licensing rules regulate numerous professions, including teaching, medicine and health care, architecture, insurance sales, engineering, and notary publics, and are administered by state and sometimes local governments. As the services of these professionals become available electronically over the Internet and therefore across state boundaries, the pressure to create national licensing regimes will grow. This transformation can already be seen in the move to create national "certificate authorities," a kind of electronic notary public for financial transactions to authenticate the identity and creditworthiness of parties who are buying and selling on the World Wide Web. Will national rules in one of these areas establish precedents that affect other areas? What will be the role of the professional societies that currently have such a profound effect on licensing rules?

Similarly, will the debate over universal access overflow from one area to another? For example, the Telecommunications Act of 1996 set up special funding for Internet access for schools, hospitals, and libraries. Meanwhile, as part of the federal government's "Reinventing Government" initiative, agencies are moving to make information and benefits available electronically to many groups, including welfare recipients and farmers. Do the rules for access in one of these areas have applicability in others? Should public funding be used to provide Internet access for farmers, rural residents, or inner-city dwellers?

Finally, legislators will have to take care as they modify and change industry-specific regulations in areas such as banking, insurance, health care, and telecommunications to ensure that the potential impact of regulations on other industries or sectors is understood and, if necessary, acted on. The digital world is too closely linked; making changes in one institution inevitably affects others.

FRACTURED GOVERNMENT

If the digital world is tightly linked, the government agencies and departments that need to deal with it are not. Most governments have organized themselves over time to mirror society's principal economic and social activities, as they developed in the past. Thus, we see ministries or departments of education, health, transportation, commerce, post (and in some countries, telecommunications), science and technology, and so forth. Each of these has not only its own bureaucracy but also its own legislative specialists and private-sector constituencies who provide political support for its budget and guide its policies. Legislative bodies tend to organize themselves along the same lines. In the United States, for example, parallel committees in the House and the Senate govern each of these areas.

For the most part, governments have not yet reorganized to meet the challenges of the digital world. In most cases, they have not even considered reorganization; instead, they have often cobbled together temporary interagency committees or advisory commissions to make recommendations. In the long run, this lack of consolidation may be a good thing, since private-sector leadership may thrive better when government is fragmented and unable to respond efficiently to new challenges. In the short run, however, this fragmentation makes it even more difficult to pass legislation that would enable electronic commerce. For example, an issue like privacy is a concern of numerous agencies and departments. Both the Treasury Department and the Federal Reserve System have a vested interest in the privacy of banking and financial records. The Department of Health and Human Services concerns itself with the privacy of medical records. The Commerce Department has an interest in privacy issues not only because of its business constituency but also because of its role as the coordinating agency for electronic commerce policies. The State Department and the Office of the U.S. Trade Representative are interested in the issue as it involves other countries or regions, such as the European Privacy Directive and its implementation in the EU. In addition, the White House, the Office of Management and Budget, the Federal Trade Commission, and other organizations in the United States are involved. This busy situation is mirrored in Congress, where many committees claim jurisdiction over privacy legislation.

The United States and many other countries have attempted to solve this problem by setting up coordinating committees of agencies, with one official designated to play the lead role. When President Clinton announced his Framework for Global Electronic Commerce in July 1997, the document was accompanied by a memorandum directing the vice president to lead a group of five government departments and agencies in a series of policy initiatives. It also asked them to work with other governments and international organizations on these initiatives.

The congressional effort has been more de facto, with the establishment of the bipartisan Congressional Internet Caucus to help form consensus on issues and then lobby fellow members for policies to promote the Internet. With more than one hundred members by May 2000, the caucus has been involved on the issues of Internet taxation, cryptography, and privacy, among others. Japan established a high-level coordinating committee in the Prime Minister's Office. Similarly, the EU established an Information Society Project office under the directorate-general responsible for telecommunications, science and technology, and the internal market. As the information infrastructure steadily becomes a larger part of national economies, governments may decide they need a more formal organization to deal with it.

ECONOMICS: NEW TERRITORY

We see the computer age everywhere except in the productivity statistics.

—Robert Solow, 1987[6]

Today, with most economists and politicians proclaiming the virtues of the "New Economy" arising from the explosion of information technology, it is startling to remember that President Kennedy once called automation and unemployment the greatest domestic challenge facing the United States, or that he appointed a National Commission on Automation and Unemployment. Although the fear of unemployment caused by information technology carried over into Europe in the 1970s and early 1980s, with the Minc-Nora Report in France and the German debate over "job-killers," it had largely abated by the 1990s. In fact, the meeting of ministers from the G-7 group of advanced industrialized nations in Brussels in February 1995 to discuss the GII appeared to resolve the issue with the G-7's affirmative declaration that the new technology would promote economic growth and employment. To be sure, there would be discontinuities based on educational attainment and other factors, but the overall picture was seen as very positive.

Policy makers until recently, however, were still confused by the debate among economists over the effects of the GII—a debate prompted by the early difficulties in measuring the productivity effects of information technology. This problem, known as the "productivity paradox," stemmed from the fact that although individual firms showed productivity gains from the use of the new computer and communications technologies, productivity advances were less clear for entire industries, and at the national level, until recently there did not appear to be any measurable effect on productivity.

Thus, some economists, such as Robert Solow and Steven Roach, found that information technology has made little or no contribution to productivity growth.[7] Others, such as Erik Brynjolfsson and Loren Hitt, believed that computers may have contributed to economic growth but that the productivity measurements used by governments were inadequate to measure the contribution.[8] Still others, such as Dan Sichel, believed that information technology was still too small a factor in the overall economy to make much of a difference, although it could make a big difference to individual firms.[9] Still others believed that it takes time for a new technology to work its way into the economy and that we have yet to see the benefits. Alan Greenspan, the chair of the Federal Reserve Board, originally took this view in 1997 in testimony before Congress when he said, "Thus, the full exploitation of . . . information and communications equipment may occur over quite a few years."[10] Greenspan compared the diffusion of information technology throughout the economy to the slow diffusion of electric motors earlier in the century. By 1999, however, Greenspan was more positive, as we shall see in Chapter 6.

If the subject of the economic impact of the Net on the economy as a whole is complex and hotly debated, the subject of the Internet's internal economics is sparsely researched. As stated by Lee McKnight and Joseph Bailey, both economists at the Massachusetts Institute of Technology, "The lack of accepted metrics for economic analysis of the Internet is increasingly problematic as the Internet grows in scale, scope, and significance to the global economy."[11] Among the factors that complicate an understanding of Internet economics have been the role of government subsidization, the perception among some that use of the Internet is (or should be) free, the complicating factor of telephone company regulation and its accompanying maze of cross-subsidization, and the lack of sound pricing mechanisms for Internet services.

Governments and international organizations, as well as industry and academicians, are working to unravel the overall economic puzzle. The Organization for Economic Cooperation and Development (OECD), in particular, has done a great deal of work. The conclusion of the OECD's 1998 study may be the best current summary of the state of the art:

> E-commerce is small in economic terms, but it has properties that are likely to make it important to a wide number of economic and social actors. As with the advent of any new technology that has the potential to be widely diffused, a number of overly optimistic and pessimistic predictions are made. . . . While it is impossible at such an early stage to confirm or reject any of these predictions . . . e-commerce . . . is likely to lead to changes that are generally beneficial and to greater economic growth.[12]

In June 1999, the U.S. Commerce Department report titled "The Emerging Digital Economy II" documented a much more positive story about the contribution of information technology and electronic commerce to economic growth, productivity, and employment.[13]

With no final answer, but with the preponderance of the evidence indicating a strong positive boost to national economies from the use of the GII, policy makers can now assume that the overall effect of the new technology will be positive.

THE CONTENT IS THE MESSAGE

If there was a seminal, provocative, twentieth-century thinker on the subject of the communications media and their role in our lives, it was the Canadian writer Marshall McLuhan. His book, *Understanding Media,* broke new ground in analyzing the impact of new electronic media such as television. With television reaching into virtually every household by the early 1960s, McLuhan was particularly influenced by its reach and the growing realization at that time that its impact on society was becoming profound. "The 'message' of any medium or technology," he said, "is the change of scale or pace or pattern that it introduces into human affairs."[14]

In some ways, McLuhan also seemed to be able to peer ahead and discern the coming of the Net as a global medium. He wrote, "If the work of the city is the remaking or translating of man into a more suitable form than his nomadic ancestors achieved, then might not our current translation of our entire lives into the spiritual form of information seem to make of the entire globe, a single consciousness?"[15] In other ways, however, McLuhan was a poor prophet. Too caught up in the odd romanticism of the 1960s, he wrote that people in developing countries would reject running water because they liked the communal benefits of fetching water each day from a common village well. He also would have made a poor financial analyst: he judged General Electric a failure because it had not discovered, as AT&T had, that it was in the business of "moving information."

But from today's perspective, McLuhan appears as a flawed Moses who could gaze across the Jordan into a dimly perceived future in the digital Promised Land but could never see it clearly or experience it himself. In his era, television, print, radio, film, and other media were totally separate and distinct, and he spent much of his effort analyzing the differences between them—why some were "hot" and others "cool." To McLuhan, the externalities of media were also an important part of their definition: the darkened world of the movie theater or the sensuous touch and feel of the telephone handset. What he did not (and could not) realize at the time was that rapidly changing technology would dissolve the distinctions and that even the externalities would change radically.

McLuhan missed the mark most when he failed to foresee that the phenomenon of convergence would collapse all media into a single phenomenon. Today, the creator of a Web site can build into that site printed text, data, music, voice, and video. The Net user can choose Internet telephony, videoconferencing, video streaming, radio narrowcasting, or text viewing. He or she can do that alone or in a large conference room, classroom, or theater with many other participants; not only are the media converged, but the externalities are now unrelated to the individual medium.

Thus, while the Net is creating the global village that McLuhan sketched, it is also obliterating individual forms of media. The result: the Net is the arch-media and its content has become the message. The Net marketer or advertiser or politician who wishes to communicate using the Net may use all or any the media tools available, but what he or she wishes to communicate is in the content of the message. Moreover, the key creators of Internet media and content—the "Web masters"—are not book publishers, film directors, musical producers, or data managers; the best of them must be all of the above and understand the skills of each. Content is again king!

This transformation is important for policy makers to consider because their focus must now be on content—not on the uniqueness of the media—as they deal with such policy issues as free speech or privacy. That which is illegal in the physical world should also be generally illegal in cyberspace. Whether that content is encased in a written sentence, an audio message, or a video clip is irrelevant. If content is fraudulent, it is illegal. If it is harmful to minors, the same rule should apply. In general, policy makers who have in the past few years created special restrictions on free speech for the Net will have to rethink those rules. For example, it would be foolish to apply rules developed for broadcast television or radio to Internet video or audio. Just as content creators have the freedom to choose what content and media they place on the Net, content users have the freedom to filter or not use what they consider to be objectionable content.

In the digital era, those who wish to develop policy for the Net will need to accept the best ideas of McLuhan but leave behind some of the intellectual prejudices and concepts of McLuhan's earlier age; they must focus on the actual realities of the newly converged media and their endless applications.

INTERNET ECOLOGY AND THE QUALITY OF LIFE

All too often in the past, environmentalists have been characterized as Luddites who have been skeptical of technological change. Real or imagined, this paradigm is being shattered by the Net, since the new information infrastructure offers many benefits for the environment while at the same time has the potential to improve the quality of life for large numbers of people.

First of all, the Net, in many instances, can replace the physical with the virtual, reducing the amount of manufacturing and processing of physical goods and thereby saving raw materials and avoiding pollutants of all types. The most obvious example, of course, could be the replacement of paper for all sorts of uses, including newspapers, magazines, books, records, mail, business data, and so forth. By 1998, for example, a 2.5-inch diskette could store 7.75 billion bits of information.

The potential for saving paper is only the most obvious impact of the new technology's environmental advantages. The use of simulation by supercomputers dramatically reduces the need to physically test everything from new commercial and military aircraft to new medications and drugs. Perhaps the most dramatic example of the potential of computer simulation is its ability to eliminate the need to test nuclear weapons and to keep unstable nuclear stockpiles safe by simulating nuclear tests and reactions.

The use of the Net for everything from E-mail to videoconferencing also reduces the need for business travel, especially air and automobile travel. E-mail also replaces physical mail, reducing both the consumption of paper and the transportation necessary to deliver it. On the other hand, and not to overstate the case, widespread use of electronic commerce will increase the need for package delivery, requiring more use of trucks and other methods of transportation, though perhaps eliminating trips to stores as well.

Most important from both the environmental standpoint and the positive effect on the quality of life, the Net makes possible telecommuting, or the possibility for employees to work in their homes. Not only does this reduce the amount of commuting—particularly by automobile, a major source of pollution—it also reduces the need for physical real estate in the form of office buildings. By 1996, it was estimated that there were already more than eight million telecommuters in the United States alone. These included not only people directly involved in the new technology, such as programmers, but everyone from salespeople to researchers to telephone-support staff. Since employers benefit directly from telecommuting because of the reduced need for office space, the trend can be expected to grow rapidly. Among the other benefits of telecommuting is the value to working parents who can perform all or part of their work at home and not have to deal with day care for young children. Another group that benefits is the severely disabled: people suffering from such ailments as severe cerebral palsy or quadriplegia, with the assistance of specially developed equipment, may now work on a variety of tasks from their homes. Future technologies promising greater ease of use will make work even easier for this group of people.

Telecommuting, or "teleworking," as it is called in Europe, also raises serious public policy questions, especially in the area of labor law—much of which was developed more than sixty years ago during the Great Depression, long before the era of the microchip. How do wage and hour rules apply to home workers? Do workplace safety rules apply to telecommuters, or will they have to modify their homes to meet the standards of the federal Occupational Safety and Health Administration (OSHA)? Will local zoning rules restricting home business use have to be changed as large numbers of people make their homes their place of business? Far-fetched as this may sound, in January 2000, the U.S. Department of Labor issued and was then forced to withdraw an OSHA directive that employers would be responsible for the home-workplace safety of telecommuters. One such government employee wondered if OSHA would require him to paint his dog yellow, since he frequently tripped over the animal. Much of this policy underbrush will need to be cleared away to allow cyberspace to thrive.

One final quality-of-life contribution of the digital age is to the elderly, particularly the homebound. E-mail in particular has allowed them a new easy means of communicating with grandchildren and other relatives and friends. Another is the rapid growth of electronic commerce: now the elderly can shop at home for groceries, medications, or gifts for grandchildren. Organizations such as ElderNet provide a Web forum for the elderly on numerous topics. Not surprisingly, the elderly are one of the fastest-growing groups of users of the Internet today.

DISTRIBUTING POWER

As Robert Keohane and Joseph Nye have observed, the information age is changing the nature of power in international relations.[16] Along with military and traditional economic power, states may now use the "soft" power of information much more effectively to influence and change other nations' behavior. Cultural content and propaganda can be disseminated even more broadly and inexpensively today, using the power of the GII. But the redistribution of power caused by the information revolution is far broader and infinitely more important than the relationship between nations. It affects the relationships between consumers and producers, between lay people and professionals, between management and workers, between governments and citizens, and between competing cultures.

These changes in the distribution of power rest on two fundamental characteristics of the digital age. First, it is much easier and cheaper now than in the past for anyone to have access to all kinds of information. Second, it is now much easier and cheaper for anyone to disseminate information broadly. These facts cannot be understated. The changes resulting from this increased ability to provide and access information will be among the most profound of the information revolution.

The first characteristic—the lower costs of access to information—means that consumers can obtain much more price and product information than ever before. Patients can look at detailed medical information from a variety of sources. Employees can access more information about their firms. Citizens can learn more about their governments—and act on that information. The second characteristic means that anyone can publish anything—poetry, art, political tracts, or music—on the Net and reach a potentially huge audience. Smaller cultures and language groups can make available their literature and culture to audiences worldwide. The effects are already visible and becoming pervasive.

For example, the availability of price and product information to consumers is fostering on-demand on-line pricing in real time. A prospective automobile purchaser can use an on-line service such as Carprices.com and review detailed information, including dealer prices and private rebates from the manufacturer to the dealer. Thus, the traditional relationship between the all-knowing, scheming auto salesperson and the ignorant, victim buyer has been shattered. Even beyond this development, however, are such trends as on-line auctions for goods, or services such as Priceline.com where purchasers bid for services ranging from airline tickets to hotel rooms to groceries. These activities are creating more competition and lowering prices and thus should generally result in more efficient markets. Moreover, the marketplace has become global, open to even more competition. A small producer in a formerly remote nation such as Peru or Pakistan no longer needs to rely solely on an agent or distributor to reach customers in other countries. A simple Web site may be sufficient.

The availability of information is also changing the relationship between professionals and their clients, such as physicians and patients. Today, a person contemplating any medical regime ranging from a surgical procedure to a new medication can view dozens of Web sites providing everything from the mortality rate for a particular operation, broken down by state, hospital, age group, condition, and individual surgeon, to the results of various double-blind studies or the side effects of different drugs. Physicians thus find themselves answering much more sophisticated questions, pondering more alternatives, reviewing their diagnoses, and perhaps altering their initial recommendations. In effect, patients can become their own second opinions, a development that obviously carries great risks as well as significant benefits. But the physicians' monopoly on knowledge is fading.

The pattern of shifting power is much the same in the workplace. The thinning out of middle management ranks during the downsizing of corporations has been noted by many observers. One reason that corporations have been able to reduce the size of this group is that the use of information technology permits the constant direct exchange of information between senior management and lower-level employees, eliminating the need for the old middle-management conduit. Thus, large institutions are flattening out as the outdated hierarchical pyramid structure is replaced by something more resembling the spokes of a wheel, with information flowing much more freely not only out from the center along the spokes, but all along the circumference of the wheel itself—between departments and individual employees. In a world of reduced product cycles, companies that have reorganized along these lines are nimbler, more responsive to customer demands, and faster to market. And within these companies, individual employees wield more power than ever before. The Net can be a powerful organizing tool for employees that has the potential to restore employee bargaining strength in an era that has seen it steadily diminished.

A similar shift is occurring between companies and their affiliates, such as suppliers and distributors. Linked together by intranets, suppliers and distributors can become integral parts of a company's development and marketing strategies, evolving into "virtual" corporations that are no longer mere appendages of the parent company.

Citizens are also learning that power can shift in their favor in their relationship with governments at all levels. Access to government information up to the present has been generally through a civil servant gateway, usually accessible only during normal working hours. Conscious of their monopoly on information—the currency of their privileged positions—civil servants are not always totally forthcoming with citizens. In the future, by contrast, most governments and their agencies can become transparent, and the civil servant will become less of a gatekeeper. Government Web sites can be navigated at any hour of the day or night.

Most questions can be quickly answered and government forms and applications can be downloaded, printed, and sometimes filed on-line.

For example, a retiree moving to the state of Florida can find on that state's Web site information on all of the following: voter registration, car registration, automobile inspection, driver's licenses, state income and other taxes, real property tax exemptions, fishing and hunting licenses, state employment, and much more. Other sites, run by civic organizations, political parties, and the press offer information on elected officials, such as their voting records and stands on key issues. Many politicians now use E-mail so that constituents can easily and inexpensively make known their views. A 1999 poll by *Wired* magazine and Merrill Lynch showed that Internet users are more likely to vote than are nonusers—and politicians have noticed. With Web publishing, small political organizations can publish their materials and make them available to a much wider audience than they once could, greatly improving the potential strength of smaller political parties and interest groups. The dark side of this is that the power of the electronic infrastructure is also open to political fringe groups that promote racial and religious hatreds and violence, giving them an audience they could not hope to reach in an earlier age. Dictatorships, such as those in Serbia and North Korea, also use the Net to spread government propaganda.

Finally, a similar shift is taking place in the cultural field. Established newspapers, magazines, book publishers, television networks, and other institutions dominated the cultural field in the past because of the great costs inherent in publishing and broadcasting; the emergence of the new information infrastructure greatly diminishes their near-monopoly. Not only are new publications springing up on the Internet almost daily, but virtually anyone can use a Web site and self-publish their own short stories, poetry, videos, or music.

This is as true for nations as for individuals. Although a few governments have felt threatened by a perceived dominance of language and material from the United States, others are moving quickly to establish their own presence on the Internet for their museums, art, folklore, music, and language. For example, anyone who wishes to learn about the languages of Lesotho, a tiny landlocked country in southern Africa that produces remarkable tapestries, can arrive from the Yahoo search engine after three clicks of a mouse at www.sil.org/ethnologue/countries/Leso. Here, one will learn that the country's principal language is Sesotho, but that Zulu is also spoken. One can access not only a tutorial on Sesotho grammar and structure on-line, but also information on the extinct language of Seroa, once spoken here. The Lesotho government has also wisely offered a link to the National Investment Corporation for those who might have an interest in investing in the country.

Lesotho is not alone out there. The Internet offers a marvelous opportunity for smaller nations and their citizens to offer their culture to the world, and many are beginning to do so. On the other hand, the free and open culture of the Internet, so representative of the values of the West and particularly of the United States, inevitably adds to the cultural assault that some perceive and fear. If Islamic fundamentalism has been at least in part a reaction to Western cultural virility, the Internet surely adds to fundamentalist concerns. However, Islamic states have so far reacted differently to the digital age: whereas Iraq has limited the use of the Internet by its citizens, Iran and Saudi Arabia have generally welcomed it. Iran's university students use it actively (perhaps contributing to their unhappiness with the fundamentalist government), and Saudi electronic commerce is now growing.

MONEY EQUALS INFORMATION

Most Americans today, having lived during an era of relative stability in the monetary system, have little awareness of what money actually is or how it can change suddenly. Europeans, Asians, and others who have personally experienced wars, civil breakdowns, and economic collapse have a better intuitive understanding of the issue, as did earlier Americans. During the relatively short history of the United States, money has taken the form of seashells, beaver skins, tobacco, gold, silver, and most recently, promises by the government. Today, the United States has a single currency, but at times in the past, the nation has had numerous currencies, including those issued by state banks and the "greenbacks" of the Civil War era, when different batches of notes had different values, depending on whether the North or the South had won recent battles.

The single currencies of the United States and other industrial countries have served them well, creating a single and constant store of value and a relatively stable trading vehicle. In the digital era, the challenge will be to maintain this constancy when virtually all money becomes bits of information that can take on different electronic forms and move at the speed of light.

When money is expressed as information in digital form, it can be transferred instantly, anywhere in the world. Ever since 1972, when the Federal Reserve Bank of San Francisco experimented with electronic payments to transfer funds, the use of electronic money has exploded.[17] Three years later, in 1975, the Social Security Administration and other government and private retirement and payroll systems began to transfer funds electronically to retirees and employees. By the middle of the 1990s, the total amount of electronic transfers had mushroomed, approaching half the size of all the paper checks written. Millions of transactions, ranging from consumers paying bills, to corporations purchasing supplies, to huge bank and government transfers, were being handled electronically. Their growth made possible the globalization of the world economy, a development that has fueled powerful economic growth. Unfortunately, it has occasionally also left governments and their citizens reeling from Asia to Latin America. Significant as they were, these electronic transactions were still made within the existing international banking and Federal Reserve settlements system.

With the advent of the Internet and electronic commerce, however, a need arose for forms of electronic money that appeared to fall outside of the settlements system. If, for example, someone wanted to spend twenty-five cents on the Internet to look at a proprietary Web site (one hosting a magazine, for example), a form of digital cash might be more useful for such a small purchase. Perhaps a consumer might wish to carry around in his or her wallet a "smart card" that could be debited by electronic vendors to make small daily purchases. Such a card could be replenished by an information appliance connected to the Internet. Although special-purpose digital payment systems for use at toll booths or mass transit fare boxes already exist, they are generally designed for a single type of transaction. Today, universal cards are being developed and tested that are both a store of value and a transaction medium. In other words, to the potential consternation of governments, they are money.

Would these new forms of cash be actual currency in a new form? If so, would they be legal or would they compete with existing currency issued by the government? How would sellers be able to trust the new currency's validity? Would users of the currency trust that it would retain its value over time and distance? What effect might its issuance have on the money supply? How might this even be measured? What kinds of institutions would the issuers be and who would regulate them?

These questions and others took on some urgency in the middle of 1998, as a worldwide credit crunch temporarily took hold, caused in part by the sudden ability of investors to move very large amounts of money easily across national borders and out of volatile regions like Latin America and Russia. As electronic commerce rapidly becomes a substantial portion of overall commerce, these issues will need to be continually addressed, not only nationally, but internationally.

THE NEW COMPETITIVE ADVANTAGE

Of all of the undercurrents connected with the digital age, perhaps the one of most interest to political leaders around the world is the seismic shift it causes not only in the actual competitive advantages of regions and nations, but in the conditions that create competitive advantage. In earlier ages, competitive advantage tended to be physically based: seventeenth-century France grew rich because of its climate and soils, nearly perfect for agriculture; Britain's maritime tradition nurtured its navy and created and sustained its empire; Saudi Arabia's oil fields and South Africa's diamonds and gold produced their wealth. On the other hand, nations with poor climates and geography and no natural resources have tended to fare poorly.

With the rise of technology and the information economies of the early twenty-first century, however, other factors began to determine competitive advantage, and the new GII is greatly accelerating this trend. The most important new determinant rests on educational systems and the harnessing of human resources to perform the tasks of the information age. Nations and regions that are able to develop the educated human capital that can deal with the new technologies will be able to leverage that strength and turn it to their economic, strategic, and social advantage.

Two countries that are quickly learning this lesson are India and Singapore. The Indian city of Bangalore has become a world-renowned center for software development because of the skills developed by many of its people. Bangaloreans are becoming wealthy by programming for companies in the United States and Europe, since distance and location have no bearing on their work. A programmer in Bangalore can telecommute to Atlanta or Seattle as easily as can a worker in the suburbs of those cities. Singapore's "IT2000: A Vision of an Intelligent Island" report recognized education and computer literacy as central to that island nation's economic development plan. Reforming and modernizing education and wiring the nation have become national priorities. The United States has also focused on connecting all schools to the Internet, and states are competing with each other to improve education at all levels to become more competitive. And within the United States, individual states are competing with each other to become more competitive. Educational reform, modernized tax laws, legal reforms, and privacy protection are among the areas in which state legislatures and governors are working.

Other factors are also critical to information-age competitiveness. These include having an advanced information infrastructure that permits cheap, fast, and reliable Internet access. To achieve this, countries will need to deregulate their existing telecommunications structures and encourage new competitors who can exploit advanced technologies. For example, developing countries are learning that wireless networks may be a more economical solution to bring telecommunications to their rural areas than building expensive physical connections. The use of public electronic kiosks, such as those developed in the province of Ontario, Canada, to deliver services may be more efficient than trying to wire every home. Of course, the problem of telecommunications competition must also be solved in industrialized countries, where the lack of competition often slows the process of modernization.

Finally, countries and regions seeking competitive advantage in the future will need to reexamine all of their government policies and regulations to create a sound overall policy environment for the development of electronic commerce. Creating this policy environment must take into account the impact that information technology has on society. We turn to this subject in Chapter 3.

3

Megaconvergence: Government and Social Services

The fog comes on little cat feet.

—Carl Sandburg

The institutional changes triggered by the digital revolution begin to creep in to organizations at first like fog—quietly and unnoticed for the most part. Even though forecasts and warnings by observers and even by institutional management may have predicted these changes, few workers or managers take notice as the first patches of change roll in. Workstations are upgraded and connected to the Internet and probably to the institution's intranet. Group-oriented software (called "groupware"), such as Lotus Notes or Novell GroupWise, is installed. Perhaps an extranet is added to connect to the institution's external constituencies. Employees and managers take a few hours of classes to learn how to incorporate these new technologies into their work.

At first, the flow and type of work in the organization remain the same. Many people may heave a sigh of relief: they have survived. That is usually the point at which the fog metaphor suddenly ends. Very soon, change hits the institution first like a violent thunderstorm, then as a cyclone.

The existing organization structure is blown away, as its activities begin to converge with the new communications and computing technologies. Skill needs change much more dramatically and rapidly. Jobs are restructured. Entirely new channels of communication with and distribution to clients, customers, suppliers, and constituents develop. The old, formal, management chain of command collapses. Firms and other organizations, such as hospitals, merge or form new strategic partnerships. Some simply close and go out of business. The foundation on which the institution has rested for years and perhaps for centuries is suddenly sucked into the maelstrom and then washed away by a flood of

65

new ideas and methods. The surviving people hope the storm will end and that stability may return, but the pace of technology and the fear of competition offer no consolation. The future looks increasingly challenging and uncertain.

This is the reality that is faced by all of the world's institutions as the new global information infrastructure (GII) and its capabilities take hold. From city halls to hospital and university boards to factory supervisors to publishers, the struggle is on to harness the new technologies. The radical institutional changes that new technology brings about also raise fundamental public policy issues. Therefore, policy makers must understand this struggle. Although the changes wrought by technology affect every institution, we will examine two categories: government and social services; and financial services, commerce and industry. In each case, we will examine both the changes themselves and the public policy issues they raise.

SOCIAL SERVICES

Health Care

If there is a single institution that could offer dramatic new benefits to humanity by adapting quickly to the new information infrastructure, it is health care. In virtually no other institution is the need for accurate and timely information frequently a life-and-death matter, and in few other institutions are the sources of information more fragmented or more archaic. Anyone who has had to physically carry his or her X-ray films from physician to physician to clinic to hospital grasps this reality immediately. So does anyone who has had an emergency illness while traveling; it is almost impossible today to retrieve a patient's health record quickly. Even when the issue is not a critical health issue, the problem of getting information from health care bureaucracies is often frustrating for patients and physicians, and even for the bureaucracies themselves, who spend far too much time and money simply dealing with information.

Health care today is an enormous web of institutions and individuals that generates by its very nature an incredible amount of information. By the end of 1995, in the United States alone, there were 600,000 physicians, 6,000 hospitals, and 1,200 medical insurance companies. That year, 4.8 billion insurance claims were filed and 1.7 billion prescriptions were filled. There were 418 million patient outpatient visits and 150 million inquiries about benefit eligibility. Health care employed 9 million people and represented about 14 percent of U.S. gross domestic product (GDP).[1] The Congressional Budget Office predicted that health care costs would grow to 18 percent of GDP in 2000, if not managed properly. This huge "system" affects virtually every employer in the country and also involves numerous government programs and agencies at the federal, state, and local levels. It also supports a massive system of education and training and the world's largest and most advanced research and development efforts at the nation's medical schools, the National Institutes of Health, and private foundations and institutes. Worldwide, particularly in the industrialized countries, the situation is much the same.

Yet despite the critical need for accurate patient information, few of the records that are generated by this "system" and its individual institutions have been digitized and even fewer are available on-line and connected to each other. In fact, for the most part, each hospital, each physician, and each insurance company lives in its own isolated information island, making decisions based on incomplete and sometimes incorrect data, instead of being able to draw on the sum total of accurate knowledge in the entire system. The results include higher costs and lower quality of care.

Consider the following single example. In 1998, pharmaceutical companies were expected to release more than 300 new cancer-fighting drugs, with approximately another 1,000 drugs in the research and development pipeline.[2] The federal government requires that each drug undergo testing in human patients, but until recently it has been extremely difficult for doctors with patients who might benefit from the new drugs to match those patients with the researchers conducting the tests, since records were kept on paper lists. Now, with the use of a secure extranet, doctors can enter cancer patients' information and have it automatically matched with a list of new drug trials. Patients can then decide if they wish to participate. Since information in the system is secure and encrypted, with access limited to the physician involved, the patient's privacy is protected.

Although this single example is illustrative, the potential impact of the Net on health care may be more usefully examined by looking at the major objectives countries have set for improving the health of their citizens and advancing their health care systems. One can then imagine how use of the Net might achieve these goals.

Most industrial countries have three overall objectives. First, countries wish to lower or at least contain the growth of health care costs. Modern information technology, especially the Net, can play a key role in this effort. Today, for example, between 15 and 40 percent of all health care costs are for unnecessary procedures that caused by a lack of information. Anyone who has had to submit to identical medical tests or procedures a few days apart because information was "not available" understands this issue immediately. A key part of the solution to this is the health information network, wherein physicians, hospitals, pharmacies, clinical laboratories, and payers such as insurance companies or government agencies can be linked together in a network using the Internet to provide a common pool of information. This pool can comprise not only alphanumeric data, but graphic information such as X-rays or magnetic-resonance images (MRIs) that can be stored, sent, and retrieved at will by anyone in the system with the proper clearances.

One such system is the Health Data Network of the Greater Dayton Hospital Association which links 5,000 physicians, 20 area hospitals, and 3 payers in the Dayton, Ohio, area. The system allows physicians to access referrals, preregister surgery patients at hospitals, and deal with insurance questions. If a patient comes to an emergency room within the association, doctors can quickly access his or her records and even navigate quickly to the most critical information. Systems like that in Dayton, which are spreading across the country, will not only save money due to their efficiency in dealing with paperwork but also reduce duplicate tests. They will also improve the quality of care for many patients. The growth of health data networks like this will also help encourage strategic partnerships and alliances between health maintenance organizations (HMOs), hospitals, physicians, and pharmacies that will further alleviate the rising costs of health care.

Another way to reduce medical costs is to prevent illness before it occurs. Although physicians and HMOs are focusing on this question themselves, a more health-conscious population is also using new digital tools to educate itself and to get information that might reveal oncoming illnesses or conditions while they are more easily and inexpensively treated or reversed. Today, dozens of Web sites, some maintained by the nation's most important medical centers and hospitals, offer a wealth of free "wellness" advice. One need not visit the Mayo Clinic in Rochester, Minnesota, to benefit from its advanced research and information: just look at www. mayohealth.com. Two clicks away from its site on aging, an older citizen can view its "Perceived Exertion Scale," which provides some simple exercise rules for the elderly to improve their health and avoid destructive side effects. Similarly, allergy sufferers who visit www.intellihealth.com, a Website sponsored jointly by Aetna U.S. Healthcare and Johns Hopkins University Hospital, find ways to keep their allergies under control. One click from the Intellihealth home page is an "Allergy Headlines" feature that offers the latest news from medical researchers on allergy treatments. Numerous other such services exist on the Internet, including chat rooms where people suffering from similar conditions can compare their treatments and reactions. The new technologies can therefore reduce costs by educating people and improving their health with easily accessible information, thus achieving the second objective most countries have established for health care: to broaden their citizens' access to it.

For most countries, the issue of access is understood in terms of people's ability to pay for health care; often it is intertwined with the issue of nationalized medicine. But "access" involves not only the highly political issue of national or socialized health care, but also the question of physical access. Even if health care were subsidized or provided by the state, would people living in rural or other remote areas be able to visit a physician? Would poor inner-city residents understand how to use the health care system properly? Would the homebound elderly get the monitoring of illnesses they need? In each of these cases, the Net will play an important role.

Michael Dertouzos, head of MIT's Laboratory for Computer Sciences, has described how medicine in the future might extend its reach far out into remote areas.[3] In his vision, a medical kiosk in a remote Alaska settlement, combined with a "smart" medical-history card, is able to monitor key indicators such as heart rate, pulse, blood pressure, and temperature. It can also transmit this information to physicians and hospitals a continent away, provide two-way video and audio between the patient and the distant physician, take and transmit X-rays, measure the patient's blood-oxygen levels, and automatically order medical transportation.

Although systems like this are still under development, telemedicine has been in use since 1958, when television was first used to communicate patient information. Since then, telemedicine has spread into every state in the United States and to many countries overseas. Reliable estimates are hard to come by, but one consultant estimates that the U.S. market for telemedicine will grow to $3 billion by 2002.

Although Alaska may not yet have the kind of kiosks that Dertouzos envisions, it does have the Alaska Telemedicine Project, a consortium of Alaskan health care providers, telecommunications carriers, the University of Alaska at Anchorage, and the state and federal governments. This consortium of forty-eight organizations, including ten Native health partner groups such as the Eastern Aleutian Tribes and the Yukon-Kuskokwim

Health Corporation, is trying to develop advanced and easy-to-use health care systems that can reach into the most remote mountain and tundra regions and islands. Alaska also hopes that its rural telemedicine system will become a model for the circumpolar region and developing countries.

Alaska's program is far from unique. States such as Texas and North Carolina have developed similar initiatives. In other countries, the story is the same. Telemedicine Canada is part of the National Telehealth Network; it uses telemedicine to bring continuing education programs to health professionals across Canada. In Europe, the Framework for European Services in Telemedicine fosters tools for planning, developing, and implementing telemedicine services. One of the more interesting international networked health projects is the Global Emergency Telemedicine Service, a program set up by the G-8 group of advanced industrialized nations and funded by the European Commission. This project will set up a worldwide, twenty-four-hour, multilingual, multidisciplinary telemedicine and telesurveillance emergency care service.

If telemedicine can benefit rural people, it can also create new forms of access for urban patients. It has the potential to improve access to health care by bringing a wide range of services into the home, including telemetry and radiology. Even a medical discipline such as dermatology can reach homebound patients, since two-way video can allow patients to be diagnosed at a distance. Perhaps one of the most useful applications is the development of health education programs in such areas as infant care that can be made available to young mothers either directly in the home or in community centers, schools, clinics, or other publicly accessible sites.

Although telemedicine can broaden access to health care, it also brings potential dangers. Web sites that offer the opportunity for on-line diagnosis by a physician may overstep medical boundaries. In April 1999, the U.S. Department of Health and Human Services issued a report, "Wired for Health and Well-Being," warning that "inaccurate or inappropriate health information and support could result in inappropriate treatment." Similarly, the American Telemedicine Association warned consumers to exercise caution in using Web sites that offer on-line diagnosis and prescribe treatment. In June 1999, the U.S. Federal Trade Commission (FTC) launched "Operation Cure All," aimed at targeting fraudulent health claims made on the Internet. By January 2000, according to the FTC, 34.7 million people were seeking health information on-line, and health information was the fifth most commonly accessed on-line information. But most users reported that they found it difficult to judge whether or not that information was trustworthy. The rapid growth of such sites suggest that Net health services will grow nevertheless, and more oversight may be needed, either by the medical community itself or by government.

The third health care objective of most countries to improve the quality of medical care. While many of the digital-age innovations already discussed can help reduce the cost of health care and broaden access, they can also improve the quality of care. Beyond them, other sophisticated techniques made possible by the new infrastructure can improve quality more broadly. For example, the Harvard Community Health Plan, with more than six hundred thousand members, used interactive technology not only to educate patients but to help them diagnose illness. Its Triage and Education System has used equipment in the patient's home to answer questions about mild illnesses and recommend a course of action.[4] At any time of day or night, the system, which included a set of illness protocols, could be asked by the patient to diagnose a particular condition. If a child had a fever, for example, the system could ask questions to determine how serious the problem was and whether there were complications. If the problem was not serious, the system could recommend a course of action and contact with the office at a later time. If the situation was serious (if the child was having trouble breathing, for example), the system would automatically alert the physician on duty, who would then call the patient. When the physician called, he or she would already have at hand much of the critical information needed to take the appropriate steps.

Perhaps the ultimate example of the Net's potential contribution to improved quality in medical care is what Dertouzos calls the "guardian angel." In the future, speculates Dertouzos, everyone would have their own digital health history module from birth, containing a complete health history and programmed with illness protocols and diagnostic techniques. Throughout a person's life, the "guardian angel" would not only be available in case of emergency with all of a person's relevant health data, but would also alert the patient to various health conditions or threats. It could warn of the dangers of becoming overweight after a gourmet tour of Burgundy, or warn of a conflict between different medications if a new drug is prescribed. Most important, the information module would be under the supervision of the individual himself or herself; the patient would control access through passwords and check the accuracy of the data stored in the module, thus protecting his or her privacy.

The innovations brought about in health care by the new information infrastructure are helping countries achieve their health care goals, but they are also causing profound changes in the structure of health care itself and in the laws and regulations that govern it. As health care organizations merge, create partnerships, and interconnect with each other, often across numerous geographical boundaries, new kinds of institutions are emerging. These new institutions and their activities often have new funding and governance models; they may also need new legislation to legitimize them. Among the public policy issues raised by the new networked health care system are the following:

—Telecommunications: Should federal, state, and local telecommunications regulations be amended to extend targeted universal-service subsidies to health care information systems?
—Research: Should federal, state, or local government funds be spent on research and development or test beds for new health care applications?
—Reimbursement: Can federal and state regulations be modified to provide for patient reimbursement under programs such as Medicare or Medicaid for telemedicine, home telemetry, and other advanced medical techniques using the Net?
—Licensure and accreditation: Should state licensing rules for health care professionals be changed to permit physicians in another jurisdiction to treat patients via telemedicine? Should Web sites that offer diagnostic services be licensed, accredited, or regulated, either by government or by professional medical groups?
—Insurance: Do health insurance regulations need to be changed to provide for payment to health care providers or patients for telemedicine services? Should state regulations be preempted by federal law?
—Medical education: Do state requirements for medical education need to be changed to provide for new educational requirements related to the new technologies?
—Privacy: Are new federal or state laws or regulations required for proper protection of the privacy of patient records in the new digital environment? Should a single federal law or set of regulations replace the patchwork of current state laws?
—Security: Are new standards required for hospitals, physicians, clinical laboratories, pharmacies, employers, insurance companies, and other health care providers and payers to protect the security of patient records?
—Legal: Are new state laws or regulations required to deal with legal issues such as the authenticity of patient records, electronic signa-

tures on medical records, or the admissibility of electronic records in court cases? Are federal and state law-enforcement authorities able to deal with health fraud and misrepresentation on the Net?

—Regulatory: Should the Food and Drug Administration or similar agencies test and regulate the software and hardware devices designed and used for medical diagnosis and treatment, much as they regulate drugs and traditional medical devices?

—International: Are there international implications for any of these issues, and if so, how are they to be resolved? One issue is clearly the privacy of patient records that are sent across national borders where different privacy regimes are in place. Another example would be the use of public funding for research into medical applications and whether foreign entities, such as corporations or universities, would be eligible to participate in such research programs. A third would be "mutual recognition agreements" to bridge different countries' health regulatory regimes for networked applications.

Many of these issues are currently making their way through state legislatures, the Congress, or the federal bureaucracy. For example, Texas has already amended its Medical Practice Act to permit telemedicine, has passed telecommunications legislation to require common carriers to promote broadband services for heath care institutions and created a fund of up to $1.5 billion to develop telemedicine and other services, and has passed laws requiring the state Medicaid agency and insurance companies to reimburse providers for appropriate telemedicine services. Other states have passed or are working on similar initiatives.

At the federal level, the Department of Health and Human Services has completed work on regulations governing the privacy of patient medical records. President Clinton announced these proposed new national rules in October 1999. The new rules were mandated by the 1996 Kennedy-Kassebaum health care reform bill, in the event that Congress did not pass new legislation. Bombarded on all sides by lobbyists, Congress failed to act, leaving the matter in the administration's hands. The proposed regulations would cover all electronic health care records and would go into effect in 2002. They would limit the use and disclosure of patient records, give individuals access to their own records, and provide ways for individuals to correct erroneous information in their files. The rules contain minor criminal penalties for violations.

The Department of Commerce is also working on general legal rules that affect electronic commerce, including health care. In the area of enforcement, the FTC in April 2000 reached settlements with three Internet companies it had charged with deception. Arizona announced similar actions. Moreover, the on-line health care private sector responded to these actions with its own agenda. In May 2000, the Health Internet Ethics Group, a consortium of twenty on-line health companies, including Healtheon/ WebMD and PlanetRX.com, announced ethical standards and privacy guidelines for health-oriented Web sites. The organization said its efforts were a first step that could eventually include implementation and enforcement. The government is also working with other countries at the United Nations and elsewhere on the international legal environment and cooperating with international projects, such as the new health applications being developed and tested by the G-8 (the members of the G-7, plus Russia).

In sum, health care systems everywhere in the world can anticipate remarkable change as they converge with digital technology—change that will transform health care institutions and change the way health care professionals and workers learn and do their jobs. These changes will reduce costs while increasing access to and improving health care. To make this possible in a timely manner, public policy in the health care field will need to be modernized.

Education

Education, it has been said, is a low-tech institution in a high-tech world. If a nineteenth-century physician were to walk into a modern hospital, for example, he or she would be totally baffled by everything—the equipment, the medications, and the treatments. But if a nineteenth-century third-grade teacher were to walk into almost any modern classroom, he or she would feel very much at home—a blackboard in front of a room filled with rows of students at their desks. In this case, the word "almost" is operative, since the revolution of technology in the classroom has recently begun in earnest.

Education worldwide is one of humanity's largest and most important institutions. In the United States alone, from preschool through graduate universities, more than 66 million students were enrolled in 1997, with more than 46 million enrolled in the grades from kindergarten to twelfth grade alone.[5] This number was expected to grow by about 4 percent by 2002. In the approximately 100,000 schools for these children, more than 3 million people were employed as teachers alone, not including administrators, union officials, textbook publishers, government bureaucrats, and others employed in the education enterprise. Total spending on K–12 education topped $340 billion in the 1996–97 school year, with about 93 percent of this funding provided by states and localities. Worldwide, according the UN World Education Report, there were more than 1.1 billion students studying from kindergarten through higher education, about one-fifth of the world's entire population. Global expenditures for education amounted to just over 5 percent of the world's entire gross national product.

In total, the United States spent more than $560 billion on preschool through university education in 1996–97, or about 7.4 percent of gross national product. This number does not count spending on professional and technical training by businesses, labor unions, municipalities, and individuals, one of the fastest-growing segments of education. In fact, this particular education segment is becoming "lifelong," as technological change drives the need for continuous learning. Moreover, education costs have been rising faster than inflation. For example, in the ten years from 1986 to 1996, the costs of tuition, room, and board at private and public universities in the United States grew by more than 20 percent, after inflation.

Quality, however, appears to be largely but not totally unrelated to the size of the expenditure, particularly in elementary and secondary education. Despite the nation's huge expenditures, educational outcomes in the K–12 sector have been deeply disappointing. Since the publication of the report "A Nation at Risk: The Imperative for Educational Reform" by the National Commission on Excellence in Education in 1983,[6] government officials, educators, businesspeople, parents, and others have all worried about the generally poor performance of American students and backed various reform efforts. Although some areas have been improved since the report was published, overall performance remains mediocre or poor, even among the best American students. For example, 13 percent of entering college students require remedial reading classes. Whereas 37 percent of German students take the equivalent of Advanced Placement classes, only 7 percent of U.S. students do. Of those, 95 percent of German students pass the final exam, whereas only 66 percent of U.S. students do.

"A Nation at Risk" made a sweeping series of recommendations for educational reform that focused heavily on the quality of teachers but also called for wide support for reform from all elements of American society. Since then, a broad but often shaky consensus has developed that places national educational goals and standards, school accountability, and systemic changes to implement these goals at the center of the reform movement. Federal legislation, in the form of the Goals 2000: Educate America Act;

legislation in almost every state; and dozens of reform efforts supported politically and often financially by teachers and their unions, parents, businesses, and educators are now falling into place to achieve these ends.

During this time, as computer and communications technologies penetrated every area of society, they also began to move into the classroom—but, oddly, with little measurable effect until recently. In 1995, the Senate Committee on Labor and Human Resources asked the Office of Technology Assessment (OTA) to report on why, despite more than a decade of investment in educational computer hardware and software, so few teachers were actually using the technology. The OTA report, "Teachers and Technology," reported that despite the installation of 5.8 million computers in the nation's schools in 1995 (one for every nine students), most teachers reported little or no use of them for instruction.[7] The most common reason was simply inadequate training for teachers, although even when computers were used, it was usually not as part of the core curriculum, but in special computer classes or laboratories. The report concluded, "Making the connection between technology and teachers . . . is one of the most important steps the nation can take to make the most of past and continuing investments in educational technology." It found that there was an integral connection between systemic reform and the proper use of technology in the classroom, which had been hindered up to that point.

To respond to this challenge, President Clinton announced in his January 1996 State of the Union address to Congress his Educational Technology Initiative, saying, "Nothing is more critical to preparing our public schools for the twenty-first century than ensuring they have the modern technology to prepare students for the information age." The President laid out four goals:

1. Provide access to modern computers for all students and teachers,
2. Connect every school in America to the "information superhighway,"
3. Develop effective software in all subject areas, and
4. Give every teacher the development he or she needs to help students use and learn through technology.[8]

Among the initiatives to achieve these goals were the creation of an Educational Technology Fund to provide matching grants for local school technology projects; federally subsidized funding for Internet access for schools; and the involvement of the nation's high-technology community through events such as "NetDay," on which local companies work with schools to provide Internet connections and new applications. On the whole, these programs have been popular, and by 1999, more than thirty thousand volunteers around the country were working to wire schools. Despite some last-minute reservations in Congress, which had created it as part of the Telecommunications Act of 1996, the new federal "E-rate" subsidy to wire schools and provide Internet connections was providing about $1.3 billion per year to schools by 1998.

In terms of pure numbers, these programs have begun to work. The National Center for Education Statistics reported that between 1994 and 1997, the number of American public schools wired for Internet access had increased from 35 percent to 78 percent, and the number of students actually using computers in school had also increased substantially. In 1984, for example, the ratio of computers to students was 1 to 125. By 1997, it was 1 to 10. The report also pointed out, however, that teachers were much more likely than students actually to use Internet functions, such as E-mail or the World Wide Web, and that schools with high minority enrollments generally had much lower rates of Internet access than schools with low minority enrollments.[9] In addition, a study by QED School Technology Research Results found that fewer than half of all the computers in schools were up to date and capable of running most of the new sophisticated software.[10]

Despite problems and false starts, the educational community bought into the notion that the use of new technologies had to be central to school reform. In his 1996 book, *Trends in Educational Technology*, Professor Donald Ely said, "The movement for restructuring education in schools across the United States has generated proposals and plans for reform of the entire education system. Virtually every proposal or plan includes educational technology as one of the major vehicles for implementing change."[11]

Around the world the situation was much the same—agreement on the need for digital technologies, but difficulties in integrating them into schools and curricula. A series of studies of forty countries sponsored by the United Nations Educational, Scientific, and Cultural Organization (UNESCO) and other international organizations showed that although the new information technologies were beginning to be used in schools, they were rarely integrated with curricula and teachers were poorly trained. Nevertheless, many countries were recognizing the critical need for educational change and for preparing young people for living and working in the information age.

Following much the same path as the United States, for example, British prime minister Tony Blair announced in 1998 a program called the National Grid for Learning, designed to give every school in the United Kingdom access to on-line information and teaching materials by 2002. He provided £450 million of government funds to pay for it and urged the business community to help. "The investment announced today will prevent a generation of children emerging who don't have these skills—the information poor," he said.[12] With varying types of programs, countries from Canada to Singapore to Japan are embarked on similar programs.

Providing computers and connecting them to the Internet, expensive as that task is, will undoubtedly be the easier part of the information revolution in education. The more difficult part will be integrating the Net into the heart of education, so that technology use becomes fully integrated into the core of the classroom curriculum. Computer literacy is only a means to the end of improving student outcomes in all fields of study, and in this regard, both the opportunities and the challenges are limitless.

For example, the Net will change forever the respective roles of students and teachers. Teachers will be transformed from the sole dispenser of information in the classroom to coaches who set goals and provide guidelines, making suggestions and motivating individual students. Students will change from passive receptacles of information to more motivated learners who seek out information from many different sources and collaborate with their peers. Teachers will be able to collaborate better with each other and with the school administration, as well as with parents, who can also have on-line access to students' work and grades. Students will have on-line access to information from all over the world and contact with other children around the world.

According to the Council of Great City Schools, for example, urban districts spend an average of only $120 per pupil on books and classroom materials, often limiting a child's information resources to a few older, outdated texts. On the Net, however, every child has access to an almost infinite variety of both primary and secondary content resources, ranging from the Central Intelligence Agency's country database, which could be used for social studies reports on a country or region, to the National Gallery of Art's Web site, a potential source for an art project. Moreover, the gap in equity between rich and poor school districts can be greatly reduced when all children have the same unlimited access to content on the Net.

One interesting example can be found at the Cottonwood Day School on the Navajo reservation in Arizona. In a program called Access Native America, run by the federal Bureau of Indian Affairs (BIA), Cottonwood's 242 students, many of whom live in homes without electricity, running water, or telephone service, found themselves chatting on-line with Pueblo students in New Mexico and Choctaw students in Mississippi after their school was connected to the Internet.[13] BIA schools, which educate fifty-three thousand children, should all be on-line before the turn of the century. For their students and other disadvantaged children, many of whom live in remote areas or are learning English as a second language, the ability to connect to other children like themselves and to have the opportunity to take on-line field trips to museums in New York—or Tokyo—opens for them an entirely new world. In a visit to the Navajo Nation in Shiprock, Arizona, on April 17, 2000, President Clinton announced new Net initiatives to benefit Native American education, including teacher training and a government–private sector initiative involving donations from such firms as Compaq, Microsoft, and Andersen Consulting.

To meet the growing demand for on-line resources, educators are producing educational Web sites at an astonishing rate. In her book *The On-line Classroom: Teaching with the Internet*, educator Eileen Cotton lists more than one hundred such Web resources.[14] One of the sites, "A Teacher's Place," provides links to more than ten thousand other sites, ranging from the National Parent-Teacher Association Web site to numerous teacher-training sites.[15] As one example, Cotton provides a sample exercise for children, titled "Ambassador to Mexico Webquest," which allows children to explore Mexico's history, geography, culture, government, and language as well as to communicate with Mexican children through E-mail. Among the resources are a burrito page, a site dealing with Mexican music (including rock), and of course, an on-line Spanish-English dictionary.

As with the broader education reform movement, the application of the new information infrastructure to elementary and secondary education is widely supported by coalitions of teachers, parents, government offices, universities, and the business community. One project, for example, the Global School Network, at www.gsn.org, was originally funded by the National Science Foundation, teachers in the city of San Diego, and Cornell University and other universities. It now also includes such high-tech partners as MCI WorldCom, Cisco Systems, and GTE Corporation. Using this network, children throughout the United States and in other countries can work collaboratively on projects involving space exploration, ecology, and energy. The high technology corporate community has focused on the education reform issue and made it a priority. The IBM Corporation alone, through its Reinventing Education project, has contributed more than $35 million to competitive experiments.

Thus, the world of elementary and secondary education has reached an exciting plateau of change. It is about to emerge from a model of education that dates back to Gutenberg, based on an agricultural, preindustrial world, and enter one based on networked technologies whose ultimate models we can only imagine. What we do know is that as technology converges with traditional forms of education, the role of the teacher will be even more creative and more central to learning. Students will emerge much better prepared to deal with the digital age, both in their careers and in their personal lives.

Higher education is also changing rapidly and dramatically. Late in 1998, for example, the creation of one of the largest universities in the world was announced: the new Governors' Open University (GOU). This Internet-based university, which began classes in 1999, was created by the Western Governors' Association, which had inaugurated the Western Governors' University in 1996. The new GOU merges this earlier venture with the Open University of the United States and the British Open University, the latter of which has already handed out one hundred thousand B.A. degrees earned over the Internet. The system will provide an on-line tutor for every twenty students; this tutor will monitor the students' progress by E-mail or telephone. Students do not need to live on campus or commute and can learn at their own pace.

By the spring 2000 semester, it was estimated that 80 percent of U.S. college students brought a computer to campus. More than one hundred universities and colleges were requiring that students have computers to matriculate, including the University of North Carolina, Chapel Hill; Wake Forest; Michigan State; and Seton Hall. Many professors were recording lectures on CD-ROM, allowing students to watch them on their own and opening up class time for discussion.

In their book *External Degrees in the Information Age*, Henry Spille, vice president of the American Council on Education (ACE), David Stewart, the former director of program development for ACE, and Eugene Sullivan of the Center for Adult Learning and Educational Credentials spell out the characteristics of higher education in the digital era:

—Students will be able to enroll and begin study at any time. There will be no set semesters.
—Students will need not attend any classes during weekdays.
—Students will not need to attend traditional classes to earn credits, but may acquire competencies through independent study, including on-the-job experience.

—Students may be able to adapt programs of study to their particular career or personal needs.

—Students will keep in touch with instructors and fellow students through interactive technology.[16]

Many universities already offer such programs in a variety of fields. For example, Stanford University is offering an M.S. degree in electrical engineering over the Internet. To be eligible, students must work at one of about three hundred high-tech companies affiliated with Stanford's engineering program, but need never leave their office desks. Stanford streams video to the students over the World Wide Web. The Regent University School of Law in Virginia is offering a postgraduate law course taught and assessed entirely over the Internet. Students download both books and case studies, which have been scanned into searchable databases, as well as lectures on such subjects as international tax law, which are recorded weekly and are downloadable as sound files. Chat rooms provide a forum for student discussions and exams are taken on-line. De Montfort University in the United Kingdom, a large university with more than thirty thousand students on four campuses, is developing a fully integrated digital library that will allow students to use a single Web site to retrieve course materials, journals, exam papers, E-mail addresses, and other materials. The system will store not only text but also digital sound, images, and video. The university is also partnering with a European Union project to create a standard for electronic descriptions of medieval manuscripts, and with Cambridge University Press on an electronic publishing system.

These developments are also causing profound changes in the nature, organization, and self-image of the university itself. For example, the Harvard University faculty and administration debated the issue of whether an on-line program would diminish the status of a Harvard degree. New York University (NYU) has created a for-profit subsidiary to develop and offer on-line courses. Already serving more than a hundred thousand full-time and continuing-education students, NYU believes it will need the profit discipline to manage its proposed investment of $20–30 million in on-line and distance education. Moreover, the line between university education and training is becoming porous, exacerbating the perennial debate over the proper role of the university. As author Don Tapscott says, "Because the digital economy is based on knowledge, work and innovation, there is a convergence between work and learning. . . . Learning has become a continual lifelong process. An expert is no longer someone who did something right once. An expert is a person who keeps up because knowledge doubles every 18 months."[17]

In this environment, not only does the university need to consider adapting its own curricula and course offerings, it also needs to consider competition in education from the private sector. The U.S. Department of Education reports that in 1995, 40 percent of all adults participated in adult education, with half taking work-related courses. Of these, more than 60 percent took courses provided by their business or professional association; only 20 percent took courses provided by colleges or universities. Interestingly, people who already had jobs were much more likely to be taking courses than those who were unemployed.[18]

These same issues are being faced not only in the United States and other industrial countries, but in the developing world. If greater access to less-expensive education can make a difference here, the impact in places like India, South Africa, and Brazil could be extraordinary. The World Bank has reported that distance education is expanding rapidly in the developing world. Thailand, for example, relies primarily on its two open universities to reach the poorest students, and in 1994, the open universities accounted for 62 percent of Thailand's higher education enrollments. South Africa's open university's reach extends far beyond its borders' and more than 10 percent of its students live in other African countries.[19]

As the United States and other countries move rapidly to bring the benefits of the Net into their schools and institutions of higher learning and deal with the fundamental changes that the Net is bringing, they must also deal with a significant series of public-policy challenges in the field of education. These range from protecting the integrity and universality of education to resolving technical issues such as intellectual property rights and the security of school records. Among the key issues are the following:

—Access: Perhaps the most important issue of all is how to ensure that all young people, rural and urban, rich and poor, have access to the new networked classrooms. Will new market mechanisms be needed to make certain this happens, or will there be a continued reliance on the regulatory models of the early twentieth century?

—Funding: How will we pay for the new technologies? Will local school districts be able to afford new technologies or will we need to increase the role of the federal government and state governments? What role, if any, will the private sector play in funding, including funding for research and development?

—Licensing: How will we license teachers and other educational professionals who are now licensed by the states? Will we need new federal licensing bodies when teaching occurs across state lines? Will there be a need for new educational requirements for teachers in order to qualify for a teaching license?

—Accreditation: How will potential students navigate the maze of state accreditation rules for schools and universities to avoid fraudulent "schools"? Will we need changes in accreditation standards to recognize the need for new offerings?

—Public control: If educational software becomes the heart of curricula for schools, how will we continue to assure public control and governance over curricula? Public-private partnerships will be key to reform and technology use, but how will we make sure that public school control remains in public hands?

—Telecommunications: Do we want to continue to maintain subsidized lower rates for telecommunications connections for schools, and if so, how do we pay for them in an era of deregulated telecommunications?

—Privacy and security: As we put student records and other information on-line, how will we protect the privacy and security of personal educational information and other sensitive school data, such as student health records or teacher employment files? Will we need national rules to achieve this, or will it be better left to the states?

—Teacher education: How can we increase spending on teacher education and training to qualify teachers for instruction in the digital era without slighting other areas?

—Objectionable content: With the widest possible student access to the Net, how can we protect children from objectionable content, such as pornography, racism, and violence? How do we balance this protection against free speech rights?

—Intellectual property: With almost unlimited amounts of content online, how do we appropriately protect the intellectual property rights of content owners without unduly restricting teachers' or students' use of materials?

—International: How do we deal with these issues in the international arena and across national borders? For example, will we develop mutual recognition agreements to validate accreditation of virtual universities and schools across international borders?

Although these issues will be difficult to deal with, they must be resolved, because the convergence of the Net and its applications in teaching and learning are already a reality. Technology is already flooding our schools and we have no choice but to harness it. As the report "Workforce 2020" points out, "America must adapt the institutions shaping its labor force to new circumstances. We cannot produce twenty-first-century knowledge workers in nineteenth-century public schools, early-twentieth-century higher education institutions, or mid-twentieth-century federal job training programs."[20]

GOVERNMENT SERVICES

Power to the people!

—1960s revolutionary slogan

Important revolutions always leave behind symbols: the Boston Tea Party; the storming of the Bastille; Chairman Mao's Long March; the Ayatollah Ruhollah Khomeini's entry into Teheran. The global revolution in government that is being brought about by the digital age will also leave a symbol for future generations, but it will be more mundane: the single click of a mouse pad accessing a page on the Net.

At the dawn of the new millennium, governments offer new promise to achieve their most fundamental and indeed their only legitimate purpose—to help people, in the words of the Declaration of Independence, in their quest for "life, liberty, and the pursuit of happiness." Liberal democracy has made extraordinary gains in the past few decades, for a variety of reasons. Although perhaps the most important has been the collapse of numerous totalitarian and authoritarian governments with the end of the Cold War, another key step forward has been the widespread dissemination and use of the new communications technologies. They are opening the eyes of millions of people worldwide to all of the benefits of democratic government. In fact, democracy and the Net appear to have a symbiotic relationship. Democratic values of free expression, respect for private enterprise and the market, and the free movements of people, ideas, goods, and money create a fertile incubator for the Net. In turn, the Net's permeating communications and information capabilities promote democratic values.

To be sure, democracy will face enormously difficult challenges in many parts of the world over the coming years. These will range from the persistence of nasty dictatorships in countries such as North Korea and Iraq, to the rise of bitter and ancient animosities in regions such as the Balkans, to a sheer lack of development and education, as in equatorial Africa. Even in these areas, however, the ability of the Internet and other technologies to permit open communications both within and from outside the countries will provide some marginal help for democratic development, as it did in the old Soviet Union under Mikhail Gorbachev's policy of glasnost. Rulers who rightly see the spread of information as a threat to their regimes, however, will do all they can to suppress the use of digital technology, except by the "party faithful," the technological elites, and the ubiquitous military and security organizations. Unable to modernize and enjoy the Net's full economic benefits, these countries will fall further behind the rest of the world.

In the democracies themselves, the Net will have greater effects on the nature of government itself, effects that can now be only guessed at. The keys to these potential changes will be access and openness. As we have seen in the cases of health care and education, the new infrastructure offers the potential for virtually everyone in society to have access to the content and services of cyberspace. In terms of government and politics, this should mean the possibility for 100 percent public participation in the political process. Some feel that this could lead to government by poll or electronic referendum. In the United States, one-time presidential candidate H. Ross Perot has already called for using the new technology in this way to read current public sentiment on any important issue. Others fear that such a system would seriously erode representative government and lead to government by popularity poll or even a kind of electronic mob rule.

A more meaningful and potentially more profound use of cyberspace in politics is its application to democratic elections. Low voter-participation rates, coupled with the high costs of fostering greater participation, have plagued many democratic countries. The Internet provides a simple solution, one that Costa Rica is embracing. Costa Rica requires its citizens to vote in national elections, but only 65 percent actually do because people are reluctant to vote anywhere except in the village where they originally registered. Even though the government spends millions to bus them back home, many simply still do not vote. On the other hand, the country has a well-developed telecommunications infrastructure with an Internet backbone and has been working at wiring every school in the country. With 30 percent of the schools already wired, the government's goal is to wire 100 percent of the nation's high schools by the 2002. With the help of Villanova University, the government is now planning to hold its national elections in the 2002 entirely on the Internet, using public kiosks in place such as the high schools—an ambitious goal.[21]

What will be the results of such a increase in the number of people voting in a country like Costa Rica? Will the additional voters, who most likely will be the country's more uneducated and rural citizens, change the balance of power? Or will the availability of information on the Internet at the same time make these voters better informed, and therefore better citizens? No one knows the answers to these questions, but the government of Costa Rica believes that the results will benefit the nation.

If access is one key to future government change, openness is the other. The ability of the Net to make all the records and proceedings of government instantly available to anyone, anywhere, without dependence on an intermediary such as a civil servant or a journalist, or without the need to make a trip to a distant government office and prowl through reams of paper, will have a great impact on the political process and on politicians and government officials themselves. At the turn of the last century, the nation needed a Lincoln Steffens or an Upton Sinclair to "rake the muck." In the future, everyone can be a muckraker, or simply an ordinary citizen using the openness of the system to do his or her business.

Already small businesses can more easily access regulations and regulatory proceedings, making it easier for them to compete with larger businesses that long have had the advantage of lawyers and lobbyists in Washington and state capitals in the United States, or in the capitals of other countries. In the future, ordinary citizens appealing a property tax assessment will be able to view tax records from their homes, making their appeals less time-consuming and more effective. Activists concerned about a health or safety issue will be able to access the files of agencies without the intervention and potential deception of a civil servant. Researchers working on subjects such as demographic trends, disease vectors, or geological explorations will be able to tap into enormously rich information resources.

On the one hand, by giving more "power to the people," openness can provide an important curb on abuses of power by government officials. On the other hand, it will also open new issues of privacy protection for individuals, and of the confidentiality and security of government records. Already, for example, the U.S. Department of Labor has inadvertently compromised the security of very sensitive economic data, potentially worth millions of dollars to investors, by accidentally releasing information prematurely. State motor-vehicle bureaus have come under fire for making information about individual motorists publicly available—sometimes for a fee.

Openness will also give new power and ammunition to political fringe groups that may or may not use it wisely. Although a small reform party trying to break into the two-party American mainstream can use the power of cyberspace to enhance its efforts for legitimate reform by recruiting members and broadcasting its platform, racist groups and anti-government groups are already using the Net's power to spread hatred and teach violence. For example, a hate group calling itself the Church of the Creator uses its Web site to indoctrinate children with racism and anti-Semitism.

The new access and openness provided by the Net is already at work. Members of Congress report being deluged with E-mail messages during debate on critical issues. They are also using E-mail themselves to communicate with constituents. The traditional press frets about Internet publications, such as the Drudge Report or Salon magazine, that report unconventional news and "scoop" old-fashioned newspapers. Newspapers and magazines have even scooped themselves by publishing material on their own Web sites before print publication and distribution.

While the democracies are embracing the Internet and welcoming its effects, other countries fear the new technologies and what they may bring. Many countries such as China and Singapore restrict use of the Internet, regulate it, and criminalize unlawful use. Myanmar offers a prison sentence of up to seventeen years for violating Internet laws. Early in 1999, China sentenced an Internet user to two years in prison for disseminating E-mail addresses to overseas organizations that the government felt were "unfriendly" to the Chinese government. Dictators everywhere seem to understand that the convergence of the digital technologies with government will sap their power in a variety of ways.

ELECTRONIC GOVERNMENT

Although it is still much too early to predict the ultimate impact of all of this on government, one thing is certain. The advent of the Internet and its ability to offer government information and services to people anywhere and at any time offers special opportunities to extend and improve those services. The potential benefits of convergence come at a particularly opportune time, as democratic governments around the world are restructuring and, in the words of David Osborne, "reinventing" themselves.[22] In the United States, at the federal level, this has taken the form of the National Performance Review, an effort spearheaded by Vice President Al Gore to modernize and streamline the activities of the federal government. Many of the states are going through the same process, as are governments around the world.

What are the reasons for all this activity and what role will the global information infrastructure play? One reason is that the end of the Cold

War has given governments new time and energy to focus on neglected issues such as antiquated bureaucracies. But there are four more compelling and more immediate reasons. First, governments everywhere find themselves under incredible cost pressures. Although for most countries tax revenues have increased with economic growth and prosperity, especially in the industrial democracies, expenditures have increased even more rapidly, as aging populations and other factors drive pension and health care costs higher every year. With the bulk of available new budget money eaten up by nondiscretionary expenses, government departments offering services must either find ways to decrease the costs of the services themselves or the costs of delivering them. Thus, if it is cheaper for a government agency to remit funds electronically rather than by check, or to offer tenders for bids electronically rather than by publication, then agencies will be highly motivated in today's climate to move toward electronic payment and publication.

The savings from administrative costs alone can be staggering. Consider that in the United States, there are more than 100 million Social Security, Medicaid, worker disability, and food-stamp accounts alone, with beneficiaries receiving monthly benefits in more than 1.2 billion transactions per year. Saving 10 cents per transaction alone—a modest estimate for these programs—would save $12 billion per year in much-needed federal funds.

Second, government faces new and complex competitive pressure from the private sector. The movement in the private sector toward "market-driven" products and customer services has greatly raised the quality of the services offered by companies to the public. Spearheaded by the graduate schools of business, the market-driven movement has preached that as many products and services become "commoditized," companies need to better understand consumer needs so that they can find specific ways to differentiate and "brand" their products.

Successful automobile companies have done this, for example, not only by making subtle changes to their products, but by offering better service. Honda, for example, goes to enormous lengths to understand its customers' service needs and then meet and even exceed them by training its staff to offer superior service. Using extensive surveys, Honda even makes tiny changes to its products, such as adjusting ever so slightly the sound made by closing the driver's side door, to satisfy customer desires.

A financial services company such as American Express has distinguished its credit-card business from that of its competitors by offering, in the company's view, the industry's best customer-service program. American Express customers with problems know they will get a fair hearing from a knowledgeable service representative, and the company bends over backward to deal with customer issues. An entertainment company such as Disney keeps crowds returning to its amusement parks by investing enormous amounts in the tidiness of the parks. Customer surveys show that people rate this characteristic of Disney's offerings higher than any other factor, including the actual entertainment, in their decisions to return.

Although this market-driven movement brought great benefits for customers and the public, it created a serious problem for governments by raising public expectations for government service, as well. In the past, when laws were written requiring governments to do everything from issue driver's licenses to provide support for crops, providing polite and efficient service to motorists and farmers was not something that legislators specified in their bills. With funding always a problem for the bureaucracies created to implement these laws, customer service was rarely at the top of the list of priorities—or even on it at all. Thus, citizens who have seen the quality of the service they receive from the private sector improve measurably are demanding the same level of service from government. A working mother, for example, who has no time during working hours to stop at her bank to make a deposit can do it at an automatic teller machine at any time of the day or night. She can even move money from one account to another from her home on her personal computer or over the telephone. She now wonders why she has do go to a crowded government office and stand in line to register a car or apply for a job during working hours.

This leads to the third reason for governments to move into the twenty-first century: technology is making possible increases in the quality of service everywhere, and government is as much of a participant in this sea change as any other institution. If college students can register for classes from their homes or dormitory rooms, why can't governments permit people to file their taxes the same way? If middle-class people can use credit or debit cards for all their purchases and improve both the convenience and the security of their funds, why can't people who receive food stamps or welfare benefits use a debit card or other electronic system? If communications companies are tending toward one-stop shopping, whereby people can satisfy all of their communications needs—local and long-distance telephone, cable television, Internet hookup—why can't there be similar one-stop shopping for people dealing with government? As technology makes these service improvements possible, both technically and economically, governments have no choice but to participate.

One-stop shopping provides obvious benefits for citizens, but it also has profound implications for government itself. In the first place, government employees of the future will need to be able to deal with a much wider variety of citizen inquiries and transactions and be more knowledgeable about government services. Of necessity, such employees will have to be empowered to do more decision-making than civil servants are currently permitted. Conversely, the rule books will need to be slimmed down or turned into software programs that give guidance to government workers.

Government organization will also be strongly affected. If a new resident of a state seeks to get a driver's license, register a car, and apply for property tax allowances and a fishing license, must he or she visit four separate government offices? If a customer needed to conduct numerous items of business with a company, that company would simply provide an account executive to handle all of the customer's needs. If government followed this path, the need for the types of functional departments into which governments are organized today might well disappear. Even the lines between jurisdictions would become blurred. A unemployed worker seeking federal job-retraining assistance, state unemployment compensation, Medicaid assistance, and perhaps local child-care help could become a more productive citizen more quickly if all this required only one teleconference-assisted kiosk session instead of five separate visits to different government offices.

The fourth and final reason for government change and restructuring is that liberal democratic governments see themselves today, to one extent or another, as key cogs in national economic development engines. If governments in the past worked to help develop natural resources or to encourage the growth of manufacturing companies or even particular industries, such as aviation, chemicals, or automobiles, today's governments see themselves as facilitators of the great economic engine of the twenty-first century—the digital technologies. Today, this role requires far more than the traditional tools of support for industries.

The old physical infrastructures—roads, rails, sea lanes, water and sewer systems, and modern gas and electric distribution systems—are still important, but they must be supplemented with a new virtual infrastructure of cable, satellite, cellular, and broadband telephone networks. Without an advanced telecommunications infrastructure and, equally important, a modern educational system and a contemporary digital system for government services, politicians and officials realize their jurisdictions will be at a competitive disadvantage with regard to other countries, regions, or states. Among the key government-service programs that are most affected by these competitive pressures are networked trading systems, customs, automated immigration systems, electronic tendering and purchasing, automated tax filings, and Internet-based regulatory and economic database systems, both for use by existing businesses and to attract new business activity.

One additional—and controversial—factor encouraging states into cyberspace is their ability to generate revenue from the information they produce. For example, both Texas and Rhode Island have given users access—for a cost—to driver and motor-vehicle information. Others charge for access to such information as tax assessments and liquor licenses. In 1997, the state of Illinois earned about $10 million selling public records. Commercial customers, such as realtors, have generally been willing to pay reasonable fees for such previously unattainable information; newspapers doing major stories on broad issues such as voter fraud or bribery have not. A number of resulting court cases will eventually determine whether these particular tolls on the information superhighway are legitimate.

What will be the more immediate result of the convergence of the new information infrastructure with government services? Examples abound, but three important sources provide a comprehensive overview—two focus on national governments and one evaluates the efforts of state governments.

National Governments

The United Kingdom's "Government.direct" green paper sets out that government's strategy for delivering central government services electronically across the United Kingdom. In its section titled "Benefits for the Citizen," it spells out the government's objectives:

All of the services will be accessible and easy to use. They will be available via terminals, either in the home or in convenient public places such as libraries, post offices and shopping centers. And they will be available alongside a full range of other services, including Citizen's Charter information, thus providing an electronic "one-stop shopping" for government. They will provide interactive guidance. . . . The services could also be available . . . for 24 hours a day, seven days a week, as appropriate. Responses will be as near to immediate as practical. . . . Citizens will have greater ease of access to the information that government holds about them, and be able to check it and initiate correction if necessary.[23]

Among the services included in the U.K. plan for electronic delivery to citizens are vehicle-license renewal, skills training and educational courses, income-tax returns, benefits claims, personal-information verification, and information provision under the country's Citizen's Charter, which spells out what government information is open to public view. The U.K. green paper also points out that the use of networked technologies in government agencies and activities such as criminal justice will also benefit citizens. For example, the London Metropolitan Police, using a U.K. Home Office Police Research Award, used digital technologies to correlate police reports around the world and thereby cracked a massive credit-card counterfeit operation based in Malaysia.[24]

The U.K. green paper goes on to point out the benefits of digital government services for business, among which are access to regulatory information, business health and safety information, market information, and electronic tax filing, including Inland Revenue, customs, and excise taxes. For example, U.K. companies will be able to access up-to-date Overseas Trade Services information on export markets, link to Commonwealth Office posts abroad, and even use teleconferencing to electronically attend overseas business and trade conferences.

The United Kingdom also plans an electronic revamping of all its national statistics. Questions dealing with subjects such as local labor markets, environmental-planning guidelines, government grants and benefits, education and health services, and transportation could all be answered on-line, in real time. The green paper concludes by stating, "The government is determined that, in addition to providing better services to businesses and the citizen, the strategy outlined in this Green Paper should also benefit all taxpayers by reducing the cost of government administration. The cost savings will come from eliminating manpower-intensive handling of paper, from government departments sharing common facilities and data and, most importantly, from the rationalisation and redesign of government processes."[25] The report concludes that all of this change will also result in lower fees for licenses and other government services and therefore will benefit the national economy. Unstated, as in other similar government documents, is the potential to reduce the size of government and the number of government workers, as their jobs converge with information technology and become part of cyberspace.

Much the same phenomenon can be observed in the United States. The Clinton administration, even before it took office, understood the forces we have been discussing that drive change in government. It sought to find a way to bring government and its services in line with the realities of the post–Cold War, high-budget-deficit environment. Although it was clear that the swollen federal bureaucracies that had been built up by both parties since the 1930s would have to be downsized (to use corporate parlance), this could not be done easily without offending traditional liberal Democratic Party constituencies, which now prominently included unions of government employees. Embracing the intellectual underpinnings built at the Democratic Leadership Council's think tank, the Progressive Policy Institute, the new Clinton administration adopted and adapted the market-driven and cost-cutting practices of the private sector, promising a number of programs "putting people first." They added to this mix the potential applications of the new information infrastructure for government and packaged everything into a major government initiative called the National Performance Review (NPR). Vice President Gore has led the NPR with the skillful help of a number of officials brought in from the private sector who understood the power and uses of the new technologies.

The NPR has proven to be a powerful initiative that is achieving many of its original goals: reducing the number of federal employees; cutting federal agency and department discretionary spending; developing and implementing innovative ways to serve citizens; stimulating federal agencies to streamline and modernize their procedures and activities; and making use of the Internet and other cyberspace technologies. A key part of the NPR has been its "Reengineering through Information Technology" initiative, which set a number of key goals for the federal government in the area of technology deployment:

— Integrate information technology into the business of government,
— Implement nationwide, integrated electronic benefits transfers,
— Develop integrated electronic access to government information and services,
— Establish a national law enforcement/public safety network,
— Provide intergovernmental tax filing, reporting, and payments processing,
— Establish an international trade data system,
— Create a national environmental data index,
— Plan, demonstrate, and provide government-wide electronic mail, and
— Develop systems to ensure privacy and security.[26]

The initiative has also called for and provided massive training and technical assistance in the new technologies for federal employees and provided special incentive programs for federal executives to spur innovation in new and advanced applications.

By the end of 1999, many of these initiatives were well underway. On December 17, 1999, Vice President Al Gore announced two new "E-government" initiatives that included an executive order directing government agencies to "promote access to government information organized not by agency, but by types of service or information that people may be seeking."[27] One-stop shopping was coming to government.

For example, as welfare reform is implemented across the United States and people on welfare move into jobs, the government has created a National Directory of New Hires, run by the Department of Health and Human Services, and accessible not only to federal employees but also to state officials running welfare, employment, training, and other programs. In addition to providing important data, this system has another, unintended benefit: States are using it to locate parents who have failed to provide child support and are then securing court orders to deduct child support from wages. For the first time, state officials can track down deadbeat parents and make certain that their children are properly cared for financially. States say that the system saves money in other ways, such as by eliminating duplicate payments for welfare, food stamps, unemployment insurance, and Medicaid. On the other hand, civil libertarians have expressed strong concerns about the potential for misuse and especially for invasion of privacy.[28]

Misuse and privacy will undoubtedly be recurring themes in discussions as new government cyberspace initiatives are developed. Among those that are completed or underway are the Securities and Exchange Commission's EDGAR program, which permits companies to file reports on-line and makes them publicly available; the Internal Revenue Service's on-line tax filing and form-downloading program; and the on-line Social Security system.

State Governments

If the federal government is moving relatively quickly to speed the convergence of digital technology with government, many of the states are moving even faster. An August 1997 study by the Progress and Freedom Foundation (PFF), titled "The Digital State," studied seven key areas in which states are using the Net. It ranked state progress in each area and drew a key preliminary conclusion about the potential use of the Internet for services by state governments: "The rise of new forms of interactive media, such as the Internet, has decentralized information storage. As a consequence, individuals are empowered to be more knowledgeable of and more involved in the affairs of their government. Attending college lectures through teleconference, monitoring the status of proposed state legislation, receiving answers to specific tax or regulatory questions—all of these activities can be done on the Internet."[29]

The areas studied by the PFF included the following:

Digital Democracy. Rated one of the most advanced areas in the study, this included citizen access to state laws, legislators and officials, and the democratic process through the Internet. Alaska was rated the most advanced state, with on-line voting on referenda, petitions, and local initiatives, as well as E-mail links to the governor, state officials, and legislators. A vast and sparsely populated state, Alaska is the ideal testing ground for remote access to government services. The Alaska congressional delegation, especially Senator Ted Stevens, has worked hard in Congress to provide federal help in building Alaska's telecommunications infrastructure.

Education. The Western states were most advanced in the area of higher education, as seen earlier in the example of the Western Governors' University, although Indiana and Michigan took first and second place in the PFF study. Indiana University offers degrees taught entirely with use of the Internet, television, and videotape. Students can also apply for student grants and loans on-line.

In the realm of elementary and secondary education, Georgia has connected almost all of the state's schools to the Internet, and Arizona publishes an electronic report card on schools that can be accessed by parents and other interested parties to assess and compare various schools.

Business Regulation. Business regulation was scored as one of the least developed areas by the states, although the web sites of Arizona, Florida, Kansas, and Maryland stood out. Florida's Department of Business and Professional Regulation, for example, offers information and forms on-line, as well as a search engine to help businesses locate important information. North Carolina, a state known for a friendly business climate, even offers a Web site in Japanese to interest Japanese investors.

Taxation. State tax authorities were given high marks by PFF for their efforts to bring the world of taxation into cyberspace. Maryland was rated the highest, with a "tax assistance" link on the state's Web site that permits taxpayers to download forms and information booklets, get questions answered, and get referred to appropriate officials. Taxes can also be filed electronically in Maryland through a third party.

Health, Welfare, and Social Services. Although many federal welfare and social service programs have "devolved" to the states in recent years, according to the PFF study, the states have not moved quickly enough to improve these services and lower their costs by using digital technology. Rated the highest, Oklahoma electronically transfers benefits in its food stamp and Temporary Assistance for Needy Families programs and has worked with the private sector to keep welfare records on-line. States have been awaiting clarification of federal rules regarding liability and other issues as they experiment with "smart card" and other on-line systems.

Law Enforcement and the Courts. States have been moving to use network technology for police officers to help spot suspects and criminals; to place court records, opinions and schedules on-line; and to use the Net for public-safety applications, such as emergency planning. The PFF study noted that the state of Washington uses an integrated criminal-justice information system that ties together police, court, and prison records. Victims of crime in the state can use the Web to learn about and download a protection order, and Supreme Court and Court of Appeals opinions are kept on-line.

Global (Electronic) Climate Change

Around the world, governments are moving critical services onto the Net. Some of the following projects are particularly interesting.

Canada. Service Ontario is a network of self-service kiosks that allow people to renew vehicle registrations, pay court and parking fines, order special license plates, search driver and vehicle records, and change their address. New Brunswick is also using public-access terminals to provide a variety of government services and is also using a networked system to provide "one-stop shopping" in government offices, eliminating the need for people to go from office to office.

Singapore. Singapore uses an extensive arrangement to permit citizens and businesses to pay all of their taxes on-line, including income taxes, goods and services taxes, and customs duties. The public can also search an "electronic valuation list" for property ownership and tax assessment information, as well as many government financial databases for business information.

Australia. Australia's Department of Employment, Education, Training, and Youth Affairs uses thousands of terminals at hundreds of job centers to allow job seekers to search a national job database maintained by the Commonwealth Employment Service. The nationwide system has helped promote a more mobile and efficient labor force.

Spain. Spain has developed a networked system for administering social security benefits. The system uses a "smart" card that not only carries data relevant to the holder's social security account but also contains a unique identification system that examines the fingerprint of citizens before giving them access to their account information.

Russia. Not to be outdone, the Russian government has also entered cyberspace. The Russian Central Bank, for example, has a "hotline" on its Internet site for customers with problems. The city of Moscow's Web site gets an estimated ten thousand hits per month (with fewer than one million Internet users in the country) seeking municipal information such as upcoming telephone-rate increases. The site allows citizens to complain directly about such problems as plumbing and street cleaning. To help in the critical fight against crime, the Russian Ministry of Justice has placed its huge database, containing more than three hundred thousand individual records, as well as national and regional court and other legal information, on the Internet for use by court officials and justice agencies. The Duma (the Russian parliament) has also voted to place all of its laws and resolutions on-line.

Brazil. To help solve its critical problem with illegal aliens, Brazil has developed SINCRE (Sistema Integrado de Controle e Registro do Estrangeiro), an automated system that uses digital imaging and networking technologies to keep track of foreigners in the country. Brazil is also developing a global automated international trade system that will allow Brazilian consulates and companies around the world to match trade leads and potential investment and export opportunities.

Seeking Answers

Taken together, these types of cyberspace applications at the state, national, regional, and international levels all aim to provide higher quality and more accessible government services, lower the costs of government, make countries or regions more competitive, and stimulate economic growth. Although these are all highly desirable goals, the road to their achievement also raises serious public-policy questions that must be resolved. Among the most important are the following:

—Privacy: With the potential to permit citizens almost complete access to government files, how will we protect the privacy of personal information, ranging from tax records to medical data to criminal information? Is it possible to define broad principles for access that apply to all types of personal information collected by government, or will the problem need to be tackled in pieces, according to the types of information? For example, will there be one standard of privacy for government medical records and another for motor-vehicle registration data? How will citizens assert their privacy rights?

—Freedom of information: Looking at the other side of the coin from privacy, how will we ensure that government officials do not unreasonably exempt certain materials from public scrutiny? How will we strike the balance between privacy and freedom of information?

—Security: Once laws are in place to protect privacy, technical and physical means of security will be needed to ensure that the privacy of information is properly protected. Among other things, this will include the need for the use of cryptography; appropriate government funding for security, and agreed-upon methods of protecting data, including those that involve the proper training and management of government employees.

—Copyright: Does government own the intellectual property rights to the data it collects and processes, or is all government information, raw or processed, in the public domain and therefore available free to the public?

—Sale of information: Do governments have the right to process information into more usable forms and then sell it to commercial or other interests? If government makes access easier for citizens, does it have the right to charge for that access? For example, is it worth an extra $5 to an automobile owner to renew his or her automobile registration from home, from the office, or from the local library rather than at a government office?

—Access: To what cost and lengths must governments go to provide equal access to networked services for all people? Will it be enough to provide terminals or kiosks in public places, such as schools or community centers, or will solutions such as mobile facilities or even publicly subsidized home equipment be required?

—Legal environment: Will citizen transactions with government over the Internet or other networks be legally valid, including electronic signatures? Government will also need to certify the validity of contracts it enters into in cyberspace, such as procurement agreements.

—Civil service: Will long-standing civil service rules need to be changed to accommodate the need for new skills for government employees and lifelong learning? In the long term, governments and the citizenry will need to deal with the far-reaching effects of the digital age on government. These will include the broader impact on government employees, their unions, and the civil service. Although smaller in number, government employees will each need to be more technically literate and more flexible and have a broader background in government services. The notion that civil servants may become "account executives" serving their citizen "clients" with one-stop shopping may seem trivial or mundane, but it may well have long-term implications for the nature of government. Particularly in the newly developing democracies in eastern Europe, Asia, or Latin America, as well as in the bureaucratic states of western Europe, a new, more modern and technically "cool" civil service may help develop bright new democratic values. Since in many countries the civil service also provides the breeding ground for politicians, a new species of political leaders may emerge in many countries, with more genuine concern for citizen rights and natural interests in assuring that government exists to serve people and not the other way around. Citizens too, treated with a new respect and encountering a higher level of intelligence, may also develop a new vision of government and its purposes, free of the unfortunate cynicism that has enveloped civil society in the United States and other countries.

What the impact will be on the nature of democracy itself will take a long time to determine. But if the earliest signs are to be believed, we will see a significant boost to open democracy being provided by the convergence of the new information infrastructure with government in all its forms and all its many important services.

4

Megaconvergence: Financial Services, Commerce, and Industry

Once, when I referred to a bank's back-end databases as technological "dinosaurs," a reporter wrote an article saying that I thought banks themselves were dinosaurs and that we wanted to compete with them. I had to spend more than a year . . . telling banks I was misquoted and that we're not really planning to set up in the banking business.

—Bill Gates[1]

Wrong. Bill Gates is missing the point. Microsoft doesn't need to set up in the banking business in order to compete with the banks. Its software, and the software, hardware, and services provided by hundreds of companies in the business of cyberspace are *becoming* the banking systems of the future, as they literally converge with the old banking industry. Not only is banking itself affected by this megaconvergence, but so are all of the financial services industries, including insurance, credit, securities, and real estate. The digital age will change fundamentally the nature of money and the way people use it. Its effects will be the most profound changes in that field since merchant banking and related financial services first began in medieval times; their impact on contemporary financial institutions and their customers will be second only in importance to the changes brought about in the realm of social services.

After people's health and freedom, and perhaps the education of their children, their main earthly concern is with their money—their financial ability to provide themselves with the goods and services they need. Americans of the past few generations, and even many Europeans and Asians of the most recent one, have taken the idea of money and the stability of the monetary system for granted, notwithstanding recent currency crises in countries from Russia to Thailand. Wars, famines, civil disorders, stock market "bubbles" and collapses, natural disasters, and even the lack of an adequate financial framework have made the history of money a tumultuous one.

Money has a number of purposes and characteristics that make it a superb object for change in the digital age. First, it is a store of value, and the ability to store things easily and at almost infinitely low cost in cyberspace is one of the key attributes of the Net. Second, money is a medium of exchange, and the ability to conduct transactions cheaply and with enormous ease is another hallmark of the Net. Third, money must be capable of movement, often with great speed and in great quantities, and the Net also provides the ability to move information at speeds orders of magnitude greater than in the past.

Since the beginning of civilization and especially since the Middle Ages, societies have experimented with and implemented all kinds of schemes to store money, to use if for transactions, and to move it around. As mentioned earlier, in the United States alone, money has taken many forms. It has been issued by the British government, by the colonial governments, by the states, and, as it is today, by the federal government. It was as recently as 1971 that the U.S. government stopped converting its currency into gold and retreated from the gold standard, backing its money instead with the "full faith and credit" of the United States government.

This history is important to review quickly, since money is not the constant it first appears to be and is therefore subject to the same raging digital storms as other institutions. Coins were invented for small cash purchases, bills for larger ones, and bank drafts, checks, and credit cards for even larger ones. The Net can supply its own, new substitutes for each of these instruments. In 1787, the new American government issued a half-penny coin, since merchants wanted the ability to price even the smallest items with great accuracy. Not only will the digital age serve the needs of the wealthy for complex banking transactions, it will also serve the poor, who rely on cash for small transactions.

In his book *A History of Money,* author Jack Weatherford quotes Anatole France as saying, "It is only the poor who pay cash, and that not from virtue, but because they are refused credit."[2] Weatherford also notes that studies of the poor, ranging from Oscar Lewis's field work on Mexican peasants to data on today's inner-city poor in the United States, show that their reliance on cash for small purchases makes their use of money far more costly to them than comparable use for the middle class or the wealthy. Whether one counts the cost to them of money lost to robbers and fraud, or the cost from the excessive charges they pay to cash checks, or the cost of purchasing items in small (and therefore more expensive) quantities, they are much worse off than their mostly cash-free wealthier fellow citizens. Cyberspace contains the means to change all this, with potentially secure means of making small transactions digitally, even for citizens receiving public assistance.

SOURCES OF CHANGE

As with education, health care, and government services, the whirlwind of change blasting banking and financial services today comes from many sources, not only technology. Walter Wriston, retired chairman of Citibank, wistfully told *Wired* magazine in October 1996, "The banking business used to have about 70 percent of the financial assets of the world. Now we have 30 percent. Do you know any industry that went from 70 down to 30 percent market share and survived?"[3] If anything, Wriston's observation is even more true today. According to the Federal Reserve, traditional U.S. bank assets were down to just 24 percent of financial assets by 1998. The reasons are many, including competition both globally and within the financial services industry.

Global Competition

The emergence of global financial markets over the past few decades and the loosening of financial regulations in many countries that prohibited the operations of foreign banks have benefited bank customers with lower costs and better services. At the same time, they have created powerful new overseas competitors for local banks, forcing them to look for ways to lower costs. Technology, of course, has played a major role in making the globalization of financial markets possible.

Inter-industry Competition

Changing customer needs and changing regulatory structures have caused a kind of convergence within the financial services industries themselves—industries that in the United States were shaped both by the Depression and by federalism. In many countries, the boundaries between banking, retail credit services, insurance, money market accounts, pension funds, securities transactions, and mortgage brokering have either partially or totally disappeared as governments have deregulated many aspects of banking and other financial services industries. By the end of 1999, the U.S. Congress had passed sweeping legislation overhauling the structure of the financial services industry, sweeping away many of the barriers between its different sectors.

This competitive environment has played a role in massive shifts in financial assets. Banking assets have fallen dramatically, but the assets of pension funds as a percentage of total financial assets, for example, climbed from 17 percent in 1980 to 28 percent in 1998. In the United States, massive numbers of citizens not only use banking services but also invest in the stock markets; own 401Ks, Individual Retirement Accounts or other retirement vehicles; finance the purchase of homes and automobiles; and use insurance vehicles for estate planning. The demand for one-stop financial shopping with the help of an expert is therefore strong, and the demand for a simple old-fashioned saving account is dying. The result is a strong wave of competitive cannibalization between all of these industries.

Shift to Capital Markets

During the past decade, with the remarkable rise of the stock market, there has been a tremendous shift in U.S. borrowing away from banks and toward the capital markets. In fact, the "dot coms" and many other high-technology companies that have built the Net illustrate the point: they raise capital by issuing stock, not by borrowing from banks. Banks have lost of great deal of their competitive advantage in lending, partly because their access to cheap funds was hurt by competition from money market funds, and partly because information technology made it easier to evaluate quickly the value of securities. This latter factor in particular boosted the public's interest in supplying the capital for business growth. This "securitization" of the financial markets has reduced the revenues and the influence of traditional banks. Since this phenomenon has also caused wild swings in the markets, because the value of securities is more transparent to the public than the value of bank assets, some think there will be a trend back to bank lending. Proponents of this view believe that the public will tire of the kinds of global financial gyrations we have been seeing for the past few years. Others, like Henry Kaufman, think the changes in banking are here to stay: "You can't put Humpty-Dumpty back together again," he says. "The nature of the markets has changed."[4]

Technology

Finally, technology itself has been a major cause of the changes in banking. As technology rapidly reduced the costs of banking and the assets needed to produce revenues, newcomers unburdened with high cost structures and expensive "roman temple" bank buildings made great headway against the traditional banks. Sophisticated computer systems that made possible money market funds and mutual funds helped steal valuable customers as well. In fields such as corporate lending and the commercial paper market, computer technology reduced or eliminated the role of intermediaries and made possible direct contact between lenders and capital consumers; a computer program can now do what a skilled bank officer did in the past. In the case of retail banking, the program and the hardware replace the teller. Even where banks managed to hold on to their retail customers, they found that the high expense ratios (noninterest expenses divided by the sum of interest and noninterest income) needed to serve most of those customers made much of the retail banking business unprofitable. Whereas traditional bank expense ratios are about 60 percent, for example, Internet banks have expense ratios below 20 percent.

Transaction Explosion

The increase in check and credit card transactions at the expense of cash transactions, or the "demonitization" of the economy, has resulted in a fantastic explosion in the number of electronic transactions made by consumers and business. This growth in transactions has also been fueled, of course, by economic growth, especially in recent years. Of the 82 billion transactions made by American consumers each year, only 35 billion are still cash transactions. Of the remaining 47 billion, more than 33 billion are check transactions and 12 billion are credit card transactions. In addition, about 3 billion business checks are written each year.[5] Control over these transactions and the revenues they may generate will fall to those institutions that develop the most cost-effective, easy-to-use, and secure systems for both consumers and businesses. Whether that control will lie with traditional banks, credit card issuers, financial services companies, or software and Internet companies themselves remains to be seen. Just as cash once was a universal system for transactions, most likely the institutions that first develop an "open" system that becomes the standard will be the winners.

CONSEQUENCES OF CHANGE

As a result of these changes in the banking environment, which have caused a period of dramatic turbulence for the world's bankers, banks are turning to technology and particularly to the Net. Broadly, the new networked banking environment will be characterized by a number of key factors.

Virtual Assets Replace Physical Assets

The banks and financial services institutions of the future will be based on the intellectual capital embedded in their networked systems and software, as well as in their employees and management. Impressive buildings and downtown locations in expensive rented space will be much less important to consumers and businesses than easy-to-use and secure Web sites and networks. Competitive advantage will be found in the use of sophisticated data-mining techniques to understand customer needs, the deployment of systems to deliver those needs, and the training and use of knowledgeable and talented account executives to offer comprehensive services.

Empowered Consumers

With the ability to use the power of the Net, consumers will gain a powerful advantage in their dealings with banking institutions. Already, mortgage-seekers surf the Net seeking the best interest rates and terms, without the assistance of sales-oriented loan officers. With direct access to all the financial markets, consumers will become more knowledgeable and able to make transactions themselves, as they are already doing with the purchase of securities. Further disintermediation will occur as software companies develop so-called intelligent agents, or programs that will find the best deals in any type of financial transaction. In the long run, this democratization will also have powerful implications for the regulation of financial markets, as nations and governments also lose power to consumers in the digital economic world.

More Barriers Dissolve

As the Internet and its future manifestations become the core of finance, the barriers between the different types of financial institutions will crumble further and faster. Consumers and businesses seeking the best possible service, without regard to geographical or regulatory boundaries, will gravitate toward those firms that offer comprehensive service. Already, American financial services companies such as Salomon Smith Barney advertise to their customers the advantage to them of a single year-end tax statement for all of their financial dealings.

Fiercer Competition

Competition will be based not only on the financial products themselves, but also on the operational aspects of the firm, such as the ease of use of its Web site or the consumer's confidence in the security of transactions. In addition, competition will be based on the quality of the firm's relationship with the customer. Since customer confidence is such an important aspect of banking, brand images will be jealously fought over and guarded, and banks will be hard-pressed to preserve their brands as software and network brands such as Intuit, Microsoft Money, and Schwab. com fight for recognition.

As with health, education, and government services, the digital bank is already here, working together with all the other trends in banking to create new institutions. Consider Citigroup, the financial conglomerate formed by the recent merger of the Citicorp bank with the Travelers Group of insurance companies. The new company also includes Salomon Smith Barney, the investment and securities firm; Diner's Club credit cards; and Primerica life insurance. Citigroup plans to build a single common distribution channel and brand for all of its electronic commerce services. Says Ed Horowitz, head of the group's electronic business efforts, "We want to be within one click, one phone call and one mile of any customers in the world. . . . That's the aspiration."[6]

One of the areas that has changed the most rapidly is mortgage shopping. Today, just by typing the word "mortgage" on an Internet search engine, a consumer can compare mortgage rates, print out payment schedules, and apply for a new mortgage on-line. Some Web sites even have zip code calculators that will tell consumers how much prices have gone up in their neighborhoods so they can better calculate the equity they will reap from the sale of their current home. One effect of the rise of Internet-based mortgage financing is greater speed in what has traditionally been a slow and cumbersome process. According to Michael Youngblood, managing director at Chase Securities, "If you need a 72-hour closing you can hit the Internet and find a borrower who will do that for you."[7] An equally important benefit for consumers is lower costs. Closing points and fees for mortgages had declined from 1.6 percent of the mortgage amount for a thirty-year mortgage in 1993 to 1.1 percent by mid-1998. Nomura Securities strategist Arthur Frank attributes this at least in part to the automated underwriting process.[8] Furthermore, mortgage brokers using the Net can make more loans using the same number of staff. One significant consequence of these efficiencies is that consumers can refinance even with higher interest rates, since their closing costs are lower.

Traditional banks extending their businesses into cyberspace will need to compete with the pure Internet banks of the future. Some of them are here: Security First Network Bank was the first all-Internet bank, operating in all fifty states, all day (and night), every day. It is federally insured and from a technical point of view, customers anywhere in the world can use it. Similar Internet banks have started in the United Kingdom, Germany, Australia, and Brazil. With their customer bases and established presence, however, the real winners should be existing financial institutions that move quickly into Net banking, such as Wells Fargo.

Network banking technologies are also beginning to benefit consumers in developing countries. In South Africa, a key platform of former president Nelson Mandela's party, the African National Congress, has been to spread the benefits of the economy to the nonwhite South Africans. Standard Bank, one of the nation's largest banks, has developed its "E-bank" service for illiterate people. Using a photo and biometric image of a fingerprint on a smart card for identification, the customer enters the card into an automatic teller machine and uses a touch screen to identify currency denominations and withdraw cash. A live teleconference connection is available for inquiries, and the bank is experimenting with wireless connections by satellite to serve remote areas with mobile terminals.

Although countries such as Singapore have invested a great deal of money and effort in networked trading systems and other financial tools, banking systems in Asia are generally behind those of Europe and the United States in moving into cyber-banking. According to the *Wall Street Journal,* this banking technology gap may have been partly responsible for Asia's financial crisis, since it is harder to hide losses and problem loans in an open networked system. Asian banks are "trailing U.S. and European banks by three to five years," according to James Fiorillo of ING Barings Securities Japan Ltd.[9]

For the foreseeable future, the impact of change will continue to be torrid in every area of financial services. On-line stock trading is becoming ubiquitous. According to *Industry Week,* "For active traders, the need to contact any sort of financial intermediary for information and execution has sharply diminished, and in a few years it won't exist at all."[10] The "day trader" who makes a living with on-line trading has befuddled the Internal Revenue Service, which is having difficulty categorizing the income and expenses of day trading for tax purposes.

A study done for the insurance industry reached the same sort of conclusion: "Insurance companies have the opportunity to sell directly to consumers, bypassing agents, lowering the cost of sales and making their products more competitive with those of banks and securities firms. They can also offer online claims filing and other interactive customer service functions, lowering the cost of conducting these activities."[11]

Technological advances in cryptography and authentication systems, smart chips and cards, and even new materials that will permit the embedding of digital technology in clothing will open up even newer financial and payment systems over the coming years. Electronic wallets, using either token or account-based systems, such as that of Cybercash, which uses an electronic gatekeeper to authenticate a customer's "cash," will become common. Digital tokens will be a form of cash, or Internet bank notes, that can be traded among individuals. Internet check and credit transactions will become the norm.

POLICY CONCERNS

The use of all of these innovations raises significant public policy issues, ranging from the preservation of the fundamental integrity of the financial and monetary system, to the need to prevent criminal activities, to protecting the privacy and consumer rights of citizens. Although many of these concerns can be addressed within the existing legal and regulatory framework, all need to be examined in the light of the new information infrastructure. Among the key issues are the following.

— System integrity: Perhaps the most important issue is the question of the protection of the integrity of the global, as well as the U.S., financial system. In recent years, there has been a great focus on the question of global risk management, particularly in light of the financial crises in Asia, Latin America, and Russia. To the extent that these crises were caused in part by the ability of investors and bankers to move huge quantities of money around the world at lightning speed, will we face even greater crises in the future when not only large traders but everyone has this ability at his or her fingertips?

— Economic management: As the amount of digital cash in the economy increases, will the Federal Reserve lose some of its ability to measure and manage the money supply? Will issuers of digital cash run afoul of the U.S. Mint and the Comptroller of the Currency? Will the government lose income from the potential loss of seignorage?

— Banking and credit regulation: How will the 1999 legislative reform of financial services interact with the digital revolution? Will regulations such as the Federal Reserve's Regulations E and Z, which govern credit-card liability and use, need to be modified? For example, will the liability rules limiting the liability of credit and debit cards be extended to cards used by food-stamp or welfare recipients? Will similar state laws need to be modified? Will new rules be needed defining banks and nonbanks, and such requirements as reserves?

— Security: How will the security of financial institutions in cyberspace be regulated? Will there be national standards for physical and digital security? Will the strongest cryptographic products be available for use by international banks and others?

— Legal: What kinds of systems will be put in place for certificate authorities and other forms of authentication? Will digital signatures and contracts be valid in every state and jurisdiction?

— Crime and money laundering: What kinds of preventive measures can be built into the system to prevent electronic crimes? Will there be new standards to insure the auditability of digital transactions? How will governments regulate on-line securities trading and prevent fraud and other abuses?

— Monopoly and antitrust: How will we ensure that competition remains strong in a globally restructured financial industry? How will we make certain that key new banking systems remain "open" rather than proprietary?

— Access: How will we ensure that the new systems are designed to include everyone, and that the poor, the rural, and the disabled have the same access to the financial system as everyone else? Can this be achieved through market mechanisms, or will we need new government programs?

— Taxation: How will electronic transactions that take place across multiple national and local jurisdictions be taxed? Are existing laws and treaties sufficient, or will new ones need to be devised?

— Privacy: Are existing banking privacy laws sufficient to protect consumers, or are new ones needed? Are the new financial privacy protections embedded in the 1999 financial services legislative overhaul sufficient to meet consumer privacy needs, or will state law override them? Is there a role for industry privacy codes that are self-policed? How will we resolve conflicting national privacy laws when international transactions are involved?

— Disclosure: How will laws defining the proper means of disclosure, as in the case of credit transactions, be applied to Internet transactions?

— Licensing: For financial professionals and companies requiring licensing, such as insurance agents, will we eliminate state licensing and move to a national system? Will companies licensed to do business in one state be permitted to offer services worldwide over the Internet?

The resolution of these issues will be difficult and time consuming. They involve significant conflicts not only between industries and companies, but also between jurisdictions, including the states, the federal government, and other nations. Will states, for example, be willing to cede their regulation of insurers to the federal government? Will nations open their financial systems to global competition? In addition, the consumer interest is sure to be heard. Fortunately, the United States is off to a good start: agencies ranging from the Federal Reserve to the Comptroller of the Currency to law enforcement are already taking action. As just one example, the Securities and Exchange Commission has set up a special unit to deal with investment scams on the Internet. It already receives more than 120 complaints each day.

At the international level, organizations ranging from the Bank for International Settlements to the World Trade Organization are active. Chapter 12 deals with these activities in more detail.

RETAIL AND DISTRIBUTION

Closely related to the Internet story of the financial industry is that of the retail and distribution sector. In retail, flowers tell the story. The virtual retail flower outlet known as 1-800-FLOWERS does business through its own flower shops and partners, through its toll-free number, and more recently, through its Internet site, which can be accessed via the World Wide Web or through proprietary systems such as America Online.

Over the past seven years, this company has seen its Internet business become its fastest-growing sector. By 1998, the Internet was generating 12–15 percent of the company's revenues—about $50 million. Some of this revenue comes through the company's ability to reach new markets: about 20 percent of its business now comes from overseas, from foreigners and Americans working abroad sending flowers to family and friends in the United States. The company says the costs of operating its on-line service are half the cost of the store operations, and it passes these savings on to its on-line customers in the form of lower service charges. Finally, the company uses the unique features of the Net to offer targeted marketing programs. For example, customers who register with them receive reminders of special occasions such as anniversaries and birthdays.

This small example captures many of the features of on-line retailing and the benefits it will bring to consumers and retailers. A comprehensive list would include the following:

—Convenience: Surveys conducted by CommerceNet and Nielsen show that convenience is the main reason by far that people shop on the Internet. Once again, in our busy society, the ability to shop twenty-four hours per day from the convenience of one's home is pushing the growth of cyberspace.

—Research ease: Today's Internet shopping malls offer enormous ease of use. Looking for an automobile model in a particular category and price range with certain features? A number of sites available now, including Edmunds.com, AutobyTel.com, and Carprices.com will narrow choices quickly and provide information on discount opportunities, nearby dealers, and financing and insurance. Electronic commerce has also revolutionized collecting. Rare book dealers, for example, now say that in minutes on-line they can locate books that once took months or even years to find. In the future, intelligent agents will actually do the search for you, powered by voice commands.

—Price competition: The Internet marketplace is the closest the world has ever come to Adam Smith's perfect market. Consumers can comparison shop in real time, and many auction services, such as Priceline.com and First Auction, allow shoppers to bid on items. Airlines can offer timely special low-cost fares to fill seats that would otherwise go unused. Small businesses can reach the same large markets as large businesses can, as entry barriers are lowered dramatically. Consumers are the beneficiaries.

—Global selection: The Internet offers a worldwide marketplace. An antiques shopper can search sites in Paris, Milan, Hong Kong, or Kyoto without leaving home. Conversely, businesses limited geographically in physical space can become worldwide exporters in cyberspace.

—Elimination of the middleman: Just as disintermediation operates in the financial services markets, so it does in retailing. Companies from Microsoft to American Airlines have learned that they can reach their customers and sell their products directly without the need for a retailer or travel agent to do it for them. This phenomenon brings manufacturers closer to customers and also cuts the costs of products and services even further.

—Consumer power: Armed with so much information about prices, product features, and services, the customer is king in cyberspace.

As consumer bulletin boards and organizations also proliferate, the ability of consumers to post complaints broadly and identify bad businesses publicly should force retailers to behave better. On-line consumer advocacy groups will grow and become more powerful, as well.

—Service: Supplementing its speed and convenience, electronic shopping offers consumers other customized services. Customers can easily choose sizes, colors, and other features of products. Once a customer's preferences are known to an on-line site, it can help narrow their searches and, if they wish, custom repeat products for them. A repeat buyer of art, for example, with a preference for antique French posters, can be offered new stock on-line, before it is made available to the public at large. A subscriber to multiple publications can receive and pay for articles only on those subjects in which he or she is interested.

—Manufacturing convergence: The ability of individuals to customize products to their liking is turning the traditional manufacturing process on its head. Rather than mass-produce thousands of items and hope to sell most of them, companies can merge their Internet marketing programs with their manufacturing operations and microproduce goods that are pre-sold. We will discuss this phenomenon and its implications for manufacturing further later in this chapter.

—Branding and advertising: The creation and maintenance of brands and brand images, a feature of retailing that dates back to the late nineteenth century and brands such as Ivory soap and Coca-Cola, will change dramatically with electronic retailing. Just as the rise of broadcast television in the 1950s changed the nature of advertising, creating powerful new national media, the Net will again cause a tectonic shift. Like the customization of manufacturing, the Net offers the opportunity for customized branding of products, aimed at individual customers with specific preferences. Thus, an airline that understands a passenger's travel habits and itineraries could offer advertising delivered only to that customer, offering services and prices that the passenger is more likely to choose.

In a sense, this dual ability of electronic commerce—to reach a worldwide market, but also to reach each individual in that market in a special way—is what makes the field so dynamic. As Francis Cairncross, senior editor of the *Economist,* says in her book *The Death of Distance,*

"Advertising will have more potential for global branding—but the audiences in each outlet will remain culturally distinct. Changes in communications will increase what companies know about their customers, will fragment advertising markets, and will shift company relations with customers from passive to active."[12]

The positive part of this equation for consumers is the added value of information about products and services and the ability to be part of a community of users. For example, a company marketing high-fidelity sound equipment can not only tailor advertising and information to meet a particular consumer's needs but can also offer an electronic bulletin board service where many users of its equipment can trade observations or complaints. As Cairncross points out, these "branded communities" will form a kind of worldwide extended family for companies, greatly extending their marketing power.

As a result of these advantages, on-line retailing, although still accounting for only about 1 percent of total retail sales, was growing at a rate of more than 200 percent annually by 1998.[13] According to the U.S. Department of Commerce in its first published statistics on retail sales, on-line sales reached $5.3 billion for the 1999 holiday season—large, but less than 1 percent of the total. Although many of the early entrants into the on-line market were entirely new firms, by 1998 many traditional retailers, particularly catalog companies such as Land's End and L.L. Bean, as well as storefront firms such as Barnes and Noble and Eddie Bauer, had entered the on-line market. These companies caught up to and passed the new companies in 1998 and accounted for 59 percent of Internet retail sales as they used the Web to supplement their existing retail channels. As giants such as WalMart and Home Depot developed their on-line capabilities, the trend was expected to accelerate.

In addition to the growth in volume, the number of households making on-line purchases doubled in 1998, to 8.7 million from 4.5 million in 1997. Although some consumers remained hesitant to shop on-line, for a variety of reasons, some of this fear dissipated as known brands such as Gap, Toys "R" Us, and even Brooks Brothers moved on-line. While the main categories of on-line sales included computers and software, hotel bookings, airline reservations, rental cars, and books, other categories were catching up: clothing, toys, music, magazine subscriptions, theater tickets, gift items, and even groceries. Whereas it had previously been commonly thought that most computer users were male, a study by Ernst and Young in 1998 showed that about one-third of on-line shoppers were women and that their numbers were growing. According to Walter Loeb, a retail analyst for Morgan Stanley Dean Witter, "Women buy multiple units of pantyhose at a time, and they are loyal to both brand and style. It makes perfect sense to buy these replenishment items on the Internet."[14]

The surge in on-line retailing is causing ripples in related fields. In 1998, on-line advertising revenues surpassed $2 billion, more than double the figures from the preceding year.[15] The traditional company Clorox, for example, was selling its Armor All brand of car cleaners on the Web site of Kelley Blue Book, the publisher of used-car resale values, thereby targeting a key, precise audience. Some advertising Web pages plant a "cookie," or software identifier, on the computers of those who visit the site, which enables them later to target the potential buyer with specific advertising material, thus raising serious privacy issues.

Internet sales are also driving growth and important changes in the distribution and package-delivery industries. Physical goods ordered on the Internet must be delivered quickly, and companies such as United Parcel Service and Federal Express are benefiting from the growth of on-line sales. An excellent example is Netgrocer.com, which offers home delivery of more than 2,500 nonperishable grocery items. Federal Express ships merchandise from a central warehouse located in Dallas, Texas, and run by a subsidiary of American Airlines. Netgrocer.com sales reached about $78 billion in 1998; the company has been highly successful among elderly and disabled consumers in southern Florida. The company also plans to generate revenue from manufacturers' advertising on its site.[16]

The public policy issues generated in the virtual retail marketplace duplicate many of those already discussed in the preceding sections: individual privacy; data security; legal contracts and signatures; consumer protection; appropriate taxation, and the jurisdictional and international aspects of all of these issues. As retailing converges not only with cyberspace itself but also with manufacturing, distribution, and financial services, even more issues will emerge. As venture capitalist Walter Forbes has pointed out, "This is the new world we are entering—a world where a marketplace exists only in time and space, where bricks and mortar retailers are an anachronism from the twentieth century, and where parking lots and suburban malls can begin to return to their rightful places as parkland and green space."[17]

MANUFACTURING AND PROCESSING

For centuries, governments have viewed their national ability to manufacture goods and to process raw materials such as crude oil or iron ore into finished products as fundamental to their strategic health. Not only have these industries provided an abundance of jobs, but they also have made possible the achievement of key economic, political, and military aspirations. Nations that cannot self-sufficiently produce, for example, such items as gasoline, automotive vehicles, aircraft, chemicals, and steel, not to mention clothing, paper, glass, and a host of other commodities, have felt inferior to those that could.

Moreover, until recently, the corporations that produced these goods felt a strong need to control every aspect of the production process, from research and development through basic manufacturing and assembly, to sales and after-market service. Such companies were vertically integrated and controlled through pyramidal hierarchies. Even as they became multinational in the years after World War II, such giants as Coca-Cola, the IBM Corporation, Siemens, Sony, General Motors, and DuPont retained this basic unified system of organization, ownership, and control. Although governments became somewhat wary as multinational corporations became ubiquitous, the old corporate manufacturing model suited government needs for political control, as well.

By the mid-1980s, however, an avalanche of forces from around the world combined to force dramatic changes in the way goods and materials were manufactured and processed—changes that were supercharged by the advent of the Internet and electronic commerce in the late 1990s. Among the key forces were economic development in Asia, Latin America, and after 1989, eastern Europe; higher levels of education in these countries, which created a new competitive workforce; the lowering of tariffs and nontariff barriers worldwide, making the international movement of goods more efficient; the development of more efficient and less expensive sea and air transport systems; the growth of the global capital market, which made overseas investment simpler; and most important, the use of advanced communications and computer systems that could link together far-flung organizations.

In addition, as we have already discussed, worldwide consumer expectations were rising during a period of intensifying competition. Manufacturers began to have to pay more attention to consumer needs, to search for constant increases in product quality, to offer new services attached to products, and to get products to market much faster than had been possible in the past. Finally, strict new environmental controls over operations in the manufacturing and process industries required development of new ways to protect the environment while still achieving other goals.

The result was the total reinvention of the manufacturing enterprise, a reinvention that turned out to be heavily dependent on the Net. In fact, as digital technology converged with the manufacturing process from the delivery of raw materials to the packaging and shipping of finished goods, the art and science of manufacturing changed irrevocably, creating wholly new kinds of institutions. Among the key characteristics of the new enterprises were the following:

—Speed to market: Reducing the time from the conception of a new product until its delivery to consumers is critical today, and not simply because one needs to beat the competitor to the marketplace. It is also important because the faster a product can be brought to market, the cheaper it will be, giving it a cost advantage over the products of slower competitors who use more research, development, and manufacturing resources. The lighting division of the General Electric Corporation (GE), for example, already solicits bids for spare parts on the Net, reducing the time for delivery from two weeks to overnight.

—"Just in time" inventory: This process, whereby the components of products to be sold are acquired with very short lead time, involves complex logistical planning and operations skills that not only reduce time to market but dramatically lower a firm's costs by minimizing the inventories that normally produce a drag on a firm's finances. The marketing of many modern products, such as electronics equipment and computers, has been compared to selling fish: they must be sold "fresh," or rot begins to set in. The use of the Net becomes critical to the survival of firms in these businesses.

—Market-driven quality: Achieving quality levels that delight customers depends not only on the elimination of defects—in itself an important customer satisfaction and cost-saving goal—but also on understanding customer needs by studying customers carefully, using in a responsible way such tools as "data mining." This method of collecting data over the Net about customer preferences also becomes an absolute necessity for companies manufacturing items ranging from automobiles to kitchen appliances.

—Virtual research and development: Firms today can improve research and development results while lowering costs and speeding time to market by the use of computer simulations to test many products and processes. Pharmaceutical and chemical firms are among the chief users of such techniques as virtual molecular modeling.

—Outsourcing: As firms have focused on their strengths in the new competitive world, they have also learned that they do not need to focus on areas of their businesses that they consider less important. In fact, they can improve the quality and reduce the cost of these operations by outsourcing them to firms for which these operations are a core business. As the *Financial Times* has said, "A decade ago, the main edition of the *Financial Times* was written and printed on one site. This was because the articles were still transmitted to the printers through pieces of paper and slugs of type. When that information became digital and practically costless, it was possible not only to separate the production from the editorial but to farm it out entirely."[18]

—Managing the supply chain: Firms that outsource on a global basis need a new way to manage the complex logistics of their supply, production, and transportation chains. Not only have the Internet, intranets, and extranets become the vehicles of choice, but firms are banding together to form new supply networks. For example, the American Textile Partnership's "Demand Activated Manufacturing Architecture" has created a standard regional database of the production capabilities of manufacturers in the southeastern United States to help manage and make more efficient the production of textiles, from raw fibers to retail products.[19] In another example, the GE lighting division system referred to earlier has prompted the formation of the GE Trading Partner Network, a Web-based system that allows GE buyers to make instant purchases from qualified suppliers.

—Protecting the environment: For process and manufacturing companies, environmental protection has become an integral part of the overall process. Production systems must be designed from the outset to deal with air and ground emissions, or companies will face enormous production delays from regulatory authorities—delays that could be devastating in today's fast-paced Net-driven environment. Similarly, production processes must be monitored with sophisticated remote sensors to avoid costly plant shutdowns that slow production. The Net will play a crucial role in these processes.

The results of all these changes in the manufacturing and processing industries have been profound already. The traditional activity structure of the large, vertically integrated corporation has been splintered. Firms look at each segment of the chain and decide where they are strong and where they are weak. Weak segments are outsourced or totally abandoned. A firm that focuses solely on its manufacturing processes may give up its packaging, distribution, or marketing functions to outside firms. It may begin to purchase components of its manufacturing operation from other firms and decentralize its assembly operations, controlling the entire process with a vast internal network connected to the Internet. With fewer fixed assets, firms can change more dynamically to meet market conditions—becoming, in effect, "virtual" corporations.

Political science professor John Zysman and author Andrew Schwartz have given these newly emerging entities a moniker: "international production networks." In the words of Zysman and Schwartz, "international production networks are relationships among firms that organize, across national borders, the research and development activities, procurement, distribution, production definition and design, manufacturing and support services in a given industry. Forms of international production networks evolving recently include large doses of contracted production provided by manufacturing services companies that organize particular activities or often the whole production value chain."[20]

An excellent example of such a network is the Automotive Network Exchange organized and run by the U.S. automobile industry.[21] Operating since November 1998, the system consists of about 1,500 members, all hooked together through Internet service providers and using common communications standards and protocols. Within the network, all participants can exchange anything from complex engineering drawings to simple E-mail. Suppliers can view specifications and updates on-line in real time and make bids accordingly. The result is not just a group of virtual companies but a virtual industry in which each player can concentrate on its strengths and become more competitive. By February 2000, Ford, General Motors, and Daimler-Chrysler had expanded the notion to create an on-line marketplace for automotive parts and raw materials. Already, other industries, such as aerospace, tire manufacturing, personal computers, airlines, and hotels, have created similar "B2B" communities on the Net.

Although all of these changes in manufacturing were not caused by the Net, they were made possible by it and they have been accelerated by it, and their impact will be felt far beyond the specific firms and industries involved. For example, the single largest employer in the United States, which was once General Motors, is now the temporary employment agency Manpower, Inc.[22] This fact reveals much both about the changes in the manufacturing industry and the stability of the new workforce. Employees in the new world of manufacturing will find employment security not in their relationship with a particular company, but in their ability constantly to refresh their skills—skills that are increasingly based in computers and computer networks.

The public policy implications of the digital revolution in manufacturing involve many of the issues that have already been discussed: data security, standards, intellectual property protection, legal signatures, and contracts and taxation. But they also go beyond these. Among the broader issues for manufacturing are the following.

—Life-long learning: How can we modify and improve our educational system to provide continuous education and therefore new opportunities for production workers whose jobs will change profoundly? The new educational system not only will have to teach specific technology skills but must also prepare production workers to deal with important new decision-making responsibilities.

—Research and development incentives: Since nations want manufacturing assets within their borders, and since they also know that profound technological changes are under way, what policies can they use to stimulate more research and development in the new digital technologies? The United States uses the research and development tax credit to some extent, whereas other countries tend to rely on direct subsidies.

—Anti-trust and competition policy: Since the new world of manufacturing will increasingly involve loose and shifting alliances among different firms in areas such as research and development and procurement, will changes be needed in competition law to permit these new arrangements? Will countries that fail to allow more mergers and alliances lose ground economically, or will countries that permit the new combinations fall victim to new and dangerous monopolies?

—Regulatory policy: How can governments work to make their regulatory agencies responsive to the digital challenge by permitting electronic submission of filings and required regulatory reports? Can the regulatory agencies be woven into the new virtual manufacturing and process networks without being co-opted?

—Trade and investment policy: How can nations serve their own best interests by adopting forward-looking international trade and investment policies that maximize their strengths in the new manufacturing world rather than looking to the old protectionist policies that sought to preserve weak companies and industries?

Megaconvergence has had a particularly global effect on manufacturing for two key reasons. First, many of the raw materials that feed into the processing industries are found in many countries, and second, cheap labor in many countries has attracted manufacturing operations. For these reasons, many of the public policy issues that result will have to be addressed in international forums ranging from the International Labor Organization to the Organization for Economic Cooperation and Development. Their activities will be discussed in Chapter 12.

CONCLUSION

This chapter and Chapter 3 began with the assertion that the convergence of cyberspace with each of society's key institutions—health care, education, government, banking and finance, and commerce and industry— was changing them irrevocably. With the institutional change would come changes in the way people worked, learned, shopped, and were treated by their physicians. Although these two chapters have covered the major institutions, others are affected as well.

Utility companies are being disaggregated into manufacturers of electricity and distributors of it. This separation is made possible by sophisticated computer networks that can measure and record complicated flows of energy. In addition, utility companies are using their investment in optical fiber, originally installed to allow them to read customers' electric meters, also to offer telecommunications and Internet access services.

Entertainment companies are learning that they are producers of content that can be used for a variety of purposes and in a variety of media. The music and video industries already have close ties through the emergence of music videos in the 1980s, and media companies are also becoming education enterprises. The proposed merger of Time Warner and America Online is a vivid example of megaconvergence. Special niches are opening up to new entrants as the costs of entry into cable networks and onto the Internet are reduced. We have seen the rise of food channels, a fishing channel, and a fashion channel; more such specialized entertainment channels appear each year. Entertainment has also begun to merge with retailing: witness Victoria's Secret's debut of its new product line over the Internet in early 1999, attracting one of the largest audiences ever to its Web site.

The news media are changing in the wake of the Internet's coverage of President Clinton's impeachment. News stories that would have been carefully fact-checked, and thus delayed somewhat, by the traditional media are now forced out by early publication on numerous Web sites. Journalism schools are now engaged in a major debate over the impact of the Internet on ethics in the profession. The Net is also changing fundamentally the economics of the news media, as newspapers and other printed media scramble to understand its impact on classified advertising and circulation.

The legal profession is also being buffeted by the same trends that physicians, teachers, and other professionals face. For example, Ralph Warner, founder of a legal Web site called Nolo.com, says, "The Internet is democratizing the practice of law."[23] His and other legal Web sites offer free legal advice and could thereby run afoul of state laws and bar association rules. The Texas Supreme Court has already closed down Web sites for practicing law without a license. Legal Web sites may also violate rules regarding legal advertising or practicing law across state lines.

Whether the institution is a government office, a bank, a professional practice, or a hospital, it is clear that we are only in the early stages of these changes. We are also in the early stages of policy-making in the Internet arena—and many of the questions are just beginning to be defined. The policy world will need to pay close attention to these questions and the individual policy topics to which we now turn.

II

Public Policy Issues

5

Digital Democracy

The modern totalitarian state relies on secrecy for the regime, but high surveillance and disclosure for all other groups. . . . The democratic society relies on publicity as a control over government, and on privacy as a shield for group and individual life. . . . Thus the constant search in democracies must be for the proper boundary line in each specific situation and for an overall equilibrium that serves to strengthen democratic institutions and processes.

—Alan F. Westin, *Privacy and Freedom*[1]

During the more than two hundred years of the American republic, public policy has generally evolved around the tensions inherent in a number of recurring conflicts. One group of concerns has been the balancing of the role of the public and private sectors, and developing appropriately tuned regulatory regimes rather than expanding state ownership of property and industry, as happened in the more ideological nations of Europe. A second has involved the tension between the needs for national security and proper law enforcement and the need to preserve the civil liberties defined in the Constitution. Another has set American internationalism—some would say interventionism—against the opposing views of isolationists and protectionists.

Other recurring tensions have arisen between individual privacy and the public's need to know; between the right of free speech and public safety or intellectual property rights; between the economic needs of the have-nots and the rights of the haves; and over the jurisdictions of the state governments and the federal government in Washington. It is the essence of democracy to seek the best balance between the conflicts of competing demands. Many individual conflicts are worked out; others are not, and legislative and legal battles continue for years and even centuries.

The coming of the digital era and the convergence of the Net with the fundamental institutions of society points a technological blowtorch at many of these conflicts and opens them up for white-hot debate. What is particularly new is that, although American public and private institutions are leading the debate, the resolution this time must be global, not American. As we have seen, the Net is borderless, and policies made in one country will fail without international acceptance or recognition.

Not only are the issues global in scope, but they are daunting in their intellectual content, as we have seen, and they are numerous. The following five chapters deal with these issues and group them arbitrarily into five broad subject areas. This chapter deals with digital democracy and covers three issues: privacy, Internet content and free speech; and the need to provide universal access. Chapter 6 examines digital economics and the issues of economic growth and productivity, the taxation of electronic commerce, international trade and investment, and antitrust and competition laws and policies.

Chapter 7 covers the technical regulatory issues that will govern the physical growth of the Net: telecommunications regulation, Internet security and especially cryptography, and standards. Chapter 8 focuses on the legal issues surrounding the digital revolution, such as the legal framework around digital contracts and signatures, consumer protection laws, and intellectual property rights. Finally, Chapter 9 will discuss national research and development policies in support of the Net.

The leitmotif that links all of these issues and often doubles their complexity is balancing the public- and private-sector roles in cyberspace. This clash is historical, cultural, and international. As earlier noted, the Internet and its underlying technologies began during the early Cold War years as government-funded projects. To some extent, they still are, although the government role in both research and development (R&D) and physical deployment becomes less important each year. By the mid-1990s, both the funding and the applications for the new information infrastructure had become mostly private.

Nevertheless, a key piece of the infrastructure was also based on heavily regulated telecommunications monopolies that had become comfortable with, or at least accepting of, government control. The computer, semiconductor, and software sectors not only were unregulated but were run by free-market entrepreneurs who cherished their independence. The stage was set for a series of skirmishes among government officials and regulators with a stake in the Internet's history, regulated companies who wanted to maintain their relatively protected positions, and the more swashbuckling capitalists of Silicon Valley, Austin, Texas, and elsewhere in the heartland who wanted to continue their unfettered successful advances in the marketplace. This last group, which included people like Bill

Gates of Microsoft, Andy Grove and Craig Barrett of the Intel Corporation, Jerry Sanders of Advanced Micro Devices, Scott McNealy of Sun Microsystems, and Michael Dell of his eponymous company, were courted by politicians in both political parties plumbing the vast untapped sources of political support and contributions in the new industry.

Although the Republicans held the home-court advantage in this public-private squabble, the Democrats came out ahead, at least initially, as a result of the Clinton administration's, and particularly Vice President Al Gore's, championing of the private-sector cause. In an extraordinary turnabout from his earlier views, when he had prodded Congress into funding advanced computing and communications programs, Gore led the administration's July 1997 declaration that "private sector leadership accounts for the explosive growth of the Internet today, and the success of electronic commerce will depend on continued private sector leadership."[2] In part, this was a reaction to the facts on the ground: the Internet had become privatized. But it was also a clever political move that the vice president hoped would pay off in terms of future political support from what he saw as the premier industry of the future.

Making the public-private balance more complicated, the information infrastructure had also become global by the mid-1990s. Thus, other governments with vastly different views of the public- and private-sector roles were evincing a strong interest. The European Union (EU) and Japan took the first steps in the 1980s. In both, the telecommunications sector was still government-owned or heavily regulated, although the process of privatizing and deregulating had begun. In both the EU and Japan, government played a much stronger role than in the United States on issues ranging from standards to privacy and security to the control of content. Again, at the outset at least, U.S. leadership seemed to take hold, and both the EU and Japan, as we shall see, embraced the idea of private leadership of the global information infrastructure. No doubt they were startled enough by the early American success and even dominance in cyberspace and its economic machine that they felt compelled to imitate American methods, at least publicly.

The initial, sweeping pronouncements by the United States and other governments that the private sector should lead the development of electronic commerce did not end the matter, however. The battlegrounds over each of the key issues of the digital age were consistently staked out by partisans of both sides. On issues ranging from privacy to telecommunications regulation to cryptography, the question of public versus private control lurked in the background. Moreover, again at least initially, the private sector did not seem to understand that in winning the first round of the debate over private-sector leadership, it had caught a hot, steaming potato. Government expected more from the private sector than mere rhetoric and it was happy to deflect the public heat from itself to private industry on issues such as privacy. The first of these potatoes to burn the private sector's hands would be the issues of individual privacy and free speech.

Although a discussion of the public policy issues swirling around the emergence of the digital age could begin with any of these issues, it seems most appropriate to begin the discussion with those issues that are most fundamental to democracy and human rights. Why? Few values are more directly important to the future success of the Net and the benefits it can bring to humanity than those of free expression, privacy, and the ability, if not the right, to access the Internet. Moreover, the failure to address these issues, more than any others, could threaten the very existence of an open Net in the future. Societies that cannot successfully deal with these questions—we see examples already of countries that are restricting these freedoms—will fall away from those that do and from the concomitant economic and social benefits. Indeed, it is reasonable to assert that the key foundation for American leadership in the coming digital century will be the openness of American society and its robust though often messy and imperfect democratic system. It is not uncommon for gurus of the wired age to compare cyberspace to the wild West, the often lawless American frontier. Yet it is clear that the strong democratic American values of freedom of expression, belief in the market economy and private property, and love of change have made possible American leadership in the digital world. Since privacy has been at the cutting edge of cyberspace issues, we will begin with a discussion of that difficult, ambiguous, and often elusive topic.

PRIVACY

No one shall be subjected to arbitrary interference with his privacy, family, home or correspondence. . . . Everyone has the right to the protection of the law against such interference.

—Universal Declaration of Human Rights, Article 12

Look in any of the world's great historical documents defining human rights, freedom, and liberty, with the exception of the 1948 Universal Declaration of Human Rights, and you will be hard pressed to find a specific mention of a right to privacy. Yet instinctively, virtually everyone understands the need for privacy, even at an early age. Surveillance, we know, is a form of social and even political control. We learn this in childhood, as we are watched by parents anxious to protect us by controlling our behavior. A basic childhood need soon evolves into the urge to shield certain actions from parents.

Moreover, the norms of virtually every human society provide for some minimal aspect of privacy for human conduct, be it for bodily functions, sexual activities, or the body itself. Within families, there are secrets between husbands and wives, between siblings, and within the extended family. Yet the broader concern with privacy is more modern.

Personal privacy was hard to achieve until relatively recently, since families lived most commonly within a single structure or room. Moreover, feudal systems of government provided no civil liberties, let alone a right to privacy. The issue of privacy as a right under siege as we know it today arose from two overall developments: the evolution of different systems of government and the rise of modern technology.

To totalitarian and authoritarian governments of every stripe, of course, the notion of an individual's right to privacy is anathema—an attack on the very legitimacy of the state. Writers from Franz Kafka to Arthur Koestler to George Orwell have documented the totalitarian state's obsessive need to violate the minds of its subjects. In his novel *The First Circle,* Aleksandr Solzhenitsyn describes Stalin's attempts to tap every telephone in the Soviet Union. The use of the block captain to spy on every family not only was used in Nazi Germany but is still in use in countries such as Cuba.

Even democratic countries, however, evolved differing norms, laws, and institutions regarding privacy. For example, Alan Westin, professor of law at Columbia University and one of the nation's leading privacy experts, points out that although the British place a very high value on personal privacy and tolerate eccentric conduct, they also have a very positive attitude toward government and the civil service that makes them more deferential to their government about things such as secrecy and surveillance.

Germans have had a different view, as Westin points out: "neither German law nor government showed high capacity, until the post–World War II period, to enforce a meaningful system of civil liberties restraints on government surveillance practices." The result, he said, is that even today in Germany, "government enjoys great rights of secrecy; but the privacy of the critic and non-conformist is still not secure."[3] Thus in both the United Kingdom and Germany, and more so in the latter, the public's trust in the government to gather and protect data is greater than its trust in the private sector to do so.

In the United States, however, a somewhat different view of privacy prevails. The American experience was forged by revolt from oppressive government, freedom from the rigid class systems of Europe, and belief in the right of private property. Written into the Bill of Rights was the Fourth Amendment, guaranteeing freedom from illegal search and seizure. The essence of American government is the complex and often purposely inefficient system of checks and balances, not only between the branches of the federal government, but also among federal, state, and local government. As Westin says, "A final value supporting privacy is the American principle of civil liberty, with its enshrinement of limits on government and private power, freedom of expression and dissent, and institutionalized mechanisms for enforcing these rights."[4] Thus, to some extent, the United States is a mirror image of the European view of privacy. Americans trust less in government to collect data and to protect it from privacy violations than do Europeans. Individualistic Americans are not entirely trustful of the private sector either, but they are less fearful of it than they are of a too-powerful government.

The other trend that defines privacy and its concerns as we enter the digital age is technology. Before technology, the ability to invade another's privacy was limited to the physical scope of the human senses—especially sight and hearing, combined with memory. By the end of the nineteenth century, that began to change dramatically. During the last two decades of that century, the inventions of the telephone, the microphone, the Dictaphone, and photography greatly extended the physical reach of the senses and created an artificial memory, no longer dependent on the physical or mental limitations of humans. People began to be aware that they were losing something, that actions that were once totally private and totally gone when they were over could be recorded at a distance, even invisibly. In 1902, the *New York Times* reported that "kodakers" lying in wait to photograph public figures was an invasion of privacy.[5]

Over the course of the twentieth century, the technology of physical surveillance improved dramatically. Telephone taps, electronic bugs, chemical dyes, photographic lenses, tiny recording devices, and other means of surveillance were not only used by governments, but became available to the public. With each technological advance came new laws and regulations to control their use, aimed at limiting the power of governments and others to spy.

Ironically, along with these technological developments came new trends in government in the United States and Europe that further threatened individual privacy. New social programs required government collection of individual data far beyond what had been needed before. These new programs ranged from the Federal Housing Administration's mortgage program, which at one time kept files on people's marital situations as part of their mortgage applications, to civil rights laws and regulations, which required collecting individual information on racial and ethnic backgrounds. It is particularly ironic, for example, that in 1964, the Federal Trade Commission (FTC) attempted to use data from federal income-tax files in business questionnaires and was forbidden to do so by Congress; today, as we shall see, the FTC is the principal federal agency charged with protecting individual privacy.

This combination of increased government data-gathering and the rise of technology, particularly computer technology, led to the first concerns about computers and privacy in the mid-1960s. Perhaps the first known warning about the dangers of computerized data collection to individual privacy rights occurred in 1961 when Bernard Benson, a computer manufacturer, spoke to the Society of Technical Writers and Publishers and said, "Where information rests is where power lies and (electronically computed) concentration of power is catastrophically dangerous."[6]

By 1965, the national concern about privacy and computers heated up considerably when the Bureau of the Budget published a report authored by a consultant named E. S. Dunn, Jr. The Dunn Report examined the numerous and overlapping data-collection efforts by government agencies and made a simple, cost-saving suggestion: eliminate redundancy and save money by setting up a National Data Center that would consolidate all government information about individuals in a single place. By crystallizing so many public privacy concerns into one issue, the Dunn Report set off a firestorm in Congress. Hearings in the House of Representatives, sponsored by Representative Cornelius Gallagher, and in the Senate, sponsored by Senator Russell Long, branded the idea a "monster" and an "octopus." Democrats and Republicans were united in indignation. The center was stillborn, but not only did government data-collection efforts by individual agencies continue to grow, private-sector organizations such as credit bureaus, banks, and mail-order houses also began to collect and use large amounts of data about individual Americans.

Meanwhile, the legal theory of privacy remained quite thin. In fact, privacy had never been legally defined as a "right" in the United States. That all changed with *Griswold v. Connecticut* in 1965, in which the Supreme

Court ruled that a Connecticut state law banning the dissemination of birth control information was a violation of the right to marital privacy. Particularly important was the majority opinion, written by Justice William O. Douglas, which said that "zones" of privacy were created by the First, Third, Fourth, Fifth, and Ninth amendments to the Constitution. In his concurring opinion, Justice Arthur Goldberg said that privacy is a fundamental right, "so rooted in the traditions and conscience of our people as to be ranked as fundamental." Although Justices Hugo Black and Potter Stewart dissented, arguing that privacy was too ambiguous a concept to be a fundamental right, a majority of the court had made history by ruling on the basic nature of the right to individual privacy for Americans.

In the two decades following the *Griswold* decision, Congress reacted to the growing concerns about computers, data collection, and privacy by passing a series of privacy-protection laws. Rather than a sweeping approach, Congress aimed at those sectors in which Americans have the greatest fears, especially government and finance. In 1970, Congress passed the Fair Credit Reporting Act, which governed disclosure of personal information by credit bureaus and required credit companies to adopt "reasonable procedures" to ensure that the personal information in their files was accurate. This was followed up in 1978 by the Right to Financial Privacy Act, which required a search warrant before banks could release personal bank records to government agencies.

Congress also began to limit the government's access to private matters. The Federal Privacy Act of 1974 required that government record-keepers adhere to the federal Code of Fair Information Practices, giving legal status to that 1973 code, which had been developed by the Department of Health, Education, and Welfare. It stated the following:

— There shall be no personal data record-keeping systems whose very existence is a secret.
— Means must be provided for a person to find out what information about himself or herself is in a record and how it is used.
— Means must be provided for a person to prevent information about himself or herself that was obtained for one purpose from being used or made available for other purposes without his or her consent.
— There must be a way for a person to correct or amend a record of identifiable information about himself or herself.
— Any organization creating, maintaining, using, or disseminating records of identifiable personal data must ensure the reliability of the

data for its intended use and must take precautions to prevent misuses of the data.[7]

Although this code originally applied only to U.S. government data, its principles became part of privacy policy in the private sector in the United States. It also was woven into the fabric of other national laws and of international law, as it merged with similar policy developments around the world. Sweden became the first country to pass a broad privacy law in 1973; Canada, the United Kingdom, Germany, France, Denmark, Norway, Austria, Luxembourg, and Australia followed soon thereafter. These governments were facing the same challenges as the United States was in dealing with modern data-collection techniques. In addition, some bore the burden of the war years, when the governments of Nazi-occupied or -allied countries had collected individual information to use as a basis for deportations and arrests. By the 1990s most of the industrial countries had passed some form of privacy law. Each embraces similar privacy principles in broad measure, but each creates very different means of monitoring and enforcement, as we shall see.

In addition, the growth of national privacy laws and concerns was being felt internationally, as the question of transborder data flow arose naturally from the issue of differing privacy standards. Thus, after more than a decade of debate, the Organization for Economic Cooperation and Development (OECD) adopted its "Guidelines Governing the Protection of Privacy and Transborder Data Flow of Personal Data" in 1980. As the preface to the document notes, "there is a danger that disparities in national legislation could hamper the free flow of personal data across borders; these flows have greatly increased in recent years and are bound to grow further with the widespread introduction of new computer and communications technology. Restrictions on these flows could cause serious disruption in important sectors of the economy."[8]

The OECD guidelines, although not legally binding, set a tone for national laws. They set forth eight personal privacy principles:

1. Personal data collection should be limited, obtained lawfully, and with the knowledge or consent of the subject;
2. Personal data should be relevant to the purposes for which it is collected, be accurate, and be kept up to date;
3. The purpose of data collection should be specified when data is collected and subsequent use limited to the fulfillment of those purposes;

4. Personal data should not be disclosed or used without the consent of the subject or with the authority of the law;
5. Personal data should be protected by reasonable security safeguards;
6. There should be a general policy of openness about personal data policies and practices;
7. Individuals should have the right to reasonable access to their own personal data and be able to challenge data relating to themselves; and
8. A data controller (for entities gathering personal data) should be accountable for complying with the above measures.

The OECD guidelines also call for member states to establish "legal, administrative, or other procedures" to protect privacy and mentions both national legislation and self-regulation by the private sector, in the form of codes of conduct, as two means to do so. They also ask member states to refrain from taking actions that would inhibit the flow of information across borders and thereby hinder international trade.

Thus, in one sense, what began as an effort by the U.S. Department of Health, Education, and Welfare to develop a government code for privacy led to much more. In the United States, Congress continued to pass privacy laws affecting data collection and use by government and other sectors. The 1988 Computer Matching and Privacy Protection Act went further than the 1974 Federal Privacy Act by regulating the matching of federal, state, and local records, and permitting an individual to examine the implications of such a match, such as the potential loss of government benefits.

In addition to these federal laws dealing with financial industry and government records, Congress passed a series of other privacy laws in this period. The Family Education Rights and Privacy Act of 1974 established the confidentiality of student records in the possession of schools. The Cable Communications Policy Act of 1984 generally prohibited cable companies from collecting information about individual consumers' viewing or buying habits, and another law was passed to prohibit the disclosure of a customer's video-rental records. Other privacy laws protect personal information in telephone company records and state motor vehicle bureaus, and there are laws protecting the privacy of both conventional and cordless telephone conversations.

Beyond the numerous federal laws and regulations are numerous state laws, some of which have their own codes of fair information practices and some of which regulate the privacy of other records, such as medical, insurance, and employment records.

This complex tapestry of privacy laws, divided along both sectoral and jurisdictional axes, is controversial. Its supporters point out that it is typical of the American approach to similar issues—limiting and decentralizing the government's powers while addressing the specific issues of greatest political concern. Its critics, on the other hand, believe the U.S. approach is inadequate. Wrote University of North Carolina professor Jeff Smith in 1994, "Although a number of privacy laws have been passed, they do not address the issues in a cohesive fashion; rather, they form a patchwork quilt."[9]

Thoughtful critics such as Smith and Marc Rotenberg, director of the Electronic Privacy Information Center in Washington, D.C., point to other models of privacy regulation, such as the United Kingdom, which requires registration of data banks; Sweden, whose Data Inspection Board licenses data banks; and Germany, which has a data commissioner who investigates complaints, inspects some data operations, and acts an a national expert on privacy. Smith favors the German approach, which he says involves less bureaucracy than the British or Swedish models.

Even as, over two decades, Congress passed numerous privacy protection laws, and even though the Supreme Court had opined on the matter of privacy, the issue was not resolved for many people. Indeed, by the early 1990s, it entered a much more critical phase. As Alan Westin said in concluding his book, "The strict surveillance system that was for centuries the conscious trademark of European authoritarianism, and which the young American republic deliberately rejected out of libertarian principles, is now being installed in the United States, not through a deliberate turn toward dictatorial policies, but as an accidental by-product of electronic data processing for social welfare and public service ends."[10]

As we look at the development of the information infrastructure in the years since Westin wrote his book, and particularly since the explosion of the Internet starting in 1993, it is obvious that he accurately predicted what was about to happen to privacy—with one large exception. What Westin did not foresee, and what no one could have foreseen, was that not only would the marriage of computers, communications, and content make it possible for government officials or a few corporate officials to have access to an infinite variety of personal data, but that anyone and even everyone could have such access. If the yesterday's nightmare was that a malevolent government official or perhaps a corporate executive could view someone's personal financial, medical, or legal records, today's is that, potentially, anyone can.

Moreover, the use of "cookies" by firms on the Internet frightens many people. Cookies are text files, saved automatically on an individual's computer and available to any Web site that computer accesses, that identify some of the Web sites visited in the past and store some information about the computer's user. They are used by companies to make transactions more efficient and to track consumer preferences. Online operators defend cookies and say they are anonymous and can be blocked by a consumer's browser. Privacy advocates see cookies as electronic Trojan horses that invade privacy. Cookies and other new technology tools that invade privacy pose especially grave and difficult public policy challenges that must be addressed, since there is already evidence of widespread abuse of such tools by both government and the private sector.

Cookies and other information-gathering techniques such as data mining came under intense criticism in early 2000 when Doubleclick, an on-line marketing firm, announced it was creating a huge database of on-line consumers' preferences, including logs of Web sites visited by individuals. Under attack from the Federal Trade Commission and consumer groups, Doubleclick withdrew its plan in March 2000 until privacy standards could be developed. Meanwhile, Predictive Networks, another on-line company, announced in May 2000 that it had developed software that would allow Internet service providers to build "digital silhouettes" of a person by tracking a consumer's every move and sending targeted advertising to him or her.

Unfortunately, egregious examples of privacy violations already abound. Two particularly bad cases involved Internal Revenue Service agents browsing taxpayer records for their personal amusement and the premature release of the Social Security Web site without proper privacy safeguards. But there are much worse examples. Consider the case of the Texas factory worker who began to receive threatening letters filled with details of her personal life. It turned out that a direct marketing company was using state prison inmates to process computer tapes containing detailed personal information on more than 90 percent of American households. A convicted rapist and burglar had viewed her file.[11] In another example, documented during hearings by the FTC, a national consumer products company was offering games for children on its Web site. To play, children had to enter information about their families' buying preferences. Worse yet, the Federal Bureau of Investigation pursued a number of cases in which pedophiles were circulating the names of children and personal information about them on the Internet. When these more sinister cases involving children came to light, Congress passed the Children's Online Privacy Protection Act (COPPA) in 1998, regulating Web sites directed toward children. The law went into effect on April 24, 2000, and bars sites from collecting personal information from children. It is enforced by the Federal Trade Commission. A number of states were considering similar legislation.

Through the late 1990s, however, public concern about incidents like these was growing, and the burgeoning growth of electronic commerce, was causing the government to take notice and to wonder if even more sweeping action was needed. In 1997 and 1998, two key developments took place. The Clinton administration announced its policy on electronic commerce, including privacy; and the FTC entered the fray.

President Clinton announced his electronic commerce policy on July 3, 1997, in a document titled "A Framework for Global Electronic Commerce." The privacy section of the document reviewed briefly the administration's work over the preceding few years on the question of on-line privacy. It included the conclusions of the Privacy Working Group of the Information Infrastructure Task Force (IITF), which in June 1995 had recommended building on and adapting the OECD's privacy guidelines for the on-line world. It also mentioned the IITF's Information Policy Committee, which just a few months earlier had released its own survey of privacy practices in the United States and had asked for public comment on the best way to implement the privacy guidelines.

Most significantly, the Clinton "Framework" document stated, "The Administration supports private sector efforts now underway to implement meaningful, consumer-friendly, self-regulatory privacy regimes. These include mechanisms for facilitating awareness and the exercise of choice online, evaluating private sector adoption of and adherence to fair information practices, and dispute resolution." The report added that the administration "anticipates that technology will offer solutions to many privacy concerns in the online environment," referring to software and hardware solutions that might provide some degree of anonymity to on-line users. The administration was thereby building on years of privacy practice in the United States and following the OECD guidelines that allowed for private-sector codes of conduct. More ominously for the business community, the report also said that "if privacy concerns are not addressed by industry through self-regulation and technology, the Administration will face increasing pressure to play a more direct role in safeguarding consumer choice regarding privacy online."[12]

Thus, the Clinton administration policy on privacy was consistent with its overall policy on electronic commerce: the private sector should lead, not the government. But there were three caveats. The first was the veiled warning that government action would come if the private sector interpreted the report as meaning that private-sector entities would not have to do anything. Second, the report singled out the issue of children's privacy for special attention worthy of a legislative solution (which resulted in COPPA). Last, the report noted that other countries were involved in similar efforts and that "disparate policies could emerge that might disrupt transborder data flows,"[13] again invoking the OECD warning to states to avoid such disruptions. To avoid the potential disruption of trade, the administration announced that it would enter into discussions with the EU, the Asia-Pacific Economic Cooperation forum (APEC), the Summit of the Americas, and its partners in the North American Free Trade Agreement and the Inter-American Telecommunications Commission of the Organization of American States.

The negotiations with the EU in particular would become critical, since the EU's privacy directive would shortly prohibit the transfer of personal data from EU member nations to countries that, in the EU's view, did not have adequate privacy protection.

The second development of the 1996–99 period was the entrance of the FTC into the on-line privacy debate. In 1997, the FTC, under Chair Robert Pitofsky, issued a staff report titled "Public Workshop on Consumer Privacy on the Global Information Infrastructure."[14] It also held a four-day hearing that focused on identifying both privacy problems and solutions, such as industry self-regulation regimes and technological tools for protecting privacy. During the hearing, Pitofsky compared the situation to the state of the advertising industry in the 1960s. At that time, the FTC had decided to try to control false advertising claims by having the advertising industry police itself. That approach had seemed to work, and Pitofsky wanted to try the same thing in the digital era.

In a hearing before the Subcommittee on Courts and Intellectual Property of the House Judiciary Committee on March 26, 1998, the FTC's associate director for credit practices in the Bureau of Consumer Protection, David Madine, spelled out his agency's interest: "The mission of the FTC is to promote the efficient functioning of the marketplace by protecting consumers from unfair or deceptive acts or practices. . . . Commerce on the Internet falls within the scope of this statutory mandate."[15] Madine went on to describe the FTC's policy on on-line privacy as one of using the commission's powers to educate and encourage the private sector to police itself. He went on to make a number of critical points:

—*Online information collection practices:* During its workshops, he said, the commission felt it developed a consensus with the private sector over four key considerations affecting online privacy: 1) Notice to consumers of how Web sites would use information collected from them; 2) Choice for consumers about how Web sites would use their information; 3) Access for consumers to information collected about them; and 4) Security for consumers from unauthorized use of their personal information.

—*Commitment to self-regulation:* The commission had learned that private industry was committed to self-regulation and in fact was actively developing new policies, procedures, and even new technologies to protect individual privacy. In addition, numerous industry groups and trade associations were developing their own privacy codes of conduct, including the mandatory posting on their Web sites of their privacy practices.

—*Children's privacy:* The commission was particularly concerned about the privacy of children on-line and was taking special actions to deal with it.

Thus, the FTC accepted the administration position on private-sector leadership and the basic privacy principles laid down in earlier U.S. government policies and in the OECD guidelines. But Madine's conclusion contained the same warning to the private sector that the administration had issued: "The Commission supports technological innovation and also encourages industry self-regulation so long as self-regulation proves meaningful and effective. . . . If . . . progress (in self-regulation) is inadequate, appropriate alternatives may need to be explored."[16]

The initial reaction of industry to the administration's acceptance of private-sector leadership on privacy policy was mixed. Some companies felt that the government position simply meant that there would be no new privacy legislation and wanted to leave it at that. To them, self-regulation meant no regulation. Others, looking at public opinion polls and fearful of the potential long-term negative consequences of inaction on the growth of electronic commerce, wanted to develop private codes. Ultimately, the more action-oriented companies won the debate, but progress was slowed and somewhat watered down by having had the debate. By 1997, however, a number of important industry codes began to emerge.

The Direct Marketing Association (DMA) had had a privacy code for years and moved to update it to meet the requirements of the digital age. In July 1999, the DMA published its "Privacy Promises: Member Compliance Guide," which listed detailed procedures its members should follow to protect consumer privacy, and indicated penalties, including expulsion from the association, to be imposed on members for violations of the guidelines. The board of directors of the American Bankers Association (ABA), representing the nation's largest banks, approved "Privacy Principles for U.S. Financial Institutions" in June 1997.[17] The association's eight principles generally reflected the code of fair information practices but did not include any method of enforcement. Although the ABA stated that the advent of electronic banking had made consumers "more attuned than ever to the need to protect personal information," it left the monitoring and enforcement of privacy practices to its member banks.

In December 1997, the Information Technology Industry Council (ITIC), an association of more than 30 of the nation's largest information-technology corporations, published its privacy principles, "The Protection of Personal Data in Electronic Commerce." This document put forth eight principles to protect consumer privacy and urged its members to adopt them and put them into practice. It also urged its high-technology members to "take the lead in making available to consumers the tools and functionalities that enable privacy choices."[18] They were referring to such devices as "anonymizers" that allow people to browse and communicate over the Internet anonymously, or devices that would notify users that a "cookie" or software identifier was being placed on their computer by a Web site and allow the user to block it. But, like the ABA's principles, the ITIC code of conduct did not provide an enforcement mechanism.

In another example, in mid-1997, the Interactive Services Association (ISA), an association of on-line service providers such as America Online and Compuserve, published a broader document, "Principles on Notice and Choice Procedures for Online Information Collection and Distribution by Online Operators." The ISA principles are more detailed and provide guidance for how on-line operators are to inform and provide choices for users about their privacy policies and options. The ISA principles also focus specifically on children's issues and on the issue of "spamming," or sending mass, unsolicited E-mail to on-line users.[19]

Finally, the private sectors in other countries were making progress on this issue.. The International Information Industry Congress (IIIC), a federation of the information technology associations of Australia, Brazil, Canada, France, Germany, Italy, Japan, New Zealand, the United Kingdom, and the United States, led the way. The IIIC had presented white papers to their governments on the subject of the global information infrastructure, including privacy, as early as 1994. Meeting in Berlin in September 1998, the IIIC published a document that dealt with privacy and called on industry to "take the lead to supplement [government legal systems] by establishing effective self-regulation programs that are sector specific, market driven, and responsive to the needs of consumers."[20] The paper went on to enunciate privacy principles similar to those established by the OECD code and called on governments not to hinder the free flow of information.

Although each of these industry codes were important steps forward for the private sector, they were not getting high marks from the U.S. government. By the middle of 1998, with public concerns about on-line privacy still high, the Clinton administration began to increase the pressure on the private sector. In May and again in July 1998, Vice President Gore called for an "Electronic Bill of Rights" and passage of legislation to prevent identity theft and safeguard personal medical and financial data. The vice president acknowledged that the private sector had made progress in self-regulation but said government needed to ensure that enforcement was effective.[21]

In June 1998, Commerce Secretary William Daley had also acknowledged the industry's progress and criticized industry codes "because they lacked enforcement mechanisms." Said Daley, "Public concern over Internet policy is so high that the government will have no choice but to intervene unless industry puts teeth in its self-regulatory plan."[22]

To round out the government's position, Pitofsky told the Subcommittee on Telecommunications, Trade, and Consumer Protection of the House Commerce Committee that the FTC had made "considerable efforts to encourage and facilitate an effective self-regulatory system," but had "not yet seen one emerge."[23] Pitofsky went on to lay out a specific legislative proposal that would set privacy standards and requirements for Web sites, including notice to consumers about privacy practices, choice for them about how their information is used, access to their own information, and steps to provide security for personal information. At the same hearing, Christine Varney, executive director of a new organization of companies and trade associations, the Online Privacy Alliance, agreed: "To increase consumer confidence in cyberspace, companies need to have an independent and trusted third party validate compliance with clearly stated policies." She said that this validation could be provided in a variety of ways, including by private-sector institutions.[24]

The Online Privacy Alliance had been created earlier that year in an effort to instill more confidence in private-sector leadership on privacy issues and to head off government regulation. Consisting initially of about 40 companies and 12 associations involved in a variety of fields, including high technology, banking and financial services, advertising, and travel and entertainment, the alliance not only adopted privacy principles similar to those generally agreed upon but also spelled out, in answer to the critics' concerns, how self-regulation could be monitored and enforced.

The alliance asserted that third parties could provide meaningful self-regulation and that privacy policies could be validated by a "seal" program—an identifiable symbol on the Web site that would assure consumers that the site followed certain privacy practices. Such seals had been in use for some time to indicate support for a number of causes, such as free speech on the Internet. Another organization had even made an attempt at a similar privacy seal, but its program was too limited in scope and not well enough known. The alliance pointed out that a seal program would need to be ubiquitous and accessible by consumers and would have to maintain high integrity. The alliance also stated that seal providers "should establish clearly defined criteria for when and how a company's seal may be revoked."[25]

In addition to the efforts of the alliance, the Better Business Bureau initiated the BBB Online service, an extension of the bureau's traditional activities into cyberspace. A user seeing a "BBB Online" seal on a Web site would know that the site met the bureau's ethical business standards. In 1998, the bureau had indicated its intention to add privacy to its concerns, and in March 1999 it did just that. On March 17, BBB Online began to offer its "trustmark" seal to Web operators that agreed to comply with the organization's privacy code. Members who failed to comply would be sanctioned with public disclosure by the bureau. Dell Computer, one of the world's largest on-line merchants, became the first company to display the seal. Privacy activists applauded the effort but said that it still didn't preclude the need for efforts by the FTC or others to enforce good privacy practices.

Despite these efforts by the private sector, tensions over privacy have continued to grow. A study by OMB Watch, a research group, found that many federal government Web sites were not disclosing their on-line privacy policies, and cited the Department of Health and Human Services, the Department of Housing and Urban Development, and the Federal Emergency Management Agency as examples. Private-sector issues also continued to bubble up. In 1999, both Intel and Microsoft were embarrassed by disclosures that their hardware and software contained undisclosed features that could permit them to track an individual computer or its owner and gather data about them. Although designed for technical-support purposes, the features were perceived by the press and public as a massive invasion of privacy.

In February 2000, Chairman Pitofsky again warned industry that, with public pressure mounting on the privacy issue and in the absence of a single federal privacy law or standard, industry might face a variety of different state rules. In fact, by early 2000, more than one hundred privacy bills had been introduced in the legislatures of forty-one states. By May 2000, laws had been passed in ten of those states: California, Washington, Idaho, Utah, Wyoming, Iowa, Missouri, Kentucky, Maryland, and Hawaii. These laws included restrictions on the dissemination of government data and limitations on the use of financial information.

Not only was the government facing public pressure to act, it was also facing a serious privacy challenge from Europe. In October 1995, the EU had adopted a privacy directive aimed at harmonizing Europe's differing privacy regimes. As we have seen, European countries had used different methods of ensuring privacy, and this had resulted in some disruption in the past. For example, the French Data Protection Commission had sought to block data from being transferred from Fiat France to Fiat's headquarters in Italy. The EU directive went into effect in October 1998.

The problem was that the directive required that data transfers to third countries be permitted only if "adequate protection of the data is afforded." The Europeans did not hide the fact that they hoped to influence U.S. policy. "The European data protection directive is therefore likely to have a significant effect . . . in the U.S.," said Heinz Zourek, a European Commission official.[26] Americans were further alarmed by comments like those of John Borking, an official in the Netherlands data-protection office, who threatened to take action against Dutch firms sending information to the United States: "My police will try to stop data streams when they can."[27] The notion of a corps of "privacy police" raised Americans' worst fears about European authoritarian tendencies; some officials also sensed trade motives in the background.

The main sticking point seemed to be the European view that the tapestry of U.S. laws regarding privacy are inadequate, and that the United States needs a regulatory official or comprehensive legal regime to oversee all privacy policy and to be able to enact sanctions against bad privacy actors. Although the administration's initial defense against the Europeans was to invoke the private sector's actions, it began to move closer to the European position as administration officials became concerned that U.S. firms would not go far enough. Overlooked to some extent by the Europeans was the fact that the United States already has an active enforcement body legally empowered to deal broadly with privacy violations: the FTC.

As argued by Washington attorneys Simon Lazarus and Brett Kappel in the *Legal Times,* Section 5 of the Federal Trade Commission Act. . . . gives the FTC broad authority to prohibit "unfair or deceptive acts or practices in or affecting commerce."[28] These are broad, flexible terms, plainly capable of providing a firm basis to redress privacy-related grievances arising in on-line commerce. As Lazarus and Kappel pointed out, the FTC has already flexed its privacy muscles, finding privacy violations and taking action in cases involving children's privacy, tax preparers, credit bureaus, and health information, among others. Sanctions available to the FTC include cease and desist orders, injunctions, and large financial penalties, as well as specific penalties in privacy laws such as COPPA. With the states having similar laws and powers, Lazarus and Kappel argued, the Europeans should be more than satisfied that the United States has an adequate legal privacy regime.

In the spring of 1999, the Commerce Department's undersecretary for international trade, David Aaron, negotiated a "safe harbor" agreement with the EU. Under this agreement, American companies that agreed to adhere voluntarily to a set of "International Safe Harbor Principles" would be immune from European action other than claims of noncompliance with the principles. Aaron and his interlocutors found it difficult, however, to reach precise agreement on such items as the definition of "reasonable" access to personal data. Even after the United States and the EU reached agreement in early 2000, American companies such as General Electric, Fidelity Investments, Home Depot, and others opposed the agreement, arguing that the Europeans had not recognized existing U.S. financial privacy laws and were creating a new trade barrier. Americans were hopeful that further actions like those of the Better Business Bureau would help resolve the matter. Meanwhile, the Europeans had refrained from taking any action. If they did, of course, they would need to take the same actions with their other trading partners, including those in many Asian and Middle Eastern countries where privacy rights are unknown; such blanket action could have significant consequences for their own trade.

The United States did take a symbolic step in March 1999, when the Clinton administration announced that it was appointing a new "chief counselor on privacy" to coordinate the administration's privacy initiatives. Whether the appointment was window dressing to appease the Europeans or another attempt to pressure the private sector to take more action remains to be seen. Congress also made another move early in 1999, as Senator Conrad Burns, co-chair of the Congressional Internet Caucus, introduced the "Online Privacy Act of 1999" to legislate specific rules.

Both parties began to take notice. A new Democratic Privacy Task Force, headed by Senator Patrick Leahy, was set up, and Republican Senator Richard Shelby announced a new bipartisan Congressional Privacy Caucus. The administration also entered the fray in May 2000 as President Clinton announced new consumer financial privacy legislation to toughen provisions in the previous year's law. At the same time, the administration announced a delay in implementing the existing regulations, citing the complexity of the new law.

That same month, an FTC survey of electronic commerce Web sites said only one in five met agency privacy guidelines, increasing pressure on the FTC to support new legislation as well. In fact, the FTC released a report calling for legislation, although Chairman Pitofsky said it would only provide "backup" for self-regulation. Clearly, both the White House and Congress expected privacy to be an issue in the 2000 elections.

Where should online privacy policy go from here? Clearly, the main aim of public policy ought to be protecting the privacy of confidential personal information. But building consumer confidence in electronic commerce should be another, parallel goal. Achieving these goals does not require building a new federal privacy bureaucracy, as some European countries have done. Those who justify this by asserting that U.S. privacy protections "range from anemic to non-existent"[29] are ill-informed and just plain wrong. Although the United States does need to modernize and strengthen its existing system and attune it to the privacy needs of a wired nation, it does not need to create coercive new government agencies. It does need to focus on sensitive areas and on the capabilities of the new technologies. A few suggestions for useful action might include the following:

- Clarify a single set of fair information practices that can be broadly accepted and put into practice for both government and the private sector. Canada has done this, for example, through the Standards Council of Canada, adopting a code as a national standard. The work of the Online Privacy Alliance is a step in the right direction, but it needs to be taken further.
- Strengthen and clarify the role of the FTC, under its existing statutes, to be the enforcer of privacy matters in the United States. The

FTC will deal with many other electronic commerce issues and it is the natural home for privacy issues. Its staff already has expertise in consumer issues and enforcement of statutes such as COPPA and it has shown that it can deal with privacy in a constructive way. Let the FTC role also be the model for the states, as they attune their consumer protection agencies to handle on-line privacy issues.

- Pass legislation to modernize privacy laws in limited areas of extreme public interest and importance. The key ones today are health care and financial privacy, where federal laws should preempt state statutes. With American mobility and travel the rule, and where families may live in one state, have children at college in others, and seek medical treatment in yet others, individual state laws are obsolete and will retard progress toward national medical-data networks that will save lives. Although health care privacy legislation failed in Congress in 1999, caught in a lobbying battle between industry and privacy advocates, the administration's proposed regulations, as described earlier, could help resolve the issue, although their final acceptance and ultimate effectiveness are far from certain. In particular, legislation must deal with the difficult issue of consumer acceptance of data collection—the "opt-in, opt-out" issue. Privacy advocates want affirmative approval—that is, consumers must "opt in"—before data collection is permitted. Most companies favor requiring consumers to "opt out," fearing most will not take any action to permit collection. The combination of new technology and perhaps financial incentives for consumers should help resolve this issue.

- Support broad private-sector efforts at self-regulation for on-line privacy such as the BBB Online "trustmark" program and the leadership of the Online Privacy Alliance. Programs using broadly recognized seals that include means for redress will help keep most businesses in compliance, particularly if they enforce their code of fair information practices and publicize the consequences to businesses that fail to comply.

- Support government and private research and development for new technologies to protect privacy, such as the Platform for Privacy Preferences (P3P) developed by the World Wide Web Consortium, which allows users to build their individual privacy preferences into their Web browsers. Once set, the system allows users to avoid Web sites with conflicting privacy practices or to negotiate with them. Another system, the Open Profiling Standard, permits an individual to control the release of data in a secure manner. Government can encourage more work like this by investing in research and development through existing government research programs in networking and high-performance computing and by requiring government agencies to use these technologies.

- Continue to work with foreign governments and with international organizations such as the OECD and the United Nations to avoid the potential disruption of trade from different privacy practices. Negotiate firmly with the Europeans and others who attempt the extraterritorial application of their own privacy laws. Adequate notice of privacy policies on Web sites and the use of technologies such as P3P should give everyone, regardless of their nationality, the choice of which sites they choose to do business with. Moreover, international organizations have a role to play in encouraging those governments that have not yet addressed the issue at all to do so.

The issue of privacy in the digital age cannot be addressed in a vacuum. Information cannot be private if it is not secure—that is, if techniques such as cryptography and biometrics cannot be used to protect it. The issue of security is a complex one and will be discussed in Chapter 7. Even more important, privacy can only exist in the broader context of a democratic society in which the issues of free speech and universal access are equally important.

FREE SPEECH

Everyone has the right to freedom of opinion and expression; this right includes freedom to hold opinions without interference and to seek, receive and impart information and ideas through any media and regardless of frontiers.
—Universal Declaration of Human Rights, Article 19

Eleanor Roosevelt never experienced the Internet, but as the person most responsible for the United Nations Universal Declaration of Human Rights, she would have felt right at home reading the pages of *Wired* magazine. Article 19 clearly foreshadowed the Internet's value as a multimedia carrier of speech across all national boundaries. Contrast the declaration's intentions with the 1998 words of Qing Guang, head of the Shanghai, China, police department's Computer Security Supervision office, whose job is to ferret out "harmful information" on the Internet: "No one is allowed to release harmful information on the Internet. You cannot send out harmful information which attacks our nation's territorial integrity, attacks our nation's independence, or attacks our socialist system."[30] China is not alone in attempting to limit the right to send and receive information.

Like privacy, free speech in cyberspace today is a major concern of governments, democratic as well as authoritarian. Unlike privacy, free speech is a less ambiguous and more directly recognized right in many countries around the world. It appears not only in the U.S. Bill of Rights but in the French Declaration of the Rights of Man, in the Council of Europe's Declaration on the Freedom of Expression and Information, in the American Declaration of the Rights and Duties of Man (adopted by the Organization of American States), and in the African Charter on Human and People's Rights (adopted by the fifty countries of the Organization for African Unity). Yet protecting the right of free speech while protecting society from truly harmful speech has proven to be one of society's most vexing problems. The advent of the digital age makes it even more problematic.

For example, whereas political speech is the key concern of authoritarian governments such as China's, other governments have other concerns. In many countries, the flood of pornography on the Net is a major issue. Unfortunately, the demand for pornography and the ease with which it can be obtained on the Internet make it one of the medium's largest and most profitable businesses. In the United States, former FCC chair Reed Hundt warned of the Internet becoming a "vast red-light district." Online pornographers have been prosecuted in a number of countries in North America and in Europe, and some countries have enacted new laws to deal with the issue. Even worse, the issue of pornography tends to be interlinked with the issue of pedophilia, since pedophiles exchange albums of child pornography over the Net. In both Europe and the United States, highly publicized cases have come to light of children being stalked on the Internet and even lured to meetings where they have been attacked. Although the numbers of these cases have been quite small, the cases themselves have horrified people and have led to strong public pressure for legislation.

Racism and hate speech are also serious issues in many countries. The German, French, and Canadian governments have prosecuted both the creators of racist Web sites and the Internet service providers (ISPs) who carried their sites, raising new questions about liability. Some Web sites published by hate groups offer bomb-making instructions and other weapons information. In the United States, militia and white supremacist groups use the Internet to recruit new members.

In some countries, especially Islamic ones, the treatment of religious and ethnic information is particularly sensitive. Some filter and block information. Some, such as Singapore, require registration and licensing of sensitive Web sites, such as those that deal with religious or ethnic matters. In others, such as France and Canada, the language used is paramount, and questions have been raised as to how to ensure that Internet speech conforms to national laws governing the use of language. Even Denmark, one of the world's most democratic countries, under the heading of "Citizen's Rights in the Information Society," says "Information Technology Must Speak Danish."[31] Furthermore, Internet slander and libel cases have already made their way to the courts.

National approaches to Net content control vary widely. In the United States, Congress has attempted to pass broad laws criminalizing the sending of "obscene" material over the Internet. To date, the Supreme Court has foiled these attempts, ruling them unconstitutional. In France, courts have ruled that ISPs have some liability for content distributed over their networks. A key case involved a top French model, Estelle Lefebure, who sued an ISP for allowing a customer to publish nude photographs of her. The judge ruled that ISPs have "the capacity to take measures to end any nuisances that the site may be causing," and was consistent with other French judicial rulings establishing liability for ISPs.[32]

In Canada, the Human Rights Commission has cited Section 13 of the Canadian Human Rights Act, which prohibits anyone from using telephone lines to spread hate messages, to try to close down a neo-Nazi Web site. The site was created by a Canadian resident but run out of San Diego, California, in an attempt to evade Canada's strict hate laws. "We don't think the Internet is a law-free zone," says Bill Pentney, general counsel of the Human Rights Commission. "We are trying to control—not the Internet—but [the author of the site] by applying Canadian laws to him."[33]

China's approach is one of the broadest: turn the Chinese national information infrastructure into a giant closed intranet. With more than 1.2 million Internet users by the end of 1998, and with that number doubling every year, the Chinese government well understands the importance of electronic commerce to its future economy. Even as the government invests in infrastructure, it is shielding its citizens from unfiltered outside content. "Such a network could tap the Web's riches but remain walled off from features deemed subversive—like pornographic sites, postings from dissidents or anything about Taiwan or Tibet."[34]

Despite all these various attempts by nations to control the cyberspace content that their citizens can see and use, the amount and variety of content of all kinds continues to explode. Americans may still access the worst kinds of pornography and Ku Klux Klan literature. The French can undoubtedly see racy photos of their favorite celebrities and read the captions in English. Chinese dissidents are finding ways to sneak messages in and out of China and even to use the Net to organize within China itself. The complexity of trying to control digital content can be seen by contrasting the existing regime for handling free speech with the nature of the Net itself.

Although the United States and other countries provide for a fundamental right to free speech, it and all other countries limit that right in a number of specific ways. For instance, various types of speech face different restrictions. Speech deemed to be obscene, pornographic, or scatological faces one set of legal restrictions. Speech that endangers public safety or national security or defense faces others. Speech that infringes on words already copyrighted faces still other prohibitions, as does speech that is libelous or slanderous. Speech that is deemed to harm public health in some way is restricted, too, as in the case of alcohol or tobacco advertising.

The subject of free speech is particularly complex because speech is also regulated according to the type of media in which it is disseminated. Private speech between adults is afforded the maximum protection, whereas speech that is broadcast over the airwaves and accessible by any radio or television set generally faces the most restrictions. Other media, including telephone conversations; mail; printed media such as books, newspapers, and magazines; cable television; public performances such as plays and concerts; sound recordings; movies; videotapes; and public and private bulletin boards all face varying degrees of regulation. Tobacco advertising, for example, is permitted in print with some restrictions but is not allowed on broadcast television.

In addition, varying degrees of liability for violations of the law have traditionally been assigned to authors, publishers, and distributors. Television broadcasters or newsstand owners are distributors of content who have control over such distribution and therefore are held accountable for broadcasting obscene words or selling pornography to minors. A telephone company is also a distributor of content, but because it cannot control what is said during a telephone conversation, it is legally exempt from such liability.

Moreover, none of this complex regulation is static or permanent. Words commonly found in books and even spoken on television today could not legally appear in print one hundred years ago. National security needs changed with the Cold War, giving rise to legal skirmishes such as the one over the publication of the Pentagon Papers during the war in Vietnam. As new technologies have been developed, such as cable television, new legislation and case law have been developed to resolve questions of liability and responsibility. Entirely new forms of content, such as software, have been invented, triggering legal battles over the right to freely copy programs. Given this complexity, it is not surprising that the struggle over what speech is free and what is not is never-ending. In the United States alone, a constant stream of free speech cases flows up to the Supreme Court.

When these knotty issues are viewed in the context of the Net, the situation becomes even more convoluted. First, as we have seen, the Internet is global and borderless by nature, and so national free speech laws provide only limited help. Whereas everyone knew (or could find out) where the Main Street Bookstore or a particular New York City broadcaster was located, it may be impossible to know where every particular Web site or E-mail originates. Second, the Internet was purposely designed to permit the entry of uncontrolled content and to be totally decentralized. Thus, there is no controlling "publisher" or "broadcaster" to be held responsible for material in cyberspace, no single controller or gatekeeper to sue, prosecute, or coerce. A bookstore owner, for example, can be compelled not to sell obscene material to minors. On the Net, however, there may or may not always be the equivalent of a bookstore owner or clerk. Moreover, unlike the traditional content industries of broadcasting, publishing, or filmmaking, the cost of Internet publishing and distribution are miniscule, allowing virtually anyone to publish or broadcast information. It costs essentially no more to send a message to one thousand people than to ten. Thus, communications can easily be one-to-one, like mail or a simple telephone call, or they may be one-to-many, like a radio or television broadcast. In the case of chat rooms, they can even be many-to-many.

In fact, cyberspace, in all its manifestations, can be all or any of the twentieth-century media. E-mail can be viewed as the equivalent of a private conversation or written correspondence between two people, or it can be a publishing service. The Internet even has an automated one-to-many E-mail service, known as a listserv, which permits anyone to publish an electronic newsletter or magazine and send it to an unlimited number of people. Internet news groups and chat rooms are amorphous electronic discussion groups in which any number of people can participate as writers and producers of written material, audio, video, or graphics, and any other number of people can participate as readers and viewers. Tens of thousands of such groups exist as global virtual communities, discussing everything from sports events, to health topics, to religion, to sensitive political or sexual topics. They can be considered public meetings, speeches, public performances, telephone conference calls, or any combination thereof.

In addition to E-mail and newsgroups, the World Wide Web itself is a form of Internet media. Encompassing text, graphics, video, and audio, the Web can transform itself into virtually any of the traditional media. People use it to receive television and radio broadcasts; they use it to send E-mail; and they use it to publish information about themselves or their activities. Finally, the Internet's file transfer protocol, which permits the transfer of large data files, can resemble a book publishing operation.

The Internet has erased the distinctions between author, publisher, and distributor. Any individual using an ISP such as America Online, Prodigy, or the Microsoft Network can produce and send virtually anything to anyone connected to the Net. It is almost impossible for an ISP to police every site and every electronic conversation. Certainly, in limited cases a publisher and a distributor can be held responsible for what is transmitted over the Net. For example, AT&T creates its own Web site and makes it available over its own network. But this is the exception; services and technologies that make it possible to send anonymous communications make it even more difficult to hold ISPs responsible for the content sent over their networks.

Thus, the policy maker who seeks to curb speech on the Internet immediately faces a number of critical obstacles: Which media rules apply to a given concern, such as pornography or hate speech? Who is liable or can be held responsible for the alleged offense? What political entity has jurisdiction in cases that cross borders, either subnational or international? Just how difficult this issue can be is illustrated by Congress's attempt to deal with the single but important issue of pornography, especially its availability to children.

By 1996, as Congress was about to pass the landmark Telecommunications Act deregulating telecommunications services, public concern about children's access to pornography was reaching new highs. Senator Dianne Feinstein of California told a group of semiconductor industry officials visiting Washington that her office was receiving more mail on that subject than any other. Pornography sites were rampant on the Internet, and many were made cunningly available to children. For example, entering the word "girls" on many search engines could lead to stomach-turning material.

In addition, several prominent cases of child molestation and rape were connected with the Internet. Although a number of such highly publicized cases had caught the public's imagination, fears of widespread child abuse via the Net were actually overblown. As business writer Don Tapscott reported in his book *Growing Up Digital: The Rise of the Net Generation,* out of 3 million cases of child abuse and more than 127,000 cases of child abandonment, the National Center for Missing and Exploited Children recorded only 23 cases of missing children involving the Internet, with only 10 involving the transfer of pornography. According to the center, "To tell children to stop using these services would be like telling them to forgo attending colleges because students are sometimes victimized on campus."[35]

Nevertheless, led by Senator James Exon of Nebraska with bipartisan support, Congress added an amendment to the Telecommunications Act called the Communications Decency Act (CDA), which criminalized the transmission of "obscene or indecent messages" to any recipient under eighteen years of age. The amendment tried to define this as a message "in terms patently offensive as measured by contemporary community standards, sexual or excretory activities or organs." The CDA was immediately challenged by the American Civil Liberties Union (ACLU) and others, including the Center for Democracy and Technology, an organization created to deal with free speech and privacy issues on the Net. Surprisingly, the Clinton administration decided to defend the CDA, undoubtedly because of its strong political support. The resulting court case became known as *Reno v. ACLU.* After an appeals court enjoined the government from enforcing the new law, the case went to the Supreme Court and was decided on June 27, 1997. Justice John Paul Stevens wrote the decision that found the CDA unconstitutional and an abridgment of the right to free speech. Since the Court's decision was an early legal landmark for the Internet, it is worth quoting Justice Stevens's opinion at some length:

Anyone with access to the Internet may take advantage of a wide variety of communication and information retrieval methods. These methods are constantly evolving and difficult to categorize precisely. . . . Taken together, these tools constitute a unique medium—known to its users as "cyberspace"—located in no particular geographical location but available to anyone, anywhere in the world. . . . It is no "exaggeration to conclude that the content on the Internet is as diverse as human thought." The Web is thus comparable from the readers' viewpoint, to both a vast library including millions of readily available and indexed publications and a sprawling mall offering goods and services. "No single organization controls any membership in the Web, nor is there any centralized point from which individual Websites or services can be blocked from the Web." Though [sexually explicit] material is widely available, users seldom encounter such content accidentally. . . . Systems have been developed to help parents control the material that may be available. . . . Technology exists by which an operator of a Web site may condition access on the verification of requested information such as a credit card number or an adult password. . . . [T]he vast democratic fora of the Internet have [not] been subject to the type of government supervision and regulation that has attended the broadcast industry. Moreover, the Internet is not as "invasive" as radio or television. . . . Communications over the Internet do not "invade" an individual's home or appear on one's computer screen unbidden.

In order to deny minors access to potentially harmful speech, the CDA effectively suppresses a large amount of speech that adults have a constitutional right to receive and to address to one another. . . . [T]he growth of the Internet has been and continues to be phenomenal. As a matter of constitutional tradition, in the absence of evidence to the contrary, we presume that governmental regulation of the content of speech is more likely to interfere with the free exchange of ideas than to encourage it. The interest in encouraging freedom of expression in a democratic society outweighs any theoretical but unproven benefit of censorship.[36]

Although the *Reno* decision reaffirmed the right to free speech on the Internet, it did not hold such speech to be totally free. It left the door slightly open to future attempts to limit Internet speech. The decision consistently attacked the vagueness of the CDA's language, implying that more limited prohibitions might be permitted. Thus, it was not surprising that Congress passed new legislation in 1998, known as CDA II, that would prohibit material "harmful to minors." Other bills sought other, narrower ways to achieve the same goal. Senator John McCain of Arizona sponsored a bill permitting schools and libraries to use software filters to block student access to certain materials, and the House of Representatives unanimously passed a bill providing substantially tougher criminal penalties for pedophiles using the Internet to find victims—a bill aimed at conduct and not at speech.

In contrast to Congress, the administration seemed to have found its bearings on the issue. When it released its "Framework for Global Electronic Commerce" on July 1, 1997, only days after the Supreme Court's *Reno* decision, it made no mention of the need for legislation to restrict content. Rather, it said,

In contrast to traditional broadcast media, the Internet promises users greater opportunity to shield themselves and their children from content they deem offensive or inappropriate. New technology, for example, may enable parents to block their children's access to sensitive information or confine their children to pre-approved websites.

To the extent, then, that effective filtering technology becomes available, content regulations traditionally imposed on radio and television would not need to be applied to the Internet. In fact, unnecessary regulation could cripple the growth and diversity of the Internet.

The Administration therefore supports industry self-regulation, adoption of competing rating systems, and development of easy-to-use technical solutions . . . to assist in screening information online.[37]

Thus, administration policy agreed with the Supreme Court conclusion, despite the fact that the administration had defended the CDA before the Supreme Court. In effect, the administration was taking the same position on free speech as it had on privacy: if the private sector would take the lead and develop good filtering technologies, education programs, and enforcement measures, no regulation would be needed, the administration said, thereby putting new pressure on the high-tech community.

It should also be noted that the administration document was much more concerned with what it saw as growing Internet content censorship in other countries. Among the concerns it expressed were those for foreign quotas to protect "domestic" content; foreign restrictions on cultural, social, or political content; and foreign restrictions on advertising. All these restrictions could "impede electronic commerce in the global environment."[38] The administration was right to be concerned.

While U.S. legislators were worrying about children and the Net, so were European politicians. In particular, the horrendous murders of a number of children in Belgium, although not directly linked to the Internet, had led to massive street demonstrations and demands that the national police focus on child safety. The same concerns were expressed in the United Kingdom, France, Germany, and the Netherlands. In addition, the American dominance of the Net and its lead in electronic commerce was making some European government officials nervous. Although none would admit it outright, some felt that drawn-out discussions over content regulations in the U.S. Congress might slow things down on one side of the Atlantic and thereby give Europe a chance to catch up. As each country began to move toward its own solutions, the European Commission in Brussels, which had been actively promoting the growth of electronic commerce, became alarmed at the possibility of widely different approaches, not only within Europe but globally. It called for a European ministerial conference to develop a pan-European policy.

With a number of non-European nations as guests and speakers, including the U.S. secretary of commerce, William Daley, the ministerial meeting was held in Bonn, Germany, on July 6–8, 1997. As it turned out, its findings were very similar to those expressed by the U.S. government in its "Framework" document. Although the resulting ministerial declaration dealt with a wide variety of electronic commerce issues, it focused heavily on content. It recognized the economic importance of content on the Internet: "Ministers recognize that content is an important sector in its own right as well as a key driver of electronic commerce. They consider therefore that the provision of high-quality European content and services represents a high economic and industrial priority."[39]

Having tipped their hats to the importance of European content, the ministers went on to state that the overall expansion of the global information infrastructure must be led by the private sector. They stressed, therefore, the role that "the private sector can play in promoting and respecting ethical standards, through properly functioning systems of self-regulation. . . . Ministers encourage industry to implement open, platform independent content ratings systems, and to propose rating services which meet the needs of different users."[40]

The ministers went further, also addressing the question of Internet service provider liability: "[I]ntermediaries like network operators and access providers should, in general, not be responsible for content. . . . In any case, third-party content hosting services should not be expected to exercise prior control on content which they have no reason to believe is illegal."[41]

Given the emotional atmosphere in many European countries concerning this subject and the potential for mischief by protectionists, the Bonn ministerial declaration was a moderating document that helped slow the rush to new Internet content restrictions. The following year, in May 1998, the Council of the EU followed up by calling for national self-regulatory frameworks to protect children using the Internet. The council said that on-line service providers should label their sites, provide warnings about potentially harmful content, and provide filtering systems for parents to use. The council also called for operators to work with public authorities to provide for sanctions for violators. A few months later, in July 1998, the European Parliament voted to approve a four-year program providing $32 million to "promote safe use of the Internet." The money would be used to help develop filtering software, other technical solutions, and education programs for parents and teachers. During the debate, proposals to have the European Commission itself develop content guidelines were rejected on the grounds that the private sector should lead these efforts.

In Asia, efforts by the United States to develop similar policy statements on content were resisted, since a number of key Asian countries, including Singapore, Malaysia, and China, had already adopted laws regulating content. The United States did conclude joint bilateral statements on electronic commerce with a number of Asian and other countries; these statements included content policy, as in the one signed with the Japanese government:

Content should be transmitted freely across national borders in response to a user's request. . . . Governments should not impose stronger restrictions on content on the Internet than exist in the real world. In instances where users do not wish to receive certain types of content, such as that which is unsuitable for children, filtering/blocking systems or other tools should be made available. On-line service providers should not be asked to monitor all the content being transmitted over their network, but should be expected to work with domestic law enforcement as well as with their international counterparts to stem the transmission of illegal content.[42]

This joint U.S.-Japan position on harmful content was based on the policy that had been developed by Japan's Ministry of International Trade and Industry (MITI) just one year earlier. In its white paper "Towards the Age of the Digital Economy," MITI had said, "Rather than restricting contents [sic], such as obscenity and violent material, which violate the public order and morals, to a greater degree than the restrictions put upon the regular media, measures will be enforced based on independent efforts by providers of information technology, as well as the technology of these providers."[43]

With governments in the major industrial countries in general agreement on the content issue, the private sector, as with the privacy issue, faced a significant challenge: to develop methods to permit individuals to regulate their own use of content. Fortunately, it had gotten off to a good start. Recognizing a potential market for filtering software, a number of software companies were already marketing filtering programs like Net Nanny, Surf Watch, and Cyber Patrol. But although these programs, if properly installed and maintained, permitted parents to control their children's Internet surfing habits, they were not foolproof, especially where ingenious and motivated youngsters were concerned.

To help make them more effective, the World Wide Web Consortium, a technical organization comprising universities and high-technology companies and based at the Massachusetts Institute of Technology (MIT), developed the Platform for Internet Content Selection (PICS), an industry-supported, open technical standard that enables both the development and use of filtering software. Using it, a number of organizations began rating and labeling sites, a practice that can help protect children but that has also led critics to charge censorship. Libraries, for example, have debated the value of filtering systems to keep pornography away from children versus their traditional support for free speech. Nevertheless, the next few years should see simplified systems that will allow parents to more easily connect their home PC browsers to a number of ratings sites offered by civic, educational, and religious groups; these parents will adjust their browsers to allow only sites with the ratings they approve. Already the Recreational Software Advisory Council provides a broad content-rating service. Thus parents, not government, will choose what their children can view.

Perhaps the leader among the business associations in the self-regulation of content had been the Interactive Services Association. As early as 1994, this association, together with the National Center for Missing and Exploited Children, published "Child Safety on the Information Highway." This educational tool for parents and teachers was an early effort that laid out guidelines for parents and, most important, created a short checklist for children called "My Rules for Online Safety." These six common sense rules suggested that children not give out personal information without their parents' approval, let their parents know if they come across information that makes them uncomfortable, not agree to get together with anyone they meet on-line without their parents' agreement, and so forth.[44] These rules were distributed widely across the country and were adopted by many boys' and girls' clubs, schools, and community organizations. They were first of many other such efforts, including a White House summit on the subject whose purpose was to enlist the high-tech industry to support new technological and educational solutions to the issue.

Overseas, both private and public efforts continued. In the United Kingdom, the media and high-tech companies created the Safety-Net Foundation, a private group, to establish a rating system and to deal with complaints about illegal material on the Internet. The private-sector International Communications Roundtable (ICRT), consisting of more than thirty influential European media and high-tech companies, developed its own white paper on the subject. The ICRT paper included its own principles distinguishing between "harmful" material, which it said could be dealt with by the private sector with filtering technologies and other means, and "illegal" content, such as child pornography. Trying to deal with the issue of liability for on-line service operators, the ICRT paper suggested the principle of "notice and take down," under which operators who received sufficient notice that material was illegal would have a reasonable time to remove it or block access to it. The ICRT companies said they would cooperate with governments to develop the technology to enable this.[45]

Another major international forum for the content issue was the OECD, which began a study of content issues in 1997. This study was to be an overview of national issues and initiatives. Meanwhile, a group of more than forty human rights and free speech groups from fourteen countries around the world began the Global Internet Liberty Campaign in 1998. Staffed and funded by the Center for Democracy and Technology in Washington, D.C., and the Open Society Institute, the organization's brochure, "Regardless of Frontiers," argued vociferously that free speech on the Internet is a strong promoter of democratic values. It should not be regulated directly or indirectly by governments, nor hindered by filtering or rating systems, said the document: "No matter what the means, government restriction on speech or access to speech of others violates basic freedom of expression protections. Filtering is inappropriate in public educational institutions and libraries."[46] This debate is being carried on now in schools, libraries, community centers, and other public organizations around the world, especially in the United States, where schools and libraries are run locally. As access to the Internet, which we discuss in the next section, becomes more ubiquitous, the debate will heat up.

Given the complexity of the content issue and its international character, where can the public policy compass be set to guide future policy? Here are a few policy suggestions:

- Activities that are illegal in the physical world should also be regarded as illegal in cyberspace and dealt with accordingly by the authorities. Creating child pornography, stealing intellectual property, committing slander or libel, or publishing classified material are crimes and should be prosecuted no matter where they appear. In practice, of course, this will be difficult, since individual cases will be nuanced and since different countries have different laws. Nevertheless, over time case law and international negotiations will be able to deal with illegal content.
- Internet content that is harmful but not illegal, such as material that is obscene, violent, hateful, or racist, should be dealt with by the private sector, using new filtering, rating, and labeling systems controlled by parents and other individuals and not by governments. Although this also seems difficult by today's standards, advances in technology and standardization, as well as rapidly growing computer literacy, will make it more effective in the future. Perhaps more important, the men and women who lead our content industry, especially filmmakers, broadcasters, and recording artists, need to reexamine their own values and consciences and decide if they really

want to continue to deluge our children in a flood of violence and sex. Without fundamental change in this broader area, the most sophisticated technology filters simply will not function.

- Governments should move very cautiously, if at all, before passing new laws and regulations aimed specifically at content on the Net. Since the Internet is both global and technically robust, broad efforts to define liability, for example, or to make the rules for Internet conduct more stringent than those for the physical world will ultimately be defeated by technology. Moreover, governments that wish to reap the economic benefits of cyberspace may well lose them if they hobble the new media with censorship. Authoritarian governments that insist on heavy-handed censorship of the Net will simply weaken themselves in the long run by stunting their own economic growth.

- Governments should provide incentives to the private sector to develop new technologies and to adopt their own codes of conduct and systems of self-enforcement. This can be done, as with the privacy issue, by providing legal safe harbors to companies that act responsibly and also by providing government research funding to aid development of content filtering, rating, and labeling systems to protect children.

- Governments that are concerned about cultural or linguistic content on the Internet should address the issue not with censorship but by encouraging their own cultural institutions to enter cyberspace. Making more national music, art, literature, folklore, and other materials available in national languages will add greatly to the cultural and educational value of the Net. A nation's prestige will be enhanced by placing its great museums and libraries on-line for the world to see, rather than by limiting its own citizens' abilities to experience other languages and cultures.

- Governments must learn that attempting to shield their citizens from the free flow of global information will be self-defeating. Technology is too ubiquitous and too sophisticated to be subverted by mere national laws. Does the Chinese government really believe it can prevent its citizens—some of the world's most technologically accomplished and literate people—from viewing Internet material? Perhaps they could, if the government banned computers and telephone lines totally, or if it terrorized people. But China's clear economic interest is in exactly the opposite direction—in encouraging Internet use. In today's world, technology trumps censorship.

- Governments must negotiate with each other more intensively to deal with questions of jurisdiction and the resolution of issues involving differing or conflicting content laws. Agreeing on a narrower content-sector issue, such as the content of advertising materials, may help provide some principles about issues such as mutual recognition, which could then be applied more broadly. In addition to bilateral and multilateral discussions on content, international organizations such as the OECD can also play an important role. In Asia, where more progress needs to be made on the issue of content regulation, the Japanese government could help by taking the lead at the APEC discussions on the Asia-Pacific Information Infrastructure, where Japan might have more credibility than the United States.

In the long run, efforts by governments to control virtual content are bound to fail. There is a strong bond between free expression and the development of the Net itself. Content providers and the Web masters will always find new technological means to defeat regulation. Moreover, open and free Net content will be one of the great spurs to democracy in the twenty-first century. As the Global Internet Liberty Campaign concluded,

The free flow of information and ideas is the very essence of the Internet. One state's restriction's on Internet content infringe upon the rights of all Internet users around the world to benefit from a free exchange of social, political, economic, cultural, scientific and personal information.

Technology will surely outpace states' efforts to restrict the free flow of information on the Internet. New methods of accessing the Internet, for example by satellite, will make territorial boundaries even less relevant to the Internet than they are today. Attempts to suppress information and communication on the Internet, therefore, not only violate international human rights laws, in the end they are likely to be futile.[47]

UNIVERSAL ACCESS

Make available, so far as possible, to all the people of the United States a rapid, efficient, Nation-wide, and world-wide wire and radio communication service with adequate facilities at reasonable prices.

—Communications Act of 1934, P.L. 416, Title 1, Sec. 1

There is a growing digital divide between those who have access to the digital economy . . . and those who don't, and that divide exists along the lines of education, income, region and race.

—President Bill Clinton[48]

Although the Communications Act of 1934, the nation's seminal telephony and broadcast law, never used the phrase "universal service," that phrase indeed became the goal for the nation's federal and state telephone regulators for the rest of the twentieth century: a telephone in every household. The doctrine was accepted not only by government but also by the private sector, in the form of the Bell Telephone System, the national private telephone monopoly that existed until 1982. That company's founding chairperson, Theodore Vail, invented and used the phrase "One System, One Policy, Universal Service" as early as 1910, not out of altruism but because market expansion, even with government regulation, was his objective.

Around the world, the industrial countries have also set objectives for universal telephone service for their national telephone carriers. Developing countries have tended to be more modest, setting a goal of universal *access*, meaning a telephone not necessarily in the home but somewhere relatively nearby and accessible. The relevant measurement here was not the percentage of households with a telephone but rather the number of telephone lines per one hundred people, a statistic known as "teledensity." This goal became United Nations policy in 1984 when the UN's so-called Maitland Report stated that "by the early part of the next century virtually the whole of mankind should be brought within easy reach of the telephone."[49] Thus, a global consensus was born that telephone service was important for a variety of reasons, including its roles in economic development and as an enabler of democracy, and for its importance in advancing public safety.

Not surprisingly, as the digital age exploded in the early 1990s, many people began to assert the need for a similar consensus about universal service or access for the new information infrastructure. In the United States, politicians in both political parties, as well as educators, corporate officials, and others, worried publicly about the development of a society composed of information haves and have-nots, one segment well educated, prosperous, and connected to the global network, and the other ignorant, poor, and disconnected. Since the telephone line was the normal link to the Net and a prerequisite for admission to the information age, the idea of universal service for telephony became a touchstone for the discussion about equipping everyone—and every nation—for the new era. Thus it is best to begin the search for consensus with a look at how well the objectives of universal service for the telephone have been achieved.

On the surface, the objective of universal telephone access in the United States and the industrial countries appears to have worked well.

By 1996, 93.9 percent of U.S. households had a telephone. The numbers were even better for other industrial nations—Canada, 98.7 percent; France, 97 percent; Japan, 96.1 percent; and Australia, 96.8 percent.[50] Underneath these high percentages in some countries, however, lay three difficult issues that would come to have great significance for policy makers dealing with the new information society. For if universal service or access for simple voice telephone service was important for so many reasons, wouldn't the same objectives apply to the new information infrastructure? If so, was the traditional view of these objectives translatable into cyberspace?

The first issue raised by universal service for telephony is that the numbers mask serious disparities within individual countries. To take the United States as the major example, the U.S. penetration level has stagnated at levels below those of developed countries. According to the International Telecommunications Union (ITU), in March 1997, more than six million U.S. households had no telephone service.[51] A 1999 study by the U.S. Department of Commerce found that fewer than 75 percent of poor rural households and just over 75 percent of poor urban households had telephones. Among African Americans, only 86 percent of households had telephones.[52] The United States was not alone in this regard, and similar discrepancies exist in other industrialized countries between rich and poor, city dwellers and rural people, as well as along other fault lines. It is clear that as countries become more dependent on their national information infrastructures for all kinds of health, education, and government services, these kinds of disparities cannot be tolerated.

The second issue is the enormous disparity between nations. The industrialized countries may fret over whether 95 or 97 percent of their citizens have telephones, but the poorest nations barely make the charts. In 1996, 43 nations had teledensities of less than 1 phone line per 100 people. The lowest-ranking, Cambodia, had a teledensity of .07, or 1 line for 1,429 people. Although developing countries such as China and India were making progress, others such as Bangladesh, Laos, Myanmar, and sadly, most African countries, were trapped below a teledensity of 1. In December 1997, the UN General Assembly committed the UN to help meet the global objective of universal access to basic telecommunications: "We are profoundly concerned at the deepening mal-distribution of access, resources and opportunities in the information and communications field. The information and technology gap and related inequities between industrialized and developing nations are widening: a new type of poverty—information poverty—looms. Most developing countries . . . are not sharing in the communication revolution."[53] Once again, if these types of dis-parities are carried over into the digital age, developing countries can and will fall even further behind, not only in economic development but most likely in the development of democracy itself.

The third issue involves government regulation and free markets, and the somewhat puzzling disparity between telephony, an industry that has been heavily regulated or actually government-owned in many countries during most of its existence, and other, unregulated high-technology in-dustries. In the United States, after almost a century of regulation, as we have seen, 93.9 percent of homes had a telephone. By contrast, in that same year, 95.2 percent of homes had a television receiver. The television receiver industry had never been regulated and had existed for only roughly half the time of the telephone industry, yet it had achieved greater pene-tration. In some other countries, the comparisons are even more striking. In 1996 in Mexico, 33.9 percent of households had a telephone, yet 86.5 percent had a television. In Ukraine, the numbers that year were similar: telephone, 39.9 percent; television, 98.4 percent. In Malaysia: telephone, 50 percent; television, 75.8 percent.[54]

Policy makers understood that there could be many explanations for these results, ranging from relative prices, to waiting times for tele-phones, to the ordinary person's obsession with television. Nevertheless, officials seeking to provide universal access to cyberspace in the digital age couldn't ignore the glaring differences in success between an industry had been heavily regulated and another governed only by market forces. Officials also could not ignore the simple fact that prices had remained relatively stable over time on the regulated side of the equation, whereas prices in the unregulated sectors, ranging from consumer electronics to computers, had declined precipitously. Thus, demand was growing for such items as televisions and personal computers, and they were diffus-ing widely. The personal computer was rapidly catching up to television's surpassing of the telephone. The number of households in the United States owning a personal computer hit the 50 percent mark in 1999.[55]

Moreover, the distinctions between regulated and unregulated indus-tries have broken down. As countries began to deregulate and privatize their telephone systems, it became even more difficult for policy makers to determine the best way to assure access for everyone to the new infor-mation society. What they did agree on almost everywhere, however, was that societies that could connect as many people as possible to the Net would prosper, and those that lagged behind would be less prosperous and less democratic. In addition, nations would have to find ways to make certain that no groups in society would be left behind, whether on the basis of income, physical location, age, disability, or other characteristics.

In seeking the solutions to these issues, governments needed to start by asking a series of critical questions:

First, what kinds of services would be included in any contemporary definition of universal access? In the older telephony era, universal service simply meant "voice grade access to the public switched network with the ability to place and receive calls"—in other words, the provision of a single voice telephone line in a household with a standard black, Western Electric, rotary-dial handset. Such amenities as color sets, touch-tone dialing, and "Princess" telephones were not a part of universal service. In developing countries, universal access has had many different meanings. In Brazil, it is defined as having a telephone within five kilometers of everyone's residence. In South Africa, it means being within thirty minutes' traveling time to a telephone. China has defined it as "one family, one telephone in urban areas and telephone services to every administrative village in rural areas."

However, in the information age, the services available are practically endless, and so are the information appliances needed to access them. Should there be universal access to E-mail alone, or also to the World Wide Web and all of its information and services? Should universal service include voice telephony over the Internet or Internet video capability? Should the provision of universal access be limited to a standard telephone line, or should it comprise a higher-speed telephone, cable, or wireless connection? What about the personal computer, the display, and the software needed to access the network, or the printer or external disk drive needed to capture information? The telephone was simple to use and required no training or special education; computers are a different story. Should Internet and computer training be provided to all as a part of a new universal service doctrine?

The second question that governments need to grapple with is how universal access would be paid for. In the telephony era, the regulated environment permitted cross-subsidization to pay for universal service: the regulatory bodies and the telephone company management set usage fees and rates in such a way that those in urban areas and those who could afford to pay for regular service subsidized the higher costs associated with providing service to those living great distances from substations or those who could not afford to pay. Rather than requiring each individual farmer to bear the cost of a long, individual line to his home, for example, which might require dozens of miles of telephone poles and wires, the cost was spread among all the users of the system, so the farmer paid the same rate as urban dwellers. In the same way, all users subsidized special low rates for the elderly or disabled, who relied on the telephone for health and safety.

Once the telephone system was deregulated, however, and market forces were left to determine prices, the subsidy mechanism for universal service in the pricing structure disappeared. As a result, countries began to turn to other financing methods, ranging from "universal service funds" created by a tax on telecommunications charges to the use of bond issues and general tax revenues. Sometimes these new policies were transparent and visible to the public, and sometimes they were hidden or disguised by governments in an attempt to avoid debate and controversy. The private sector also began to play a role by underwriting the cost of access in public places such as schools, libraries, and community centers. Perhaps the most important policies available were those of governments that promoted competition and innovation, which drive down prices and make access more affordable to everyone.

The third question facing governments is, What groups or individuals in society will be eligible to receive the benefits of universal access policies, and how will they receive them? Will the traditional groups benefiting from universal service be maintained, including the rural, the elderly, and the disabled? Or will new groups be added, such as low-income people, racial or ethnic minorities, students, and medical personnel? If groups such as students are added, for example, would the definition of universal service in a country like the United States shift to mean access in a classroom, rather than service in the home? Will access in the workplace also count as individual access? The July 1999 Department of Commerce report "Falling Through the Net" showed that whereas 27 percent of whites could access the Internet from home, only 9.2 percent of blacks could do so. When connections from school or work were included, however, the numbers jumped to 38 percent for whites and 19 percent for blacks, narrowing the gap somewhat. Are there lessons for policy here regarding the importance of connecting schools, for example?

As the first Clinton administration took office in 1993, it decided to tackle these questions as part of its initiative on the National Information Infrastructure (NII). The administration included as part of its 1994 NII "Agenda for Action" a statement calling for a new definition of "expanded universal service." It called for the National Telecommunications and Information Administration in the Department of Commerce to hold hearings and work with state regulatory commissions and others to "give all Americans who desire it easy affordable access to advanced communications and information services."[56]

To get ideas from the nongovernmental sector, the administration also set up the National Information Infrastructure Advisory Council, consisting of experts from the fields of high technology, education, health care, business, libraries, and other fields. This council studied the issue of universal access and issued its report, titled "Common Ground," in March 1995.[57] Although the council left as many questions unanswered as it answered, it set down five important principles that guide the U.S. debate over this question.

First, the council rejected the traditional notion of universal *service* from the regulated world in favor of universal *access* that provides ubiquitous, convenient, and affordable connections to the national information infrastructure. Second, it rejected regulation to achieve universal access in favor of private-sector leadership and the use of competition to drive innovation and lower prices. Third, the council rejected the idea of an absolute definition for levels of access, but said that rapidly changing technologies required that the definition evolve along with technology. Fourth, it set as a requirement that access be provided to schools, public libraries and other institutions that serve the community. And finally, the council warned that if the private-sector mechanism were to fail to achieve universal access, government incentives and subsidies would have to be considered. Thus, as in the cases of privacy and free speech, pressure was placed on the private sector to help solve the problem.

The timing of the council's report was propitious, since Congress was in the midst of its debate over reforming the more than sixty-year-old Communications Act. The overall conclusions of the administration and its advisory council regarding the primary reliance on competition to achieve universal access seemed to mesh well with the objectives of Congress, since the latter was trying to deregulate telecommunications more broadly. However, as part of the overall "balance" in the new act between those who wanted to abolish all regulation and those who wanted to retain it, a compromise was also reached on universal service. Section 254 of the Telecommunications Act of 1996, which required common carriers to contribute to a Universal Service Fund, was amended to set up a new "E-rate" program to "ensure that health care providers for rural areas, elementary and secondary school classrooms, and libraries have affordable access to modern telecommunications services that will enable them to provide medical and education services to all parts of the Nation."[58] What happened to the new program provides an interesting case study in the complex politics of providing universal access in the digital era.

Dutifully following the congressional mandate, the FCC issued its Universal Service Order in May 1997, setting up the new "E-rate" program.

The FCC required telecommunications carriers to contribute to the Universal Service Fund for the E-rate, capping the program at $2.2 billion per year. Schools and libraries would then solicit competitive bids for equipment and services, such as Internet connections, with discounts of up to 90 percent subsidized by the program. Under the FCC's order, the cost of the new program to the carriers would be more than offset by the overall benefits of deregulation. Unfortunately for the E-rate, the long-distance and wireless carriers did not all see it that way and when the program began in mid-1997, some of them began to pass along the costs of the new charge to residential and business customers as a separate item on their service bills. American telephone bills were already clogged with a long list of taxes, charges and fees, both federal and state, which made telephone service one of the most heavily taxed products in the country. A typical monthly telephone bill for $19.53 from Bell South, for example, contained fifteen different taxes and government-imposed "fees," totaling $7.90—a tax rate of over 40 percent. (In May 2000, Congress moved finally to eliminate the federal excise tax on telephone service, which dated back to the Spanish-American War.)

The outraged letters to Congress from telephone customers about the new tax were not long in coming, and soon members of both parties were denouncing the new tax. A bipartisan group of members on the Senate and House commerce committees wrote the chair of the FCC telling him to suspend the program and calling it an unconstitutional hidden tax not properly passed by Congress. Congressman John Dingell of Michigan also attacked the head of the new organization set up to administer the program, who was being paid a yearly salary of $200,000. Said Dingell, "We did not vote to have the FCC set up a giant bureaucracy headed by someone paid as much as the President." After congressional hearings and moves to take the matter through the courts, the FCC scaled the 1998 program back to approximately half of its original size. But by mid-1999, the furor had died down; the program was popular with schools, and the FCC's commissioners voted 3 to 2 to boost the program back to the original $2.2 billion.

"The Strange Case of the E-Rate," as Christopher DeMuth, president of the American Enterprise Institute, called it in a research paper,[59] is only one example of the contradictions and controversies involved in attempting to provide universal service for advanced information services in a world shifting from regulated monopoly to free markets and from the voice telephone to the Net. Other examples that will be discussed in more detail in Chapter 7, include the use of access charges paid by long-distance carriers to local telephone companies to provide universal service, and the exclusion of ISPs from having to pay access charges. Each of these issues sets various sectors of the information industry against each other in a lobbying collision between themselves and all the interest groups on each side.

The issue has also provided a rich mine for researchers and academics on both sides of the question. Speaking of the new subsidies for universal service, A. Michael Noll, professor of communications at the University of Southern California, said, "[T]he wisdom of using the telephone bill as a means to support social programs must be questioned. History tells us that Federal pork barrels have a way of growing and can rarely be closed once opened. . . . The intent of the Telecommunications Act of 1996 was to foster competition. The result of the Act is to create new subsidies and to make explicit all the old subsidies. However, subsidies are inconsistent with competition."[60] Lawrence Gasman, a senior fellow at the Cato Institute, was more blunt: "[U]niversal service programs are largely payoffs to politically influential groups. Markets alone would ensure that the benefits of the information age were widely shared, even among the poor. Congress should simply eliminate universal service subsidies."[61] According to Gasman, attempts to subsidize universal service actually harm the more widespread use of advanced technology, since they discourage competition, slow the development and introduction of new technologies, and keep prices artificially high.

On the other hand, Herbert Dordick, professor of communication at the University of California at San Diego, writes, "The promise of information abundance, so necessary in a democracy, can be met only by guaranteeing universal and equitable access to uncensored sources of information. To achieve this, we may have to define our traditional notion of common carriage and make a commitment to minimizing or even outlawing 'communication redlining.' "[62] Battle lines on the issue seem to fall along old political fault lines.

Thus it is surprising that the view of the need for continued government intervention to provide a form of universal service was supported not only by Vice President Gore but also by former House Speaker Newt Gingrich, who called for a tax credit to make a personal computer available to every family. The Department of Commerce's study mentioned earlier also seem to buttress the need for some action, showing strong and growing income and racial divides between those who are on-line and those who are not.

Trying to bridge the gap between private and public initiatives, the Clinton administration announced on February 2, 2000, a new budget initiative to close the digital divide. Among its key provisions were $2 billion in tax incentives over to encourage private-sector donations of computers and training, $150 million for training of new teachers, and $100 million to create community technology centers in low-income areas. During April of that year, the president visited disadvantaged towns from East Palo Alto, California, to Shiprock, New Mexico, to announce partnerships with such companies as Hewlett-Packard, Novell, and Qualcomm.

Other scholars point to the international digital divide, citing the growing information gap between rich and poor nations. In his book *Info Rich—Info Poor*, Trevor Haywood says, "The continuing capacity to innovate and to create distinctive stocks of information is what now gives one nation an advantage over another. . . . Nations build up important knowledge surpluses by investing in ongoing programmes of pure and applied research, funded by both public and private investment or partnerships of both."[63]

The OECD stated the problem most starkly in its report titled "The Economic and Social Impact of Electronic Commerce: Preliminary Findings and Research Agenda": "Visions of a global-based knowledge economy and universal electronic commerce characterized by the 'death of distance' must be tempered by the reality that half the world's population has never made a telephone call, much less accessed the Internet."[64]

A nation's information capability, of course, goes far beyond the provision of universal access to its citizens, but widespread use of cyberspace is a prerequisite to admission to the information society. Different countries and regions are experimenting with different ways to achieve it. For example, the EU, even as it moved toward telecommunications competition in 1998, stated its intention to continue universal service requirements for basic telephony. In Chile, where telecommunications has been deregulated, a universal service fund based on a tax on telecommunications revenues provides funding. The same is true in such countries as France, Peru, and Australia.

Other countries have solutions such as the use of access charges to fund universal service and direct financial assistance to disadvantaged groups such as the elderly homebound or the disabled. The private sector is also playing an increasingly important role. With the advent of the Internet and advanced information services, it is no longer possible for the local telephone company to be the only mechanism for providing universal access. Although the local telephone connection is a prerequisite for access to the information infrastructure, that is all it is. Computer hardware and software, peripheral equipment such as a printer, a modem, and a disk, CD-ROM, or DVD drive and other services are also part of the overall picture. Like Theodore Vail at the beginning of the twentieth century, the people running the high-technology companies that produce these products and services increasingly understand that universal access is a goal that is totally compatible with their business interests. Giving away computers and software to schools, libraries, and other community and cultural institutions is not just a philanthropic activity, it is a wise long-term business strategy.

Thus, IBM, Microsoft, AT&T, Hewlett-Packard, Sun Microsystems, and other companies have initiated substantial programs to donate personal computers, software, and other products and services to schools, libraries, and other public institutions. Some offer discounts; others simply give away equipment and services. Some have programs that encourage employees to become active in volunteering for these types of organizations and then permit them to make gifts on behalf of the company. Others have elaborate programs involving competitions for funds. IBM's Reinventing Education Program contributes both equipment and technical expertise to schools proposing new uses of technology to reform education, not just to connect to the Internet. MCI WorldCom, together with a number of other companies, supports a Schools on the Web program providing teacher training and computer equipment. Microsoft is donating its software to upgrade the technology and access of the nation's libraries. AT&T's Learning Network program provides free Internet access to classrooms. More recently, the cable television industry has joined the fray, as cable modems are becoming an important component of access to the network. Established job-training programs across the nation, such as those run by the Urban League and others, are also shifting the focus of their training to Internet-related jobs.

On the international level, international organizations are also beginning to throw their weight behind a variety of programs to aid information-anemic countries. A good example is the World Bank's InfoDev program for information development. Through this program, World Bank experts help countries achieve a consensus on subjects related to their information infrastructures and help them devise policy strategies, including the reform of their telecommunications systems. Using funds from the World Bank and private-sector funds provided by such firms as AT&T and IBM, InfoDev also tests applications of digital technology to combat such problems as illiteracy, urban decay, illness and malnutrition, and environmental degradation. Among the projects that have been sponsored are ones that develop self-sustaining community centers to provide information services to urban and rural communities.

Such programs have great promise because of the enormous potential of human capital everywhere in the world. Says computer scientist Michael Dertouzos of MIT, "Spending $200 million a year for ten years in, say, Sri Lanka for information kiosks, terrestrial communications, training programs, software and equipment could start a chain reaction that would eventually move a good part of that country's workforce and schoolchildren onto the Information Marketplace."[65]

Given the wide range of views about what constitutes "universal service" in the information age, as well as how it could be achieved, policy makers are left with many options. Certainly there is a mandate for "universal access" based on the widespread agreement over its critical importance to economies and societies in the twenty-first century. But the subject of broad citizen access to the Net is so critical to the future success of whole societies that nations must be bold and adopt imaginative new policies to achieve it. Setting a goal of 100 percent access may be reaching for the moon—but so was reaching for the moon. Nations can meet the test of greatness only if they set the highest goals. Therefore, among the policy options that nations should consider, debate and adopt are the following:

- Develop, adopt, and publicize a national goal for "universal access" to the global information infrastructure for every citizen—100 percent access. Through every means that democratic governments use—speeches, hearings, white papers, political campaigns—make sure every citizen understands how important this will be for them and for their children.
- Base the policy of universal access first and foremost on the principle of competition. Competition is driving the acceleration of innovation and the decreases in prices that are shaping the information infrastructure. If government policies increase competition, the flow of new products and services and lower prices that make universal access possible will roll out at an even faster rate. Government's principal tools to drive competition include further and faster deregulation of telecommunications and broadcasting and the prudent use of antitrust and competition laws to prevent new monopolies from developing. International competition will also be spurred by continuing trade initiatives to lower the remaining tariffs and eliminate nontariff barriers on high-tech goods and services.
- Use a backup system of limited and temporary government intervention measures to jump-start universal access in institutions such

as schools, hospitals, libraries, community centers, and assisted living and nursing home facilities. Rather than using hidden cross-subsidies, such as those buried in the telephone system, use universal service funds that are openly funded by general tax revenues. Hidden subsidies disguised as fees or charges will be discovered and will make the public unnecessarily cynical about the overall goal. Open debates, such as those over other uses of tax revenues, will educate the public and make the information age part of the ongoing debate about national priorities, as is already the case with issues such as health care, agricultural support, education, and law enforcement. Above all, make these policies transparent, so that all citizens understand them.

- Help create the broad social and economic infrastructure in which universal access can thrive. People who are illiterate will not be able to use a computer, even if it is given to them without charge. Governments at all levels should continue to press for education reform so that children are ready to use cyberspace productively, not as an education aim in itself but as an enabler of overall education. For adults, governments should work with the private sector to create training programs that are available to citizens at no charge. Furthermore, tax policy should support the national universal access objective by stimulating competition and not distorting the growth of the Net by favoring one technology over another, or one method of commerce over another. (Tax policy is discussed in more detail in Chapter 6.)
- Encourage companies to give away more equipment, software, and services and to offer free expertise to schools and other institutions, as well as directly to young people. One stimulus is tax incentives at the federal, state, or local level. As already mentioned, companies are already engaged in these activities, but the surface of their potential has barely been scratched. Companies will naturally want to spread the use of their products and services to prepare the market. But even companies not directly producing equipment or software can become involved. Semiconductor companies will see the markets for their products—the raw materials of the cyber age—expand if universal access becomes a reality. Content producers such as newspaper or book publishers will see the same result. Even the film industry, which has done so much recently to damage society with the harmful effects of its films on young people, could partly redeem itself by contributing to this effort.

- Create partnerships between industry, government, foundations, universities, and organizations such as the Urban League to run training programs in the inner city and remote rural regions. These programs could include job training but should also include simple training on how to use an information kiosk, how to surf the World Wide Web, or how to send and receive E-mail. Every citizen should know how to perform these simple digital functions.

- Work together with industry to develop a universal E-mail program, including a permanent E-mail address for every citizen and E-mail address portability. Although such a system is technically difficult, it is far from impossible and will provide benefits to every user of the global information infrastructure. Such a goal should also include the development of numerous alternative means to receive and send E-mail, such as via their television sets with a set-top box, via direct satellite systems and hand-held mobile devices, or through equipment available publicly at information kiosks located in post offices, supermarkets, libraries, and government buildings. With telephony over the Internet soon to become a widespread reality, perhaps a permanent telephone number could be combined with a permanent E-mail address.

- Internationally, governments should work bilaterally and multilaterally to help the developing countries enter the digital age. Far from altruism, providing assistance would be to their own benefit, since digitally adept developing countries will become both markets and suppliers of new and inexpensive goods to the citizens of developed countries. Some international organizations such as the OECD, the ITU, and the World Bank are already involved in pressing the need for global universal access, but others need to become energized. The World Health Organization could do more to spread the benefits of the information age in the health field. The International Labor Organization could increase its efforts to educate governments and people about the critical role of electronic commerce in the future of work and employment. Although the G-8 (the G-7 group of advanced industrialized nations, plus Russia) has made a start, it should proclaim a policy of global universal access and work with the UN and other agencies to help achieve it.

Achieving the goal of global universal access will not be easy. Some will say it is unrealistic and impossible. But if the new digital age has taught us anything, it is that great leaps of the imagination can be and are being translated into reality daily. After all, just a few years ago, the Internet was used only by a handful of researchers. Why should we not set the bar high? For centuries, politicians have promised their citizens all sorts of things, many of them unobtainable, many of them unimportant. With information the key to economic and democratic progress, why not offer to the citizens of the world a goal that is both obtainable and also very important?

CONCLUSION

The Net will be a forum for democratization in the twenty-first century if we deploy it properly and safeguard individual rights. In June 1999, Amnesty International's executive director, William F. Schulz, said, "The Internet has been a major factor in raising awareness (of human rights) because it has allowed information to flow freely in and out of countries with censor-heavy government."[66]

Regarding China, the *Washington Post* reported, "Despite official Chinese efforts to control the Internet and limit its use as a method of disseminating news, rumors, lies and truths unfavorable to China's government, a growing army of Chinese web surfers is scaling fire walls, posting radical criticisms of government policy and engaging in deep, unregulated discussions of China's fate."[67]

The 1948 Universal Declaration of Human Rights set forth a series of rights that together constitute a definition of democracy. They seem to have anticipated the global interconnectivity of the Internet and how that would be a new fountain of democratic rights. But only if we can assure that the rights of privacy, of freedom of expression, and of access for all can be achieved will the Net fulfill its potential as an engine of democracy.

There is a natural and robust symbiosis between democracy and the Net. Each nurtures the other. But the relationship is not absolute and not immutable. As the Net evolves, its creators and users must pay proper respect to democratic values, especially those of free speech, privacy, and equal access for all. If the private sector and government fail to do so, the resulting weakening of democratic values will in turn retard the growth of the Net, along with its social and economic benefits.

6

Digital Economics

Information technologies have begun to alter the manner in which we do business and create value, often in ways not readily foreseeable even five years ago. . . . The recent years' remarkable surge in the availability of real-time information has enabled business management to remove large swaths of inventory safety stocks and worker redundancies and has armed workers with detailed data to fine tune product specifications to most individual customer needs . . . [and] fostered marked reductions in delivery lead times. . . . This, in turn, has reduced the relative size of the overall capital structure required to turn out our goods and services, and, as a consequence, has apparently added to growth of multifactor productivity, and thus to labor productivity acceleration.

—Alan Greenspan, May 1999[1]

In cyberspace, the Invisible Hand has carpal tunnel syndrome.

—A cynical and witty economist.

By 1999, even Federal Reserve Board chair Alan Greenspan seemed to have embraced enthusiastically the economic benefits of the Net—albeit in his typically understated manner. Greenspan was a late convert, having just two years earlier questioned whether all the investment in new technology had created any benefits in the form of productivity improvement. In fact, even as investors, businesses, and governments had seen and experienced enormous economic benefits arising from the digital age and structured their portfolios and their policies accordingly, economists and financial experts had been arguing endlessly about whether there were any benefits at all.

For example, J. Bradford De Long, a professor of economics at the University of California at Berkeley, argued that the idea of a "new economy" shaped by the information age was much like earlier "revolutions," such as Henry Ford's manufacturing revolution. "[A] technological revolution is not an economic revolution," he argued, asserting that the speed of Moore's Law will slow and the information industry will mature, much as others have in the past.[2]

Daniel Sichel, a Federal Reserve economist, studied the impact of computers on productivity and concluded, "In recent decades, U.S. businesses have spent billions on information technology. . . . In the midst of this rapid computerization, . . . however, the economy's measured productivity performance has been lackluster."[3] His use of the word "measured" is critical here, since many believe that economists are not yet adequately measuring the contribution that information technology makes. Sichel believes that the total investment in information technology, though it seems large, is still small compared to the overall economy and therefore makes little difference in measuring the entire economy's performance in an area like productivity.

In fact, the measurement issue and the size issue are two of three questions that have arisen to explain the productivity paradox discussed in Chapter 2. The third, and the one that had been offered by Alan Greenspan prior to 1998, is the issue of diffusion: that it takes years for a new technology to be accepted and used throughout the economy. Until it is diffused, its benefits, including its contribution to productivity and economic growth, are meager. Perhaps, as a witty economist has paraphrased Adam Smith, the invisible hand does suffer from a form of cyber-arthritis.

In contrast to these skeptical views, Wall Street and most governments have been overwhelmingly bullish on the contribution of the new information infrastructure to the global economy. A key portfolio manager at Fidelity Investments in Boston, on the first day that the Dow Jones Industrial Average closed above 10,000, said, "Look around the globe. The U.S. economy has the highest percentage of spending on information technology. And which economy is the strongest? The U.S."[4] Similar views are offered in government statements, though often a bit less exuberantly, from Washington to Beijing, and by international organizations and regional groups from the European Union (EU) to the Asia-Pacific Economic Cooperation group (APEC).

Where does the truth lie? Can so many noted economists have been wrong in the past? Did Wall Street create a high-technology bubble based on false assumptions? If so, why are so many individual businesses and other institutions spending huge amounts of money so they can participate in the digital age? Why are governments competing with one another in the rush to cyberspace? It is worth examining each side, since government economic and financial policies, ranging from tax policy to international trade and investment policies, must be based on a realistic set of assumptions about the global information infrastructure (GII) and the world economy. Although the latest economic data from the U.S. government seem to settle the argument in favor of information technology, it is worthwhile to review the debate.

To begin the discussion, it is important to note that businesses and other institutions have been investing in and using information and communications technologies for many years. Mainframe computers came into relatively wide use during the 1950s. The introduction of the IBM System 360 in 1964 made them ubiquitous by the end of that decade. Coupled with advances such as optical character recognition that made automated check-clearing possible, as well as the rise of data communications and the use of private networks by the 1970s, computing and communications were obviously making some industries, such as banking, much more productive. The head of AT&T estimated in the 1960s, for example, that without automated switching and toll systems, the Bell Telephone System would have been required to hire every female high-school graduate in the nation to serve a telephone operators. (At the time, of course, almost all operators were women. Moreover, he failed to note that if all calls had to be handled manually, the cost of phone service would have been so high that many fewer calls would have been made.)

Despite the anecdotal evidence in numerous firms and industries, economists had never really agreed about the overall economic effects—positive or negative—of all this automation. If they had found the economic results of early computerization difficult to measure, they faced a much more complex problem by the early 1990s, as commercial use of the Internet began to take hold.

Their first problem is that the internal economics of the Internet and its family of networks is barely understood. For one thing, the Internet began as one type of economic creature and later metamorphosed into another while retaining some of the characteristics of the first. What began as a federally funded government and academic network for researchers seemed "free" to those users. Moreover, these early users engendered an entire culture that saw the Internet as a free public medium. Although it was certainly true that the Internet's ARPANET and NSFNET ancestors were supported by the government, they were not "free" in an economic sense; someone else (the taxpayers) footed the cost. Moreover, by the mid-1990s, with the commercialization of the Internet, government support became a small fraction of the overall cost. Nevertheless, the notion that the Internet and its services should be "free" persists to this day in many Internet communities. To complicate the matter further, many Internet services are offered free to users. By the end of 1999, free services on the Internet included voice mail, music, E-mail, and even greeting cards. For example, a company called Net Zero offered no-cost Internet connection service and signed up more than a million people. It hoped to become profitable through advertising revenues. Thus, with many of its underlying costs buried in public funding or cross-subsidized by other products and services, it is difficult to sort out the real underlying "cost" to any particular user.

Additionally, the technological complexity of the Internet makes economic analysis difficult. As one economic student of the Internet has said, "Access to the Internet is a minor economic miracle that is often taken for granted."[5] The Internet "cloud" that economists must analyze is composed of many-layered and interconnected networks, each with its own complex cost structures. These networks—some regulated and some not—are composed of communications lines that may be owned outright or leased and routers or computerized switches. They also include the servers owned by hundreds of thousands of users, the personal computers or other appliances that offer access, all the software that makes the network and the applications run, and the substantial human capital behind it all. Much of the valuation of a software firm, for example, reflects the company's star programmers.

Individual users and the Internet service providers (ISPs) that offer access also face a tangled maze of both regulated and competitive rules for interconnection fees, resale charges, access charges, and universal service fees. As the Federal Communications Commission and state regulatory agencies try desperately to keep up with new legislation and technologies, these rules change. In addition, cases involving most of these rules make their way through the courts, and the legal outcomes also create economic change.

Furthermore, the technology continues to explode. Thus, yesterday's high-bandwidth technology, ISDN (Information Services Digital Network, a technology that is now obsolete), and the underlying cost structure for it give way to today's high-bandwidth technologies—digital subscriber lines (DSL) and cable modems, dramatically changing bandwidth economics. Companies developing and offering these technologies rise and fall in an ever-changing competitive landscape. Convergence itself creates new forms of competition, with regional and long distance telephone companies, cable companies, utilities, and others engaged in a massive merger exercise to provide the competitive communications services of the future.

Intensive use of the Net has also created controversy over network congestion, a key factor for the future economics of the Internet. The traditional regional telephone companies have charged that low-priced Internet access charges spur people to inefficient overuse of the Internet, which in turn causes congestion on their public switched networks, interfering with telephone calls. The studies that the phone companies have produced to document this have been challenged by ISPs, who countercharge that fairer interconnection rules would ease any congestion that exists.

Not only is there great difficulty in measuring the economic basis of the Net's infrastructure, measuring and understanding the economic value of its content and services is also extraordinarily complex. How much is a particular piece of information worth? Can it be worth more at one instant than another? If so, how much value is there in the speed with which it can be transmitted, or in the reliability of its carriage? Given the huge volume of information now accessible on-line, content has become a much more significant part of the Net's economic equation. Similarly, the availability of services, such as the ability to use electronic commerce to buy and sell goods or to offer professional services, also adds to the new economic equation.

Finally, the underlying characteristics of the Internet "cloud" that users value and are willing to pay for is changing. Whereas the earliest users wanted mere access, today's users want more bandwidth and faster speed—and are willing to pay for it. Other features that users now desire, and may be willing to pay for, include security, reliability, priority (the ability to displace other users during periods of congestion), and anonymity.

Some economists believe that a more rational Net pricing system would provide different prices levels based on the user's transmission priorities. Guaranteed instant service would cost more than a lower-priority transmission. These economists believe that such pricing would create a more efficient and rational infrastructure, and that the complexity of implementing such a system would not be much greater than the switched telephone system's billing and traffic-management system.

In sum, with the internal economics of the Internet still relatively unformed, and its effects so new, measuring its broader economic impact with precision is difficult, if not impossible. Yet a number of clues hint at the overall external economic impact of information technology, especially as it has developed in the past few years.

As noted earlier, economists had debated for some time about their failure to note any productivity improvements resulting from the use of information and communications technologies. Some attributed this to measurement difficulties, some to the time it takes for technology to diffuse throughout the economy, and some to the relatively small percentage of total capital stock represented by the new technologies. Although productivity gains had been hard to measure at the national level, they clearly existed at the firm level, since managements had been making increasingly large investments in computers, communications, and most recently, electronic commerce. As we have seen, many companies are now doing a large proportion of their business electronically.

Recent studies have also shown that productivity gains exist at the industry-wide level. Some studies have indicated that the railroad, telecommunications, and steel industries have made above-average productivity gains at the same time they were making large investments in information technology.[6] Some of the most intriguing effects have been noted in the electric utilities industry, where large investments have been made to integrate technology into operations, automating many processes and improving service while reducing labor input. The result: electric utility productivity improved at a rate 50 percent greater than for total manufacturing in the most recent period studied.[7]

What seems to have been the reason for this discrepancy in productivity rates? More recent studies seem to indicate two important factors. First, institutions are now realizing that the new digital technologies don't yield their best results when simply grafted on to an existing organization. They do the most to improve an organization's performance when the organization makes radical changes to maximize their use. As economics professors Erik Brynjolfsson and Loren Hitt point out, the greatest benefits of technology are realized "when computer investment is coupled with other complementary investments: new strategies, new business processes and new organizations."[8]

These benefits are analogous to those encountered when electricity came into use at the beginning of the twentieth century. At first, electricity simply replaced whale oil, kerosene, and candles to provide lighting. Then industries began to install single electric motors in a machine shop to replace a steam engine. Although there may have been small savings from these innovations, the big savings came later, as electricity allowed the total redeployment and organization of machinery and operators in factories, resulting in great productivity gains. Similarly, computers and communications for the first few generations of their use were merely appended to businesses and other institutions, whose fundamental organizations and services remained unchanged. The rise of networked technologies has jump-started and accelerated a wide variety of new trends—making organizations market-driven, providing innovative new customer services, reducing cycle time and time to market, improving the quality of products and services, and laying the groundwork for the mass customization of products.

Brynjolfsson and Hitt argue that the definition of productivity must be broadened to include measurements not only of the number of products rolling out of a factory, but also of such intangibles as "product quality, timeliness, customization, convenience, [and] variety," among other things.[9] They go on to predict that the payoff from investment in information technology, combined with organizational and strategic changes, may be much higher than generally thought. Wall Street obviously agrees, given the high multiples not only of the Internet stocks themselves but of companies that are moving rapidly to integrate electronic commerce into their operations.

Governments also agree. The most recent Department of Commerce study of this issue made a number of key points. In the realm of productivity, from 1990 to 1997, worker productivity (technically, the gross product originating/worker) grew at 10.4 percent annually in information-technology-producing industries. In information-technology-using industries, it grew at 2.4 percent annually, compared to 0.5 percent for industries that do not as yet use information technologies. The information technology industry was responsible for 35 percent of U.S. economic growth in the years 1995–98. And from 1996 to 1998, falling prices in the information-technology industry reduced U.S. inflation by 0.7 percentage points.[10]

Internationally, the most recent Organization for Economic Cooperation and Development (OECD) study on the economic impact of electronic commerce concludes that "E-commerce has the potential to provide the productivity gains that 'prove' the worth of information and communication technologies." The study goes on to state that job gains from electronic commerce will generally outweigh job losses and that the use of the new technologies will be generally beneficial to countries in reaching their social as well as economic goals.[11] Reports and studies issued by numerous individual countries support this conclusion, and most nations are developing policies that are supportive of their national information infrastructures.

That the effects of the digital revolution are truly international is also accepted by Greenspan, as he mentioned in his speech to the Federal Reserve Bank of Chicago: "Technology is also damping inflation through its effect on international trade, where technology developments and a move to a less constrained world trading order have progressively broken down barriers to cross-border trade. All else equal, the enhanced competition in tradable goods enables excess capacity previously bottled up in one country to augment worldwide supply and exert restraint on prices in all countries' markets."[12]

Although Greenspan has now accepted the positive economic role of the new technologies, he cautions wisely that the jury is still out on a final verdict. He also agrees to some extent with De Long that we should also be wary of "new economy" prophets. The world also entered a remarkable new technological era at the beginning of the last century, with the outpouring of electric power, radio, telephony, and motor vehicles. The optimism of that period was dramatically shattered by depression and wars, which were made worse by technology. Today's digital technologies are full of economic promise. The remarkable productivity increases in the information-technology industries are beginning to show up in all of the industries that use such technology. But the future promise of these productivity gains will be fulfilled only if governments and the private sector work together to apply wisely their understanding of the new technologies. As Paul Romer, professor of economics at Stanford University, has said, "It isn't so much that we have a new economy, as we have a new understanding of the importance of technology in the economy."[13]

Given this new understanding and the powerful international consensus that now exists on the contributions that the Net will make to productivity, economic growth, and employment, nations have turned to questions of economic management, i.e., how to exploit that growth while at the same time encouraging it. Three principal questions have arisen: how to tax the phenomenon of global electronic commerce, how to treat it from the standpoint of tariffs and international trade, and how to deal with competition and monopoly.

TAXATION

Just as one to two hundred years ago economic discussions were dominated by the "corn tax," reflecting the importance of grain for the national economy, today the dominant issue should be how governments can adjust their tax base in line with the . . . information society and the increasing importance of information transmission for economic production and consumption.

—*The New Wealth of Nations: Taxing Cyberspace*[14]

The old saying about death and taxes is half true: only death is certain. Governments and their tax collectors have struggled for centuries to navigate the shifting sands of economies and tax structures. As feudal and agricultural societies became industrial and manufacturing ones, the older taxes on serfs, farm goods, and property were replaced or supplemented by taxes on industrial goods and processes. As automobiles and telephones became key parts of the economic landscape, governments found ways to tax them. As commerce became more international, and companies moved from one country to another, governments constructed international tax rules and a complex network of tax treaties. The world of taxation is a constant struggle for survival. A nation that continued to rely on a tax on horses and wagons for its revenues would have been in serious trouble by 1930.

Today, tax collectors at every level of government are worried about electronic commerce. As electronic commerce becomes ubiquitous, will the sales and income generated from it escape taxation? Moreover, as electronic commerce replaces physical commerce (for example, as Internet book sales displace the sales of books in traditional stores), will the income- and sales-tax revenues from traditional sources shrink? Since cyberspace is borderless, how will jurisdictions determine whether transactions take place within their borders? How can tax collections be administered in a virtual world of anonymous electronic cash and potentially unauditable and untraceable records? How will a region like Europe, which relies on a value-added tax (VAT) imposed on each stage of manufacturing, collect the tax from electronic commerce customers or prevent their citizens from avoiding taxation by ordering goods electronically from countries without a VAT?

The complexity of the issue can be seen in one example: Who has the right to collect income tax from telecommuters? The general U.S. rule is that the income of a nonresident is taxed in the state where the work is performed. What, then, if a worker in Nebraska performs services on his or her home computer for a firm in New York City? New York City takes the position that if this worker visits New York only once, and if the company has no office in Nebraska, then the worker is liable for New York income tax. Distinctions such as this one, multiplied by fifty states and countless other jurisdictions, will eventually make national rules a necessity.

As the *Economist* noted in an article subtitled "The Tap Runs Dry," "The Internet eliminated not just national borders but also the identity of firms and individuals doing business. As a result, the Net will open up opportunities to exploit tax differences . . . and to dodge taxes altogether."[15]

In response, governments and their revenue officials from Austin to Brussels have been scrambling to keep ahead of the digital wave. Some have proposed new sales taxes on electronic sales. Some have extended or supplemented their existing telecommunications taxes with new taxes or charges on Internet access or telephone service. The United States has done this, for example, to fund Internet hookups for schools. Some countries, including the United States, have advocated a moratorium on new taxes until the new medium is better understood and agreement can be reached on a single method of taxation.

Perhaps the most radical proposal has been the so-called bit tax. This idea has been proposed by a number of economists and, most important, by an independent committee appointed by the European Commission and headed by Luc Soete, an economist at the University of Limburg in Maastricht, the Netherlands. The basic notion of the bit tax, which would focus on the technology rather than the physical product of an electronic commerce transaction, is summed up in a book co-authored by Soete, *The New Wealth of Nations: Taxing Cyberspace*:

In Adam Smith's time, the wealth of nations was a function of the division of labor and the extent of the market. Today the new wealth of nations is a function of information and communications technologies. The trillions of digital bits of information pulsing through global networks . . . make up the raw material of the new economy. . . . It is important that the new wealth be accessible by governments, so that government can perform its traditional functions. . . .

The new tax base is that myriad of transactions, images, voice, text and data—all carried over global telecommunications, cable and satellite networks. . . . Just as some of the old tax base came from taxes on goods and transportation vehicles moving on the nation's rail lines and highways, so too can the new tax be found in the new distribution system of the new economy: the networks of the new economy."[16]

In addition to the obvious benefit of providing revenues, say bit tax advocates, such a tax would fulfill other purposes. For one thing, they argue, it would force people to use information more efficiently and therefore ease congestion on the Internet—the same goal sought by those who would impose a graduated pricing structure on the Internet. For another, bit tax advocates say, the proceeds of such a tax could be used not only for traditional social purposes, such as to fund social security or insurance programs, they could also help eliminate the digital have and have-not problem by providing revenues for Internet access and information services for those who could not otherwise afford them.

Although the bit tax may seem to be a "silver bullet" solution to the tax problems of cyberspace, few economists, tax experts, or politicians favor it. In Brussels, the EU commissioner for taxation stated in 1997 that there would be no need for a bit tax in Europe. Why these unfavor-

able reviews? Since a bit tax would shift the tax base to the new information infrastructure, it could also be the bullet that kills the digital
golden goose and retards the growth of the very phenomenon that appears to be the economic engine of the future. Another serious drawback
is that not all bits of information are alike or have the same value. Some
bits may be worth literally billions of dollars, whereas others may be almost worthless. Much information is time sensitive and may be extremely
valuable one minute and worthless the next. Taxing every bit at the same
rate makes no sense, and trying to fix value to individual bits or transmissions would be hopeless. Finally, since cyberspace is borderless, countries without a bit tax would simply become information and commerce
havens, making the tax impossible to collect.

Since the simple approach offers little possibility of success, governments and international organizations have been studying the tax issues
and observing the progress of electronic commerce. Many, though not
all, seem to agree on one overriding principle: tax neutrality. Electronic
commerce transactions should be subject to the same tax burden as physical transactions—no more and no less. Achieving this objective in practice can be complicated, however, and raises a number of issues. On both
the national and international levels, three basic issues have been identified: the nexus, or place of taxation; the classification of on-line transactions; and tax administration and compliance.

Nexus

The problem tax collectors face in determining who has jurisdiction over
a particular transaction can be illustrated by the French customer who
buys American-made shrink-wrapped software in Paris. He or she pays
a French VAT. If the same customer downloads the same software over
the Internet, however, American tax rates apply to the transaction. And
if an American customer in Wyoming orders the software through the
mail from a software company that has no "substantial presence" in
Wyoming, then no tax is due at all.

Under current rules at both the state and international levels, a tax
"nexus" is deemed to exist for a business if it maintains a "substantial
presence" within a jurisdiction. Not surprisingly, an enormous amount
of law and regulation exists on this subject. In a seminal paper on the
taxation of electronic commerce, the U.S. Department of the Treasury
dealt with the question of whether or not an electronic business maintained a "presence" for tax purposes in a jurisdiction:

Persons engaged in electronic commerce could be located anywhere in the world and their customers will be ignorant of, or indifferent to, their location. . . . Therefore, it is necessary to clarify the application of U.S. trade or business and permanent establishment concepts to persons engaged in electronic commerce. . . . For example, to the extent that the activities of a person engaged in electronic commerce are equivalent to the mere solicitation of orders from U.S. customers, without any other U.S. activity, it may not be appropriate to treat such activities as a U.S. trade or business. . . . Another example is the treatment of foreign persons who maintain or utilize a computer server in the United States. Again, it is useful to review the treatment of existing, traditional, commercial activities and consider whether any existing exclusions from permanent establishment treatment should apply in this situation.

For example, a permanent establishment generally does not include the use of facilities solely for the purpose of storage, display, or delivery of goods or merchandise. . . . For a business which sells information instead of goods, a computer server might be considered the equivalent of a warehouse."[17]

The first critical observation from the Treasury paper is that existing regulations can be applied to this aspect of electronic commerce taxation without an unusual amount of difficulty. A totally new body of tax law is not needed to deal with electronic commerce. Second, according to the Treasury, existing rules do offer a solid framework for resolving the questions of tax jurisdiction. Unless a company or person has a physical presence that exceeds some minimum threshold in a jurisdiction, tax jurisdiction lies in its country or state of residence under current rules.

For example, the U.S. Supreme Court, in its decision in *Quill Corp. v North Dakota,* upheld the standard that a business must have local employees or real property within a state to be deemed to have a substantial presence in that state for tax purposes. It is under this rule that mail-order houses ship items without collecting state or local sales taxes to states in which they do not meet this test. The same rules can also be generally applied to electronic sales, which are generally analogous for tax purposes to mail-order catalog sales.

Similar rules are already accepted internationally, as pointed out in the Treasury paper. The OECD Model Tax Convention states, "It has come to be accepted in international fiscal matters that until an enterprise of another State sets up a permanent establishment in another State, it should not properly be regarded as participating in the economic life of that other State to the extent that it comes within the jurisdiction of that other State's taxing rights."[18] This view is also accepted in tax treaties between the United States and its trading partners.

The issue is extremely complex, however, and is far from resolved. Since almost all tax rules preceded the development of cyberspace, many existing laws and regulations may have unintended consequences. For example, the law is somewhat fuzzy on the question of whether or not the use of a local ISP within a jurisdiction through a contractual relationship constitutes a local presence. A recent complex German tax case involving an oil pipeline in Germany controlled by a computer in the Netherlands seemed to increase the risk that servers and telecommunications equipment constitute a permanent establishment for property-tax purposes.[19] Nevertheless, the existing body of U.S. and international tax law makes the important point that the computer servers and telecommunications lines necessary to perform an electronic transaction do not in themselves pass the threshold necessary for their owners to be taxed in the jurisdiction where they operate. The Treasury paper further establishes that these existing rules can be applied to electronic commerce. Thus, although many technical issues of jurisdiction remain to be resolved, as do the unique interests of governments with different tax bases and systems, these principles go a long way toward addressing the nexus issue.

Classification

Perhaps as vexing as the issue of nexus is the issue of the classification of online transactions for tax purposes. Classification is important because different types or classes of transactions are treated differently for tax purposes. For example, some states tax the sales of goods but not of services. The purchase of a newspaper from a newsstand is the sale of a good. But what is the purchase of an on-line subscription to a newspaper, especially when it might involve customization of the news? Is that a good or a service? Moreover, the right to distribute copies of the newspaper might involve the license of copyrighted material and royalty income, with still different tax consequences. The Treasury paper mentioned above also describes the main issues involved in classification:

Any type of information that can be digitized, such as computer programs, books, music or images, can be transferred electronically. . . . The purchaser of a digitized image [such as a photograph] could obtain the right to use a single copy of the image, the right to reproduce ten copies of the image for use in a corporate report, the right to reproduce the image for use in an academic work that is expected to have a limited press run, or the right to reproduce the image in a mass circulation magazine. Depending on the facts and circumstances, some of these transactions may be viewed as the equivalent of the purchase of a physical copy or copies of the photograph, while other of these transactions would result in royalty income because they involve payments for the use of or the privilege of using copyrights or similar property in the United States, which could be taxable in the United States.[20]

Electronic classification issues collide with copyright law and the tax treatment of royalties as opposed to sales of goods. Most jurisdictions have treated the sale of shrink-wrapped software as the sale of a good, since the disk on which the software is recorded is tangible. But the sale also involves a contract between the buyer and seller involving the seller's copyright ownership of the software. Generally, the purchaser agrees not to make unauthorized copies of the software, and perhaps agrees to certain other conditions, such as not to decompile the software. In the electronic downloading of software, despite the lack of a tangible disk, the substance of the transaction may be the same.

For tax purposes, however, sales income, royalties, and services income can be and are taxed differently in different jurisdictions. The rates may be different, as may be the nexus. For example, services tend to be taxed where the service is performed, not at the point of consumption of the service, whereas royalties may be taxed where the royalty is paid.

As in the case of nexus, existing tax rules can help clarify this issue, although not completely. For example, the U.S. Internal Revenue Service issued regulations on the classification of computer-program transactions in November 1996. These regulations treat most computer-program transactions as sales, unless they involve the right to reproduce and distribute the program. Other countries, such as Canada and Australia, also take this approach, as has the OECD. On the other hand, the European Commission announced in June 1998 that it would treat the sale of downloaded products such as software as services for tax purposes, putting EU member nations at odds with other countries. Clearly, the reason behind the EU's decision to tax in this manner is the economic impact of the VAT, since the EU wishes to apply VAT to online sales.

The U.S. tax code deals at length with the distinctions between sales and services. As the Treasury paper points out,

Although many commercial transactions involve elements of both the provision of tangible property and the performance of services, these transactions are generally classified in accordance with their predominant characteristic. For example, a transaction involving the performance of professional services may result in the provision of a letter or other document. . . . The provision of the tangible property is treated as incidental to the performance of the services. In contrast, if a retail establishment sells a suit to a customer but agrees to make slight alterations as part of the purchase prices, the performance of services would be viewed as an integral part of a transaction consisting of the sale of goods.[21]

Despite the fact that existing rules provide a rough blueprint for dealing with tax-classification rules in cyberspace, many issues will still need to be resolved, as services ranging from telemedicine to living encyclopedias are offered over the Net. Although many of these issues will be decided by tax authorities on a case-by-case basis in the near term, there is a longer-range need for international agreement on a uniform system of classification. Uniform treatment is important not only for tax purposes but also for international trade.

Tax Administration and Compliance

A third issue confronting tax professionals is administration and compliance. Although the issues of nexus and classification are critically important, ultimately transactions must be accounted for and taxes must actually be collected. In some ways, tax authorities anticipate that electronic commerce could actually improve accountability since, in an accounted electronic system, "the central record of transactions, if it is available for examination on audit, will permit tax administrators to match payments and receipts to specific taxpayers."[22] A serious problem arises, however, from unaccounted systems, which will use electronic cash, especially for small transactions. Although this problem also exists for traditional businesses, such as restaurants and grocery stores, it offers more difficult challenges in cyberspace, where other methods of verifying business volume, such as checks of inventory, may not readily exist.

A similar problem arises from the ability of on-line business to be transacted anonymously, when parties may wish to use their legitimate right to preserve their privacy, leaving no clear trace of who bought and who sold. Since attempts to require some type of residual identification by regulating or controlling various digital-identification techniques may run afoul of government privacy objectives, this problem may also be particularly difficult to resolve.

A third issue arises from the phenomenon of "disintermediation." Since the new information infrastructure will allow parties to eliminate intermediaries and do business directly with each other, trusted and regulated institutions that have traditionally played a role in tax collection and administration, such as banks, may be excluded from many transactions. Since commercial banks assist government revenue agencies not only through record-keeping and reporting requirements but also through withholding requirements, substitutes may have to be found.

Some observers have suggested that ISPs might act in these capacities, by withholding taxes, for example. But as the IBM Corporation has pointed out, "As a practical matter, an ISP will have no way of knowing, particularly in the case of an internet transaction, that the subscriber has visited a particular site, much less purchased goods or services. . . . An obligation to collect and remit use taxes would not be imposed on a telephone company or other common carrier if the transaction were conducted by conventional means. There is no reason that an ISP should be held to a different obligation."[23] Nevertheless, some states have been exploring this approach. In fact, the governments in twenty states and the District of Columbia have already moved to impose at least one tax on electronic commerce. These taxes differ from each other and range from 4 percent in South Dakota to up to 8.25 percent in Texas.[24] Cities have also been eager to join in the hunt for new revenues. Mark Schwartz, president of the National League of Cities, said in July 1997 that "hard-pressed cities should have the ability to tax Internet and electronic transactions."[25] With a total of more than thirty thousand taxing jurisdictions in the United States and another ten thousand in Canada, the prospect of thousands of different taxes on electronic commerce could easily stop the new medium in its tracks.

Recognizing this possibility, and eager to foster economic development generated by new technologies in their own states, governors Pete Wilson of California and George Pataki of New York announced, with the public support of their tax authorities, that their states would not pursue new taxes on electronic commerce. The Clinton administration took the same approach in its July 1997 Framework for Global Electronic Commerce: "The Administration is also concerned about possible moves by state and local tax authorities to target electronic commerce and Internet access. The uncertainties associated with such taxes and the inconsistencies among them could stifle the development of electronic commerce. . . . No new taxes should be applied to electronic commerce and . . . states and local governments should cooperate to develop a uniform, simple approach to the taxation of electronic commerce, based on existing principles of taxation."[26] The administration also stated that it would work with the OECD, the primary forum for cooperation on international taxation, on this issue.

In 1997, Representative Christopher Cox (R-Calif.) and Senator Ron Wyden (D-Ore.) introduced joint bills in the House and the Senate to impose an indefinite moratorium on subnational taxes on electronic commerce in the United States. Supported by the high-technology trade associations and companies, as well as by the administration, but opposed by many states and cities, the legislation passed in 1998, although the moratorium was limited to three years. The legislation also created a joint state-federal Advisory Commission on Electronic Commerce to work on a common approach to the issue. The commission was chaired by Governor John Gilmore (R-Va.) and began its work in Williamsburg, Virginia, in June 1999. In November 1999, Governor Gilmore unveiled his own plan to ban all taxes on Internet sales and services and also to end the federal excise tax on telephone service. To compensate states for lost revenues, Gilmore's plan would have imposed a new 1 percent federal tax on telephone service.

The Gilmore Commission—comprising business representatives and federal and state officials—split on the basic issue of whether Net sales should be taxed. Although a March 30, 2000, vote favored a tax-free Internet, the vote was short of the thirteen-vote "supermajority" margin that Congress had required. Governor Gilmore and the corporate executives on the commission from AT&T, America Online, MCI World-Com, and others backed a permanent ban on taxing Net commerce. The National Governors Association, led by Utah governor Mike Leavitt, and the Clinton administration favored tax simplification among the nation's thirty thousand tax jurisdictions to permit collection of some tax. With the failure of the commission, Congress in mid-2000 was considering another temporary moratorium to allow more time to work out a compromise. The House of Representatives passed a five-year extension of the moratorium on new Internet taxes on May 10, 2000, but did not prevent states from collecting sales taxes. Some senators, led by Senator John McCain, chair of the influential Commerce Committee, favored a completely tax-free Net.

Governments of other countries are also active in trying to resolve electronic-commerce tax issues. Of particular importance is the position of the EU, since it and the United State currently account for the great bulk of the world's electronic-commerce transactions. After the July 1997 European Ministerial Conference on Global Information Networks, the ministers issued the Bonn Declaration, which declared, "Ministers support the principle of non-discriminatory taxes on the use of Global Information Networks. They agree that tax issues of electronic commerce call for international cooperation and where appropriate coordination in order to avoid distortion of competition."[27] The reference to competition illustrates the special EU concern that electronic-commerce customers will try to avoid paying a VAT by purchasing goods from countries with no VAT. The ministerial meeting also rejected the idea of a bit tax, warned against complex administrative requirements, and called for the harmonization of payment for VATs on goods ordered electronically. The ministers also agreed that the OECD and the World Trade Organization (WTO) should be the principal international bodies to coordinate a uniform international system for the taxation of electronic commerce.

Since the Bonn ministerial meeting, however, a significant tax issue has emerged from the EU. As mentioned above, in June 1998 the European Commission announced that electronic sales of software and other digital products would be taxed not as goods but as services. Since the designation of tax jurisdiction for services is different from that of goods, the EU's position was intended to help keep its VAT tax viable for electronic transactions. But the EU ruling is in conflict with U.S. policy and with the position of the OECD, whose Committee on Fiscal Affairs had declared in November 1997 that the classification of a good or service should not depend on whether it was distributed electronically or physically.

Canada, Australia, and Japan have also issued reports dealing with the taxation of electronic commerce, and each agrees with the basic principle that the taxation of electronic commerce should be neutral with respect to physical transactions. Each concluded that further studies are necessary to deal with tax avoidance, jurisdiction, and administrative issues such as withholding and auditability. The Canadian report also states that "new or additional taxes [on electronic commerce] would not serve to capture additional tax revenue for the country. Rather they would remove the incentive for corporations to continue doing business in Canada . . . affecting employment and hindering the development of electronic commerce initiatives."[28] While rejecting new taxes such as a bit tax, the Canadian report expressed concern about the potential loss of tax revenues and called for efforts to deal with such questions as jurisdiction, nonreporting of taxes, withholding, and transfer pricing. Canada, like the United States and the EU, called for international cooperation, especially within the OECD.

The OECD's approach to electronic-commerce taxation was summed up by Secretary-General Donald J. Johnston in a 1998 London speech: "the OECD does not have proposals for tax free electronic commerce nor for 'bit' taxes or any other special taxes, just an assurance that the existing tax principles will be applied, no more, no less."[29] Jeffrey Owens, head of fiscal affairs for the OECD, supplemented these remarks: "We believe existing taxation rules can be applied to this new form of doing business. We consider it an attractive base for tax authorities, but we want to make sure electronic commerce develops and that this [tax] doesn't act as a barrier."[30]

With these basic objectives in mind, the OECD's Committee on Fiscal Affairs is examining a number of key tax issues from an international standpoint:

1. What is the impact of electronic commerce on traditional source and residency concepts in international taxation? How should the concept of permanent establishment be applied to electronic commerce?
2. How can income from electronic transfers of technology be classified? Is it business profit or royalties, and is there an erosion of source taxation?
3. Does electronic commerce change established principles for transfer taxing or change the structures of multinational enterprises in ways that affect intercompany transactions?
4. How does electronic commerce affect the concept of the VAT? Is there a need to change the definitions of goods and services, as goods lose their physical identity, or to change the place of supply and place of establishment rules to prevent avoidance of the VAT?
5. Are tax administration rules and procedures adequate to deal with electronic commerce or will there be compliance difficulties or opportunities created for fraud that will require new compliance techniques?

On the whole, the private sector supports the direction of electronic-commerce tax policy being pursued by governments and international organizations like the OECD. High-technology trade associations in the United States and abroad have expressed their opposition to new taxes on electronic commerce while calling for equal tax treatment for electronic commerce with traditional transactions. For example, the Computer Systems Policy Project (CSPP), an organization of U.S. computer systems companies, has favored tax neutrality for electronic commerce and "believes it is critical to develop a broad domestic and international consensus on neutral tax methodologies."[31] The CSPP lobbied in favor of the state tax moratorium in the United States and is supporting international efforts such as the OECD's.

The International Information Industry Congress (IIIC), an organization of the major high-technology trade associations from the United States, Europe, Japan, Canada, Brazil, Australia, and elsewhere, has issued a paper that also calls for tax neutrality for electronic commerce and the application of existing tax rules with six aims: be consistent with the principles of international taxation; be neutral with regard to other forms of commerce; be consistent across tax jurisdictions; avoid double taxation; minimize compliance costs; and be simpler to administer and easier to understand."[32]

It is clear that individual governments and the international community have a great deal of work to do on the details of taxation. But it is also clear that they are already in fundamental agreement on numerous basic points that provide a blueprint for both national and international action:

- Electronic commerce is a driver of economic growth and has the potential to generate substantial tax revenues.
- Premature passage of new taxes on electronic commerce at different levels of government could create a chaotic tax regime, retard the growth of the Net, and limit its economic benefits.
- Existing tax laws and regulations, at both the national and international levels, can and are being applied to electronic commerce transactions. A totally new tax system does not need to be invented.
- Taxes applied to electronic commerce should be neutral from a technology standpoint—that is, electronic transactions should be taxed in the same way as physical transactions, with no advantage or disadvantage. Additionally, double taxation of electronic commerce must be avoided where different jurisdictions are involved in transactions, particularly at the international level.
- Although tax jurisdiction and classification involve a number of new issues in electronic commerce, the answers can, for most part, be found in existing tax law. Where they are not, as in issues involving the precise definitions of residency and permanent establishment, or the application of the VAT, national and international agreements are needed to deal with the issue.
- In the United States, state governments and other tax jurisdictions must work over time to create nationally applicable rules for sales and income taxes to be collected on the Net. Failure to do so within a reasonable period will begin to distort the deployment and use of electronic commerce, favoring some regions and disadvantaging others, and forcing business to make decisions based on tax policies.
- National and international studies and agreements are also needed to resolve the issues involved in tax administration and compliance, including record-keeping, withholding, reporting, disintermediation, and verification.
- Internationally, the OECD should remain the principal organization dealing with the tax issue. In addition to promoting the principles listed above, it must also seek a tax system that is both certain and transparent to all participants. The OECD can also play a role in helping developing countries deal with taxes, perhaps with the help of the United Nations agencies.

How to tax electronic commerce is a difficult issue, and one for which tax attorneys will undoubtedly bill hundreds of thousands of hours to clients all over the world. But it is first and foremost a complex technical issue that requires not a great deal of new invention but a lot of technical tinkering and engineering—divorced to the greatest extent possible from political concerns.

INTERNATIONAL TRADE

The electronic marketplace has . . . a global rather than a national or regional dimension. . . . This reality means that governments are being pushed to work together, plan together, and pool their efforts as never before. . . . [N]o country, developing or developed, has an interest in building walls against technology or investment flows from outside—flows that will determine whether it is equipped to participate in the new global economy, or is left behind. This represents a sea-change in the global trading system.

—Renato Ruggerio, former WTO director-general[33]

Traditionally, trade issues divided nations as they sought to protect their own economic bases and the local industries on which they rested. Whether the issue was the exploitation of natural resources or the protection of manufacturing industries, protective tariffs and nontariff barriers were the principal tools that governments used to shelter their workers and industrialists.

Since the end of World War II, the vector of international trade policy has been in the direction of free trade, as countries warily tested out the notion that trade was not a zero-sum game, and that tariff-lowering exercises would result in regional and global economic growth. The free-trade proposition proved itself, far beyond most people's expectations. But even as it succeeded, not only within regions that dismantled protectionist systems, such as the EU, but also on a global basis, powerful protectionist forces have continued to fight holding actions. The emergence of the Net and electronic commerce gives a strong boost to globalization and the free-traders and deals a body blow to the protectionists.

A substantial part of the trade agenda of the world's leading economies now deals with the Net. Why? In the words of the office of the U.S. Trade Representative, "The growth of the Internet brings with it new jobs, and better paying jobs. In the United States, in 1996, 7.4 million people worked in information technology industries and in information technology-related occupations. The positive effect on jobs is particularly apparent in the software and services industries, in which employment doubled to 1.2

million with an average annual wage of $56,000; employment in these industries is expected to double again by 2002."[34]

Similarly, Stefano Micossi, director-general of internal market for the EU, has said, "We are beginning to think of electronic commerce as the third pillar of the European Union, along with the euro and the internal market."[35] Although these statements should not be interpreted as saying that there are no important disputes about the implementation of electronic commerce, it is a fact that national, regional, and global trade agendas are increasingly preoccupied with the future of the digital age. It is high on the trade programs of regional groups such as the EU and APEC, and of the key international trade organizations, including the WTO and the OECD.

The digital trade agenda is a broad one that includes issues ranging from privacy to intellectual property and standards. Many of these issues are covered in other sections of this book; this section will deal with issues of tariffs and nontariff barriers.

Today, the U.S. Trade Representative lists five specific trade objectives for electronic commerce: to create a tariff-free zone for the Internet, to make electronic commerce a seamless global marketplace, to oppose the creation by foreign governments of nontariff trade barriers, to eliminate barriers to access to advanced communications services, and to address issues of consumer confidence in electronic commerce. This section will focus on the first of these proposals, that for a duty-free Internet, and on the negotiations on the General Agreement on Trade in Services (GATS). It will also cover the International Technology Agreement, which is eliminating tariffs altogether on most high-technology products, the building blocks and plumbing of the Net. A fourth subject, the Agreement on Basic Telecommunications, is also quite important; it will be discussed in Chapter 7, which focuses on telecommunications.

The International Technology Agreement began as a gleam in the eyes of a number of high-technology companies in the early 1990s. Tariffs on high-technology products had come down during the preceding decades, but the systems of tariff rates and classification in place were complex and becoming increasingly unworkable. The result was not only a high annual customs bill for the global high-technology industry but an administrative nightmare that was becoming worse. A Digital Equipment Corporation executive told a subcommittee of the U.S. House Ways and Means Committee, "The fact is, our industry is now in an information revolution. . . . What this means is that the products and innovations that emerge from this revolution are utilizing the same digital technology to perform multiple functions within single units, using as just one example a laptop computer that can simultaneously serve as a fax machine, telephone, television, radio, and video machine, all while the user is typing a letter or cranking out numbers on a spreadsheet. These are all digital functions." He went on to point out that "the worst-case scenario could foresee an ambitious Customs official . . . classifying a wide range of products into some high-tariff category."[36] The obvious answer was to eliminate tariffs altogether and remove not only the duties themselves but also the administrative burdens. Tariff elimination would also remove the opportunities for official customs mischief, such as the dubious reclassification of certain products to yield higher tariffs.

By 1995, as the growth of the Net and its importance to national economies began to become apparent, a broad private- and public-sector coalition had formed with the leadership of the Information Technology Industry Council. There was strong backing for an agreement that would eliminate duties altogether on computer hardware, semiconductors, semiconductor manufacturing equipment, computer and telecommunications software, telecommunications equipment, and parts and components for each of these categories. One important fact that bolstered this advocacy was that the world's top five exporters of information-technology products were also the top five importers—the United States, Japan, Singapore, the United Kingdom, and Germany.

In January 1995, the information technology associations of the United States, Japan, and Europe, and a few months later, Canada, agreed that "to achieve market access necessary to build the GII, all tariffs affecting information technology and telecommunications technology products and components, including semiconductors, must be eliminated."[37] The duty-free project took the name of the International Technology Agreement (ITA).

Later that year, in November, more than 120 American and European business leaders attending the Transatlantic Business Dialogue in Seville, Spain, also advocated the zero-tariff plan, which was endorsed jointly the following month by the governments of the United States and the EU. The Japanese government, as a major exporter of high-technology goods, also joined in agreement. Even smaller countries who were net importers of equipment and would lose tariff revenues, had begun to see the importance of electronic commerce and to understand how its underlying infrastructure could be made less expensive for use by their own industries through the elimination of duties.

Despite a number of negotiating difficulties, including a last-minute attempt by the EU to link the ITA to the unrelated U.S.-Japan semiconductor agreement, the ITA was signed at the WTO ministerial meeting in Singapore in December 1996. Twenty-eight countries signed, representing more than 80 percent of world trade in the covered high-technology products. By March 1997, an additional fourteen nations had signed, raising the total covered to more than 90 percent. The signatories agreed to eliminate duties by January 1, 2000, on the long list of approved products, which included virtually all of those originally envisioned. Significantly, television receivers were not included, mostly because of opposition from European television set manufacturers. This would soon cause a problem, when customs inspectors in the United Kingdom attempted to reclassify personal computers with multimedia capacity as television sets, proof that the earlier "worst-case scenario" nightmares described by the computer industry had been justified.

With the ITA in hand, the industry moved to expand its coverage to more products, an objective the U.S. government accepted. Among the new objectives for expansion of the ITA were the acceleration of duty elimination; the addition of certain products to the agreement, including such items as instruments, control mechanisms, some laser products, and manufacturing equipment; and agreement on some standards and testing issues. The list also included duty-free treatment for content delivered over the Internet.

The effort of the United States formally to seek, or reaffirm, duty-free treatment for Internet-delivered goods and services began in July 1997 with President Clinton's directive to the U.S. Trade Representative to "secure agreement within the next 12 months that all products and services delivered across the Internet not be subject to tariffs."[38] The president's Framework for Global Electronic Commerce, issued that same day, had also expressed concern that the duty-free principle should be established quickly, before other nations, at the urging of local vested interests, attempted to impose tariffs. (The president's directive also called for other trade measures, including expansion of the ITA, and removal of other barriers in the areas of standards and testing and access to local markets.)

After a study to determine that no precedents existed in WTO countries for placing tariffs on electronic transactions, the United States made its formal proposal to the WTO members on February 6, 1998: "Currently no Member of the WTO considers electronic transmission as importations for customs duties and, thus, no member imposes customs duties on them. The United States delegation would like to inscribe on the agenda of the General Council the proposal that WTO Members should agree to continue this current practice so that the absence of customs duties on electronic transmission would remain."[39]

By framing the proposal as mere recognition of current practice, the U.S. delegation hoped to avoid opening a larger debate about other aspects of electronic commerce. As U.S. Ambassador Rita Hayes said in her presentation to the WTO General Council, "an agreement regarding our customs duty practices does not set a precedent for our practices in other areas, such as taxes or regulation."[40] She went on to point out that not only were there currently no customs duties on any electronic transmissions, including telephone calls, faxes, or data transmissions, but that there was not even a tariff classification for them. She said that there was much work for the WTO to undertake on trade matters in electronic commerce, and that this positive action would be a good way to begin such a work program.

The U.S. effort was successful, and at the ministerial conference of the WTO in May 1998, the ministers declared that "Members will continue their current practice of not imposing customs duties on electronic transmissions."[41] The ministers also agreed to begin a work program on electronic commerce. By stating that the duty-free commitment was made "without prejudice to the outcome of the work program," the ministers hedged their bets.

The overall work program agreed to by the WTO General Council included a number of important future steps:

1. *Services:* A review of market access and nondiscriminatory treatment for network, content, and information-services providers, as well as a review of the GATS negotiations in considering package-delivery services—an item key to electronic commerce.
2. *Goods:* A review of using electronic commerce to facilitate customs transactions, to comply with government health, safety, and consumer protection standards and to enhance opportunities for small and medium-sized businesses, particularly in developing countries.
3. *Government procurement:* An agreement to use electronic commerce to streamline the administrative provision of the Government Procurement Agreement (which committed countries to open government contracts to foreign suppliers) and to open-bid opportunities.
4. *Trade and development:* An agreement to use electronic commerce to help developing nations participate in trade negotiations and meet their implementation commitments.

The first results of the work program appeared in July 1998, when the WTO Secretariat reported that the GATS covered electronic services transactions: "The Agreement makes no distinction between the different technological means by which a service may be delivered—whether in person, by mail, by telephone or across the Internet."[42] This meant that a company supplying financial services across a border would have the same rights to do so electronically as it would physically. However, the Secretariat suggested further study of the question of the supply of Internet access services. At an information-technology symposium at the WTO in Geneva on July 16, 1999, many national delegations expressed support for electronic-commerce trade liberalization.

Electronic commerce was also on the agenda of the WTO ministerial meeting in Seattle in November 1999, where members considered an extension of the duty moratorium and the work program, as well as debated the classification of digital products as goods or services. Little was accomplished in Seattle, however, because of riots and demonstrations by protesters.

In addition to the WTO's electronic-commerce work program, complementary efforts are under way in a number of other trade groups. The OECD is looking at electronic-commerce trade statistics and an analysis of goods and services actually supplied over the Internet. It is also holding workshops for developing countries. Both the World Bank and the United Nations Commission on Trade and Development are also working on trade issues for developing nations.

Regional groups are also at work. The Free Trade Areas of the Americas has established an "expert committee" to look at the impact of electronic commerce on trade obligations as well as study the environment for and the benefits to be derived from electronic commerce. APEC is also examining a variety of trade issues, including how to expand infrastructure and how to provide assistance for small and medium-sized enterprises.

In sum, excellent progress has been made by governments, with important leadership by the United States, to deal with the trade issues created by the Net. Among the key tasks remaining are to include in the ITA all the products used in constructing the Net by completing a second ITA agreement and, under the framework of the GATS agreement and through other arrangements, to clarify the status of services provided in electronic commerce. These include such issues as the rights of access for Internet service providers and information providers and dealing with problems remaining in the electronic provision of other services such as banking, insurance, and package delivery. Beyond these pure trade issues are many other international issues; chief among them are the global regulatory schemes for telecommunications, which is one of the topics of Chapter 7.

ANTITRUST AND COMPETITION

As the internal economics of the Net begin to stabilize and be better understood, economists will be better able to measure their characteristics and their external effects—on productivity, economic growth, employment, and international trade. This understanding will help to resolve issues like taxation and international trade rules. Other economic issues will become more important: first among them will be competition policy and antitrust regulation, for a variety of reasons.

For one thing, as regulation in areas like telecommunications fades, governments will find it necessary to use antitrust law increasingly as the tool of choice to control excesses in the industry. For another, it is clear that monopolies or near-monopolies will appear from time to time as companies develop "killer" products that become standards and dominate the industry or a sector of it. Determining whether firms with monopoly power abuse their position with unfair commercial practices will become a major government activity. The outlines of the emergence of major antitrust wars can be seen already in a number of cases.

The Department of Justice case against Microsoft is the most prominent of ongoing cases and is an early and critical test of how the antitrust laws apply in the high-technology world of intellectual property rights, globalization, new and relatively undefined markets, rapid innovation, and de facto standards. After persistent complaints from a number of competitors, the Department of Justice charged the company with illegal monopolization. Spurning opportunities to settle the case on what would later appear to have been favorable terms for Microsoft, the company chose to fight in court, where the depositions of Chairman Bill Gates, in particular, appeared arrogant and conveyed a sense that mere government rules had no place in the world of high technology. Meanwhile, the EU announced a similar inquiry into Microsoft's behavior.

Federal judge Thomas Penfield Jackson in late 1999 ruled that Microsoft was a monopoly that had used its market power illegally to coerce its customers, and that it had harmed both competitors and consumers. In May 2000, the Department of Justice, joined by the attorneys general of nineteen states, presented its view to Judge Jackson that the appropriate remedy for the company's actions was to split Microsoft into two companies: one for operating systems and one for applications. Each of the new companies would also face a period of restrictions on its ability to enter the other's markets. Judge Jackson ruled that Microsoft had violated the antitrust laws and accepted the Justice Department's recommendation that it should be split into two companies. The case is now on appeal to the Supreme Court.

Although the final outcome of the case is likely to remain unresolved for some time while it is appealed, the case has already offered some lessons. In comparison with the earlier, more than decade-long antitrust case against IBM, the Microsoft case showed that antitrust issues could be handled in court in a reasonable amount of time. Judge Jackson seemed to have learned well the lessons of the IBM case. Observers could also infer from the case that companies that achieve monopolies through innovation, whose products become a de facto standard because of their universal appeal to consumers, will not face prosecution under antitrust laws, but those who use their market power illegally, as Microsoft had, will be subject to penalty. This was an important message, since standardization, including standards based on the ownership of intellectual property rights, is a key ingredient of the Net.

More difficult to perceive from the Microsoft case was exactly how consumers had been harmed. Although innovations ranging from Netscape's Navigator browser to Novell's applications had been negatively affected by Microsoft's conduct, no one can know exactly what the market might have produced in the way of invention and pricing advantages if Microsoft had obeyed the law.

The case also left unanswered questions about public opinion. Earlier monopolists such as John D. Rockefeller and J. P. Morgan were disliked by the public. Bill Gates was not, and the public climate in Washington reflected that. Republican members of Congress defended the company and President Clinton welcomed Gates to the White House only a few days after the company's loss in court. One could not have imagined Theodore Roosevelt welcoming the steel trust or sugar barons.

The remedy proposed by Assistant Attorney General Joel Klein nevertheless appeared to be the right one. To do nothing would be to accept illegal conduct. To place a series of permanent restrictions and limitations on Microsoft would lead to complex regulation and never-ending squabbles about the implementation of the remedies. A breakup would be a relatively clean solution, allowing Microsoft's shareholders ultimately to recover their investments, and introducing two eager new participants in the marketplace.

The ultimate effect of the case itself on the broader industry and of the remedies imposed by Jackson on Microsoft may not be known for years. Rapid market and technology changes will also blur the effects of the case. Moreover, the matter is already spilling over into the international arena; the EU competition authorities and numerous private firms have expressed interest in filing their own claims against Microsoft.

Another key competition issue involves the "convergence" mergers and the issues they raise. The largest so far is the pending supermerger between America Online (AOL) and Time Warner, which would create a company worth more than $150 billion and bring together the worlds of the Internet, content provision, and cable. Microsoft has already pointed out that the deal will put it at a disadvantage in the area of providing access to broadband services. Many observers expect Microsoft to counter the merger, if it is approved, by moving closer to AT&T, whose earlier mergers with TCI and MediaOne Group were worth more than $110 million and made AT&T the largest cable operator in the United States. Both giants were expected to offer comprehensive services to users, including telephone, cable, and Internet access along with other content and service offerings. One immediate policy shift resulting from the AOL–Time Warner deal was AOL's sudden dropping of its call for open access to AT&T's cable services.

In July 2000, the Department of Justice surprised Wall Street by blocking the proposed merger of Sprint with MCI WorldCom. Although it had already approved a long string of giant telecommunications mergers, the department appeared to be signaling a new concern about concentration.

Other key mergers in the Net world included the merger of Britain's Vodafone Airtouch with Germany's Mannesmann, linking a communications company with a content provider; that of SBC Communications with Ameritech; and that of Bell Atlantic with GTE. Each of these mergers has received scrutiny not only from the Department of Justice, the Federal Trade Commission, and, in some cases, the Federal Communications Commission, but also from the competition authorities of the European Union in Brussels and those in other countries.

In fact, interest in antitrust is growing worldwide. More than eighty nations now have antitrust laws, many passed in the last decade. The United Kingdom's new Competition Act, for example, went into effect in March 2000, the first reform of Britain's competition policies in a quarter-century. Stephen Byers, U.K. secretary of state for trade and industry, speaking of electronic commerce and globalization, said, "In the new economy, we need strong competition, enforced by a tough but intelligent competition regime."[43]

As more disputes over competition arise from issues of both conduct and mergers, and as the regulatory solutions recede, the courts and the government will have to become more involved. These issues involve complex technical issues, and with the exception of Jackson's conduct of the Microsoft case, courts have been notoriously slow in resolving them, a fatal offense in an industry where companies and technologies rise and fall with lightning speed. Moreover, the industries involved are global, making it even more difficult to measure and control them.

In addition, as the Microsoft case illustrates, prices have continued to fall in most high-technology arenas, and consumers appear to have benefited overall. It is always difficult to prove how consumers might have benefited in an alternative but more competitive universe. Aspiring monopolies can point out that the biggest networks are the most efficient and bring the most benefits to consumers. They can also point to the low entry barriers to new companies in the industry and to the need for cooperation and alliances among companies. Indeed, Congress relaxed the antitrust laws in 1993 to permit joint research and production efforts. Nonetheless, while digital combinations such as the new "B2B" online markets should lower costs and therefore, prices, regulators are already scrutinizing such deals as the automobile industry online parts exchange.

Nevertheless, economists, government officials, the courts, and the antitrust bar should prepare themselves for new waves of cases. In a 1999 speech, Robert Pitofsky, chair of the Federal Trade Commission said, "Prior application in the antitrust laws to high-tech industries raises some of the most challenging questions that we have seen in a long time. As with any adjustment to new facts or proposed law, a cautious approach is called for. But abandoning antitrust principles in this growing and increasingly important sector of the economy seems like the wrong direction to go."[44] Finally, economic measurements generally and worldwide need to be developed and improved by economists and adopted by governments. Wise economic policies rest on sound data.

As the Net continues to expand around the globe, Metcalfe's Law, also known as the law of network effects, may exert the most important economic impact. This law states that each time an individual user connects to a network, that economic value is created exponentially. With the price and performance of Net components falling dramatically, and bandwidth and other advanced functions just beginning to come on line, we are still in the Net's economic infancy. What economic benefits its adolescence may bring, we can only now guess. But we can be sure that they will be accompanied by new and difficult economic policy issues.

7

Physical and Technical Infrastructure

Commission law has been tried. Not just in the telecosm but in command and control economies around the globe. Like communism, Commission law has failed. . . . Markets constantly probe new technology, try out new forms of supply, and assess demand with a determination, precision and persistence that no commission can ever match.

—Peter Huber, *Law and Disorder in Cyberspace*[1]

Two great and inexorable trends are shaping the future of the Net's physical form and the role that governments around the world are playing in its development. One trend, like a universe collapsing, is the convergence of all the media and their supporting industries—local and long-distance telephone, cable and broadcast television, and Internet access and services—into a single digital phenomenon. The other, like a universe exploding, is the transformation of communications based on limiting physical resources, such as scarce spectrum, expensive telephone lines, and clumsy switches, into a microelectronic world of unlimited bandwidth, global communications pathways, and practically infinite information-storage capability.

Together, these two ferocious forces are tearing apart and rebuilding the companies and industries that have provided telephone, television, and other communications services for many years. Almost every day, new mergers—and often quick divorces—are announced—between software companies, long-distance carriers, "Baby Bells," cable giants, cellular telephone firms, and television broadcasters. The players range from giants such as AT&T, AOL, Time Warner, and Bell Atlantic to tiny software and network startups looking for a serendipitous link to give them a leg up in today's supercharged communications and information marketplace.

If these forces are restructuring industry, they are having at least as great an effect on government regulators. Born with the introduction and the early deployment of telephones around the turn of the last century, the regulation of communications was based on the notion that telephony was a natural monopoly, with a need for only one twisted pair of wires to each home. Later, broadcast radio and television and, still later, cable were seen as separate entities, but also as oligopolistic, and thus were also regulated. Governments of most other countries went further than did the United States, keeping for themselves the ownership and provision of communications services.

By the mid-1980s, however, the technological storms had also begun to spawn political and regulatory ones. What was once a "natural monopoly" now seemed quite unnatural, and a great wave of liberalization and deregulation began. The Telecommunications Act of 1996 in the United States, the liberalization of telecommunications in the European Union (EU) in January 1998, and the 1997 signing of the Global Agreement on Basic Telecommunications by the nations of the World Trade Organization (WTO), began to revolutionize the legal basis for regulatory structures. The purpose of each of these steps was to replace regulation with competition; the actual reality of each was quite different and more complex, and would take years if not decades in some countries to produce results. The combination of evolving technology and the outcome of the regulatory wars would largely determine the physical and technical form of the Net.

But other factors besides regulatory changes were at work. If the security, reliability, and integrity of the network had been a priority for the older, switched telephone system, it was even more important for the new infrastructure. For one thing, many of society's most important institutions, including those in government and banking, would depend on the constant accessibility and perfect reliability of this new infrastructure. For another, the millions of consumers who would use electronic commerce would want a high level of security for their transactions to protect their personal privacy as well as the security of their data. A number of network outages, reports of network congestion, and well-publicized security breaches raised a number of questions that led to the formation of a presidential commission in the United States. In mid-2000, the virus known as "I love you" had infected thousands of computers around the world, caused more than $6 billion in damages, and greatly escalated security concerns.

The search for security also led the private sector into a major clash with government, particularly in the United States. Cryptography, the science of encoding and decoding information, had become the principal tool for providing security for communications and transactions over the Internet, as well as performing other key functions. Unfortunately, its widespread use made it much more difficult, and impossible in some cases, for law enforcement and national security officials to intercept communications between criminals and terrorists and to uncover physical evidence of crimes. Government thus tried to restrict the use of cryptography, producing a serious clash between the high-technology industry and the civil liberties community on the one hand, and the national law enforcement and national security communities on the other.

A final, critical issue affecting the future technical form of the digital infrastructure is the question of standards. Since the value of a network grows exponentially with the number of people who can access and use it, the ability of everyone to be interconnected and for various networks and devices to be interoperable is key. With companies all vying to establish the standard and thereby their own dominance, universal interoperability is no easy task. It is further complicated by the fact that nations and even regional organizations, such as the EU, recognize that standards are critical to national leadership in cyberspace. As a result, government policies designed to set standards or at least to establish favorable terms and conditions to benefit their own country have created further difficulties.

This chapter, therefore, examines the three relatively technical issues of telecommunications regulation, security, and standards, and discusses how their resolution at both national and international levels will affect the future information infrastructure.

TELECOMMUNICATIONS POLICY

To tens of millions of Americans who grew up in the roughly seven decades between 1913 and 1982, there was but one great private American telephone company. Its Wall Street symbol was the letter "T" and its financial endurance, through dozens of economic cycles, made it America's favorite stock. Its reputation for customer service and its broad commitment to ethical business dealings enhanced its popularity. Its unique partnership with government as the world's largest regulated monopoly moderated its growth somewhat but preserved its profitability and its business health. The history and evolution of the American Telephone and Telegraph Company, or AT&T, from a regulated "natural" monopoly into a modern digital age communications competitor is a metaphor for the shifting plates of the massive telecommunications industry in the era of the Internet.

The Pivotal AT&T

Although AT&T was founded in 1885, its modern origins, and the origins of the long-lived system of telephone regulation in the United States, were contained in an obscure and legalistic 1913 letter from one of its vice presidents, N. C. Kingsbury, to President Woodrow Wilson's attorney general, James C. McReynolds. The 1913 Kingsbury "commitment," as it came to be known, created the regulated monopoly telephone system that proved so resilient, and ultimately so difficult to change. As one commentary states, "The letter delineated the parameters for a privately financed and owned monopoly for telephony that would be acceptable to both political parties and sellable to the electorate—a de facto monopoly, if not in law, in exchange for AT&T's best efforts to provide universal, affordable service (for the urban population at least), with progressive improvements in service and technical proficiency."[2]

The letter had its own origins in the era of cutthroat competition that was crippling the young AT&T during the height of the Progressive Era. After the expiration of the original Bell telephone patents, which AT&T had purchased, in the mid-1890s, the company encountered fierce competition from numerous local competitors. Many cities had duplicative and wasteful competing telephone systems, and predatory business practices and occasionally even violence directed at competitors were not uncommon. At the same time, monopolies in a variety of industries were under attack from President Theodore Roosevelt and the Progressives, who used the new Sherman Antitrust Act of 1890 to battle what they saw as monoliths that strangled the American consumer. Outright nationalization of the telephone system was a possibility. By 1909, AT&T was under legal attack by competitors and the subject of an investigation by the Department of Justice.

If AT&T had fought these legal attacks through the courts, while keeping up the pressure on competitors, as other industries had done, the future world of telephony would have been altered significantly. But Theodore Vail, the visionary chair of AT&T's board of directors, decided to strike a bold deal with the government. He offered to submit the company to regulation and to provide universal service in exchange for remaining private and, implicitly, avoiding further investigation and prosecution. It was an innovative suggestion, and one that appealed to the new Democratic administration in Washington. It was also not inevitable.

Although the United States, in contrast with Europe, had historically avoided government ownership of key industries (with occasional exceptions), it had also been quite suspicious of regulation. James Madison had written in the Federalist Papers that "[e]very new regulation concerning commerce or revenue, or in a manner affecting the value of the different species of property, presents a new harvest to those who watch the change, and can trace it to its consequences; a harvest reaped not by themselves but by the toils and cares of the great body of their fellow citizens."[3] In the case of telephony, Madison's words would ring true for decades, as telephone company officials, government regulators, communications lawyers, and lobbyists all built careers and sometimes fortunes on the complex ins and outs of communications regulation.

For the first two decades after 1913, AT&T was regulated by the Interstate Commerce Commission (ICC) and by the states. The ICC's priorities lay clearly with the nation's growing transportation system, and it allowed AT&T to operate relatively freely, within the confines of the Kingsbury commitment, which kept AT&T out of the territory of its competitors and allowed them to connect with AT&T's long-distance facilities. But with the coming of the Franklin Roosevelt administration and the New Deal in 1933, the need for a more effective regulator of telephony and the new radio broadcasting industry was recognized, and the 1934 Communications Act established the Federal Communications Commission (FCC). In this early manifestation of convergence, both wired and wireless communications were brought under the same regulator, and the notion of "common carriage" was established. For telephony, AT&T's Long Lines organization provided both interstate and intrastate long-distance service, the Bell Telephone operating companies provided local service, Western Electric manufactured the equipment, and Bell Telephone Laboratories did the research and development.

With a few bumps in the road, the system worked extremely well for many years. Bell Labs became the nation's foremost private research laboratory, inventing the transistor and the communications satellite; Western Electric equipment was known for its reliability, if not its diversity; and the Bell Telephone companies enjoyed a sound reputation for service. AT&T and Western Electric also became one of the nation's foremost defense contractors, contributing significantly to the technologies of Cold War defense systems and even collaborating with the International Business Machines Corporation (IBM) on an early example of convergence—the SAGE early-warning radar system deployed on the nation's far northern borders. Bell system companies also became well known for civic involvement, firmly enmeshing themselves and their executives in the political and social life of the nation.

But advancing technology and the corrosive effects of monopoly began to take their toll on the 1913 structure. By the 1950s and early 1960s, the computer industry took its place in the industrial pantheon, and as its mainframe computers began to communicate with each other, questions arose about the nature of common carriage. Microwave technology also advanced, and the FCC's Above 590 decision in 1959 opened a Pandora's box of new competition. In that decision, the FCC ruled that firms owning rights-of-way, such as railroads and pipeline companies, could provide their own microwave facilities for their own communications needs. Although they could not yet interconnect their systems with Bell's common carrier lines, the actions of these firms started an inexorable process of building telephony competition. New manufacturing firms arose to build microwave equipment, and in 1963, the tiny Microwave Communications, Inc. (MCI) applied to the FCC to build a microwave system between Chicago and St. Louis to serve business customers with specialized services. Despite bitter opposition from AT&T, the FCC approved the MCI plan in 1969, allowing it to become a "specialized common carrier." Today, of course, MCI WorldCom spans the globe.

While AT&T continued to fight to make it difficult or, for some, impossible for competing companies to interconnect with its network, the interconnection issue was taking other forms. To protect its network from harm (or at least that was the reason the company gave), AT&T forbade the interconnection of any device with its network (families who had installed illicit extra extensions in their homes nervously wondered if AT&T could detect them). This "no foreign attachment" policy was ultimately brought down by a humble device—a piece of plastic equipment that fit over a telephone mouthpiece, called the "Hush-A-Phone," that people working in noisy areas could use to make themselves heard. AT&T forbade its use. The Hush-A-Phone company took its case to court and won. Although the decision allowed only mechanical and not electrical devices to attach, it opened the floodgates for future decisions, since the Supreme Court raised dreaded antitrust issues in its decision.

Perhaps the greatest long-term challenge to AT&T came not from its new long-distance challengers or from firms beginning to sell equipment to interconnect with the network, but from another arena—the new computer industry. Under the terms of a 1956 consent decree in which AT&T had agreed to stay out of noncommunications businesses (even agreeing to divest itself of Western Electric's motion-picture-sound business), the company had not entered the nascent but growing computer business. This decision changed AT&T's destiny. Bell Laboratories had done pioneering work in computers and microelectronics; AT&T's future electronic switching systems would essentially be computers; and computers were playing a major role in running the massive Bell Telephone System—operating the network, keeping track of long-distance calls, and billing customers.

In 1966, in its own book *Business Information Systems,* the company said, "Computers, of course, are not new to the Bell system. We participated in both their development and the growth of their applications. For some time, computers and their associated equipment have been processing payrolls, rating tolls, billing customers and performing other functions."[4] Indeed, without the consent decree, AT&T might have been an early challenger to IBM, changing the future of both telephony and computing and perhaps bringing convergence much earlier.

In that same year, the FCC opened the first of three proceedings known as the Computer Inquiries, which were aimed at defining the boundaries between communications and common carriage on the one hand, and computing on the other. The commission wanted to know what it could regulate and what it could not, and what AT&T was permitted to do in the new world of data communications. Initially, in Computer Inquiry I, the FCC tried to distinguish between pure data communications, pure data processing, and so-called hybrid services where data might be transformed in some way during communications. But as soon as the FCC thought it had resolved the issue, technology quickly moved to moot its solutions, and it was left with complex problems relating to definitions of services, rates, subsidies, interconnection, and more. The Above 590 decision and Hush-A-Phone had raised early questions about the future of regulation, but the Computer Inquiries blew the issue wide open. The U.S. telecommunications regulatory system was looking more and more obsolete, but regulatory change was coming very slowly.

One of the most respected observers of this period, former regulator Henry Geller, noted, "One would look in vain at the 1934 Communications Act to find any vision of our telecommunications approach. . . . It is ludicrous that in the digital age, our policy is based upon a sixty-year-old act that is, in turn, based on an outmoded 1910 ICC approach, which is itself derived from the railroad situation at that time. For much too long, the United States has acted as if it had no vision of what should be done about the far-reaching technology and market changes now fully underway."[5] Geller knew of what he spoke; he had served as general counsel of the FCC from 1964 to 1970, and as assistant secretary of commerce for communications and information from 1971 to 1978.

As the FCC tinkered with the regulations and attempted to fit late-twentieth-century technology into a nineteenth-century regulatory model, other areas of the U.S. government began to notice the changes. In 1969, President Richard Nixon set up a White House Office of Telecommunications Policy (OTP) to take a broader look at the U.S. stake in this issue. In 1978, early in the presidency of Jimmy Carter, the OTP was replaced by the National Telecommunications and Information Administration (NTIA) in the Commerce Department. The Departments of Defense and State, as well as the U.S. Trade Representative, also became involved as the strategic and international implications of telecommunications and information policy became clearer. Congress also became a battleground, as AT&T sought to counter efforts to permit competition, as with the "Bell Bill" of 1976, and as its competitors sought to weaken it, as with the 1981 legislative battle over "enhanced services."

But it was the Department of Justice that was ultimately the major player and catalyst for change. Its 1974 antitrust case ended with the settlement of that case and the modified final judgment (MFJ) of federal district court judge Harold Greene. In 1982, AT&T agreed to divest itself of the Bell operating companies; the "Baby Bells" that were created would remain regulated incumbents for local service. AT&T kept its long-distance business, as well as Western Electric and Bell Labs. A few years later, Western Electric and Bell Laboratories would be spun off as well (with Western Electric morphing into the new Lucent Technologies). Judge Greene temporarily replaced the FCC as the telephony regulator, but he too would become overwhelmed by new technological and market changes—and burgeoning competitive forces that were about to flood the regulatory gates.

In the long-distance field, competition brought lower prices relatively quickly. From 1983 to 1989, the consumer price index for interstate telephone tolls dropped 9.8 percent per year.[6] This clear economic benefit made the argument for competition much more palatable for politicians. With AT&T suddenly on their side, the political muscle of the long-distance carriers seeking entry into the local telephone business increased dramatically. Technological and regulatory changes in other parts of the communications industry were also in the wind.

Cable companies were growing rapidly and in a state of regulatory flux. They were also seen as a potential source of competition in telecommunications, if their networks could be reengineered to operate competitively. Local telephone service competitors (known in telephony jargon as CLECs, or competitive local exchange carriers) were beginning to spring up to compete with the Baby Bells, particularly for business customers in the major cities. Large corporations were eager to build their own single networks to be used for both voice and data services. These increasingly global businesses were also combining their telecommunications and computing departments into a single operation and beginning to outsource these operations to companies like IBM, EDS, and Computer Associates. Electric utilities were installing fiber optic cables into every home to read electrical meters, and some saw the unused portion of that fiber—so-called dark fiber—as another potential source of telephone competition. Finally, the Baby Bells themselves were eager to break out of the legal straitjacket of the federal court judgment and enter businesses such as telephone-equipment manufacturing and long-distance service.

The Telecommunications Act of 1996

When the Clinton administration took office in 1993, as we have seen, a final element was added—the National Information Infrastructure (NII) initiative, the plan to build the "information superhighway." Among other things, it envisioned more competition in telecommunications to help jump-start the NII.

The result of all of this activity was the multiyear effort in Congress to amend the Communications Act of 1934 to open the system to more competition. After a long and bruising battle, Congress passed the Telecommunications Act of 1996. On the surface, it appeared to meet its objectives, and the early reviews were favorable. Congress was congratulated for its courage in overcoming the objections of lobbyists on all sides and passing the new law.

The Telecommunications Act did a number of things. It permitted the Baby Bells to enter long-distance, equipment manufacturing, and other businesses—but with many complicated legal conditions. It allowed the long-distance carriers to enter the local telephone business—but also with many conditions. It allowed the cable and utility industries to enter the local telephone markets. It defined the conditions for interconnection and established complex safeguards for competition. In other words, although the act paid homage to competition in the broadest ways, it also created a legal nightmare (or dream, for the communications lawyers who could anticipate billing thousands of hours). In its willingness to find a compromise between the opposing parties that would permit a bill to pass, Congress made the conditions for opening competition too complex. The new law gave so many openings to court actions that the long-distance companies might never be able to enter the local telephone business in a reasonable period of time, or vice versa.

Moreover, since Congress could not agree on, or did not understand, several key issues, it fudged them or left them unresolved. One was the issue of universal service and how it could be funded in a competitive environment. This issue was left to a commission and subsequent FCC action over a two-year period. The other issue was the status of advanced telecommunications services, such as broadband (like a wider pipe, it permits more information to be transmitted at a higher speed), voice, graphics, data, or video communications: the bill simply directed the FCC to "initiate a notice of inquiry, within thirty months after enactment." Thus, the FCC would have many years to worry about advanced telecommunications services, even as the number of Internet users was doubling every month.

Thus, the Telecommunications Act of 1996 had two major flaws. First, it was so complex that rather than reduce regulation, it actually increased the amount of FCC oversight and court activity. Second, like much government action, it focused on the wrong conflict and tried to solve the wrong problem. It was narrowly concerned with the relatively parochial fight between the local telephone companies and the long-distance carriers and overlooked the new information infrastructure and the Internet that would soon threaten the entire switched telephone system with obsolescence. It also left many new questions unanswered: Should Internet telephony be regulated in some manner? Should the exemption from access charges enjoyed by Internet service providers be eliminated? How could the need for new broadband services be met?

As a matter of fact, the Telecommunications Act mentioned the Internet only twice. One section was the amendment to keep obscenity off of the Internet—the Communications Decency Act. The other mentioned the need to connect schools to the Internet. As an official of the U.S. Telephone Association said in 1998, "The debate in 1995, when they originally did the act, was all about local telephone service vs. long distance. Now it's about Internet vs. telephony. This is the market responding to reality, and the public policy is 100 miles behind."[7]

The immediate result of the act was not the hoped-for competition between the Baby Bells and the long distance companies. In fact, by mid-2000 only one Bell operating company had won FCC approval to enter the long-distance market. Instead the act set off a feeding frenzy of mergers among the Baby Bells themselves (as between Bell Atlantic and Nynex) and between the long-distance carriers and both cable companies, such as TCI and MediaOne, and overseas carriers, such as British Telecomm. Other merger players were software companies, broadcasters, media companies, and Internet players such as America Online. The outcomes of these mergers and their benefits or lack thereof for consumers remains to be seen. But the regulation labyrinth remains a major impediment.

Meanwhile the needs of Internet users and electronic commerce were slow to be met. By 1999, the higher-bandwidth home telephone connections to the Internet (so-called digital subscriber lines, or DSLs) offered by local telephone companies were still rare and expensive. In contrast, and almost in spite of the Telecommunications Act, broadband cable connections were moving ahead more quickly: almost 750,000 cable modems were in use in 1999. While the Bell operating companies were busy fighting the long-distance companies in Congress, at the FCC, and in the courts, their cable competitors began to take the lead in advanced services.

As academicians W. Russell Neuman, Lee McKnight, and Richard J. Solomon point out in their book *The Gordian Knot,* "The Telecommunications Act of 1996 . . . contains more than 100 pages of detailed legal mandates and prohibitions in an ill-advised attempt to micromanage the transition to deregulation rather than cut the knot. The Act calls for more than 90 bureaucratic inquiries, evaluations and rulings by the FCC—which are likely to drag on for years. . . . The Act will only delay and distort the process unnecessarily."[8] This halfway effort, or partial liberalization, as Columbia University professor Eli Noam calls it, has slowed progress not only in the United States but in other nations that have tried it as well:

Deregulation does not necessarily lead to a diverse market. The result can be a deregulated monopoly or, conversely, a tightly regulated multicarrier system. The experiences in the United States and the United Kingdom, two of the most liberalized markets, reveal that more rather than less regulation emerged, at least initially after markets were opened. . . . Partial liberalization requires that interconnection arrangements be set, access charges determined, and a level playing field secured. In some cases, cross-subsidization from monopolistic to competitive services must be prevented. Under liberalization competitors may receive preferential treatment in order to protect competition in its infancy. All this leads to considerable regulatory complexity; no system is more lawyer intensive than partial liberalization.[9]

Noam, who wrote these words a year before the passage of the Telecommunications Act, was prophetic.

International Actions

Other countries, trying to achieve the same goals as the United States—more innovative services and lower prices for consumers—are following a similar path, some with more success, some with less. The United Kingdom moved to privatize and liberalize its telecommunications system before the United States and has been successful in lowering prices for consumers. Japan, Australia, New Zealand, and others have tried to follow. As of January 1998, the EU moved to liberalize telecommunications within all of its member countries, and has adopted rules similar to those in the United States.

But different countries have used different methods. According to Don Cruickshank, former director-general of the U.K Office of Telecommunications, which oversaw liberalization in the United Kingdom, "The U.K. has many competitive local exchange providers because it focused on pricing, not rules, to achieve competition."[10] Cruickshank believes that the United Kingdom's approach of eliminating price regulation, subsidies, access charges, and all restrictions on the scope of business and relying on competition or antitrust laws to restrain monopoly behavior brings about more rapid change than the U.S. system. Japan's experience with liberalization, however, has in some ways been like the United States's. In 1997, two of Japan's largest telecommunications companies, Japan Telecom and International Telecom Japan, a domestic and an international carrier, respectively, merged. NTT, the merged entity's primary competitor and the dominant company in the Japanese market, continues to enjoy a privileged position. Other countries are beginning to experiment with variants that fit their local needs.

In a worldwide effort, the nations of the World Trade Organization (WTO), after a decade of discussions and negotiations that began before the birth of the World Wide Web, concluded the Agreement on Basic Telecommunications. This agreement took so long to negotiate, in part, because the $600 billion size of the worldwide telecommunications industry made many nations cautious in their approach. But the main reason was government ownership in most parts of the world: "After decades of cartel- and monopoly-supplied telecommunications services (both domestic and international), it will take carefully crafted agreements to enable public telephone operators (PTOs) to make the transition to a competitive market. Some governments, as well as many PTOs, are fearful of losing revenues generated by monopoly systems. Many of the PTOs will therefore oppose this transition."[11] Many governments were afraid, not only of the loss of revenue, but of the loss of jobs that would result from competition: in many countries, the PTO was one of the largest employers in the country. Privatization would lead to trimming of the bloated public payrolls, and the politicians would be blamed.

Nevertheless, the agreement was concluded on February 17, 1997. In the end, governments recognized that the new technologies were rapidly making the old system obsolete, regardless of the regulators' actions. As economist Cynthia Belz pointed out, "Excessive regulation and artificially high international rates have created an engine of their own destruction. Technological innovations are giving consumers the power to bypass overpriced systems at the same time as bloated profit margins are attracting competition from entrepreneurial firms. Even before the WTO agreement was concluded, digital technologies and demanding consumers were tearing down market barriers, undermining monopolies once seen as unassailable, and forcing governments to open up."[12]

The Agreement on Basic Telecommunications gives foreign companies access to local telecommunications markets, permits investment by foreigners in national telecommunications companies, and perhaps most important, establishes a series of pro-competitive regulatory commitments in a legally binding Reference Paper. To quote U.S. Trade Representative Charlene Barshefsky, whose skilled team negotiated the agreement, "The Reference Paper commits foreign countries to establish independent regulatory bodies, guarantees that our companies will be able to interconnect with networks in foreign countries at fair prices, forbids anti-competitive practices such as cross-subsidization, and mandates transparency of government regulations and licensing."[13] Led by House Commerce Committee chair Thomas Bliley of Virginia and Senate Commerce Committee chair John McCain of Arizona, Congress gave bipartisan support to the agreement.

The Agreement was signed by 70 nations and covers more than 95 percent of the world's telecommunications revenues. Even though the liberalization principles in the Reference Paper may take years if not decades to find their way into national law and practice in many countries, their inclusion in the agreement creates an important international benchmark. It marks an extraordinary worldwide acceptance of the mutually reinforcing powers of technology and competition. With the digital age in its infancy, the remaining regulators and their political and industrial allies will face even more difficult and ultimately losing battles in the future.

Policy Goals

What should be our telecommunications policy goals for the future? Given the broadly accepted economic importance of electronic commerce, how can government policy work to meet individual consumer and business goals?

Consumer needs are well defined: inexpensive flat-rate pricing for home Internet access, more bandwidth for faster connections and advanced applications such as video, widespread access in public spaces such as schools and libraries, and endless mobility in the form of wireless connectivity. Business and institutional objectives also place emphasis on the availability of competitive services. In a study done by the *Economist* Intelligence Unit, more than half of the companies studied desired to derive a substantial portion of their "need [for] information technology functionality from the networks of competing service providers."[14] Most corporations, forced to compete themselves, understand well the role of competition in driving innovation and lowering prices.

The FCC also recognizes these goals. In its working paper "Digital Tornado: The Internet and Telecommunications Policy," the FCC articulated three policy goals:

1. Promote competition in voice, video, and interactive services;
2. Facilitate network investment and technological innovation; and
3. Allow all citizens to benefit from advanced technologies.

Having stated these goals, the paper goes on to decry the FCC's basic lack of authority to reach them: "The [Tele]Communications Act [of 1996] provides little direct guidance as to whether the Commission has authority to regulate Internet-based-services." Conversely, it continues, "nothing in the Act expressly limits the FCC's authority to regulate services and facilities connected with the Internet."[15] Not surprisingly, opposing forces are pushing the commission in both directions. The local exchange carriers, for example, have pressed the FCC to apply to Internet service providers (ISPs) the same access charges that the long-distance carriers pay. They have argued that this is necessary to pay for future investment in new lines and to relieve congestion on the telephone network they say is caused by heavy Internet usage.

The ISPs and their allies in the computer and software industries have argued the opposite case, pointing out that the Internet has actually created huge new revenues for local telephone companies in the form of second telephone lines that people use for home Internet connections. They also charge that the telephone companies are not investing in new technologies: "Because the ILECs' [incumbent local exchange carriers, i.e., the Baby Bells] networks were designed to carry voice traffic, they provide frustratingly slow connections to the World Wide Web, and are entirely inadequate for emerging multimedia applications. . . . The Internet Access Coalition believes that consumers must have access to high-bandwidth, "data-friendly" communications services. . . . The best means by which the [FCC] could achieve this goal is . . . to facilitate the entry of competitive providers."[16]

With no clear statutory guidance, even from the recent Telecommunications Act, and a murky regulatory record on the exact nature of ISPs, the FCC, while taking a general hands-off view of the Internet, has been somewhat ambiguous about its future direction. This has spurred some action from Congress, including a letter from Senator McCain and Representative Christopher Cox of California asking that the FCC "work with us on legislation to clarify the 1934 Communications Act to make it clear that the FCC will not regulate the Internet or impose access charges on Internet service."[17] Cox and McCain cited the "thousands of e-mails and phone calls from concerned Internet users." Clearly a new political force was shaping up that could eventually match the political muscle that the telephone companies had built with years of political contributions to key members of Congress.

Given the deadlock in the existing system, can anything be done to move more rapidly toward the new services that consumers and businesses want? A variety of proposals has been offered. Henry Geller favors "open entry and all-out competition," more deregulation, and allowing effective interconnection with existing carriers. But Geller still sees a need for "residual regulation for such things as interconnection, standardization rules, and targeted subsidies for the universal service concept."[18] Eli Noam believes that "systems integrators" will emerge that will package communications services for individuals as well as for businesses, providing a de facto resolution of many regulatory issues: "Today, systems integrators exist only for large customers. . . . The next step is for systems integrators to emerge that assemble individualized networks for personal use and offer them directly to end users. . . . Systems integrators, competing with one another for customers, will act as users' agents vis-à-vis carriers. The need for government intervention can be expected to decline substantially."[19] Under Noam's vision, a future monthly consumer communications and information bill might look like the following:

Global Info Corporation
Invoice: April 2005
For: A. Customer, universal comm. # *qxyz@glocomm*

Flat rate worldwide voice telephone:	$ 2.00
Flat rate multi-conference video:	8.00
Cable service: 680 channels:	10.00
Unlimited wireless Internet access:	6.00
Secure shopping service fee:	1.00
Bill presentation platform:	1.50
Special orders (6 events):	12.00
Music programming:	2.50
Universal Access Fee:	1.00
Total:	$44.00

Such bills will likely be characterized by lower rates, simplicity, comprehensiveness and a sharp reduction in telecommunications taxes. Nevertheless, both Geller and Noam believe that some residual telecommunications regulation is necessary.

The Progress and Freedom Foundation (PFF), in another twist on policy, has favored legislation "specifically eliminating any and all federal and state regulatory authority over any "advanced information service [including] the Internet, Internet access services, on-line services, information services [such as voice mail] . . . or any value-added services."[20] A bill to achieve this result was introduced in the Senate. The measure has been strongly opposed by the computer industry and ISPs for fear that the local telephone companies would be able to cross-subsidize their newly unregulated advanced services businesses with their still-regulated local telephone service business. Viewed this way, the PFF measure would be another half-step toward full competition.

A much more radical proposal has been made by Peter Huber, a senior fellow at the Manhattan Institute for Policy Research. Huber proposes abolishing the FCC altogether. He equates it with the central planning of communist states: "Commission law has been tried. . . . Like Communism, commission law has failed. It is rigid, slow, and—despite all the earnest expertise of bureaucrats—ignorant. Market forces, mediated by common law, elicit information faster and more reliably. Markets constantly probe new technology, try out new forms of supply, assess demand with a determination, precision and persistence that no commission can ever match."[21] Despite Huber's somewhat intemperate language, his proposal could be seen as a wake-up call to a world so changed by digital technology that a total break with the past must be considered. Perhaps we are so much prisoners of the past that we have difficulty seeing beyond the narrow confines of the regulatory box in which we are trapped.

Finally, in a variation of Huber's view, Neumann, McKnight and Solomon propose what may be the most interesting solution. They argue not for totally abolishing regulation, nor for lumbering on with residual regulations. Instead, they propose setting a date—a digital deadline—for complete deregulation based on the creation of an "open communications infrastructure" that would provide worldwide, interoperable access to any type of device, wired or wireless. They believe that the countdown of the clock would drive rapid competition and that the antitrust laws would replace FCC regulation to deal with bad actors and would-be monopolists. One weakness in their argument is that they leave such details as how to provide universal access to future policymakers.

Nevertheless, their argument—and Huber's—are convincing. Trying to maintain and even extend the FCC's outmoded telecommunications regulatory regime in the face of torrential technological change is like trying to stop an earthquake by sitting on a fault line. As most governments around the world have moved away from monopoly and toward deregulation, the United States could seize the moment and leave the nineteenth-century regulatory paradigm completely behind by working toward elimination of the FCC and as many of its regulations as possible. The necessary remainder could be folded into the NTIA and the NIST in the Commerce Department, with the Federal Trade Commission (FTC) overseeing consumer protection issues such as "slamming" and the Department of Justice overseeing issues of competition and monopoly.

The FCC itself recognizes how the digital age and the forces of technology, competition, and convergence are forcing it to change. In a five-year plan unveiled in May 2000 called "A New FCC for the 21st Century," the agency laid out four core functions: fostering competition, protecting consumers, managing the nation's airwaves, and promoting opportunities for everyone to benefit.[22] The first two functions are clearly responsibilities of the Department of Justice and the FTC; the third can be handled by the Commerce Department, and the last one should be a shared responsibility of the Departments of Commerce, Education, and Labor.

For example, the Department of Justice's antitrust case against AT&T brought sweeping change to the telecommunications industry—arguably a greater impact than any FCC action. In fact, as was asserted in Chapter 6, antitrust law is more suited to the digital age than is regulation in general. The Sherman Antitrust Act itself is short and simple, and its enforcement requires the Justice Department or the FTC to persuade a court that a company has violated the act's provisions—a procedure that assures less political intervention in the process than if an independent agency oversaw it. Moreover, the remedy can be relatively simple and clean: breakup of the offender rather than decades of complex regulatory procedures.

With U.S. leadership in abandoning regulation, the rest of the world will follow. As Frances Cairncross, senior editor of the *Economist,* says, "By the end of the century, few countries in the developed world will have a single monopoly telephone operator, a limited number of television channels, or serious restrictions on cable services. Ten years into the next century, communications will be much like any other industry: consumers will have won."[23]

SECURITY AND CRYPTOGRAPHY

[A]s the threat of nuclear war has diminished, new technologies have appeared that render physical geography less relevant and our domestic sanctuary less secure. Today, a computer can cause switches or valves to open and close, move funds from one account to another, or convey a military order almost as quickly over thousands of miles as it can from next door. . . . A false or malicious computer message can traverse multiple national borders, leaping from jurisdiction to jurisdiction to avoid identification, complicate lawful pursuit, or escape retribution.

—President's Commission on Critical Infrastructure Protection[24]

Although the issue of Net security has been under intense scrutiny by government at least since 1996, 2000 was the year in which the issue really exploded into the public consciousness. Beginning with the Y2K threat on January 1, with warnings from the Federal Bureau of Investigation (FBI) about related "piggy-back" attacks by cyber-terrorists; continuing with the "denial of service" hacker attacks in February, which overwhelmed many electronic-commerce Web sites; and culminating in the "I love you" virus in May that caused billions of dollars in damages to user files, the public began to wonder how vulnerable the Net was. The facts that the turning of the new year event passed virtually without incident and that the other events were over relatively quickly didn't dispel people's unease about the potential fragility of the new medium.

Perhaps the best indicator of the government's deep concerns about the security of the Net is the fact that the report of the President's Commission on Critical Infrastructure Protection was published almost a year before the President's Framework for Global Electronic Commerce. Ironically, neither document pays more than brief lip service to the central role that cryptography plays in protecting the security of information and transactions that pass over the networks of the global information infrastructure. Protect security, yes, the government seemed to be saying, but not too much security in the hands of individuals who might impede law-enforcement agencies or foreign-intelligence-gathering activities. This schizophrenia about cryptography is a leitmotif that runs throughout the subject of network security.

As the world's leading user of the Net, the United States is potentially the most vulnerable nation in terms of threats to its economic and governmental infrastructures. These threats are of three types: threats to national security in the form of cyber-military or terrorist attacks; threats to businesses and other institutions in the form of physical attacks or various forms of cyber-crime; and threats to individuals, such as loss of privacy or being targeted by cyber-thieves.

The President's Commission on Critical Infrastructure Protection was formed in 1996 to assess the potential new threat to the nation's infrastructure—and by implication to some of the nation's most important businesses and institutions—posed by the country's new dependence on networks. In part, the commission's work was stimulated by physical terrorist attacks against the U.S. military, the U.S. government, and the private sector, such as the bombing of the World Trade Center in New York City. But it was also driven by the convergence of the nation's key infrastructures—energy, banking and finance, information and communications, physical distribution, and vital human services—with the Net.

Recent developments in these sectors—some unrelated to technology—have created a new dependence on the Net. As the commission pointed out in one area, "Disparities in prices across the country are primarily responsible for the recent restructuring of the electric power industry and the natural gas industry. New information systems for electronic commerce, for data interchange and for improving operational efficiencies are now essential business elements of the energy infrastructure. . . . The reliability of electricity has become more critical to our nation's competitiveness and standard of living in the Information Age."[25] Thus, economic and social needs had made the nation's infrastructure more dependent on the Net. In turn, the Net, as it grew, was more dependent on the proper functioning of other infrastructures such as electricity, natural gas, physical distribution, and telecommunications. Critical sectors are more dependent on each other, and all are dependent on the information infrastructure. An attack on one could be an attack on all.

The commission's findings were sobering. In addition to the classical physical threats posed by natural events and accidents, blunders and errors, and insider sabotage by disgruntled employees, for example, it found new types of cyber-threats ranging from recreational hackers to cyber-criminals to outright cyber-terrorism, industrial espionage, and information warfare. In light of the revelations in the spring of 1999 regarding the alleged theft of U.S. nuclear secrets by China, sometimes by downloading information surreptitiously from government computers, the commission's work seemed right on target, if a bit late. In fact, a report written by two People's Liberation Army officers in China in 1999 singled out information warfare as an unconventional way to defeat the United States in a war.

The commission made a number of recommendations for action by both the private and public sectors. Its efforts also resulted in a number of new activities and organizations. In May 1998, President Clinton signed a new executive order, Presidential Decision Directive (PDD) 63, creating the National Infrastructure Protection Center. Housed within the FBI, the center would coordinate federal activities on infrastructure security, coordinate the federal response to incidents, and investigate attacks. In addition, a lead federal agency was assigned for each private-sector infrastructure, such as banking, to lessen vulnerability and deal with threats. Said the president, "Our economy is increasingly reliant upon interdependent and cyber-supported infrastructures and non-traditional attacks . . . may be capable of significantly harming both our military power and our economy. Any interruptions or manipulations of these critical functions must be brief, infrequent, manageable, geographically isolated and minimally detrimental to the welfare of the United States."[26]

The PDD went on to state that government mandates and new regulations were to be avoided and would be used only in unusual circumstances. This was in line with the main conclusion of his commission about the respective roles of government and the private sector: "In the interconnected cyber-oriented world of today, the responsibility for infrastructure assurance cannot be divided along traditional lines between government and the private sector or allocated among levels of government. The need to forge a partnership between all players—to achieve joint, integrated and complementary action—is more acute than ever."[27]

The government stopped well short of mandated standards or regulations—which industry opposed—to cover such issues as the physical security of buildings and computing and communications equipment; physical protection, backup, and recovery plans for data files; and the use of firewalls, key recovery systems, and other means of providing security in the private sector. It did, however, recommend more education and cross-industry discussions of these techniques. In fact, the marketplace has been active in developing and selling many of them to businesses. Numerous companies offer such products and services as firewall protection for intranets and recovery services in the event of natural disasters or man-made attacks.

Although the commission's work provided a good start by educating businesses and the public, and the creation of a government watchdog brought bureaucrats' attention to the problem, the warnings of danger to the infrastructure had increased by 1999. The U.S. government was becoming so concerned about the threat of cyber-terrorism or outright warfare that it proposed a system under which the government would monitor the Net—a seemingly impossible task and one opposed by civil libertarians. Whether or not it would really be needed would probably not be known until an actual incident occurred. Meanwhile, defense researchers at the Pentagon and elsewhere were examining the offensive as well as defensive uses of information warfare, and its legal implications. A Defense Science Board report in December 1999 made a series of recommendations for improving national security.[28] Moreover, the government was concerned as the year 2000 approached that hackers or cybercriminals might use the cover of the nation's distraction with the "Y2K bug" to commit on-line crimes or disrupt basic infrastructure systems.

To examine the issue further, President Clinton signed in August 1999 his Executive Order No. 13,333, establishing the Interagency Working Group on Unlawful Conduct on the Internet. The working group published its report, "The Electronic Frontier: The Challenge of Unlawful Conduct Involving the Use of the Internet" in March 2000.[29] The report covered the existing legal framework as well as the respective roles of government and the private sector. It identified significant challenges for government, including the ability to hire, train, and retain skilled professionals, and for the private sector, including education for computer users on how to protect their security. In particular, the report identified gaps in existing laws and in the ability to coordinate between state and local government, as well as between international entities. It also stressed the need for both the private sector and government agencies to publicize security threats and methods of protection to businesses, schools, and individuals.

On the whole, the United States has been fortunate. The most feared attacks have not taken place—attacks sponsored by governments or terrorists that would do permanent damage. Instead, there have been numerous smaller cyber-crimes and hacker attacks, aimed at individuals or institutions and involving actions such as theft and fraud. In fact, a joint survey by the FBI and the Computer Security Institute showed that almost one-third of the companies surveyed each had lost millions of dollars to security breaches. Even more—over 40 percent—said that unauthorized parties had used their information systems. Many of these go unreported because institutions such as banks and securities firms do not wish to advertise their vulnerabilities. It is to this threat to individual and business security that we will now turn.

Perhaps the greatest inhibitors to electronic commerce today are the public's fears of a lack of security and of the loss of privacy and the consequences, such as the theft of financial resources, should one's bank account information become available over the Internet. To some extent, the fear is exaggerated. People who unthinkingly hand their credit card to a waiter they've never seen before, who then disappears with the card into a back room, should worry about that before they worry about using their credit card on-line. But although Internet crime has been relatively limited to date, there is no question that the Net is a fertile ground for crimes of all sorts, particularly financial crimes. Failure to prepare for them will ensure that they happen.

To build the same trust in the electronic world that exists when a customer walks into a known retailer or bank, people must feel that their data is protected. They must believe that the electronic party with whom they are dealing is really the entity they think it is, and they must believe that no unauthorized person will be able to see their data or use it without their knowledge. Many legal and technological developments are needed to make this sense of security possible in the broadest sense (some of which we will discuss in Chapter 8), and the key to satisfying both of these conditions is the use of cryptography. Unfortunately, the unfettered use of cryptography is one of the most divisive issues of the digital age. It has set off a triangular war between government, industry, and civil libertarians.

Cryptography is a mathematical technique that has been used for many years. Early forms of it were used by the ancient Egyptians and Phoenicians to hide state secrets. Modern encryption takes advantage of the fact that it is very difficult and time-consuming to factor the product of two large prime numbers. By using mathematical algorithms to generate ciphers—i.e., to encrypt information—a person sending data can be virtually assured that it cannot be read by anyone except the person to whom it is sent, provided he or she has the key to decrypt the message. The bigger the numbers used in the algorithm, the more complex, expensive, and time-consuming the calculations are, and the more secure the original information is.

There are two types of encryption: private key and public key. Private-key encryption is the type used by consumers when they send their credit-card information over the Net during an electronic transaction to a retailer or a bank. In this method, both parties use the same "private" key to encode and decode messages. The message is encrypted as it is sent and decoded when it is received; in between, along the transmission path, is a hash of digital garble that no one can read. Private-key encryption builds consumer trust in electronic commerce.

The second kind of encryption, public-key encryption, builds another kind of trust. In public-key encryption, each user has two keys—one private and one public, and they are related to each other mathematically. Thus, public-key encryption allows parties on the Net to encrypt messages with a public key and decode them with a private key. It is more complex and expensive than private-key encryption, since it requires more calculations, and it enables an important application: it permits a message sent over the Internet to carry a unique electronic "signature" that identifies the sender, like an electronic fingerprint. In legal business terms, it "authenticates" the party, assuring a retailer, for example, that the buyer is really who he or she says. Many electronic commerce applications use both private- and public-key encryption, but the system is transparent to the users, and normally neither a buyer nor a seller, neither the sender nor the receiver, is aware that encryption has taken place.

For some time, cryptography using a 40-bit key provided adequate security for most individual and institutional needs. When it was demonstrated to be simple to "break," however, many businesses moved to a 56-bit algorithm known as the Data Encryption Standard (DES), developed by IBM and the National Security Agency in the 1970s. In 1998, two cryptographers broke DES in 56 hours using a single personal computer, prompting the market to demand even stronger encryption products.[30] Today, according to the Business Software Alliance, the software industry's key trade association, "[t]he worldwide standard is 128-bit encryption"—i.e., that is the level of encryption with which commercial users begin to feel secure.[31] There is only one small problem: the general export of 128-bit encryption technology by U.S. companies to customers overseas has been prohibited by law. The government has even tried to restrict its use domestically.

The government view of encryption and its power was born during World War II. According to the historian Paul Johnson, "The real significance of the Battle of Midway . . . was that it was won primarily by the Allied success in code-breaking. . . . Thereafter, the Allies knew the positions of all Japanese capital ships nearly all the time. . . . [C]ode-breaking alone raised [Japanese] shipping losses by one-third."[32] The same successes applied to the war in Europe, where the British had broken the Nazi codes and used their information to great advantage. After the war, the secret "Venona" program of the U.S. government provided evidence of atomic theft by Julius and Ethel Rosenberg. For almost half a century, the role of encryption in the Rosenberg case was kept secret by the government. In fact, during the Cold War, America's code-making and code-breaking techniques were the nation's most closely guarded secrets, on a par with nuclear ones. Even the budget of the National Security Agency

(NSA), the organization responsible for global eavesdropping, was secret. Thus, the ability to maintain American encryption superiority became one of the two or three most important jewels of the nation's arsenal.

As the deputy director of the NSA testified at a hearing before a House subcommittee,

NSA intercepts and analyzes the communications signals of our foreign adversaries, many of which are guarded by codes and other complex electronic countermeasures. From these signals, we produce vital intelligence reports. . . . Very often time is of the essence. Intelligence is perishable. . . . Passage of legislation that immediately decontrols the export of strong encryption . . . will greatly complicate our exploitation of foreign targets and the timely delivery of intelligence to decision makers because it will take too long to decrypt a message—if indeed we can decrypt it at all.[33]

Moreover, the FBI and local law-enforcement agencies are in a constant technological struggle with criminals, who have become more sophisticated in their ability to hide their activities. Drug dealers with unlimited funds, for example, were using sophisticated telecommunications equipment with encryption capability to conduct their business. Child pornographers have been caught with encrypted files. The Department of Justice testified at the same hearing that

[c]ourt-authorized wiretaps have proven to be one of the most successful law enforcement tools in preventing and prosecuting serious crimes, including drug trafficking and terrorism. . . . But if non-recoverable encryption proliferates, these critical law enforcement tools would be nullified. Thus, for example, even if the government satisfies the rigorous legal and procedural requirements for obtaining a wiretap order, the wiretap would be worthless if the intercepted communications of the targeted criminals amount to an unintelligible jumble of noises or symbols. Or we might legally seize the computers of a terrorist and be unable to read the data identifying his or her targets, plans and co-conspirators.[34]

In response to the national security and law-enforcement concerns, the computer and software industries have replied that strong encryption is absolutely necessary to protect security on the Net today, and that export controls are no help in any event. According to the trade group Americans for Computer Privacy, "a December 1997 study conducted by Trusted Information Systems found that 656 non-American encryption products are available from 29 foreign countries . . . located as far from the U.S. as China and as close as Mexico."[35] The Cato Institute, in a study published in November 1998, cites as examples of this the International Data Encryption Algorithm (IDEA) system, which uses a 128-bit key and is owned by a Swiss company, and GOST, a 256-bit system originating in Russia.[36] Thus, says the industry, unilateral U.S. export controls are futile.

Since the U.S. government knew unilateral controls would not work, it concluded an international agreement on the control of cryptography. After announcing in the fall of 1998 some liberalization of export controls on cryptography that fall under existing U.S. laws and international agreements, the Clinton administration concluded the so-called Wassenaar Agreement on encryption in December 1998, under which more than thirty key U.S. trading partners agreed to control strong encryption products. (Wassenaar is the successor to the North Atlantic Treaty Organization coordinating committee that controlled exports during the Cold War.) The EU also began to work to harmonize the export-control policies of its members. But industry was not impressed: "[I]f it were truly possible to achieve universal agreement that was fairly enforced, industry would no doubt be supportive. But Wassenaar only has 33 members and does not include encryption-producing countries such as China, India, South Africa or Israel. . . . Some of the member nations will promulgate regulations that are less restrictive than those of the United States, thus providing those nations with a competitive advantage over domestic encryption manufacturers. In short, the Wassenaar Arrangement is a toothless tiger."[37] Industry's position on export controls left a bitter taste in the mouths of many government and law-enforcement officials, who openly and angrily stated that industry was driven on this issue strictly by greed and not by any concerns about the public good.

But industry had an important ally that occupied the moral high ground on this and other issues—the civil liberties community. It had already expressed its concerns about free speech on the Net and was also deeply concerned about the individual right to privacy. The American Civil Liberties Union and other organizations saw encryption as the best technique to protect that right; these organizations supported industry's push for deregulated encryption. Testifying before Congress, an official of the Center for Democracy and Technology stated, "In early 1999, it is more clear than ever that the widespread use of encryption is of critical importance for public safety, national security, and law enforcement in the Information Age. The flow of sensitive information over the Internet leaves people increasingly vulnerable to the prying eyes of potential criminals, terrorists or even foreign governments. Encryption gives people an easy and inexpensive way to protect that information."[38]

Yet when the issue is framed that way, those arguing for the free use of cryptography could be seen as supporting strict security, which in fact had been the conclusion of the nation's (then) most exhaustive study of the subject of encryption export controls a few years earlier. Sponsored by the National Research Council, this report said,

For both law enforcement and national security, cryptography is a two-edged sword. The public debate has tended to draw lines that frame the policy issues as the privacy of individuals and businesses against the needs of national security and law enforcement. While such a dichotomy does have a kernel of truth, when viewed in the large, this dichotomy is misleading. If cryptography can protect the trade secrets and proprietary information of business and thereby reduce industrial espionage (which it can), it also supports . . . the job of law enforcement. If cryptography can help protect nationally critical information systems and networks against unauthorized penetration (which it can), it also supports the national security of the United States.[39]

Unfortunately, the encryption debate had not been framed this way and the antagonists remained locked in a bitter struggle. For a time, it seemed that encryption key escrow systems might have been the answer. This idea grew from the government's ill-fated "Clipper Chip" proposal in the mid-1990s, which would have involved the mandatory use of an electronic "trap door" in every encryption system by which the government would be able, in criminal or national security cases, to access the encryption key. Civil liberties and industry groups defeated the proposal for mandatory systems, which was broadly deemed an assault on domestic civil liberties and far beyond the scope of export controls. In response, industry suggested the rapid development of voluntary "key escrow systems," equivalent to a homeowner's leaving a key to his home with a neighbor when going on vacation so that, in an emergency, the neighbor can enter the house. In a key escrow system, a trusted third party, such as a bank, can hold the keys used by many businesses. If the company loses its key, it can retrieve it from the bank. If the government needs the key, it can also retrieve it, with a legal search warrant. Some companies argued that the marketplace would soon demand key escrow systems for business reasons, and that governments should work to encourage them. Shortly thereafter, a number of commercial key escrow systems were put on the market, but they were not widely accepted by industry. So although key escrow is still a possible partial solution to the encryption issue, it is developing very slowly.

The courts have also become entangled in the encryption debate. Two computer activists used another legal tool—the First Amendment—to argue in court that the computer source code that makes up encryption software is like any other computer source code and is thus protected by the First Amendment as free speech. Therefore, they said, export controls are "an impermissible prior restraint on speech." A lower court and a federal appeals court have agreed. In handing down her decision, Judge Betty Fletcher said, "Government attempts to control encryption . . . may well implicate not only the First Amendment rights of cryptographers . . .

but also the constitutional rights of each of us as potential recipients of encryption's bounty."[40]

The case is headed for the Supreme Court, where it will raise serious issues of national security. If the notion that all computer source code is protected as free speech is upheld, for example, it could mean that the software that allows the cheaper, easier, and more rapid development of nuclear weapons is similarly protected. Could no software secret fall under the protection of the government? Such a notion is troubling. As the *Washington Post*—normally not an advocate of government secrecy—pointed out in an editorial, "The government's interest in controlling the spread of strong encryption is a real one that cannot be dismissed blithely."[41]

Congress has also continued to wrestle with the encryption issue. In 1999, as he had done in past years, Representative Bob Goodlatte of Virginia introduced his so-called SAFE (Security and Freedom Through Encryption) bill, which would totally decontrol cryptography exports—and which was denounced by FBI director Louis Freeh and other law-enforcement and national security officials. Similarly, Senator McCain introduced his own bill that would liberalize export controls and decontrol the export of products using a key length of 64 bits or less while maintaining tight controls on stronger encryption products. In addition, in the fall of 1999, the Department of Justice said it would ask Congress for new legislation permitting the FBI to make covert entry to premises to permit installation of devices on computers to provide access to plain text—with a court order.

The terms of the debate changed dramatically again in September 1999 when the administration announced that it was effectively eliminating almost all export controls on encryption. In other words, it was accepting the substance of the SAFE bill. The administration balanced this announcement, however, with a proposal sent to Congress for a "Cyberspace Electronic Security Act" (CESA). This bill would authorize recovery agents (firms or government entities that perform security services for others and therefore have access to those companies' encryption keys) to disclose recovery information to law enforcement agencies, thus providing them with access to plain text. The bill would also provide privacy protections for security keys and authorize funding for a centralized technical resource within the FBI to deal with criminal use of encryption.

Whether or not the terms and conditions of CESA would prove acceptable to the law-enforcement community and its supporters in Congress remains an open question. Freeh has said that every encryption product "should have a feature in that product . . . that will respond to court order.

And this should be true for the holder of a network's security and everyone else."[42] He went on to say that government should not leave it to industry to decide whether or not each encryption product should be so equipped. This sounded very much like the government's earlier failed "Clipper chip" proposal. The FBI also asked for funding for encryption research.

Even given the tangled web of the administration, Congress, and the courts, and strong advocacy and lobbying from industry, the civil liberties community, and law-enforcement organizations, it appears that we are now moving closer toward a resolution of the encryption dilemma. Without progress on the issue, the development of electronic commerce would be retarded, as the public and businesses alike worry more about the security of the information they transmit. The ultimate solution must take into account the needs of both the public and business and the important needs of law enforcement and national security.

Unfortunately, we live in an age when the likelihood of terrorist attacks and internationally organized criminal activities is real. We cannot afford to disarm ourselves. Although it is true, as industry argues, that export controls will not fully prevent terrorists and criminals from using cryptography, the purpose of export controls generally had never been totally to prohibit anything. Export controls simply make the purchase and use of various products—including encryption—more expensive and more difficult for malefactors to obtain and thereby slow down their proliferation.

Therefore, the U.S. government and concerned foreign governments should take the following steps:

- Encourage the use of encryption products—including strong encryption—by citizens and legitimate businesses and impose no government controls on domestic use. This is the best way to protect the security of individuals, businesses, and critical infrastructures.
- Continue to liberalize the export controls on encryption products, making strong encryption freely available to friendly nations and their citizens, but do not totally deregulate the export of cryptography, especially to terrorist nations and criminal users.
- Recruit and retain a corps of skilled and dedicated people who are available 24 hours a day to intervene in security incidents.
- Encourage the private sector to improve security technology. Ease of use is important but security should not be sacrificed inordinately in order to attain it. For example, future operating systems should make it more difficult for users to open executable files, in order to

foil viruses. Intelligent filters and "virtual fuses" could limit or stop suspected malicious Net traffic, such as denial-of-service attacks.

- Encourage the user community to develop a culture that promotes security and increases the use of safety measures, such installing firewalls. Recruit universities to help with this effort.
- Improve and increase research on cryptography, especially on new tools and technical capabilities for national security agencies and law enforcement. The FBI should disseminate information on the use of these capabilities to state and local law-enforcement agencies. Knowledge about the tools and technological capabilities of law enforcement should be restricted, so criminals cannot evade the law.
- Promote the use of techniques such as key escrow and recovery systems by using them in its own operations and sharing new knowledge with the private sector.
- Pass legislation to assist law-enforcement efforts in using the judicial system to get access to decoded text under a court order. Legislation to clarify the Wiretap Act is especially needed.
- Pass legislation that creates new and substantial criminal penalties for those who use encryption in committing a federal crime, and encourage the states to pass similar laws to cover the use of encryption in state crimes.

As the use of encryption spreads and the technology advances, the government will need to continuously update its laws and regulations. New technologies will surely emerge that will substitute for some encryption applications. Biometric technologies such as electronic fingerprinting and retinal scanning, for example, will augment and perhaps replace the authentication functions of encryption. Such new technologies will have significant implications for government, particularly in the area of civil liberties. Governments will need to ensure that its measures are technology-neutral, so that it does not inadvertently favor one technology over another.

STANDARDS

Achieving interoperability in the presence of diversity, heterogeneity, and change call for the widespread adoption of common standards. . . . The American approach to information infrastructure development places the government in the role of enabler and the private sector in the role of investor and innovator.

—Lewis M. Branscomb and Brian Kahin, *Standards Processes and Objectives for the National Information Infrastructure*[43]

If cryptography is one of the most heated and topical policy subjects in the development of the information infrastructure, standards are perhaps the most obscure for the public. Nevertheless, standards are still critical to the development of the Net and therefore merit attention. Although many of the most important standards issues have already been settled, new ones continue to arise as companies, industries, and nations seek to bolster their competitive advantage through the use of standards.

The principal organization charged with developing standards to make the Internet itself work well is the Internet Engineering Task Force (IETF). The IETF, in its own words, is a "loosely self-organized group of people" who develop new standard specifications for the Internet, as well as make other engineering contributions. Founded in 1986, the IETF has grown to become an open international community of researchers, network designers and operators, and vendors who work on standards and protocols in a number of areas, including applications, network management, routing, security, and transport. The IETF works with its sister organizations, the Internet Architecture Board and the Internet Engineering Steering Group, to develop standards and get them widely accepted throughout the Internet community.[44]

The scope of the IETF's work is immense. In the first three quarters of 1999, it completed work on almost two hundred standards in areas such as public key encryption, domain-name security, encryption key storage, packet transmission, remote network management, and the fight against spam, or mass, unsolicited E-mail. At the end of 1999, almost a hundred other standards were on the IETF's agenda and under discussion.

The development of many of these standards is a routine technical matter, but others involve serious controversy. For example, the IETF has engaged in a long and contentious debate about whether to build wiretapping capabilities into the Internet. Some argue that this step is necessary to comply with U.S. law, whereas others believe it would be an egregious invasion of privacy. Nevertheless, the IETF, along with the other technical organizations, has done a good job of Internet standards development.

The road to relatively smooth operation, however, was not always so clear. As the World Wide Web began to explode in the early 1990s, many observers raised concerns about the terms and conditions of interoperability and the roadblocks that were blocking its achievement. There was special concern about how many different devices and types of software would connect to the growing information infrastructure. Both government and those in industry quickly came to recognize a critical need to resolve key issues by bringing many other industry standards groups to the table—including those from cable and broadcast television, photography, publishing, and consumer electronics.

In fact, the Internet's infancy and the burgeoning activity surrounding it were overshadowed by the single issue of interoperability. For years, a major failure of the computer industry had been its inability to allow the hardware and software of different manufacturers to interact with each other. Although this problem even then was a nuisance and created added expenses for many users, it did not become a critical issue until everyone *could* be interconnected. Suddenly, with the coming of the national information infrastructure, not only would computer hardware and software have to be compatible, but they would also have to interconnect with the public switched telephone network, private networks of all types, wireless networks and devices, television sets, cameras, and new types of information appliances. Software applications of all types would also have to be compatible with each other, as well as with the underlying operating systems and other software.

The communications protocols of the Internet (the TCP/IP protocols, discussed in Chapter 1) permitted smooth transmission across the web of networks, but they did not provide complete interoperability. Information appliances such as personal computers, workstations, hand-held devices, and television set-top boxes would need to be interoperable with the networks and with software applications. Applications such as E-mail, security techniques, voice mail, electronic publishing, and database software would all need to work with one another. Networks, including the switched telephone system, private "intelligent" networks, cable, and wireless, would all have to be compatible.

As the leading computer systems association, the Computer Systems Policy Project (CSPP), stated in 1994, "Interoperability is not a luxury—it is an essential element for meeting many of the goals that have been articulated for the NII [national information infrastructure]."[45] In the computer industry, work on this issue had begun some years earlier: in the mid-1980s, private data networks had begun to proliferate and computer users had begun to complain about the incompatibility of equipment not only from different manufacturers but even, in some instances, from the same maker.

As a result, the International Standards Organization (ISO), the worldwide body that brings together the standards organizations of the world's countries, had developed the Open Systems Interconnection standard (OSI). This broad standard created a layered architecture specifying standards for seven types of interoperability, including physical connections, network interoperability, and application compatibility. Some believe OSI helped push innovation and competition in the industry: "Standards define what is expected and what is allowed, enabling smaller companies to enter the market and larger companies to focus their unique strengths in creating new products and services. . . . Standards of interoperability (such as OSI) also give users the freedom to change vendors and technologies, allowing them to buy the best solutions for their needs with confidence they can work together."[46] Others point out that OSI failed ultimately in the marketplace because international politics within the ISO caused too many compromises, resulting in so many options for implementation that OSI did not achieve the comprehensive interoperability that TCP/IP did.

But OSI was only a small beginning—and it was limited to computers. In the early 1990s, many interfaces between networks were simply not open. Progress on standards for applications interoperability in areas such as multimedia and telephony was slow, in some cases because of technical complexities, and in others simply because of the proliferation of standards bodies and industry associations. The telephone companies, the computer industry, and the television and motion picture industries, for example, all have their own standards-setting organizations. Additionally, standards accepted nationally must be accepted at the international level by the ISO and the International Electrotechnical Committee (IEC).

Part of the problem was eased in 1994 and 1995 when the American National Standards Institute (ANSI), the umbrella body for all U.S. standards organizations, set up the Information Infrastructure Standards Panel (IISP), the purpose of which was to bring together all interested standards-making bodies voluntarily, not only from the U.S., but from anywhere in the world. The IISP facilitates the identification of key standards issues and seeks resolution of them by working through the existing standards bodies such as the IETF. To date, more than 30 standards organizations belong to the IISP, representing such industries as computers, telephony, cable, media, financial services, and electrical manufacturing. As a result of their work, many standards barriers have been overcome.

Nevertheless, many issues remain. Some involve competition and antitrust law: for example, to make software programs and hardware compatible so that users can freely use different equipment and applications together, the application program interface (API), or software that allows two different software programs to work in sync, must be open. Its technical specifications must also be published in a timely manner so that software developers have the opportunity to write compatible software code for new applications. Changes in specifications must be announced publicly in a timely manner. This subject, in fact, has been a major part of the Microsoft antitrust case.

Another issue involves intellectual property rights and concerns the nature of these open interfaces. Some have argued essentially that intellectual property embedded in open interfaces must be public and not subject to royalties by the inventing companies. Sun Microsystems and Japanese companies such as Fujitsu have taken this position. Others point out—and have so far carried the day—that an open interface can make use of proprietary technology and still be "open." To do so, the intellectual property rights—patents or copyrights—involved in the technology must be available for use by all on reasonable terms and conditions (i.e., royalties). Thus, an inventor is motivated to develop new technology for an interface, since he or she can expect some reward.

These issues of competition policy and licensing of technology have also become weapons in the race between nations to develop and reap the rewards of the Net. Since a great majority of the innovations for this infrastructure, including technology that becomes embodied in standards, originated in the United States, other countries and their industries have reason to want to weaken the control that the American inventors have over them. The Japanese government, for example, has been active around the world in attempting to weaken intellectual property protection, particularly copyrights on software. This will be dealt with in more detail in Chapter 8.

In the standards arena, a key battle between the United States and Japan began in the mid-1980s when the Japanese government, lobbied by its television and consumer electronics industries, pushed hard for international adoption of a standard for high-definition television (HDTV). This proposal set off a decade-long struggle over the HDTV standard that raised a number of serious issues, including not only the potential Japanese dominance of this important future technology, but also the larger issue of when to set a standard in the fast-moving digital world.

The proposed Japanese standard was an analog one, and as U.S. companies pointed out, the world was rapidly becoming digital. Setting an analog standard so early in the game could retard the growth of the new digital technologies and impede the coming convergence between computing and television. The Reagan and Bush administrations both wanted to avoid premature government acceptance of a standard that would not only help Japanese industry but also undercut the digital advances being made by U.S. high-technology companies. In 1990, a cabinet-level decision was made by the Bush administration not to proceed with the standard. After more years of internecine warfare between the television and computer industries, the FCC gave its approval in 1997 to a flexible HDTV standard that would facilitate both the development of HDTV broadcasting and the convergence of television with computing.

Technological nationalism raised its head again in the mid-1990s when the European Telecommunications Standards Institute (ETSI) attempted to mandate the licensing, under its own terms and conditions, for any technology that became embedded in a standard. This dispute nearly sparked a trade war between the United States and the Europeans and even involved the White House's bringing pressure on the European Commission in Brussels to influence the ETSI. The ETSI proposal was finally defeated when some European countries withdrew their support for it.

But the tension between intellectual property rights and standards in the world of the Net is one of the most difficult to resolve. As Harvard professor Lewis Branscomb and researcher Brian Kahin have pointed out, "This is not a simple matter. There are complex strategic issues on the standards side, and unresolved and controversial issues of both substantive law and policy and administrative process on the intellectual property side."[47]

Tension also exists between the private and public sectors on the issue of standards. In the United States, most standards are developed, driven, and set by the private sector, in standards-setting bodies that follow legal procedures. Although some U.S. standards are set by government, such as technical telephone-industry standards set by the FCC or general measurement and time standards set by the National Institute for Standards and Technology (NIST), the private standards-setting process is jealously guarded by U.S. industry. The FCC sits in on IISP meetings, for instance, but as an observer not a participant. The federal government also participates as a user of information technology.

In other countries, by contrast, government bodies often control standards. This setup can facilitate the use of standards as a nontariff barrier to trade. For example, a standard may be set that favors a local company and thus creates an unfair trade advantage. Additionally, once a standard is established, a testing procedure is usually required to make certain that products meet the standard. This testing may be for health or safety reasons, or it may be to make certain that, for example, use of a different voltage does not damage other equipment. At present, most countries require their own testing procedures to certify a product, even if that product has been tested and passed by another nation's testing laboratories. Thus, an imported product can face a testing maze, sometimes purposely created, that allows a local product to get an unfair early start in the marketplace. The EU solved the issue of conflicting standards for information-technology equipment to be attached to the telephone system a decade ago through a common scheme of homologation, or permitting the acceptance of one national test in all EU member states.

Now, a number of industries are calling for an international regime of "one standard, one test," that would eliminate the duplicative testing of the same product in many different countries. This scheme would establish, with WTO blessing, reciprocal recognition of test results for all participating national certification bodies; passing one nation's test would exempt a product from duplicate testing in other member countries. If this regime were administered by the IEC, its thirty-eight member countries, who account for a large part of world trade in information-technology products, would benefit from a reduced need for testing. Although establishment of such a regime would face a difficult hurdle in overcoming the mandatory testing of pharmaceuticals and drug products in every country, it should be acceptable to the vast majority of nations.

In sum, many parts of the standards issue for the global information infrastructure seem to have been resolved. The Net is, for the most part, interoperable. Although complex and difficult individual issues involving standards are sure to arise in the future, including some difficult antitrust issues, at this point none of them will be overriding.

Above all, the issue of standards highlights the need for international solutions to digital-age issues. With the value of each country's network directly proportional to the number of people and institutions worldwide who can interconnect with it, compatibility and connectivity must be global. The same is true for the telecommunications and security issues discussed in the preceding sections of this chapter.

Building the physical and technical infrastructure for cyberspace also involves issues beyond those discussed in this chapter, however. The domain name system for the Internet must continue to be improved, decentralized, and internationalized. Countries will need to develop portability and permanency for E-mail addresses and telephone numbers. The issue of anti-circumvention, or preventing unauthorized copying of material from DVDs and other electronic products, must be resolved.

Many more standards also need to be set in areas ranging from financial transactions to high-definition television to security. Spectrum issues involving the future development of wireless connectivity must be resolved. All of these and more are beyond the scope of this book, but all will demand cooperation between the public and private sectors on a global scale.

8

Legal Framework

The rules for . . . [horses] did not adequately apply to . . . [manufactured goods]. . . .
The law of toasters, televisions and chain saws is not appropriate for . . . on-line
databases, artificial intelligence systems, software, multimedia, and Internet trade
information.
— from a draft U.S. "Computer Information Transactions Act.[1]"

Before the late 1930s, most commercial and contract law in the United
States had been developed for an agrarian society that was more concerned about disputes involving sick mules or infested grain than it was
about sales issues involving warranties on automobiles or refrigerators.
By 1935, horse-drawn ice-wagons were in full retreat and trucks were
beginning to deliver refrigerators to dealers as fast as Depression-era
people could buy them. Meanwhile, a debate raged among the nation's
lawyers and judges over the adoption of a new code of commercial law.
Some argued that the old rules were good enough and that courts and ju-
ries could use common sense to adapt existing commercial law to the
new realities. Others argued for a totally new commercial code. The re-
formers won, and the result was a new section of the Uniform Commercial Code governing the sale of goods: Article 2.

Today we are at a similar turning point. As the National Conference
of Commissioners on Uniform State Laws, the body responsible for
American commercial law, points out,

The economy has changed again. Goods-based transactions remain important,
but transactions in intangibles of computer information are a central element of
commerce. . . . Transactions in computer information are governed today by a
complex, often inconsistent or uncertain blend of different aspects of state common law, rules of federal common law, and by various statutes, most of which
were designed for other subject matter, such as Article 2 which focuses on sale of
goods, rather than on licenses of computer information. This mismatch of legal
rules and the uncertainty of outcome adds complexity and cost to transactions.[2]

The shift to a digital economy directly affects the laws governing sales of goods and services, but it also affects many other areas of commercial law. Among the key issues that need resolution are those dealing with electronic "writings": Is an electronic or digital signature legally binding? Is an electronic contract valid? How can one affix the exact time of the formation of an electronic contract or authenticate the identity of a party to the contract?

Can a will or last testament or a deed to real property be drawn up electronically? How can an electronic document be notarized? Are electronic writings admissible as evidence in court? How can jurisdiction be determined in the event of a dispute? What intellectual property rights exist in cyberspace? Where a number of jurisdictions exist, either within a country or across national borders, whose consumer protection laws apply? Can government agencies use electronic contracting and bidding procedures and, if so, what special rules might apply to them?

All of these issues and more are currently being actively debated and acted on at every level of government in much of the world. In the United States, the fifty states and groups such as the National Conference of Commissioners on Uniform State Laws and the American Law Institute are drafting and passing new acts and model laws. In Europe, Asia, and Latin American, national governments and regional organizations such as the European Union (EU) are doing the same. And at the international level, the United Nations Conference on International Trade Law has been developing model laws and codes that can be used by countries as they draft their own rules. Since it will be particularly important that these new laws and codes be consistent across national borders, international cooperation will be critical. Without it, consumers and businesses will have little legal certainty on which to depend and many will be reluctant to engage in electronic transactions.

This chapter will deal with attempts at the many different levels of government to develop an appropriate legal framework for the digital era—both within countries and internationally. Since intellectual property law is an especially important aspect of the legal issue, it will be dealt with separately from the broader legal-framework discussion.

ELECTRONIC CONTRACTS

Government Principles

Laws and rules begin with broad principles. The Clinton administration suggested some in its Framework for Global Electronic Commerce document issued in July 1997 and urged that these principles be adopted by all nations as "a start to defining an international set of uniform commercial principles for electronic commerce." Its first principle is that "parties should be free to order the contractual relationship between themselves as they see fit."[3] Perhaps the most fundamental idea regarding electronic contracts, this means that private contractual relationships, with their terms and conditions, should continue to be voluntary and not determined by unnecessary government regulations, as some countries and jurisdictions might be tempted to impose.

The administration's second suggested legal principle deals with technology: "Rules should be technology neutral and forward looking" (i.e., the rules established should neither assume nor require a particular technology nor should they hinder the use or development of technologies in the future). The reason for this principle is twofold. First, technology is changing so rapidly that it would make little sense to lock in the current state of affairs by requiring that a particular form of technology be used. For example, at present digital signatures that make use of public-key encryption are the best and most commonly used method of authenticating the identity of parties doing business on the Internet. But it would be foolish to mandate legally the use of digital signatures for this purpose, since other methods, such as biometrics, electronic fingerprints, or retinal scans are in the late stages of development and could prove to be more effective and less expensive in the long run.

The second reason for this principle is to prevent nations from attempting to use the legal code, as well as technical standards developed by their own companies, to favor technologies that they themselves are developing and exploiting. As we saw in Chapter 7, this technique for establishing competitive advantage has already been at work in the standards world; it could cause mischief in the legal arena, as well.

The administration's third principle is that "existing rules should be modified and new rules should be adopted only as necessary or substantially desirable to support the use of electronic technologies." This harkens back to the notion that existing law should be relied on wherever and whenever possible. It confirms the administration's view that an entirely new body of law is not only unnecessary to deal with the issues involved in electronic commerce, but would probably cause more problems than it would resolve. In fact, some earlier observers had suggested that an entirely new body of law, such as the law of the sea, might be needed for the Net. The administration has rejected that notion for now, and so have the EU and other key governments active in electronic commerce policy issues.

Finally, the administration's fourth legal "principle" is not a principle at all, but the recognition of an important fact. It said, "[T]he process should involve the high-tech commercial sector as well as businesses that have not yet moved online." This statement made two points. It confirmed the administration's overall view that the private sector must lead, and in the case of a legal framework that would ultimately have to be adopted by politicians and passed into law, at least participate. But the statement also made an important and subtle observation about conditions at the time. The technology companies directly involved in the creation of the new information infrastructure—computer, software, communications, and media companies—had been deeply involved in the policy-making debates and processes. But those companies that would be the ultimate users of cyberspace—retailers, banks, airlines, insurers, manufacturers, and so forth—had generally been quiet and too often were absent from the policy table.

A number of reasons account for this absence. First and foremost, many businesses were only beginning to dip their toes into the digital waters. As we have seen in Chapter 4, for example, insurance companies during this period had established Web sites but hadn't yet really figured out how to sell and service insurance over the Internet. In anticipation that that would change, it was imperative that insurance companies play a role in the discussions about the legal framework. Few industries relied so heavily on complex legal constructs and contracts and would need clear and predictable rules in cyberspace. But second, even as they began to do business electronically, many of these companies lacked the expertise to participate in the discussions. Eventually they would develop it, however, so they needed to be at the table.

Private-Sector Principles

The administration's principles for a new legal framework for electronic commerce were a good beginning and soon the high-technology sector and other industries began to add thoughts of their own. In addition to the administration's four principles, a number of others that are central to the debate emerged from organizations such as the Computer Systems Policy Project and the Coalition of Service Industries, a group comprising financial service organizations as well as high-tech firms. The first important principle is that electronic signatures and documents should have the same legal standing as physical signatures and documents, except in certain cases where a handwritten signature is especially critical, such as those required for wills, health care powers of attorney, or whenever a once-in-a-lifetime financial or health care matter is involved, such as the signing of an irrevocable trust. Similarly, documents should not be denied legal status in any legal procedure merely because they or the signatures on them are electronic.

Another principle to emerge, connected to the preceding one, is that the parties that authenticate or certify electronic signatures and documents at the voluntary bidding of contracting parties (so-called certificate authorities, a kind of electronic notary), be trustworthy. To ensure this, they should be required to meet some minimal accreditation standards, such as appropriate insurance or bonding requirements. Furthermore, licensing requirements should be minimal and involve only those standards needed to ensure integrity and reliability. According to this principle, because some countries might wish these electronic "notaries" to be government officials, whereas others might prefer regulated "trusted" private parties, such as banks, it would be better to leave this level of detail to the marketplace. In any case, a variety of authenticators should be available to customers, offering different services and at different prices, but with some minimal assurance of trustworthiness. These standards for certificate authorities should also be accepted internationally, so that transactions can take place across national borders without complications.

Yet another principle emerged in the area of jurisdiction. The best way to resolve this issue, the private sector has asserted, is to leave the choice of law and jurisdiction to the parties entering into electronic contracts. These contracts could include binding provisions governing the choice of both law and forum. Absent this, courts should assert jurisdiction only when a party's presence is sufficiently substantial. Legislators should resist the temptation to develop new rules of jurisdiction for cyberspace. Within the United States, current rules and traditions of jurisdiction can apply with little if any changes.

One notion that has emerged that helps resolve jurisdictional issues to some extent is that contracting parties in cyberspace should to the extent possible use on-line dispute-resolution mechanisms to eliminate the logistical problem associated with traditional litigation—travel and lodging costs, time lost, etc. These on-line methods might involve compulsory arbitration or the use of some third party. For example, in the United States, the Better Business Bureau's BBB Online service provides the means for consumers to seek redress when they have an issue with an on-line business.

Finally, governments and industry must wrestle with the broader issue of consumer protection, including rules for fair and nondiscriminatory advertising and rules governing such areas as pricing, disclosures, and warranties. Although every nation's own laws, norms, and culture affect this area, some global predictability is needed for electronic commerce. In the view of the chief executive officers of the computer industry, "[b]asic consumer protections must be established for this new electronic medium and international rules are required to provide certainty about how and what consumer laws will be applied to a given transaction. Similarly, predictable rules are needed to determine where and how disputes may be resolved and agreements enforced."[4]

Developing Laws: Electronic Signatures

With general agreement on many of these principles to be found across government and geographical boundaries, a wide variety of governments and organizations have been working to turn the principles into new and functional laws for electronic commerce. These activities are taking place at both the state and the national levels in the United States and at the national government level in other countries, including such diverse places as the United Kingdom, Japan, Malaysia, and Peru. Of particular importance, major activities are also under way at various regional and international forums, including the EU, the Organization for Economic Cooperation and Development (OECD), and the United Nations Conference on International Trade Law (UNCITRAL).

Because state law governs commercial transactions in the United States, the states have taken the lead in a number of legal areas, especially regarding digital or electronic signatures. By the middle of 1998, according to the *Electronic Commerce and Law Report,* all but three states—Arkansas, South Carolina, and South Dakota—had either considered or enacted some form of electronic authentication law.[5] But the states passed widely differing laws, creating a cumbersome and unpredictable situation for parties who wished to use digital or electronic signatures in the borderless world of electronic commerce.

In fact, a study conducted for the Internet Law and Policy Forum (ILPF) demonstrated that the differences between the new state laws dealing with digital and electronic signatures were not merely cosmetic or minor, but very basic. The ILPF study identified four distinct categories of new laws.[6]

Prescriptive Laws. Prescriptive laws recognize and make legal only a single, specific regulatory framework for digital signatures, using a public key infrastructure (PKI) encryption licensing scheme. In this structure, a subscriber obtains a certificate of authenticity from a certificate authority (an independent third party) that attests to the identity of the subscriber. The subscriber then uses this encrypted certificate to do business on the Net. These so-called thick laws may also dictate duties between parties to a contract and prescribe standards for liability. The licensing of certificate authorities is "voluntary," but unlicensed agents may face greater liability and other legal disadvantages.

The state of Utah, in a commendable effort to be an early leader in the field, passed such a prescriptive into law in 1995, and it became the model for this approach. Unfortunately, the Utah law came too early, and diverged from the key legal principles that were developed by the federal government and industry a few years later. For instance, it is not technology neutral, since it mandates PKI digital encryption technology for electronic signatures, and it takes much of the control over terms and conditions out of the hands of the contracting parties and the private sector. Only two other states—Minnesota and Washington—have enacted laws like Utah's, and Washington's law permits some small amount of deviation from its specificity.

Criteria-Based Laws. Criteria-based laws—often called thin laws—do not choose and mandate a particular technology but rather set broad criteria for electronic signatures that satisfy needs for security and trust. The law then authorizes a state agency to approve any technology meeting the criteria. Examples of the criteria for an electronic signature are that it be unique to and under the control of the person using it, and that it be verifiable and closely linked to the data so that data cannot be changed after a signature is affixed to it.

California is the prime example of a state with a criteria-based law. The California law's greater sophistication arises from the state's strong industrial and academic technology base and its participation in drafting the law. The law is technology neutral, recognizing immediately both PKI-encrypted digital signatures as well as signature dynamics (a technique in which a "signature digest" captures the handwriting measurements and characteristics of a person, links them to the signature, and transmits them along with it). The California law also says that "any individual or company can . . . petition the California Department of Information Technology to review [a proposed] technology" to be added to the approved list.[7] As of mid-1997, ten states had followed California's lead and passed laws with criteria-based approaches.

Signature-Enabling Laws. Signature-enabling laws, very general thin laws, simply state that any kind of electronic mark that is intended to au-

thenticate a "writing" (such as a contract) by satisfying a signature requirement is permitted. They give electronic signatures the same legal status as written signatures. Massachusetts and Florida, which both have
passed signature-enabling laws, were both concerned about distorting the
future market for electronic commerce and wanted to make their laws as
technology-neutral as possible. Although their laws left many issues unresolved, they decided to leave those issues for resolution by the marketplace and future technologies rather than by regulation. Massachusetts
also tried to make its law more consistent with similar statutes being developed at the international level. More than twenty states have passed
signature-enabling laws.

Hybrid Laws. A few states have attempted to draw from what they believe to be the best elements in all or some of these other types of laws.
The most prominent example is Illinois, which provides for broad recognition of electronic signatures but also creates a PKI digital-signature
regime. Unlike Utah's, however, the Illinois law is broader and applies to
electronic signatures generally. Four other states have followed Illinois'
lead.

Electronic Commerce Laws for the Future

As good a beginning as these various electronic signature efforts by the
states are, they have a number of significant shortcomings. First, they are
after all effective only within the boundaries of the states in which they
are enacted. Most do not even mention the issue of jurisdiction or the effect of their laws in other states. When they do, it is merely to assert rec-
iprocity with states that pass the same laws, ignoring the question of resolving differences. Second, there are significant differences between the
many laws, leaving those who wish to do business on the Net in somewhat of a legal limbo in a number of areas. Finally, these laws generally
ignore the existence of foreign legal systems and the global nature of
electronic commerce. They do not begin to deal with the issues of international and extraterritorial law. As the American Bar Association pointed
out, with international coordination or harmonization, "those engaging
in international electronic commerce may consider themselves to be entering unexplored, uncharted and ungoverned areas."[8]

A number of particularly significant efforts are being made above the
state level to deal with these issues. The most important is the activity
of the National Conference of Commissioners on Uniform State Laws

(NCCUSL). With representatives from the legal community in every state, NCCUSL is the 107-year-old body that works to assure legal uniformity among the states. It develops acts that the states then pass into law and works very closely with groups such as the American Law Institute and the American Bar Association.

NCCUSL has drafted two important acts: the Uniform Electronic Transactions Act (UETA) and the Uniform Computer Information Transactions Act (UCITA). Both were slated for discussion and adoption at NCCUSL's annual meeting in Denver in July 1999. Following that, they were targeted for introduction and passage in all state legislatures as well as in the District of Columbia, Puerto Rico, and the U.S. Virgin Islands. Taken together, they provide a broad legal framework for electronic commerce that would provide predictability and uniformity anywhere in the United States and generally meet the principles discussed earlier. On March 14, 2000, Virginia became the first state to approve UCITA when a bill enacting it was signed by Governor James S. Gilmore.

The UETA provides the basis for a uniform state statute governing the use of electronic records and signatures. It covers the legal recognition of electronic records and signatures, their attribution and effect, electronic notarization and retention, the rules for admissibility in evidence, and the time and place of sending and receipt. It also covers specific issues such as the use of electronic documents and signatures by government agencies and items that are excluded from the electronic arena, such as wills and testaments.

The 291-page UCITA deals with the commercial law governing computer information transactions. It began life as an attempt to modernize Article 2B of the Uniform Commercial Code, which dealt with licensing. NCCUSL wanted to resolve some issues related to the sale of shrink-wrapped software applications. As the NCCUSL members wrestled with this issue, they realized that it was much broader and involved the entire issue of electronic information transactions. In the end, NCCUSL invested more than four years of activity on UCITA and the work of hundreds of lawyers. Basically, UCITA accepted the Clinton administration legal framework principles, even though some NCCUSL members had argued otherwise:

There are many who have argued for a regulatory approach to transactions in this industry that would differ from the contract law approach applied to any other field of commerce. UCITA adheres to the norm of United States commercial law: freedom of contract is the philosophy of commerce. UCITA leaves in place basic consumer protection laws and adds several new consumer and licensee protections that extend beyond current law. However, the principle remains that markets and agreements control subject to unconscionability, fundamental public policy and supplemental principles.[9]

If a major change in contract law resulted from UCITA, it stems from the fact that transactions involving contracts for information are different from contracts involving the sale of goods. The sale of goods "focuses on rights to a tangible item, while the other [i.e., the sale of information] focuses on intangibles and rights in intangibles."[10] As UCITA points out, in a sale of goods, the buyer owns the subject matter and that ownership creates exclusive rights in the specific item being purchased. In the case of information, however, the buyer may acquire the digital form of the information or even a physical diskette, but does not own the underlying information or rights associated with it. These are determined by the terms of the electronic contract and by the laws governing intellectual property rights, especially those dealing with copyright issues. In Chapter 6, we saw how such distinctions might affect tax law and the tax liabilities of buyers and sellers. Now we will examine how they affect the fundamental legal environment.

In addition to the impact of intellectual property law, UCITA also points out that the First Amendment and free speech protections are central to computer information transactions. Since computer information is content, which in reality is a form of "speech," electronic contracts can be influenced not only by intellectual property law but also by the First Amendment. For example, UCITA establishes the right of a court to invalidate a contract term that might conflict with fundamental public policy in this area.

UCITA is also in agreement with the administration's recommendations for a legal framework in that it agrees with the principle of permitting individuals to set contract terms without governmental interference. Key in this regard is Section 109, which permits parties to a contract to choose a jurisdiction for possible disputes that may arise between them.

UCITA is carefully coordinated with UETA and includes, among others, the following subjects: legal recognition of electronic records and authentication, choice of law and forum, contract formation in general, use of electronic agents, offer and acceptance, pretransaction disclosures, electronic errors and consumer defenses, delivery terms, warranty, ownership and transfers, financing, performance, and damages. Together with UETA, UCITA provides a firm basis for building a legal structure for electronic commerce.

In addition to the construction of this legal structure at the state level, legislative and regulatory activity is also ongoing at the federal level. A key issue has been whether or not the federal government should pre-empt the states on issues like electronic signatures with federal legislation. Debate over this issue has been the most serious impediment to a broad federal bill dealing with the subject of electronic signatures. The federal government has made progress, however, on this and on the issue of electronic transactions for government agencies.

For some time, a number of agencies, including the Food and Drug Administration and the Department of Defense, had been developing electronic signature and authentication methods that would allow them to complete transactions, such as purchasing and filing of reports, electronically and still meet their legal obligations. In 1998, Congress passed legislation enabling electronic signatures for virtually all federal agencies. Sponsored by Senator Spencer Abraham of Michigan and Representative Anna Eshoo of California, this legislation is technology neutral and provides a broad framework for agencies to follow. Although the congressional committees studying the legislation had earlier favored an approach more like Utah's, testimony from the head of the Information Technology Division of the state of Massachusetts, Dan Greenwood, led them to shape the bill along the lines of the Massachusetts signature-enabling law. Said Greenwood, "Given the rapid growth, number of options and dynamic change that characterize the electronic commerce marketplace, federal legislation of this type must stop short of picking technology winners and losers."[11]

After the passage of the federal electronic signatures legislation, Congress passed a broader technology-neutral bill to cover not only federal agencies but most electronic transactions. While a variety of issues made final passage difficult, including the issues of state preemption, privacy concerns related to the third-party certificate authorities, and consumer activist concerns about fraud and other issues, the "Electronic Signature in Global and National Commerce Act" was passed and signed into law by President Clinton on June 30, 2000.

In the international arena, the situation is much like the dilemma in the United States created by the myriad state laws. At the national level around the world, dozens of countries have passed or are in the final stages of considering laws that deal with the legal framework for electronic commerce, particularly digital- or electronic-signature laws. Among the key nations doing so are Germany, Korea, Spain, Malaysia, Italy, Argentina, Chile, Netherlands, the United Kingdom, and Denmark. Unfortunately, most of these countries' efforts have been uncoordinated and are often, like the early Utah law, over-regulatory and favor a single technology.

The German Digital Signature Act, for example, adopted in mid-1997, essentially imposes a licensing scheme for certificate authorities under a PKI approach. It imposes detailed regulatory requirements on certificate authorities in areas such as fees, liability, technical standards, privacy, and criminal sanctions. On the positive side, it does provide for recognition of systems outside of Germany, although basically only those within the EU; other countries would be eligible for recognition through treaties.

In contrast to the German law, Spain's, based on the revision of its penal code, is much more general. It prescribes little government intervention and is more like the Massachusetts law. Italy's statute, on the other hand, confers enormous power on the Italian National Council of Notaries, a large and politically potent group that would essentially control certificate authorities. Malaysia's law, like Germany's, adheres to a particular technological approach but takes an even more regulatory approach. As one expert observer says, this mixing bowl of new laws

suggests ongoing disappointment for the international actor who desires a predictable legal environment within which to conduct electronic commerce. Not only do these various efforts suggest a legal landscape comprised of widely varied treatment of digital authentication issues, but they indicate that a seeming preference for vigorous state intervention in the emerging infrastructure appears to be, if not ascendant, at least widely contemplated. This could very well create not just disharmony but outright conflict between the increasing number of national jurisdictions that are intent upon dealing with digital authentication legislatively.[12]

Fortunately, despite the fragmented efforts at the national level around the world, a number of significant international efforts under way may bring some global order to the legal framework issue. For example, the ministers of the member states of the Asia-Pacific Economic Cooperation forum (APEC) set up a working group on electronic commerce during their meeting in November 1997. APEC had been working on the issue of digital signatures for a number of years and in late 1998 published its "Blueprint for Action on Electronic Commerce." In that document, Japan contributed to the discussion on electronic signatures by recommending that future electronic-signature legislation within APEC be minimal; that the government role be merely to facilitate electronic signatures; that laws be technology neutral; and that international barriers not be raised to cross-border transactions. Canada and Singapore also reported on their June 1998 demonstration of the interoperability of their PKI systems.[13]

In addition to APEC, at the regional level, the EU is also working on a method of harmonizing electronic signatures across its member states. On May 13, 1998, the European Commission revealed its proposed directive on a common framework for electronic signatures. In contrast to the German law discussed earlier, the commission's proposed directive is more general and technology neutral, allowing for "legal recognition of electronic signatures irrespective of the technology used [e.g., digital signatures using asymmetric cryptography or biometrics]. It establishes only minimal requirements in such areas as liability and certification and expresses alarm that the diverging national laws within the EU "could create a serious barrier to communications and business."[14]

Above the regional level, other international organizations are also at work. The OECD completed a paper titled "Certification in the Electronic Environment" in August 1997 that warned of the dangers of conflicting national laws, which it said could become significant trade barriers. A year later, in October 1998, the OECD completed "A Global Action Plan for Business with Government toward Electronic Commerce," which called for a number of international actions in the electronic-signature area. It said, "Digital certification is an embryonic sector that needs to be addressed, common definitions further refined, etc. . . . Self-regulation should be given preference to avoid the lock-in effect of inflexible and potentially incompatible government regulation."[15] The paper went on to encourage member governments to work with UNCITRAL in its efforts to standardize electronic signatures law.

UNCITRAL has a strong track record in the area of digital legal framework. As the United Nations body that develops model laws for nations (a sort of international NCCUSL), UNICTRAL completed work on a "Model Law on Electronic Commerce" in 1996. This model law was aimed at removing legal obstacles to the use of electronic communications. It conferred legal status on the contents of data messages, allowed them to serve as "original" documents, prohibited the inadmissibility of electronic documents, and set some technology-neutral standards for electronic attribution.

Following its work on the electronic commerce model law, UNCITRAL turned its attention to electronic signatures. Initially, the UNCITRAL drafters favored a thick approach like the Utah law. Recent advances in technology plus some constructive lobbying by the U.S. State Department led the drafters to accept two key principles favored by the Clinton administration: technology neutrality and the freedom of parties to choose the method of authentication they both desire. The model law would also require countries to refrain from erecting trade barriers and to treat foreign providers and users of authentication technologies no less favorably than local ones. By early 1999, UNCITRAL was making good progress, but even after UN acceptance, the model law will have to be enacted into legislation in each country.

CONSUMER PROTECTION

Beyond the issues of providing a legal framework for electronic documents, contracts, and signatures lies the broader legal issue of consumer protection in cyberspace. Robert Pitofsky, chair of the Federal Trade Commission (FTC), set out the digital consumer issue at an FTC workshop:

> But what if the products don't arrive, or if the wrong product is delivered, or somehow the advertising, marketing or sale by the seller is inconsistent with the laws of the consumer's country? . . . [T]he informal nature of the medium, the lack of personal contact between buyer and seller, the geographic dispersion of sellers, create new opportunities and unprecedented opportunities for consumer abuse through fraud and deception—opportunities so great that if not effectively addressed, they can undermine the full development of global competition itself. How do we monitor the Internet, and deal with cross-border fraud?[16]

The FTC has already begun to play an active role in the United States, especially on the issue of privacy, as we saw in Chapter 5, but also on issues related to fraud and deceptive advertising, and particularly where children are involved. The Securities and Exchange Commission (SEC), the Department of Commerce, the U.S. Postal Inspection Service, the Internal Revenue Service, and other government agencies have also been active in trying to protect consumers from Internet-based fraud. For example, the SEC has prosecuted companies and individuals suspected of securities fraud on the Internet. Going one step further, in May 2000 the Federal Bureau of Investigation and the National White Collar Crime Center jointly announced a new Internet Fraud Complaint Center (IFCC) Web site. The IFCC provides consumers with an easy-to-use mechanism to report suspected on-line crime. While the administration's "Framework for Global Electronic Commerce" called for private-sector self-regulation to address many of these issues, it also pointed out that government action was appropriate where cases of consumer fraud were involved.

Indeed, the private sector had been quite active in working out self-regulating efforts in the consumer area to head off more government regulation. A number of self-regulatory programs have sprung up, including the CPA WebTrust seal of the American Institute of Certified Public Accountants (AICPA) and the Better Business Bureau's BBB Online seal program, which was discussed in Chapter 5. Begun in 1998, the AICPA program requires that businesses displaying its seal satisfy a number of key criteria, including disclosure of business practices and certification by a certified public accountant.

The Better Business Bureau, which had been identified more with Main Street than with cyberspace, began its BBB Online program in 1997. It offers a seal that permits consumers to find reliable, trustworthy businesses on-line that meet Better Business Bureau criteria. In addition, the service offers a search engine through which consumers can find businesses with the seal and provides vital consumer-focused information about the company, such as whom to contact in the event of a dispute. The service even offers a dispute-resolution mechanism for consumers. As of mid-1999, more than 3,000 businesses had qualified to display the BBB Online seal.

Many consumer issues are still unresolved, one of the most vexing being the case of advertising. Since all advertising in cyberspace can reach any country, whose laws apply? Most countries have laws forbidding the use of false or inaccurate advertising and some, such as the United States, also have self-regulatory schemes. In the United States, the National Advertising Association enforces the rules. But many countries also restrict advertising language, frequency, and duration, and place further restrictions on certain types of advertising, such as that for alcoholic beverages, tobacco, and medications. Advertisements may offend cultural concerns in some countries: many Islamic countries, for example, are especially sensitive to portrayals of religion or sexuality. The administration's framework document directs federal agencies such as the departments of State and Commerce, the U. S. Trade Representative, the FTC, and others to work both bilaterally and multilaterally to reach agreements with countries on advertising issues like these. Whether or not there is a resolution to these issues and how long it will take to reach agreements are open questions.

Nonetheless, the tremendous difficulties involved in creating a global and coherent legal framework for the digital age suggest that new mechanisms may be needed to create them. Nations and their political subdivisions have been at work for years on a framework for the relatively narrow area of electronic signatures alone, and without a reasonable solution yet in sight. How will they tackle in a timely manner the broader and more difficult issues of consumer protection? Can nations afford to wait while not one but literally dozens of international and regional organizations constantly reinvent the wheel and develop their own frameworks, which then have to be revised and harmonized with those of others?

Or should governments simply agree to cede control of this issue (and perhaps others) to one international organization with broad coverage, such as the World Trade Organization? Or would it make more sense to establish a new international body with almost universal coverage? Since governments have not yet reorganized themselves to deal with the realities of the digital age, it seems unlikely that they are ready to cede control to any other entity, nor is it yet clear that such action is needed.

DIGITAL PROPERTY: THE END OF COPYRIGHT?

[P]otentially everything on the Net, captured as electronic bits, is intellectual property: e-mail "conversations," banner ads, movies and video clips, legal documents, databases of consumer information . . . to say nothing of traditional packaged content, such as videos, images and news articles. . . . Who owns all these things? Who controls their use? Who has the right to benefit?

—Esther Dyson, *Release 2.0*[17]

From the very beginning, people began to realize that the Net was a giant, uncontrolled copying machine. But if everything on the Net was intellectual property in one form or another, did that mean that all the property on the Net could be owned by anyone and everyone—free of charge? Or could owners of digital property fence and protect it, as owners of real property and tangible goods had done for centuries? As one early observer wrote about this odd property of the Net, "There's land, lots of land. We are told that the digital revolution is going to open up a lot of territory. Money's to be made by using it, subdividing it, selling it, farming it. . . . The opposite may, of course, be equally true. There are those who believe that the digital revolution . . . will destroy private property. Owners of large information estates like Time-Warner and TCI will soon find themselves pushed out of their protective enclosures. They will be forced to live in a new electronic wilderness, where hackers and directors of information systems are equal."[18]

The result of this peculiar situation has been a particularly bitter struggle between traditional copyright owners—publishing companies, motion picture producers, software developers, recording studios, and the like—and those favoring unlimited access to information on the Net—librarians, educators, and foreign interests (countries and their companies) that are copyright-poor. As civil libertarian Mike Godwin points out in *Cyber Rights,* "Protecting one's economic interests and one's individual liberties is important . . . so fights over issues such as the balance between copyright and free speech tend to generate a lot of strong emotions like anger and fear."[19]

One gauge of the intensity of the debate is that the section on intellectual property protection in the Clinton administration's "Framework for Global Electronic Commerce" is the longest single section in the report. This should not be too surprising, however, since the public policy debate over intellectual property has been stoked continuously for the past half-millennium. The birth of the digital age has merely ignited it and set off a four-alarm fire.

Before Johannes Gutenberg—and even after him for many years in most countries—copyright simply didn't exist. When William Shakespeare wrote and produced his plays at the end of the sixteenth century, he had no copyright protection at all—not from others' publishing or performing his plays, nor even to prevent others from making changes in them. Copyright law did not come into being in England until 1709. China, the world's most populous nation, did not begin to offer intellectual property protection until the early 1990s, as it entered the world trading system and countries like the United States began to complain about piracy.

The authors of the American Constitution did recognize the importance of intellectual property, and they wrote it into Article 1, Section 8: "The Congress shall have the Power To . . . promote the Progress of Science and the useful Arts, by securing for limited Times to Authors and Inventors the exclusive Right to their respective Writings and Discoveries." Congress passed the first Copyright Act in 1790 and has continued to amend both copyright and patent law right up to the present day. Generally, debate about the law always returns to its fundamental inherent conflict: Do intellectual property laws exist to benefit authors and inventors by protecting their financial interests in their creations, or do they exist to benefit the public by encouraging the widespread use and open flow of inventions and ideas? Some argue that the Constitution clearly intends to protect authors and inventors, since it speaks of their "exclusive rights." Others argue the opposite, citing the document's aim of promoting "the progress of science and the useful arts" and its limiting of the exclusive right to a fixed period, so as to avoid a perpetual monopoly.

Both sides are right, of course, leading to tensions between these two not always compatible aims. To understand how the digital world upsets the intellectual property apple cart, it is first necessary to understand the elements of intellectual property law. Of the variety of forms of intellectual property, three are most relevant to the Net: copyright, patents, and trademarks.

The most important of these three is copyright. Copyright law protects works of authorship, including such items as books, sound recordings, motion pictures, and computer software. In most countries, the bestowal of a copyright gives the owner the exclusive right to copy and reproduce, publicly perform, change, and make publicly available the work. Copyright owners copyright the *expression* of their ideas—in words, musical notation, or programming code, for example—not the idea itself. Thus, the film *Titanic* can be copyrighted, but the idea of a film about a doomed romance aboard the ship *Titanic* cannot. Copyrights are also issued in a single country, so the author of a book of poems who wishes to maintain global exclusive rights for him or herself will file for copyright in many different countries. Copyright is also limited in time; its length varies from country to country. In the United States it lasts for fifty years, in the EU for 70 years. Terms vary from country to country as well, with some nations more interested in economic rights and others in "moral" rights—that is, the author's literary interest in seeing that his or her work is not bowdlerized or altered.

Internationally, copyrights are governed by the 1886 Berne Convention for the Protection of Literary and Artistic Works. A United Nations agency, the World Intellectual Property Organization (WIPO), administers cooperation and harmonization on intellectual property law worldwide. The Berne Convention has been updated constantly, most recently in 1997. Copyright law around the world is also revised as technology advances. For example, during the past decade, computer programs gained formal copyright protection as literary works in a number of international treaties and directives, including the Agreement on Trade-Related Aspects of Intellectual Property Rights, which was part of the Uruguay Round of the General Agreement on Tariffs and Trade in 1994, and the European Software Directive of 1991.

Unlike copyrights, patents protect inventions as well as processes. They are also issued within a country and, unlike copyrights, which exist as soon as a work is written, patents must be applied for so that a government search can be undertaken to ensure that the invention is truly a new effort. Internationally, patent rules are governed by the 1883 Paris Convention for the Protection of Industrial Property. It, too, has been regularly revised under the auspices of WIPO.

Constant disputes arise between high-technology companies over patents involving the physical infrastructure of the digital age, but patent policies enter into the digital debate principally over the issue of the patentability of software. Since processes can be patented, certain computer programs, such as a utility that governs the operation of an inventory system or a machine-tool operation, can also be patented. Thus, a particular type of program for searching the Internet may be patented. Patent protection for software is also becoming more important to many companies as hardware inventions are increasingly embedded in software. Some argue, however, that patents provide too much protection for software and issuing them is therefore not in the public interest.

Finally, trademarks are the names or symbols used mainly by businesses to identify or "brand" their products and services. Companies can build up substantial "goodwill" for their products and services over time through the use of a well-known mark, and thus trademark ownership is quite important to businesses. Trademarks must also be registered in each country in which the owner wishes to use them. The 1891 Madrid Agreement Concerning the International Registration of Marks is the governing international agreement on trademarks.

Issues Raised by the Digital Age

The emergence of the Net has opened up new trademark issues. Businesses that wish to expand their operations into another country often find the equivalent of their name or trademark already in use. In the past, various accommodations could be worked out between businesses, or companies might simply use a somewhat different name in order to do business in a particular country. The problem on the Net arises since everything on it is global. The domain name "coke.com," for example, appears everywhere in the world, since it is the Web address for Coca-Cola's home page.

Not surprisingly, numerous disputes have erupted over the ownership of such domain names. Some view them as source identifiers, like street addresses, which are not normally protected by intellectual property law. Courts have recognized, however, that the misuse of a domain name is not in the public interest when it misleads people to think they are doing business with one entity while in fact they are dealing with another. The domain-name dilemma has become a major issue for companies as they choose new brand names and logos for their products and services. Although the addition of new, top-level domain names (to supplement the existing ones, such as .com, .org, .net, .edu, and .gov) may help, it will not mollify those who want to use the ".com" domain, which is the most popular, much as "800" numbers are preferable to "888" numbers for toll-free calls.

Although the patent and trademark issues are important, copyright is by far the most serious of the intellectual property issues raised by the Net. The reasons are simple: the stakes in copyright are by far the greatest. On the one side, the content-owning industries, already plagued by massive piracy of their products, see the potential for a quantum leap in illegal copying over the Internet. They fear theft not only in the traditional form of piracy by professional thieves but also by ordinary people not even aware they are committing a crime by printing out material they find on the Net. In fact, most people are unaware that copying a professional photograph, an audio tape, or a software application is an infringement of copyright. The motion picture, music publishing, and software industries, for instance, spend millions of dollars each year to educate the public about this issue and thereby to try to stem the tide of illegal copying.

For example, Jack Valenti, president of the Motion Picture Association of America (MPAA), told a Chicago audience in July 1998 that intellectual property then accounted for about 4 percent of the U.S. gross domestic product and that up to $20 billion per year was lost to piracy. Of this, the MPAA estimates that the U.S. motion picture industry loses about $2.5 billion per year.[20] What the MPAA and its members fear even more than the current form of professional piracy, however, is a digital future in which the mass production facilities of thieves reproducing and selling videotapes would be replaced by ordinary citizens innocently copying and transmitting DVDs or downloading films over a future broadband Internet. Even these motion picture industry statistics, however, are dwarfed by those of the software industry. The recording industry faced this challenge early in 2000 as thousands of young people downloaded music files in the perfect-sounding MP3 format with the new software called Napster, thereby obtaining free digital copies of recordings by popular musical groups. A study released in June 1999 by the Business Software Alliance, an association of the nation's largest software firms, stated that one of every four software applications in use were illegal and that software piracy cost the industry $11 billion in 1998.[21] Moreover, the report stated, this piracy cost the U.S. economy more than 100,000 lost jobs and almost $1 billion in lost tax revenues. Clearly, the ability easily to transmit and download software across the Net was contributing to these losses and would become the major component in the future. The same fears were expressed by music, book, and newspaper publishers, as well as by the giant corporate content owners such as Disney, Time Warner, Reed Elsevier, and Bertelsmann.

Arrayed against the copyright owners has been a broad coalition of librarians, educators, scholars, and some industries that depend on the broadest and freest possible circulation of information or that have some economic interest in weaker intellectual property protection. As Pamela Samuelson, a professor of law and information management at the University of California at Berkeley, put it, "An 'information society' in which all information is kept under high-tech lock and key, available only under terms and conditions dictated by a licenser, would not be worthy of the name."[22] The problem for the parties on this side of the debate has been that their interests have diverged somewhat. For example, the libraries, which have many interests, have been principally concerned about preservation of the "first sale" doctrine, under which they may purchase a book and then lend it to multiple readers. How, they ask, can this doctrine be preserved in the digital environment?

Educators and scholars, also with many different interests, are principally concerned with the "fair use" doctrine, which defines, for example, how teachers or scholars may make use of excerpts from copyrighted material in teaching and research without infringing the copyright. Some corporations, such as the telephone companies and other network providers, are especially interested in how to avoid any liability for the potential copyright infringements committed by their users. Other corporations, such as some Japanese computer companies, wish to legalize technical mechanisms such as the "decompilation" (or deciphering a program's source code, or programming code, to permit reengineering of the program) of software code to avoid copyright infringement. This would allow them to make free use of software belonging to American or other companies.

All in all, there are four major issues to be resolved: fair use, temporary copies, infringement liability, and anti-circumvention.

Fair Use. The fair use doctrine in copyright law permits journalists, teachers, literary critics and reviewers, researchers, and scientists to reproduce limited portions of copyrighted works. According to copyright law, this must done in such a way as to not diminish the rights of the owner. In fact, normally it is in the interests of the owner to allow such use, since authors normally wish to be reviewed by critics and cited by scholars. Most copyright experts believe the fair use doctrine has worked well over the years, encouraging creativity, assisting in the educational process, and spreading knowledge.

A great many court decisions have been handed down that define the limits of the fair use doctrine in the physical world. For example, teachers cannot copy entire chapters from textbooks and distribute them to students. The problem arises in the digital arena, as more materials are digitized and become available over the Net. Some educators believe these types of material should be available to everyone free of charge. Although reasonably priced educational materials are an important social goal, allowing free use of copyrighted materials would also destroy the economic incentive for authors to create new materials. Over the years, a good balance for fair use has been developed between content owners and users, and this same balance can and should be preserved in the future digital environment.

Temporary Copies. The issue of temporary or transient copies is a more difficult one. In the normal course of operations on the Net, temporary copies of content are often made and used for various technical purposes, such as during transmission. Copies of software transmitted over the Net may be made on the hard drive of a desktop computer and may remain there even after the software finishes its job. "Caching" is a technique whereby a temporary copy of a Web site is made on a person's personal computer to save the time of downloading the site a second time. Mirroring is a similar technique that involves duplication of very busy Web sites on different servers, allowing more people to access the site. When the National Aeronautics and Space Administration (NASA) posted pictures on its Web site of its Mars landing robot, a number of computer companies "mirrored" the site as a public service so that the hundreds of thousand of people who wished to see Mars could do so. In this case the mirroring was legal, since NASA is a public agency and, in any event, gave its permission for the site to be mirrored. But are all these temporary copies legal, or does their use or very existence create some liability for copyright infringement?

The issue is of particular importance to the operators of networks who fear that they could be held liable for copyright infringement just in the normal course of their operations. As in the case of fair use, the answer seems to be in finding the correct balance. The use of temporary copies that are needed for the internal functioning of a network or its underlying equipment or software, and do not have any independent purpose, should not subject the user to any liability for copyright infringement. On the other hand, temporary copies that do have some economic value of their own, such as the unauthorized reuse of a piece of software, should require the permission of the owner and could subject an unauthorized user to copyright infringement liability. Over time, the courts will have to deal with the many permutations and shades of gray in this phenomenon.

Infringement Liability. The broader issue of liability is of particular concern to network providers and telecommunications companies. Today, telephone companies are not legally liable for the conversations that their customers have over telephone lines. The telephone companies and the network providers argue that the same principle should apply on the Net. If a subscriber to an Internet service provider (ISP) posts material on a Web site for children that illegally reproduces a copyrighted children's story, for example, does the ISP have any liability for the infringement, or does the local telecommunications carrier whose lines may carry the data? Should network providers and telecommunications carriers have to police their systems for such possible violations? The network providers clearly answer "no," but the copyright owners, who fear massive copyright violations, have implied that that answer may be "yes." What, they ask, if a carrier did know about a copyright violation and took no action to deal with it? What if unscrupulous network providers even encouraged violations, or let it be known that they would look the other way? What if the Web site operator was impossible to find in the course of a lawsuit?

On this issue, too, it will take many years to work out a body of law to deal with most circumstances, but some principles that can help resolve it have already been written into law. It seems reasonable that telecommunications operators and other network providers should not be held liable for flows of content on their systems over which they have no control or knowledge. Nor should they be expected to police the content that moves over their systems for copyright or other potential violations of law. On the other hand, when a carrier or network provider receives formal notice from an author or other copyright owner of infringing material on its system, it should remove or block access to it within a reasonable time. If it does not, perhaps because it does not wish to lose the financial benefits it derives from the site, the carrier or provider may become liable. Carriers and network providers may fear that they could incur another liability if they remove material that is later found to be legal, since they may have deprived their customer of some economic benefit. In this case, the complaining author should be liable, particularly if he or she knowingly misrepresented the facts in order to have a site blocked.

Anti-circumvention. No digital intellectual property issue has set off as complicated an internecine battle between segments of the high-technology industry than the issue of anti-circumvention. Fearful of the wholesale copying of digital content in the future, the motion picture industry and others came up with a simple solution—that is, simple for them. They decided to persuade Congress to pass legislation to require the manufacturers of every device capable of making digital copies to include in their products a standardized technology that would prevent that device from making unauthorized copies by circumventing the protective features built into the original. Although this solution might have been acceptable to the manufacturers of single-use products, such as DVD players, it was certainly not acceptable to manufacturers of other, general-purpose products. For example, the personal computer industry argued that it would face additional costs and technical problems if such a solution were mandated by law. It also pointed out that a single technical standard for anti-circumvention simply would not work.

The motion picture industry failed in its bid to get Congress to mandate a single solution, but its campaign did raise the interest of the computer industry in the subject. Technical experts in both industries are now working together on the issue.

Government Action

As these issues were developing, the international intellectual property community took early action to deal with some of them. In December 1996, representatives of the nations who signed the Berne Convention came together in a diplomatic conference in Geneva and approved two new treaties to protect copyright in the digital age. The Clinton administration played a major role in the adoption of the new treaties and was criticized by some for representing too strongly the interests of copyright owners. Telecommunications carriers and network providers were particularly concerned about the administration's position on liability and attempted to get Congress to delay the diplomatic conference, but without success. Nevertheless, key compromises were made in Geneva that allowed Congress to pass legislation bringing U.S. law in line with the new treaties. Perhaps the most important compromise removed the question of liability from the treaty's purview; liability is left for national law to deal with.

To implement the new treaties, Congress passed the Digital Millennium Copyright Act (DMCA) in October 1998, surprising many who thought that the broad gaps between different parties could never be bridged. The law prohibits the circumvention of any technical protection measures used by copyright holders to restrict access and prohibits the manufacture of any device primarily designed to defeat protection measures.

The law made no basic changes to the fair use doctrine but added some exemptions for scholars and teachers for the use of copyrighted works in digitized research papers or classroom materials. The law also exempts on-line service providers and telecommunications carriers from liability for copyright infringement based solely on use of the carrier's or provider's system. It provides a "take-down" mechanism when carriers and providers are formally notified about infringement by a copyright holder. This new take-down law was used in May 2000 when the rock group Metallica notified Napster of its view that more than 300,000 Napster users were infringing Metallica's copyrights. Napster said it would comply with the DMCA and remove the offending names, but offered to reinstate customers who were wrongfully denied service.

The law also permits authorized institutions, such as libraries, to make up to three digital preservation copies of a copyrighted work and electronically to "loan" those copies to other qualifying institutions. It also created a two-year period during which the government would study how the fair use and other provisions were working.

Adoption of the new treaties and passage of the Digital Millennium Copyright Act were major steps forward for both the United States and the international community in advancing intellectual property law for the digital age. Nevertheless, many issues remain unresolved. For example, the governance of Internet domain names remains controversial, although some progress has been made. Protection for databases, involving the extension of copyright protection to a database that has in some way been ordered or manipulated, must still be worked out.

Moreover, agreeing on a new treaty is one thing. Putting it in force and seeing to it that countries implement and especially enforce it is another. The United States and other nations face years of negotiation on the treaty issues.

Furthermore, as the Net develops new issues will emerge. Computer guru Esther Dyson has suggested, for example, that new ways of making money will appear. "Businesses who make content will have to figure out ways other than selling copies to make money, and they will."[23] Among the methods she suggests are electronic intellectual services, memberships, product support, spin-off goods, and sponsorships; these "products" will engender business conflicts of their own, of course.

In conclusion, much work remains. Progress has been particularly slow and difficult on issues such as electronic signatures, contracts, and consumer issues. Venues are unclear and include a number of national and international bodies, some of which are regional and some of which overlap. Some have legal authority; some do not. Perhaps it is time to begin thinking about the creation of a new international body, or the greater empowerment of an existing one. This body could hammer out, adopt, and put into practice some legal rules of the road that will provide the transparency and certainty that consumers and businesses will need to confidently use electronic commerce. Although it is too early to propose seriously that such a body actually be created, the discussion of it might spur the existing international bureaucracies to faster action.

9

Research and the National Interest

The current boom in information technology is built on basic research in computer science carried out more than a decade ago. There is an urgent need to replenish the knowledge base.
— "Information Technology Research: Investing in Our Future"[1]

The development and use of the atomic bombs that ended World War II sent shock waves far beyond Hiroshima, Nagasaki, and Alamogordo, New Mexico. In the months and years after 1945, government leaders and industrialists in capitals from Washington to Moscow experienced a common revelation: In the future, national security and the national interest would depend more than ever on research and the ability to engineer the abstract ideas of basic science into practical reality.

To be sure, it was more than nuclear fission that was responsible for this new insight. Numerous inventions and technical advances had helped fight and win the war, including radar, encryption devices, rocketry, radio transmission, aeronautics, navigation, and sonar. Many others were just beginning to emerge, such as jet aircraft, nuclear energy, and an obscure device called the "stored program computer." Advances in fields such as metallurgy, mathematics, avionics, physics, and electrical engineering were responsible. All of this progress had been made possible by a unique wartime collaboration, especially in the United States and the United Kingdom, between government, industry, academia, and labor. University professors worked side by side with military officers, government officials, industry executives, technical experts, and labor union officials on the Manhattan Project, on code-breaking, and on aircraft development and manufacturing, among other things.

Near the end of the war in 1944, President Franklin Roosevelt asked his top science adviser, Vannevar Bush, what lessons could be learned from the wartime experience with science and technology that could be used in peacetime. Bush was a towering figure, a former electrical engineering professor from the Massachusetts Institute of Technology (MIT) who had directed the nation's wartime research and development activities as director of the Office of Scientific Research and Development and chair of the president's National Defense Research Committee. His answer to the president came in his report "Science: The Endless Frontier," a visionary work that still dominates national thinking about the role of science and government in society.

In addition to its key role in the national defense, said Bush in his report, scientific research should be supported by government "for the improvement of the national health, the creation of new enterprises bringing new jobs, and the betterment of the national standard of living."[2] Bush's recommendations led directly to the formation of the National Science Foundation (NSF) and later to the establishment of the National Institutes of Health (NIH), two government agencies that became heavily involved in the growth of the digital age. The NSF played a key role in the creation of the Internet; the NIH created one of the most powerful medical information tools on the Net, and also uses the Net for basic medical research.

For years after the war, however, the Cold War tilted U.S. research and development policy priorities heavily toward defense. The lion's share of funding went to the Pentagon, either directly to the services' procurement programs or through the Department of Defense's Advanced Projects Research Agency (ARPA) and other national defense agencies such as the National Security Agency or the Atomic Energy Commission. Although the NSF funded primarily non-defense-related programs proposed by universities, some NSF funding did help defense efforts, such as that for mathematics and science teaching after the Soviet launch of *Sputnik,* or for foreign-language teaching. The growth of the space program under the National Aeronautics and Space Administration (NASA) also became a major source of research and development funding. The Atomic Energy Commission, which later became the Department of Energy, established its own network of government laboratories for nuclear research and development, some in collaboration with universities, and some managed by private companies, such as the Sandia Laboratories in New Mexico. Much later, as supercomputing became more central to the nation's nuclear program, the Department of Energy's role would become key.

At the same time, private research and development funded by corporations was making substantial and more than sufficient progress in the broader civilian areas that Bush's report suggested were key. Bell Laboratories at AT&T was highly visible after its inventions of the transistor and the communications satellite, but labs at DuPont, General Electric, IBM, and elsewhere were turning out new ideas and products in droves throughout the 1950s and 1960s. These companies and dozens of other American firms were the masters of the world economy throughout those decades. No real need was seen for any significant and direct government involvement in civilian or applied research and none was proposed.

The earliest calls for more government funding of civilian scientific research came not from the United States, but from Europe, where they were prompted by the very success of American industry. In the 1960s, Jean-Jacques Servain-Schreiber published his book, *Le Defi Americaine.* In it, he warned of a tidal wave of American industrial products overwhelming Europe and creating a new kind of economic colonialism. He especially feared the robust American multinational companies such as General Electric, Ford Motor, and IBM, which he said were stealing Europe's talented young scientists and engineers and hiring them to work in their plants and laboratories in Europe or luring them to the United States. This "brain drain" quickly became an issue in Europe.

The remedy for this, thought many Europeans, was national research and development programs and government assistance to European industry to challenge the American upstarts. Soon, government support programs for technology, especially in areas such as computers, semiconductors, and telecommunications surfaced in the United Kingdom, France, and Germany. Companies such as ICL in Britain, Bull in France, and Siemens in Germany, and even a short-lived trans-European entity called Unidata, received government financial support as "national champions" and benefited from protectionist measures aimed at American competitors, including the government-approved merger of local firms. These financial support programs were later adopted and institutionalized by the growing new European Community bureaucracy in Brussels to become more permanent financial-support programs for research in these fields.

The first of these Europe-wide programs directed at the new computing and telecommunications fields was the European Strategic Program for Research and Development (ESPRIT). Begun in 1982, ESPRIT created government-supported research and development projects that brought together private companies, government monopolies, such as the public telephone and telegraph companies, or PTT's, and local universities. For example, an automobile manufacturer, a computer maker, and a university software researcher might work together on a protocol for manufacturing software. When these projects were challenged by non-Europeans as an unfair government subsidy, European officials replied that the U.S. defense research programs had generated much civilian technology and were therefore a critical hidden subsidy that the Europeans were merely countering.

By the 1970s, Japan had also begun government support of research in information technology. Fearing that its export-based economy would need more fuel as its older shipbuilding and automobile industries slowed, the Japanese government also came up with a plan for support of its high-technology industries. This plan began with protectionist support in the form of government subsidies and other assistance for the computer and semiconductor industries, made up of firms such as Toshiba, Fujitsu, Hitachi, and Oki. The powerful Japanese Ministry of International Trade and Industry (MITI), for example, provided 70 billion yen to help Japanese companies catch up in computers. NTT, the Japanese government telecommunications monopoly, assisted this development financially and then purchased exclusively from Japanese suppliers in order to weaken American competitors. NTT's tactics, along with those of other Japanese government-owned entities, were challenged by U.S. trade negotiators at the Tokyo Round of the General Agreement on Tariffs and Trade (GATT) in the 1970s. The ensuing negotiation resulted in a new GATT government procurement code that banned these practices and mandated bidding open to all, including foreign companies, for most government contracts. The Japanese financial-support programs for research and development in these high-tech fields were later broadened and made permanent.

The European programs never seemed to work well, however, and European companies fell further behind in the information technology race. The Japanese programs, on the other hand, seemed to Americans by the late 1970s to be working all too well. Japanese exports in highly visible products, especially consumer electronics and semiconductors, were flooding the United States. Worst of all, the American semiconductor industry, considered to be at the heart of the new Silicon Valley phenomenon, was in trouble. The industry that had invented and exploited brilliantly the integrated circuit appeared to be losing the key battle for the important dynamic random-access memory (DRAM) chip. MITI funding of 200 million yen, combined with some questionable trade and pricing practices, had helped Japanese companies develop the DRAM chip and exploit worldwide markets. Intel, America's leading chip maker, was in deep trouble and had to be rescued by IBM, which provided capital by taking an equity interest in the company, saying it was important to help preserve an American supplier. The Department of Defense was also deeply concerned, since semiconductors were central to so many weapons systems.

As a result, Intel and its U.S. competitors formed the Semiconductor Industry Association (SIA), which enlisted U.S. government help in fighting what it saw as trade law violations by the Japanese government and Japanese industry. The result of ensuing U.S.-Japanese negotiations was a semiconductor agreement between the two countries, which called for more procurement of U.S. semiconductors by Japanese companies. But the SIA members also looked beyond the immediate trade problem to the real long-range problem for U.S. industry: the mounting cost of research and development. Without government involvement, the research push could not be sustained. That involvement came in the form of partnerships between government, private companies, and university engineering departments, and also in the formation in the 1980s of Sematech, a cooperative research and development effort funded by government and the private sector to cooperate in areas of common interest, such as metrology and other areas of pre-competitive research.

Meanwhile, other high-technology industries were growing concerned about what they saw as a new lack of American competitiveness. Companies in industries such as photography and imaging, telecommunications, aircraft, automobiles, pharmaceuticals, and chemicals were alarmed about the future; their concerns were shared by the major research universities and by some labor unions. President Ronald Reagan appointed a commission to look at the issue of competitiveness and in 1986, John Young, the chairman of Hewlett-Packard and the head of the president's commission, issued a bleak report, citing serious deficiencies in U.S. education, tax policy, science policy, and other areas. One important result was the formation of the Council on Competitiveness, an organization of university presidents, corporate chief executive officers, and labor union leaders, which was charged with devising solutions to the problem. The Council on Competitiveness immediately ran into a political problem, however.

A consensus was emerging that the nation needed to spend more money on research and development and especially on applied research, as opposed to basic research. Although indirect policies such as a research and development tax credit might help stimulate more such spending by private industry, many thought that the government would have to spend money on this area directly. On the surface, the notion seemed to be in line with Vannevar Bush's 1945 pronouncement about using federal science policy to create jobs and help business. Japan had used this tool to make itself so competitive.

But in 1986, such direct government funding appeared to be "industrial policy," a form of government intervention in the economy that was anathema during the Reagan era. The basic philosophy of the Reagan administration was that an environment of lower taxes and less govern-ment regulation and intervention—not direct subsidies for civilian re-search and development—was the best way to stimulate innovation. Moreover, in these climactic years of the Cold War, few wished to divert funding for research and development away from higher-priority defense programs such as the Strategic Defense Initiative. Nevertheless, technol-ogy planners in the Pentagon were growing increasingly concerned about the national competitiveness "crisis" and warned that the United States might lag behind in technologies and products needed by the military, such as advanced integrated circuits or flat-panel displays. It was for this reason that the administration had funded Sematech. The Pentagon did not wish to find out during a crisis that it was dependent on foreign sup-pliers for those products.

An important group of Reagan and Bush administration officials finally recognized the critical role of technological competitiveness in the nation's strategic posture overall and fought to establish a variety of programs. These officials included the White House science advisers George Key-worth and Bill Graham, Commerce Department officials Thomas Murrin and Robert White, and Energy Department official Deborah Wince-Smith. Their collective legacy included the doubling of the federal basic research budget, the founding of the Advanced Technology Program in 1988 under the National Institute for Standards and Technology (NIST) in the De-partment of Commerce; and the establishment of the high-performance computing program as an interagency effort (with the strong support of then-senator Al Gore of Tennessee and Representative George Brown of California). The Reagan-Bush years also evidenced a greater coordination of federal departments on matters related to technology, including key trade issues.

The issue of competitiveness continued to intensify, and in 1990, Pres-ident George Bush's science adviser, Allen Bromley, issued a report defin-ing new goals for U.S. technology policy that owed a great deal to Van-nevar Bush's original thinking. Bromley said that U.S. technology policy ought to aim to produce a quality, well-educated workforce, a financial environment conducive to investment in technology, an applied science environment where technology can be quickly translated into quality products, an efficient infrastructure for transferring information, and a supportive legal and regulatory climate. Bromley also called for partner-ships between government, industry, and universities to achieve these goals, with cooperation from state and regional governments.[3]

While these programs were focusing on technology in general, center stage was being occupied by the computer and telecommunications industries. Even though the World Wide Web had not yet been invented, the Advanced Research Projects Agency Network (ARPANET) and the National Science Foundation Network (NSFNET) were already flourishing as tools for the defense and university research communities. In 1991 (the year Timothy Berners-Lee invented the World Wide Web), there were more than one million hosts on the Internet. Corporations had also begun to use the Net, and in 1992, the NSF formally lifted its ban on commercial use of the Internet. Science policy was shifting in favor of more federal involvement in civilian technologies because of competitiveness concerns, just as convergence between computing and communications was beginning and just as the Internet was about to explode. This conjunction was about to bear congressional and federal fruit.

In 1990, Gore and others had sponsored a bill to create a National Research and Education Network (NREN), intended to provide federal funds to upgrade the Internet to serve better education in particular. Although not a new network in itself, the NREN project, as Harvard researcher Brian Kahin has pointed out, had two main objectives: "the NREN is simply a tool that enables agencies to carry out their mission better," and "the NREN is a basic research and prototyping program on fiber optics, network design, switches and protocols."[4] The NREN was a tool because it cut across the different federal agencies involved in the new network efforts and set priorities among them. Thus, it involved the departments of Defense and Commerce, the NSF, and other agencies using the new technologies such as the departments of Education and Agriculture, the Corporation for Public Broadcasting, the Rural Electrification Administration, and the Patent Office.

The NREN's research elements were also important to the high-tech industries. The Bush administration had already proposed most of them in its High Performance Computing Initiative. In fact, the administration had few substantive differences with Gore, although both sides wanted credit for an initiative they believed would be politically welcome. In December 1990, the chief executive officers of the nation's leading computer systems firms had met with administration officials to discuss the federal research program. The following year, their association, the Computer Systems Policy Project (CSPP), endorsed the federal effort as a critical undertaking, saying it would "advance research in high performance computing and networking technologies as well as increase the use of high performance computers to solve important science and engineering programs." Moreover, they said, it could "advance the development of technologies to help solve a wide range of social and economic problems and improve the competitiveness of U.S. industry by providing the foundation for a national communications and information infrastructure."[5] Thus, the business executives were stressing the importance of the program both as a tool to strengthen U.S. competitiveness in the civilian sector but also as an effort to focus on applied research in fields such as health, education, and manufacturing.

The High Performance Computing and Communications Act of 1991 passed both houses of Congress unanimously and provided initially for funding of $469 million to be spread among the various agencies. The NSF, ARPA, and other agencies could then make grants or contract with private parties such as universities or corporations. Thus, from a congressional standpoint, Gore had in fact played a major role in creating the modern Net, just as he later claimed in 1999. In fact, he had championed high technology for years, from the House of Representatives and from the Senate. Since his tenure, no one in either of those bodies has played as singular a role as he did.

In 1992 an election was upon the nation, and the Clinton-Gore team saw federal technology programs linking the public and private sectors as an important "New Democrat" idea that could win votes. In the summer of 1992, Gore and Brown introduced the Information Infrastructure Technology Act to enhance the high-performance computing and communications efforts. The Clinton campaign developed positions on technology and sought advice from the high-tech industries. The Bush administration generally supported this effort and also responded by enhancing the Advanced Technology Program (ATP) that they had piloted in 1990 with $9 million.

After the election of 1992, the Clinton administration came to Washington, having promised to generate federal support for technology, particularly in the area of computing. After an initial glitch, when Vice President Gore debated Robert Allen, the chairman of AT&T, at the post-election economic summit in Little Rock over whether the government or the private sector should build the new information infrastructure, the administration moved ahead with a number of federal research and development programs. Most were aimed squarely at the new information infrastructure and further development of the Net.

First, proposed funding for the high-performance computing and communications program was more than doubled, to over $1 billion. Research on supercomputing was deemed particularly important, so the NSF provided support for supercomputer centers involving both universities and the private sector. The Department of Energy's laboratories also began to play major role in the development of supercomputing. In addition to basic research on computing and networks, applied research was promoted in fields such as health and education, bringing the NIH and other agencies into the technology mix.

Second, the ATP, begun in the previous administration, was expanded to create partnerships between the federal government, large and small companies, universities, community colleges, and local governments in new technology areas. Third, the Technology Reinvestment Program was established in the Department of Defense, creating federal grants for companies seeking to convert defense technology programs into civilian ones. One key program, for example, sought to convert networking techniques used in defense manufacturing into broad civilian use as a standard for on-line production.

Fourth, cooperative research and development agreements were expanded and developed between the Department of Energy's research laboratories and private companies in order to help the laboratories convert some of their defense efforts to civilian use. Although these types of agreements had been used successfully by the NSF in the past, difficult contractual issues arose when using them with other agencies. Issues such as the ownership of intellectual property ownership issues had to be and were worked out, as in the agreement between a research consortium of the semiconductor industry and the government's Sandia National Laboratory.

Fifth, the National Institute of Standards and Technology published its research reports on new applications for the emerging information infrastructure. The reports helped dispel the notion—becoming popular at the time—that the principal use for the new technology would be for interactive television and pointed out that the key technical challenge would be providing "full connectivity at many different points on the network, and interoperability between networks and services."[6]

Finally, the National Cooperative Research Act of 1989 was extended by legislation to provide protection from antitrust prosecution by the government for companies that banded together in research cooperatives to work on common development and production programs.

These efforts, although generally popular in the communities they affected, did meet with significant problems. For example, given its focus on reducing the budget deficit, the administration struggled to find the funding it needed. As it pushed for a large tax increase, Republican critics such as Representative Robert Walker of Pennsylvania, chair of the House Science Committee, charged that the administration was giving away taxpayer money to support private applied research. Additionally, within agencies such as the Department of Defense, officials more concerned about the readiness of the armed forces questioned funding priorities for advanced research.

Not surprisingly, politics entered the picture as well. Republicans charged favoritism in the awarding of grants of contracts. Where scientifically disciplined peer review was used to select winners, as with the ATP, this criticism was easy to rebut. Where other selection methods were used, as in the Technology Reinvestment Program (which did seem to produce an unusually large number of contracts in the vote-rich state of California), the criticism was harder to deflect. In fact, the Technology Reinvestment Program had to be renamed and reinvented as a result.

Furthermore, Congress grew concerned that programs created to help the cause of American competitiveness could be used by foreign companies in the absence of a specific prohibition on foreign participation. Thus Representative Thomas J. Manton of New York introduced legislation to prohibit the participation of any non-American company in these government-supported programs. The Manton Amendment raised red flags for American companies and U.S. trade officials, though. Originally, the European Union had also banned participation in their programs by American companies. Pressure from American companies with large investments in Europe and from Washington, however, had persuaded the Europeans to revise their policies to permit at least some American participation. Even Japan was beginning to allow companies such as IBM into its government-sponsored research programs. Moreover, some European companies with U.S. subsidiaries were expressing interest in the U.S. programs.

After some negotiation, a formula was developed that permitted non-American entities to participate if they made a substantial contribution in the form of U.S. operations and jobs—and, of course, the actual development would have to be done in the United States. Nevertheless, this issue continued to be controversial, and participants often had to deal with strict contractual obligations that would force them to use any technology generated by the program only in the United States.

By the end of the 1990s, a number of factors had calmed American concerns about U.S. competitiveness, including American domination of the Net. In addition, key industries such as semiconductors had made dramatic turnarounds, and in most cases direct government help was no longer needed. Sematech, for example, had voluntarily given up its government funding by 1998. In addition, a great deal of government funding was now being directed toward government Net applications themselves: the president's memorandum to heads of agencies in 1997 called on "all executive departments and agencies to promote efforts domestically and internationally to make the Internet a secure environment for commerce. This includes ensuring secure and reliable telecommunications networks; ensuring an effective means for protecting the information systems attached to these networks; [and] ensuring an effective means for authenticating and guaranteeing confidentiality of electronic information."[7] These were formidable technical tasks.

Nevertheless, government, university, and private sector research circles agreed that the research and development partnerships that had helped develop the key advanced information and communications technologies underlying the Net had worked so well that they ought to be continued. In 1996, the Council on Competitiveness issued a report on U.S. research and development policy that concluded, "The Council's central finding is that [research and development] partnerships hold the key to meeting the challenge of the transition that our nation now faces."[8] The report, signed by seventy-five of the nation's leading corporate, university, and government research scientists, went on to say that the partnerships it envisioned were cooperative arrangements of companies, government agencies, universities, and laboratories pooling resources in pursuit of shared research and development objectives.

Of the Net and its underlying technologies, the report said,

Many government-industrial-academic partnerships during the past three decades . . . have helped establish a foundation for the explosive growth now characterizing this sector. The Internet, seeded initially by the technology and resources of the Advanced Research Projects Agency . . . is a vivid example of progression from a government-sponsored to a market-driven network. Today, however, the combined impact of competitive pressures, escalating costs and the globalization of markets puts a greater premium on industry-to-industry strategic partnerships rather than government-industry links.[9]

The report also warned, however, that U.S. preeminence in this field should not be taken for granted and that new mechanisms would need to be found for future partnerships involving government.

In fact, in 1996, a consortium of universities and high-technology companies announced a partnership called Internet II, whose purpose was to develop the broadband backbone for the future Internet and prototypes for applications that would run on it. Shortly thereafter, the U.S. government announced its Next Generation Internet (NGI) program to provide government funding for the same goal.

These two interrelated projects provide a good model for the use of government funding in research and development partnerships in the future. Testifying before a Senate committee, John Gibbons, assistant to the president for science and technology, justified the continuing federal role in Net research:

There are those who ask why are we making Federal investments in a next generation Internet when the private sector is clearly making the current generation Internet a commercial success. Despite the dramatic and global growth of the Internet, we realize that there are still stiff challenges to be met if we are to fully harness its enormous potential. . . . The Federal government is among those whose increased requirements for high-speed communications and advanced applications cannot be accommodated by the current technology. . . . There is a consensus among experts outside the Federal government. . . . not only on the need for NGI research, but also about the unique role of the Federal government in stimulating investment and collaboration for the NGI.[10]

Congress apparently agreed and in 1998 authorized $142 million for the NGI program over two years. The program involved at least seven government agencies: ARPA, NASA, the NSF, NIST, the NIH, the Department of Energy, and the Environmental Protection Agency. Its three principal aims were experimental research on advanced technologies in areas such as routing and security; development of the next generation Internet fabric by testing NGI sites; and development of revolutionary applications in areas such as health care, emergency management, and environmental protection.

As the year 2000 approached, two unrelated events jarred U.S. government support of information technology and communications research. The first was the onset of the presidential election season. Vice President Gore had labored for many years on behalf of high-technology industry and the Republicans decided to "triangulate" his leading position on the issue. Incidentally, of course, they were also eyeing the potentially huge political contributions from the deep pockets of high-tech corporations and executives. They attacked first on the Y2K issue, using legislation limiting liability for Y2K events to force the administration and the vice president to choose between trial lawyers, who opposed the legislation, and high-tech companies, who supported it.

The Republicans' opening for attack came from the second and unexpected event—a report from the president's own Information Technology Advisory Committee. In February 1999, the committee had submitted a report to the administration critical of federal information technology research programs:

After careful review of the Federal programs, this Committee has concluded that federal support for research in information technology is seriously inadequate. Research programs intended to maintain the flow of new ideas in information technology and train the next generation of researchers are funding only a small fraction of the research that is needed. . . . [C]ompounding this problem, Federal agency managers . . . have naturally favored research supporting the short-term goals of their mission over long-term, high-risk investigations. . . . [T]he sum of such decisions threatens the long-term welfare of the nation.[11]

The report pointed out that although statistics showed that private-sector information-technology research and development had doubled in ten years to an annual level of $30 billion in 1998, the numbers were misleading: "Over 90 percent of information technology [research and development] expenditures are allocated to product development, with the major portion of the remaining expenditures going toward near term, applied research."[12] The report went on to state that although the absolute private research and development numbers had grown, research and development as a portion of revenue had declined from 9 to 7 percent. Industry, pushed by commodity products, short product cycles, competitive pricing pressures, and high startup costs for newcomers, was not investing in long-term research.

The report concluded with a call for dramatically increased federal spending for basic information technology research:

Past government investments in high-risk research have helped fuel the intense pace of the information technology marketplace. The U.S. has the most energetic, viable and productive technology transfer mechanism in the world. Ideas freely flow from . . . national labs to existing and new companies. In 1998, over 12 billion dollars were invested by venture funds in new companies. The basic feedstock for these investments has been government support of basic information technology research. If this feedstock is allowed to deplete, this economic growth engine could slow or disappear.[13]

The committee made specific recommendations in its report for large increases in federal spending on information technology research and development and for shifting the focus from applied and near-term research to basic research. It recommended the creation of a strategic initiative that would increase the funding base by almost $1.4 billion.

Not surprisingly, the administration moved quickly to respond to the committee's report. It accepted the committee's recommendation and in April 1999 announced its "IT²" proposal increasing the government's investment in information technology research by 28 percent, to $1.8 billion for fiscal year 2000 and focusing it on long-term research. The new program was submitted to Congress as part of the president's budget for 2000.

Not to be outdone, the Republicans in Congress raised the ante. By June, Congressman F. James Sensenbrenner of Wisconsin, chair of the House Science Committee, had introduced his own legislation, the Networking and Information Technology Research and Development Act. It authorized almost $5 billion over five years for a variety of information technology basic research programs. It also proposed to establish a $95 million program to support internships for students in information technology and to make permanent the investment tax credit for private research and development. In support of its recommendation, the House Science Committee said, "[A]s the Nation's dependence on the Internet . . . increases, current federal programs and support for fundamental research in [information technology] are seriously inadequate."[14] By early 2000, the administration upped the ante again. The president's budget for fiscal year 2000 provided $2.268 billion for information-technology research and development, an increase of 36 percent over the prior year.

The net result of the competition between the administration and Congress over information technology research and development funding seemed to be a reaffirmation by both sides of Vannevar Bush's original 1945 notions of the role of the federal government in science. The ideological battles over science policy appeared to be over—at least for a time.

Although the United States, the European Union, and Japan continue to act in their own national interests by funding advanced research in computing and telecommunications to promote the development of the Net, they have also found it in their interests to cooperate in certain areas, for a number of reasons. The most important is the borderless nature of the Net and that fact that its value increases exponentially with the number of people and institutions connected to it. Therefore, it is in the interest of all countries to encourage research and development that will result in more people worldwide being able to connect.

Secondly, there are important applications for which international cooperation is essential, including weather prediction, environmental studies, health care and medical research, and emergency management. In each of these areas, seamless applications across national boundaries benefit everyone. It was with this fact in mind that the G-7 group of advanced industrialized nations met in Naples in 1994 and approved a cooperative plan for supporting the global information infrastructure that was finalized the following year.

The result was the G-7 GII Pilot Projects, which are aimed at developing an international consensus on common principles for applications, access, and interoperability. The G-7 countries agreed to identify projects and obstacles to applications, to create model programs, and to exchange information. Eleven projects were chosen, each to be coordinated by one country: education, electronic libraries, emergency management, environmental management, global marketplace, government on-line, health care applications, interoperability for broadband networks, maritime information systems, and multimedia museums and art galleries. The emergency management project, for example, is known as the Global Emergency Management Information Network Initiative (GEMINI), and its mission is to develop a global emergency management information network that provides electronic access to all emergency management knowledge and experience to anyone, anytime, anywhere. This involves not only assisting nations to develop their own national information networks but also working to develop global technical standards for exchanging emergency management information and to provide interconnectivity.

In addition to the member governments of the G-7, the World Bank is also providing funding for research and development for these projects through its InfoDev program. InfoDev is also funding research on similar projects for developing nations. Among the development projects InfoDev has funded are environment and information in Central America, telecommunications and information centers in Ghana, connectivity between health organizations for AIDS research in Southeast Asia, and information systems in rural development in Peru.

Nations with the resources to do so will continue to use science and technology policy to improve their competitive position with regard to the Net. For the United States in particular, the use of federal funding to stimulate partnerships between government agencies and laboratories, universities, and corporations should remain a priority. This research should be aimed principally at basic science. As a side benefit, it should help train new young scientists with up-to-date knowledge in the fields of information technology and telecommunications. The disposition of these funds should be as far removed from the political process as possible, administered by agencies such as the NSF and subjected to strict peer review. Foreign entities should be allowed to participate as they make substantial contributions to the national economy. Some funding should be used to fund international projects, such as the G-7 program, that provide mutual benefits and demonstrate the global nature of the Net.

III

Governance—Public and Private

10

The U.S. Government

Government can have a profound effect on the growth of commerce on the Internet. . . . Knowing when to act and—at least as important—when not to act—will be crucial.

—President William J. Clinton[1]

With both the impact of the Net on different sectors of society and the public policy issues it raises identified, the next question is, how are governments approaching these issues? Are the actions they are taking effective? Do Net-related issues fall naturally into political categories or are they nonpartisan? Are governments organized properly to carry out this task? Are there better methods of dealing with Net-related issues? What are the international organizations doing and are their efforts adequate? With the private sector assigned the leading role, what if any innovative actions is that sector taking to deal with these issues? Are they effective? The next few chapters deal with these public policy questions in terms of the U.S. government, foreign governments, international organizations, and the private sector.

As the new millennium opened, the United States was no longer just the leader of the "free world," but by common consensus, it was also the world's only superpower. In the millennium's first issue of the *Wilson Quarterly*, sociologist Seymour Martin Lipset wrote, "At the dawn of the new century, the United States finds itself in a position of surprising dominance around the world. It has been a triumph of ideas and values perhaps even more than of power."[2]

The core values of which Lipset wrote were democracy, the freedom of expression, the openness of American society to change and its acceptance of diversity, and respect for private property and the work ethic. This fertile brew of values provided the incubator for the high technology on which much of American supremacy rested—especially the Net.

285

As Don Heath, president of the Internet Society, told a *New York Times* reporter, "If the United States government had tried to come up with a scheme to spread its brand of political liberalism around the world, it couldn't have invented a better model than the Internet."[3] The profound link between the Net and globalization—the worldwide evolution of liberal capitalism and democracy—provided a strong stimulus to the U.S. government and American politicians to work to strengthen the core values and foster the growth of the Net.

Thus, the U.S. government provides by far the most important example of government efforts to stimulate, exploit, and cope with the digital age. America's acknowledged pivotal leadership in the development and use of the Net and the size of the U.S. economy makes its policies toward the Net almost irresistible to other nations. Once the U.S. government had decided that the leadership of cyberspace issues should be with the private sector, for example, it was difficult if not impossible for any other industrial nation to decide otherwise. Among the less obvious reasons for examining the U.S. experience are the unique interest of many of its key political leaders in the subject and the political structure of the United States as a federal democracy, with state and local interests to resolve. To understand these themes, it is worth reviewing briefly the actions the U.S. government has taken and how it is currently organized to deal with the issue.

REVIEWING POLICIES SO FAR

Whatever its grades in other areas, the U.S. government deserves an "A" for its overall efforts to support the emerging information infrastructure. This grade is as much due to what the government did not do—that is, yield to the temptation to regulate the Net. Furthermore, it is high in spite of some notable failures, particularly the failure to deregulate telecommunications totally.

Presidential Administrations

Although much of the credit is due to the Clinton administration, the broad policy framework and funding have their origins in earlier times and with preceding administrations. Among the early key efforts, as we have seen, were the Defense Department's Advanced Research Projects Agency (ARPA) funding of the early Internet technologies in the 1960s, the ongoing National Science Foundation funding of computer and network research, Department of Defense funding of advanced semiconductor and communications technology work, and Department of Energy funding of supercomputing in the national laboratories and several universities. These government research efforts played a major role in creating the scientific basis for the underlying digital technologies.

In addition, the Federal Communications Commission's support of competition in telecommunications was a second and parallel track that also helped lay the groundwork for the new information infrastructure by creating a more affordable and innovative telecommunications system. Flawed and limited as they were, the commission's deregulatory actions over a few decades helped create dozens of innovative new companies and new products and services for consumers and businesses.

As we have also seen, beginning with the Bush administration's high-performance computing initiative and with congressional support spearheaded by then-senator Al Gore, more funding for civilian research had also became available. The new Clinton administration, principally because of Vice President Gore's special interest in the area, had moved quickly to accelerate the federal government's efforts to advance what was then called the "national information infrastructure." In September 1993, the administration published "The National Information Infrastructure: Agenda for Action." This document, building on earlier work on high-performance computing and national information policy, listed nine major goals along with action items for each. The nine goals were

1. Promote private sector investment (following Al Gore's postelection debate with the AT&T chairperson about whether the private sector or government should fund and build the new infrastructure, the administration had heard loudly and clearly from the high-tech industry and wanted to highlight its acceptance of their message);
2. Extend the "universal service" concept to ensure that information resources are available to all at affordable prices;
3. Promote technological innovation and new applications;
4. Promote seamless, interactive, user-driven operation;
5. Ensure information security and network reliability;
6. Improve management of the radio frequency spectrum;
7. Protect intellectual property rights;
8. Coordinate with other levels of government and with other bodies; and
9. Provide access to government information and improve government procurement.[4]

Among the key actions contemplated were revision of tax policies, review of encryption policies, and implementation of government high-performance computing research. Some of the goals meshed well with other related programs. For example, reforming the government procurement process to provide for on-line government purchasing was also part of Gore's "reinventing government" program.

From an organizational standpoint, the White House decided not to create a new agency to implement its agenda, but to create a virtual team of existing government departments to coordinate the effort: the Information Infrastructure Task Force (IITF), chaired by Secretary of Commerce Ron Brown. Staff for the IITF was provided by the National Telecommunications and Information Administration (NTIA) in the Department of Commerce, headed by Larry Irving, a former member of the staff of the House Telecommunication Subcommittee and also a Clinton loyalist. The IITF pushed the agenda throughout the government in the first Clinton administration and worked on the major initiatives, especially telecommunications policy and the reform legislation in Congress. It also focused on security issues and information policy, including intellectual property, privacy protection, and the use of government information.

The IITF also initiated government work on applications, carried out by the National Institute for Standards and Technology (NIST) and headed by Arati Prabhakar, a talented young researcher who was assistant secretary of commerce and director of the NIST. Prabhakar had worked at ARPA and had been the first female graduate of the California Institute of Technology. The NIST published two studies, "Putting the Information Infrastructure to Work," and "The Information Infrastructure: Reaching Society's Goals."[5] The first of these studies focused on applications in areas such as education and lifelong learning, health care, libraries, manufacturing, electronic commerce, and government services. The second dealt with energy resources, the disabled, transportation, telecommuting, emergency management, and cultural institutions. Although these studies did not necessarily break any new ground, they publicized and helped the public understand the broad reach of digital technology at a time when most people saw interactive television as its biggest and perhaps only application.

After Brown's death the IITF was chaired by Secretary of Commerce William Daley and received guidance from the White House Office of Science and Technology Policy, headed by Neil Lane, and the National Economic Council, where another talented staff member, Tom Kalil, oversaw policy issues. The IITF's work focused on three areas: telecommunications policy; information policy, including privacy and intellectual property rights; and applications and technology, especially aimed at health information applications and government information.

Sensitive to industry concerns, the administration also appointed a private-sector group in 1993, the National Information Infrastructure Advisory Committee (NIIAC), for a term of two years. Headed by the chairpersons of Silicon Graphics and National Public Radio, Ed Mc-Cracken and Delano Lewis, respectively, the NIIAC comprised thirty-seven members from industry, labor, the universities, public-interest groups, and state and local governments. During its existence, the NIIAC held numerous public forums and gave advice on key issues such as universal access. It also highlighted the views of groups such as the disabled that might not otherwise have been heard. The NIIAC brought many new players into the debate over the Net and mobilized groups that had not yet realized the importance of the new technology to their interests, or how it would affect them over the coming years.

The White House also set an early example for government by establishing its own creative Web site in 1993. Mike Nelson, the talented young White House staff member (and geophysicist) who served as Gore's expert on the Internet, took pride in showing visitors to the Old Executive Office Building the image of the virtual Socks, the Clinton's pet cat. Other government agencies, eager to keep pace, followed quickly with their own Web sites.

In 1994, Gore also took the subject overseas when he addressed the International Telecommunications Union in Buenos Aires in March. He laid out the U.S. government's five principles for what he now termed the "global" information infrastructure:

1. Encourage private investment;
2. Promote competition;
3. Create a flexible regulatory framework that can keep pace with rapid technological and market changes;
4. Provide open access to the network for all information providers; and
5. Ensure universal service;

These principles quickly became U.S. government policy and were embedded in a number of international negotiations and agreements in bilateral, regional, and multilateral forums. With unusual speed, they were also accepted by many foreign governments.

By 1997, as the commercial uses of the Net boomed, the administration narrowed its focus somewhat and turned the spotlight on electronic commerce, even as it continued to support research and development projects. The administration's July 1997 "Framework for Global Electronic Commerce" and the accompanying memorandum from the president to his agency and department heads was followed by the formation of the Working Group on Electronic Commerce. (Although this working group was technically formed in 1995, it was not active until 1997.) Its first annual report was published in November 1998. That report recounted the progress that had so far been achieved on the issue, including four major pieces of legislation passed by Congress the previous year to promote electronic commerce:

1. The Digital Millennium Copyright Act, to protect on-line copyrighted material and to bring the United States into line with the new copyright treaty of the World Intellectual Property Organization (WIPO; discussed in Chapter 6);
2. The Government Paperwork Elimination Act, to encourage government use of electronic commerce;
3. The Children's Online Privacy Protection Act, to protect the privacy of children on-line; and
4. The Internet Tax Freedom Act, to develop a reasonable on-line taxation system during a three-year moratorium on new Internet taxes.[6]

Of the legislative work on the Net, Ira Magaziner, the White House's lead player on electronic commerce, said, "I think it's a good bipartisan record."[7] Nevertheless, the administration did not mention congressional passage of a bill drafted by Republican senator Daniel Coats of Indiana and Republican representative Michael Oxley of Ohio to require commercial Web sites to ensure that only adults can access material deemed harmful to minors. The administration was ambiguous about the effort, concerned about the constitutionality of the measure, and opposed to regulation, yet it was extremely sensitive to parent's growing concerns about children's access to pornographic and violent materials.

The annual report also listed the administration's international accomplishments in electronic commerce, which, when taken together, were quite impressive:

—A World Trade Organization agreement to refrain from imposing customs duties on electronic commerce transactions;
—An Organization for Economic Cooperation and Development (OECD) declaration supporting U.S. on-line taxation principles and an OECD affirmation of an international authentication regime;

—An affirmation at the Brussels Global Standards Conference that the private sector should lead in the development of Internet technical standards;

—An agreement of the Basel Committee on Banking Supervision to adopt a nonregulatory approach to electronic payment systems; and

—A number of bilateral agreements with countries such as France, Japan, and Ireland to support a nonregulatory approach to the Net and the free flow of information.

Finally, the annual report also cited a number of important actions by the private sector, such as industry agreements and new techniques to protect on-line privacy, to filter objectionable content and to manage the Internet domain-name system.

Thus, the administration had shunned any new government organization or department to deal with the Net. This was in line with both the administration's views on "reinventing government" and Republican wishes to control the size of the federal government. Rather, it achieved its objectives with a virtual team combining the Department of Commerce, the White House Office of Science and Technology Policy, and the National Economic Council (which also served as the vice president's eyes and ears on the program). With this trusted political team overseeing the effort, a variety of federal agencies and departments worked on many aspects of Net public policy and research and development programs.

Agencies and Cabinet Departments. The White House housed a number of agencies with policy roles, including the Office of Management and Budget, which oversees government privacy and information policy, and the National Security Council, which oversees export controls for cryptography and computers, especially those related to supercomputing. In addition, the Office of the Vice President under Chief Domestic Policy Adviser David Beier oversaw electronic commerce policy broadly, especially in sensitive areas such as content control, privacy protection, and universal access.

The Office of the United States Trade Representative (USTR; technically part of the White House) under the leadership of Charlene Barshefsky built a powerful group of international trade agreements that strengthened electronic commerce, including the Global Agreement on Basic Telecommunications and the International Technology Agreement. The USTR, under the leadership of former assistant U.S. trade representative Donald Abelson, had also negotiated significant bilateral agreements on electronic commerce with a number of countries and pressed the World Trade Organization to take the lead on developing a work program that advances U.S. interests.

The Department of Commerce included numerous agencies working on Net-related issues and programs. Secretary Daley himself devoted a great deal of time to the electronic commerce issue, which was coordinated by Eliot Maxwell. The NTIA acted as the secretariat for the IITF, developed the administration's telecommunications policies, and issued special studies, such as its "Digital Divide" report on universal access.[8] The Technology Administration developed policy on Net research and development efforts and on U.S. competitiveness. The Bureau of Export Administration oversaw and administered export controls on high-technology exports, including computers, telecommunications equipment, and cryptographic products. The NIST administered the advanced technology program of research grants and also participated in Net standards-setting activities in the United States and around the world. The Patent and Trademark Office, formerly under the aggressive leadership of Bruce Lehmann, developed key policies on intellectual property, particularly Net copyright policy, and was a strong advocate for U.S. copyright policies overseas. In addition, the Commerce Department's general counsel, Andy Pincus, played an important role, particularly in the legal framework discussions and on issues related to consumer protection and security.

The Department of Defense played a major role in Net research and development from the earliest days through ARPA, especially its Information Technology Office. In fact, ARPA played a major role on the IITF. The armed services were involved with research in areas such as integrated circuits and in their own development and acquisition programs.

The Department of Energy's Office of Science and Technology under Martha Krebs performed research in advanced scientific computing. The department's Office of Strategic Computing and Simulation did critical work in supercomputing, and the national laboratories participated in the high-performance computing programs, often jointly with universities and more often with private companies in cooperative research and development agreements (CRADAs). In fact, the Department's advanced supercomputing initiative (ASCI) was by far the largest initiative of its type in the world.

The Department of Health and Human Services was responsible for health care privacy issues, and its National Institutes of Health and National Library of Medicine participated in both health care applications research and the high-performance computing programs, including the "Next Generation Internet" and "Internet Squared" programs.

The Department of Justice's Antitrust Division under Assistant Attorney General Joel Klein enforced the antitrust laws and prosecuted a high-profile suit against Microsoft. It also oversees proposed mergers and acquisitions of companies involved with the Net. The department's criminal division and the Federal Bureau of Investigation (FBI) also are concerned with Net crime and have played an important role in overall security matters and especially policy concerning encryption. The new National Information Protection Center was housed within the FBI.

The Department of State's Bureau of International Communications and Information Policy, headed by Vonya McCann, developed policy in these areas and dealt with other governments in important areas such as satellite and broadcast policy, negotiating new agreements as necesary. The department's Advisory Committee on International Communications and Information Policy provided a forum for private-sector advice.

The Department of the Treasury's Office of Tax Policy developed government policy in Net taxation and the undersecretary for international affairs represents those views overseas. The department's international tax counsel, Joseph Guttenberg, wrote the Treasury's paper on Net taxation. The Comptroller of the Currency played a key role in developing policy on electronic banking and payments systems and enforced them through its banking supervision operations. The Treasury also worked closely with the FBI and other law-enforcement agencies in dealing with Internet financial crimes, such as money laundering.

Independent Agencies. In addition to the executive departments, a number of independent agencies have also been deeply involved in developing and enforcing information infrastructure policies. The Federal Communications Commission (FCC) was responsible for regulations and enforcement dealing with telecommunications, broadcasting, and cable and wireless communications. First under Reed Hundt, and then under William Kennard, the FCC was been very active in electronic commerce and Internet matters, often taking its lead from Gore. The FCC backed and help shape the Telecommunications Act of 1996, helped develop and now implements the so-called E-rate to wire schools and hospitals to the Internet, and has pressed for faster broadband access. It helped devise a compromise solution to the high-definition television standards issue and played a key role in international telecommunications negotiations.

The Federal Trade Commission, under chairman Robert Pitofsky, has been very aggressive in developing privacy and consumer protection policies for electronic commerce. It did this both by educating the public and the key Internet constituencies through a series of workshops and by citing a number of companies for violating rules in areas ranging from children's privacy to medical fraud on the Internet. Although some in the private sector may fear the commission's reach, its efforts have made comprehensive new and onerous regulations in these areas unnecessary—so far. The commission also has a role in approving proposed mergers and acquisitions by companies involved with the Net.

The National Science Foundation (NSF) played the lead role in federally supported research and development for the Net. Its central position in the high-performance computing and communications initiative is only one example. Aside from its programs' substantive contributions to high-performance computing and communications and other research work, the NSF's impeccable scientific procedures for reviewing and choosing projects has earned it great praise and generally kept politics out of the research laboratories.

The Federal Reserve System's Board of Governors, led by Alan Greenspan, generated rules on the electronic transfer of funds and electronic payments systems. Greenspan himself has played an important role in articulating and defining the economics of the new digital technologies. The General Services Administration, through its office of electronic commerce, was responsible for converting government procurement to the Internet. Its goal was to cover the electronic purchasing of four million items by 2000. And, finally, the National Aeronautics and Space Administration (NASA) provided a key application test area for advanced computing and communications research and development. NASA is a participant in the administration's "Next Generation Internet" research program.

Thus, while the federal government has not had a permanent institution to oversee digital age policies, it has done well to date with a virtual government-wide organization of like-minded people, propelled in large part by Vice President Gore. Their principal achievement has been forbearance from regulation and allowing the private sector to lead. It is unclear, however, whether a future administration, perhaps headed by a president or vice president without similar interests and abilities, could do as well without a more permanent institutional arrangement.

Congress

The main contribution of Congress, by contrast, has been to do little to harm the Net and to follow the administration's lead, working generally in a bipartisan fashion. There are a variety of reasons for this. Former Republican Speaker of the House Newt Gingrich realized at an early stage how important the Internet would be, and he initiated several innovative programs, such as the Library of Congress "Thomas" server to allow people to access legislation on-line. He also startled his Republican colleagues at one point by calling for the government to provide a free computer for every child. Gingrich's peers, however, did not pick up his theme. After he left Congress, no single Republican champion of the Internet emerged to challenge Gore, and therefore Congress did not do as much as the administration to set the digital age tone.

Another reason for congressional inaction has been that digital age issues do not break down easily along traditional party lines. As James Boyle, professor of law at American University, said, "Congress still hasn't come to terms with the politics and morality of the Internet."[9] For one thing, while the Net businesspeople who have become wealthy with stock options might appear to be a natural Republican constituency, many of them tend to be social liberals (although economic conservatives) and clear products of the 1960s. (One term used to describe them has been "bohemian bourgeoisie.") For another, the issues cannot easily be sorted into one ideological pile or another. Encryption can be perceived as a business issue to promote commerce or as a national security and law-enforcement issue to promote law and order. Both are traditional Republican causes. Censorship of pornography and privacy protection are also issues that cut a number of ways politically.

Equally important, perhaps, is the fractured congressional committee system as viewed from the age of the Net. Unlike more clearly defined areas such as agriculture, defense, or taxation, there is no obvious committee to oversee and push Net policy issues in Congress. The House Commerce Committee, the House Science Committee, and the Senate Committee on Commerce, Science, and Transportation, all with some oversight over telecommunications, broadcasting, science, and technology, probably come the closest, as a group. They oversee FCC activities, as well as advanced research in computing and communications and encryption policy.

But other committees have equally important responsibilities in other areas of Net public policy. The Senate Finance Committee and the House Ways and Means Committee oversee the taxation of electronic commerce and international trade issues, such as the U.S. role in World Trade Organization negotiations on Net-related issues. The Senate Banking Committee and the House Committee on Banking and Financial Services oversee policy on such areas as electronic payments systems, electronic funds transfer, and electronic banking and financial services. The House and Senate Judiciary Committees oversee intellectual property protection, including digital copyright and trademark issues, as well as competition and antitrust laws. With law-enforcement interests, they are also involved in encryption policy.

The Senate Government Affairs Committee and the House Government Reform and Oversight Committee oversee government information policies and government use of electronic commerce. The Senate Armed Services Committee and the House National Security Committee oversee Department of Defense spending and policies on advanced computing and communications research and development. Because of their national security role, they have also interposed themselves into the debate over encryption policies. And the House and Senate Appropriations committees must approve all government research and development spending on both programs and agencies such as the NSF, the advanced technology program, and ARPA research programs.

Without a single natural leader—Democrat or Republican—to coalesce its views, therefore, Congress has not been able to articulate as clear a vision of how its wants the Net to develop as the administration has. One important attempt to develop this leadership has been the Congressional Internet Caucus, a group of members—many from states home to key high-technology constituencies, such as California and Washington—with Internet interests. This bipartisan caucus, founded in 1996 and co-chaired by Representatives Bob Goodlatte and Rick Boucher of Virginia and Senators Conrad Burns of Montana and Patrick Leahy of Vermont, had grown to more than 130 members by the end of 1999. But although the caucus has occasionally been effective, as on the passage of the Internet tax moratorium, it has not yet developed as comprehensive a set of policy objectives, as the Administration has. Congress needs one or two highly visible advocates for the Net whom the public will recognize and—over time—respect.

As Net issues have gained in importance and public visibility, and especially as the new wealth of Net entrepreneurs and companies has created a potentially new source of political contributions, members of Congress and other politicians have become more interested. The industry's new clout, in fact, has resulted in both political parties, led by House Republican leader Richard Armey and House Minority leader Richard Gephardt, offering somewhat different versions of "E-agendas," including a variety of favorable tax measures.

Many members have also begun making pilgrimages to Silicon Valley and other centers of high-technology to meet with high-tech executives and to establish their credentials. Individual members in both parties are also beginning to accumulate expertise in digital issues, including, as already mentioned, Leahy and Goodlatte, as well as others such as Senator John McCain of Arizona, who chairs the Senate Commerce Committee; Representative Billy Tauzin of Louisiana, who chairs the House Telecommunications Subcommittee; Representative David Dreier of California; Senator Ron Wyden of Oregon; Representative Christopher Cox of California; and Representative Tom Davis of Virginia.

State Governments

In addition to the federal government, state governments have been important players in developing Internet policy in the United States. The number of proposals for new state laws related to the Internet has skyrocketed during the past five years. According to Paul Rusinoff, state policy counsel for the Internet Alliance, "We saw some of the first bills dealing with the Internet in 1995. There were three of them. Last year, the association looked at over 700."[10] In 1999, state legislatures considered between 1,200 and 1,500 such Internet issues. Among the key ones have been control over content directed at children, banning of unsolicited E-mail (spam), banning on-line gambling (a proposed federal law banning gambling failed to pass Congress in 1998), legalizing digital signatures and contracts, liberalizing state telecommunications laws, and promoting state government use of electronic commerce. Many states would probably also be considering numerous electronic commerce taxation proposals were it not for the federal moratorium on them.

Like Congress, state governments and legislatures tend to be divided about the Net. On the one hand, they want to promote its use in state government and to make their state Internet-friendly to attract new business and investment. On the other hand, they also see a rich new source of tax revenue and they fear the reactions of constituents regarding privacy and content such as pornography and violence. In addition, they are concerned that the borderless nature of the Internet will dilute state power and focus more power in Washington, where a single law can cover the entire nation. Among other things, the Net exacerbates the current historical debate over federalism. Just as the states are beginning to see the Supreme Court return some of their power from Washington after a century of growing federal power, the Net threatens to kill the new trend. Moreover, even city governments have become involved. The case of the city of Portland's requiring AT&T to offer open access to its cable system is an important example of a city issue with profound national implications.

CREATING POLICY FOR THE FUTURE

Overall for the future, the U.S. government faces five key issues regarding its role in the coming digital age.

Federal Government Organization

The basic American government approach to the digital age should continue to recognize private-sector leadership. Nevertheless, it is necessary to have a powerful voice in the government to keep repeating this message, no matter what administration or party is in power. Such a voice is also needed to help take whatever government actions are necessary to enable and promote the use of the Net, such as liberalizing export control regimes, lifting telecommunications regulations, or transforming banking or insurance regulation.

The United States government certainly does not need another Department of Agriculture, with its mythological "one employee per farmer," but it does need some permanent government institution to oversee public policy needs in the digital age. The impact of the Net on the American economy and on society is so great that it would be irresponsible not to have a single focal point. The model for this should not be a new government department, but rather a small office in the White House, consisting of fewer than ten people. This office would be responsible for coordinating the development of government policy and giving advice to the president on Net policies. It could provide the National Economic Council with a regular update on the impact of the Net on the U.S. economy and society, thus engaging the key cabinet members on the issue.

The office would also develop the administration's legislative initiatives as needed and work with the key congressional committees and members of Congress to achieve passage of the initiatives. It would coordinate work with the independent agencies such as the Federal Trade Commission (FTC) and others to clarify administration policies and to work with them to resolve issues. The office would also work with the private sector to continue to press companies and other private institutions to act responsibly and actively support measures such as privacy protection and content control. The president's Information Technology Advisory Committee should be broadened to focus not only on research and development, but on a more comprehensive range of public policy issues, forming a more permanent version of the NIIAC. Finally, the office would also work with state governments as needed to help resolve issues of federalism—i.e., at which level, state or federal, action is best taken.

The new White House office would not have any effect on existing government organizations except that it might take some of its employees from the NTIA in the Department of Commerce and perhaps one from the White House Office of Science and Technology Policy. As discussed in Chapter 7, the FCC would be dismantled and the Department of Justice, the FTC, the NTIA, and the NIST might have future responsibility for the needed remnants. Thus, there would be no need to increase the number of federal employees. The office would also publish an annual report, providing Congress and the public with a baseline of data on the progress and impact of the Net on the American economy and society.

Beyond these modest changes, the federal government needs to consider the longer-range issue of government organization for the twenty-first century. The issues revolving around the Net are critical but are only one component of the new challenges that government faces; the others include the growing importance of health, education and aging issues, and the globalization of the economy. Perhaps a blue-ribbon, bipartisan commission of senior public figures is needed to look at this broader question.

Federalism

The emergence of the Net comes just as American government is in the midst of a historic shift in power from the federal government to the states. After more than half a century of expanding federal government power, actions by Congress and the executive branch have shifted both powers and government programs back to the states. The Supreme Court has upheld this shift in a number of decisions over the past few years. Most recently it did so in cases that limit the rights of people to sue state governments for state "violations" of federal laws, such as the Fair Labor Standards Act or the Family and Medical Leave Act, and in a case that reversed federal legislation permitting rape victims to sue in federal court.

A problem arises where Internet issues are concerned, however, since the Net does not recognize state or any other boundaries and must find a more comprehensive legal existence elsewhere. First among the issues raised is that of taxation. The federal government has not yet sought to impose its own sales tax, but it may have to before long, because a maze of widely differing state tax rules, as we have seen, are a formidable barrier to electronic commerce. Another critical area is the issue of professional licensing. With most professionals, such as doctors, lawyers, engineers, and architects, licensed locally by the states, how can such people offer their services on the Net in a rationally and legally predictable way? Related to the issue of professional licensing is the issue of educational accreditation for schools and universities, also currently a state function; as more and more educational institutions offer courses and degrees over the Internet, the existing structure of state accreditation will become impossibly outdated.

Another series of state-federal issues is related to telecommuting and the labor and workplace rules that govern it. Will employers of telecommuting workers be accountable to state governments and regulations or to the federal government as they offer services across the United States? Another group of questions involves businesses that are licensed and regulated by state government, such as insurance. Should state insurance regulation be replaced by federal regulation? As we have already seen, the legal environment and such issues as electronic signatures and contracts are also issues involving potential federal preemption of state laws. Finally, there are many other areas involved, including state regulation of telecommunications and the provision of universal access. If ever there was a constitutional test of the interstate commerce clause of the Constitution, the Net will provide it.

What is to be done? Perhaps the best way to approach the question is to begin by asking what is in the best interests of the individual states. First, it is important that each state have a legal and policy environment that supports the development of the Net and of electronic commerce. In the twenty-first century, such an environment will be an absolute prerequisite for the creation of jobs and a healthy economy in general. States that ignore the need for a sound legal framework or states that simply try to wring new tax revenues from Net activities will simply not thrive economically.

Second, it will be important for each state that all the other states have similar policies. The Net economy is not a zero-sum game. The more people and businesses that are connected to and actively use the Net, the more valuable it becomes to each player. Although states may compete with each other for digital businesses and jobs with innovative new incentives, all states will prosper less if some states fall behind in Net policy and law.

Third, it is important for states to move quickly on policy issues. The Net is happening *now*. Business and commercial decisions are being made that will determine for some time the configuration of the digital world. It is not in the states' interest to wait years to develop synchronous policies. The traditional method of developing uniform state laws has been ponderously slow. Fortunately, it appears to be nearing the end of the national process with regard to electronic signatures and electronic contracts, but state legislatures will still need to act.

What is needed now is for the governors of the fifty states to take the initiative and develop a comprehensive policy framework for the states that involves both individual and coordinated state legislation when needed, or federal legislation, drafted by the states, when it is needed. The National Governors Association (NGA) has a good basis for beginning this process. It has established an Information Technology Task Force that understands the challenges of the digital age. To quote its co-chair, Governor Jim Geringer of Wyoming, "Our government agencies are still structured on a model that was suited for a time in the past, not one that is prepared to meet the challenges of today or the future."[11]

To date, the work of the NGA's Information Technology Task Force has been concerned principally with four issues: the Y2K problem, state government use of electronic commerce, Internet taxation, and the legalization of electronic signatures.[12] Although each of these issues is important, only the electronic signature issue involves a new policy issue. Many of the truly key policy issues are not covered. The NGA should prioritize a list of issues that are important to the states and review their progress. Those that are mature, such as the electronic signature and electronic contracting issues coming out of the National Council of Commissioners on Uniform State Law, could be handled in an expeditious manner by the state legislatures with strong backing by the governors. Those that need work might be worked on jointly by the Information Technology Task Force. They might recommend joint or coordinated action by state legislatures, or they might recommend federal legislation that the governors might draft and help push through Congress. Either way, the states would retain control over their policy environments but still recognize that the Net will demand nationwide action on policy issues. If the governors fail to act, the federal government will slowly but surely act for them, pressured by the private sector.

National Sovereignty

If the U.S. government faces an inward challenge of federalism in dealing with the states, it also faces the outward-looking challenge of sovereignty as the Net spreads worldwide. Moreover, the challenge to sovereignty is a reciprocal one. Where U.S. and foreign laws differ, as over consumer issues dealing with advertising, disclosures, or the sale of specific products, such as medications or alcohol, companies adhering to U.S. law may violate another country's sovereignty—and vice versa.

In the past, sovereignty issues have been dealt with a number of ways. Countries have developed bilateral arrangements such as treaties of freedom of commerce and navigation or tax treaties to resolve such issues. They have also turned to multilateral and regional institutions such as the OECD, WIPO, or the World Trade Organization, and they have developed international treaties such as the Law of the Sea Agreement or the Wassenaar Agreement. Unfortunately, they have not always reached consensus and angry disputes have resulted. The United States has tried to extend its extraterritorial arm, for example, in areas such as export controls and attempted to force other countries' private sectors to obey U.S. export control laws. The Reagan administration's efforts to stop European companies from providing equipment and supplies for the Soviet gas pipeline to western Europe in the early 1980s was such an example. The Europeans have made similar attempts at extraterritoriality, most recently by trying to export their privacy laws to the United States and other countries.

Today, with the United States at the height of its international power, economically and strategically, the issue is especially sensitive, since any efforts to exploit American domination of cyberspace technology to extend American sovereignty over the Net will be resisted overseas. American Net hegemony could become a rallying cry for opponents in countries from France to China. Therefore, the task of developing a transparent and predictable international policy order for the Net will be long and difficult for American diplomacy. There will be no easy answer; instead, there will be a number of incremental steps.

First, the United States should continue its current efforts to negotiate bilateral agreements and to support specific regional and international agreements on issues such as trade, taxation, and telecommunications. Second, it should continue and intensify international discussions at the appropriate forums, such as the OECD and the Asia-Pacific Economic Cooperation group, on the more difficult long-range issues such as content regulation and privacy protection. The first principal in these discussions should also continue to be self-regulation and private-sector leadership, to avoid direct clashes of international legal regimes. This will mean helping to nurture private-sector institutions in other countries where they have not normally taken on this kind of role. Such nurturing efforts are not new for the United States, which helped to develop important private institutions such as labor unions and business associations overseas during the Cold War. If, for example, an institution such as the Better Business Bureau's BBB Online could grow and be effective around the world, and operate as a mediator or even arbiter in business-consumer disputes, the need for laws, with their potential for conflict, would be lessened. A more powerful international arbitration body may also be needed to deal with on-line consumer issues and resolve disputes independently of governments. Such a mechanism could be faster and more efficient for consumers.

Since the importance of the antitrust laws will grow with continuing deregulation, the United States should also continue to press other governments to enforce existing statutes and to pass new ones when needed. During the past decade the number of countries with antitrust laws grew to about eighty, and global enforcement was also improved. Although bilateral arrangements now exist, it may be that a more formal multilateral antitrust framework may be needed in the future.

In the sphere of international relations, the National Security Council should initiate a study involving the Departments of State, Defense, and Commerce to examine the implications of the digital age for overall foreign policy. The study should concern itself with direct security threats from cyber-terrorists and cyber-warfare, threats that may develop from the growing disparity between the "wired" nations and those that are left behind, and threats from the misuse of technology. It should also examine the key measurements of U.S. world leadership of the Net and determine how the government's international policy-making apparatus should be adjusted to deal with a digital world.

Finally, the National Economic Council should regularly re-examine and prioritize the issues involving potential international conflicts and put the necessary firepower behind such conflicts to resolve them before they explode. A key task of the new White House Office for Net Policy ought to be to report to the council on progress on these issues.

Representative Democracy

A number of political leaders, such as Ross Perot, former head of the Reform Party, have called for the use of the Internet as a kind of constant and instant referendum on the issues of the day. In this school of thought, the way to determine U.S. policy on an issue such as the war in Kosovo or the possible privatization of Social Security is to let every citizen vote on it through the Internet. Such a system would radically change the American form of government from a representative democracy to a direct democracy, or what in an earlier age might have been called a "dictatorship of the proletariat." But such a system is simply not needed.

The brilliance of the Net is that it can empower the ordinary citizen politically in new ways and yet maintain the system of government we have in place. That system provides for majority rule, but with a thoughtful look at minority opinion and, as a rule, shielded from the passions of the moment. We do not need instant referenda or government by polling to achieve this. Already, citizens are learning more than they have ever known about their government and about how to influence it. For example, Web sites such as voter.com sponsored by a variety of liberal and conservative organizations offer citizens a wide-open door to a whole range of political groups and information. The Net makes it incredibly easy to read an article in the newspaper and instantly send an E-mail about it to a member of Congress—or to all of them. Just as doctors will be more challenged by an educated citizenry about their diagnoses and recommended treatments, so will politicians be more challenged about how they are running the nation—or their state, county, or city. The Net also allows people to associate with each other in ways that didn't exist before. From this may arise not only new special-interest groups or temporary lobbying teams, but perhaps permanently new political parties.

Thus, the Net is not so much a challenge to political life as it is an enhancement of it. If in the future, all telephone calls become local, then perhaps all government will also become local and close enough for everyone to understand and to influence.

The Private Sector

In the end, the greatest challenge for the U.S. government may be its greatest temptation: to seize control of the Net back from the private sector and to regulate it. Historically, restraint and forbearance from regulation has not been one of government's greatest virtues. With a booming economy and a technologically savvy government in the 1990s, the government remained virtuous and allowed the private sector to lead the development and control of the Net, with astonishingly good results. In the future, this trend could be reversed.

For example, egregious incidents such as the Oklahoma City bombing, the high-school shootings in Littleton, Colorado, or the spree of hate killings in Illinois, Indiana, and California in the summer of 1999 could convince people that violent or sexual content on the Net requires strong government regulation. Similarly, a series of serious privacy violations could also lead to regulation. A significant economic downturn, with sharp falls in technology stocks and high-tech company bankruptcies, could also stimulate calls for regulation. Moves in other countries toward increased regulation might also not be able to be resisted in the United States.

To prevent this, the private sector, with government prodding, must work harder to build public trust and permanent institutions that people can turn to solve their Net problems. For example, the technology for protecting privacy and permitting parents and schools to control what children have access to must constantly be strengthened. Institutions that enforce business codes such as the Online Privacy Alliance and the BBB OnLine service must also be given permanency and backing by as much of the private sector as possible. New software security features need to be widely disseminated to prevent widespread damage from viruses. Without strong actions from the private sector, it is inevitable that government will backslide and move to control the digital age.

11

Governments Worldwide

In reality, despite a certain discourse on the seemingly unavoidable withdrawal of the State, throughout the world public powers are actively assisting in the development of new technologies and services, as we can see in the United States.
—Lionel Jospin, prime minister of France[1]

French Prime Minister Lionel Jospin captured with Gallic sarcasm a mood that is endemic to governments around the world. For most, it is painful to accept the notion that a development as important as the Net should be left to the private sector, and that the government role should be minimal. Many, like Jospin, look hopefully for any clue, no matter how insignificant, that might reveal the hidden hand of government in the United States. Nevertheless, most governments that have developed comprehensive policy papers on the digital age at least pay lip service to the overall need for private-sector leadership.

This chapter will examine the policy platforms that governments around the world have developed to deal with the information society. It will not attempt to cover every government or region, nor will it discuss every policy of the governments that it does cover. Rather, it will examine representative governments and clusters of policy that reveal patterns of policy making and government dilemmas around the world. International and regional organizations such as the United Nations or the World Trade Organization will be discussed in Chapter 12.

A number of critical themes emerge from an examination of foreign governments' Net policy development. The first is the tense tug-of-war between the private and public sectors. Many nations are barely emerging from socialist frameworks in which many economic institutions have been owned by the state. Some still support numerous state-owned enterprises. For them, the notion that an omnipresent national entity such as the Net could be developed and owned privately is anathema. Even

306

more alien to them is the idea that issues such as personal privacy or regulation of content on the Internet could be self-governing by privately owned entities, or even by nonprofit institutions outside the central government, such as universities or professional organizations. These governments simply cannot let go.

A second theme is that while governments are looking to the United States for policy guidance and ideas, they also fear U.S. domination of the Net. These fears are economic, cultural, political, and strategic. They must be viewed in the broader context of increasing American military and economic power after the collapse of the Soviet Union. The post–Gulf War, post-Kosovo world has created universal fears of American power but also produced responses that vary greatly from friendly to adversarial nations.

Another theme that emerges is a schizophrenia about the power of the Net itself. Although nations want to master the Net and reap its economic advantages, they also want to control its political, social, and cultural powers. This manifests itself more or less benignly in nations such as Canada, but it has more serious repercussions in countries such as China. In some nations, it has greatly retarded the development of the electronic medium.

A fourth theme involves the potential new openness that governments suddenly find themselves anticipating. Transparency is not a chief characteristic of most governments around the world; secrecy is the norm. But for many of the reasons discussed in earlier chapters, governments will increasingly live in a digital goldfish bowl. Civil servants who not only commanded great power but who, in many countries, earned their living by selling government information and actions, will become increasingly irrelevant. This change is also sparking negative reactions in some countries.

Furthermore, although most governments see the nurturing of the Net as a key priority for themselves, few if any have reorganized themselves significantly to deal with it. Those that have taken some organizational steps have mimicked the American method of creating an interdepartmental task force or coordinating agency to development digital policy. Whether or not this will change remains to be seen.

Finally, developing countries in particular see the Internet as a tool to leap into the twenty-first century. But they also see it as a kind of genie or mirage on the horizon that will be difficult for them to conjure without substantial outside help, in the form of either private investment or international assistance. Without it, they see themselves forever parked on the wrong side of the digital tracks.

CANADA

Canada provides one of the most interesting case studies for the development of the information society. An advanced industrial country with a creative, diverse, and well-educated population spread over a vast territory, it is fertile ground for the Net. But Canada, adjacent to the U.S. giant, has cultural concerns that far predate the advent of the new information infrastructure—concerns that are often at odds with its economic interests. As Marc Raboy, professor of communication at the University of Montreal, has said,

Debate over communication policy has been one of the dominant themes of Canadian social discourse since the early days of radio broadcasting. Communication, in Canada, has been seen variously as a binding force for national unity, a vehicle for social development, and an instrument of cultural affirmation. In contrast, policy has also sought to promote the development of Canadian communication industries. In this respect, more so than in Europe or the United States, where one or the other pole has conventionally dominated, in Canada communication has evolved according to the push and pull between economics and culture.[2]

Thus, Canada began its public policy debate about the digital age in the context of a government and society pulled in different cultural directions, as evidenced by a number of public laws and government departments. Separate telecommunications and broadcasting acts call for strengthening Canada's economy and promoting its international competitiveness while also maintaining Canada's cultural identity and sovereignty. Canada's Department of Industry seeks to achieve the former, while its Department of Heritage is responsible for the latter. The Canadian Radio-Television and Telecommunications Commission (CRTC), an independent body much like the American Federal Communications Commission, seeks to do both, injecting into Canadian broadcasting values that include dual-language facility and respect for Canada's multicultural and multiethnic population.

In addition to the cultural debate, Canada is also dealing with the question of public versus private ownership and the question of deregulation and liberalization of telecommunications. Canadian broadcasting includes both public and private ownership, with the bulk of public funding coming from the national government in Ottawa and a smaller amount, mostly for educational television, from provincial governments. The telecommunications system is private, with Bell Canada as the largest player. Canada began the introduction of competition into telecommunications in 1994, but the actual removal of barriers to competition has been slow and painful, as in the United States. In addition, foreign ownership of broadcasting and telecommunications entities is restricted, adding an additional complication to Canada's attempts to globalize its economy. Canada has sought special exemptions for cultural reasons from a number of international agreements, including the North American Free Trade Agreement and the World Trade Organization (WTO) Agreement on Basic Telecommunications.

In this complex and meaty policy stew, the Canadian government began its approach to the information age by appointing an Information Highway Advisory Committee (IHAC) in 1994, a group composed of private-sector experts from the worlds of telecommunications, broadcasting, computing, content, and other sectors of the economy and society. Its biggest problem was dealing with the cultural and economic dichotomy. In the midst of IHAC's deliberations, in February 1995, the Canadian government played out its own tensions over the issue at the meeting of the ministers of the G-7 group of advanced industrialized nations on the global information infrastructure in Brussels.

At the meeting, Heritage Minister Michel Dupuy told the delegates that the new information infrastructure "has the most prestigious cultural showcase of all time. It will reach the largest imaginable audience and permit the most wide-ranging intercultural communication ever. . . . We must prevent the creation of any form of cultural monopoly on the information highway."[3] On the other hand, Industry Minister John Manley said that Canada's telecommunications framework "places Canada at the forefront of countries with pro-market regimes."[4] Both ministers, however, called for the assembled governments to address the content issue, which, with European support, they did in the closing communiqué.

IHAC completed its work in September 1995 and published its final report, "Connection, Community, Content: The Challenge of the Information Highway." It contained hundreds of recommendations that fell into a framework of three broad policy objectives and five operating principles:

—Creating jobs through innovation and investment;
—Reinforcing Canadian sovereignty and cultural identity;
—Ensuring universal access at a reasonable cost;
—An interconnected and interoperable network of networks;
—Collaborative public and private-sector development;
—Competition in facilities, products and services;
—Privacy protection and network security; and

—Lifelong learning as a key element of Canada's information super-highway.[5]

The Canadian government issued its response to the IHAC report and other studies done by the CRTC on May 23, 1996, in its report, "Building the Information Society: Moving Canada into the 21st Century," and summarized its policy recommendations in August 1996 in its "Convergence Policy Statement."[6] The statement enumerated specific policies for liberalizing and deregulating both telecommunications and cable television, ensuring competition in telecommunications and broadcasting, providing open standards for interoperability, and all the while achieving Canada's cultural objectives. On this last point, the government listed a number of specific ideas.

For example, it stated that "[a]s navigational systems for programming and distribution undertakings are introduced, they must facilitate advantageous access to Canadian programming and access to French language services."[7] The government report also discussed the difficulties of making sure that new content on the information infrastructure meets the content requirements of Canadian laws. It pointed out that the new technology will permit individuals "to have access to programming to be delivered to them and only to them at a specific time" and said the government would continue to review the content implications of this from legal, regulatory, and legislative viewpoints.[8]

Telecommunications and cultural policy have provided the major plotline for Canadian policy makers, but other issues have also been important. The IHAC report also listed universal access as a major objective, and Canada's Coalition for Public Information, a group representing libraries, educational institutions, and publishers, made more detailed recommendations. The coalition called for both private and public resources to be allocated to provide access to basic services to all people, including those in rural and remote areas and those who are handicapped. It also called for free public access points to be located in libraries and community centers, as well as community networks.[9] These recommendations are being carried out throughout Canada, often with the assistance of provincial governments. For example, in Ontario, public access terminals provide citizens with a variety of on-line government services, including job information and motor-vehicle registration. The government's 1997 budget included $30 million (Canadian) over three years to extend the Community Access Program to create public access points for Canadians in five thousand communities.

Canada is also focusing on the area of research and development. Canadian national laboratories have been collaborating with the private sector in a number of research areas, including interoperability for wired and wireless services, the delivery of multimedia services to remote regions by satellite, wireless broadband services, and advanced applications. The government budget for 1997 included $800 million (Canadian) over five years to modernize the research infrastructure, especially for Canada's national research and academic network, called CANARIE. It also included $50 million (Canadian) to set up the Canada Health Information System to connect health care providers, government planners, and individuals.

In other areas of the policy framework, the Canadian government is also working on an electronic signature law, new privacy legislation, and the revision of the national legal code to make it "media neutral." The government has also resisted a rush into new taxation of electronic commerce. Rather, the minister of national revenue released a 1998 report that focuses on the technical aspects of tax collection in a digital environment, including such topics as reporting issues, jurisdictional issues, maintenance of records, and collection points. The report specifically states, "Governments should avoid placing undue regulation and restrictions on, and should avoid undue taxation of electronic commerce."[10] The report also calls for tax neutrality, i.e., making no distinction between electronic and physical commerce, and recommends that Canada participate in international negotiations to deal with global tax issues.

So the Canadian government has generally taken a practical and balanced approach to the development of the Net and the implementation of electronic commerce. Like the United States, it needs to deregulate its telecommunications, cable, and broadcasting systems faster and should rely more on competition laws to combat monopoly behavior. Canada, which has a rich culture, should focus more energy on finding ways to display that culture to the world over the new media than it now does on trying to prevent the entry into Canada of the alien culture south of its border. Canada's use of public access points also provides a sound model for other countries, particularly developing ones.

In 1997, IHAC published its final report, "Preparing Canada for a Digital World," and seemed to accept these conclusions. On content, IHAC urged the federal government and industry together to "ensure the availability of a wider range of Canadian content reflecting Canada's distinctive cultural realities and linguistic duality."[11] The report also stressed the importance of universal access and the potential for Canadian global leadership. Finally, the report called for one government organizational action: "The federal minister responsible for the Information Highway, in concert with his/her provincial and territorial counterparts, should undertake the task of establishing a formal mechanism to review performance and to assess Canada's overall progress in developing a knowledge economy and information society."[12]

ASIA

Japan

If Ruth Benedict were writing her classic work about Japan, *The Chrysanthemum and the Sword*, today, she might call it "The Sony and the Missing Microsoft." Wildly successful in building a consumer electronics industry that is still the world leader, Japan has failed to build a correspondingly successful software industry. Such ironies emerge in each of the key Japanese industries that make up the new information infrastructure.

Home to many of the world's most creative artists, writers, and filmmakers, Japan's media industry still does not have the global reach of either U.S. or European media industries. Japan began to dominate world semiconductor markets two decades ago but lost its lead to American, Korean, and Taiwanese ingenuity. The moderate success of Japan's computer industry is marred both by earlier protectionist policies and by glaring episodes of industrial espionage in the 1970s. Japan has one of the world's most modern telecommunications systems, yet Japanese Net use has been limited until recently because of the high costs of telecommunications and Internet access caused by the persistence of monopoly.

Against this backdrop, Japan is nevertheless one of the world's key Net users and producers. In 1998, the Japanese Ministry of Posts and Telecommunications (MPT) estimated that about 17 million Japanese people were Internet users, or about 10 percent of the world's total users. The MPT also reported that the Internet household penetration rate was about 10 percent, compared to about 37 percent in the United States.[13] Moreover, the size of the market for electronic commerce doubled from 1997 to 1998, when it reached almost 2.6 trillion yen—an amount equivalent to about one-fourth of the U.S. estimated 1998 total of $102 billion.[14] One sign of the Japanese fascination with the Net is that Japanese is the second most common language used in cyberspace, with Japanese 7.2 percent higher than all languages but English.[15] Another sign is the use of the Net by Japanese farmers to sell products on-line—avoiding a cumbersome distribution system. By mid-2000, the Japanese electronic-commerce market was also being stimulated by the use of new and more accessible cell phones connected to the Net.

Thus, with a creative and motivated population that is eager to use on-line services, Japan's digital development up till now has been slowed by a government bureaucracy that finds it difficult to get out of the way. As three California scholars have observed, "The development of Japan's plans for a future information infrastructure hearken back to its past patterns of successful postwar economic development, involving many of the same actors involved in the creation and growth of the domestic consumer electronics, computer and semiconductor industries."[16] This plodding bureaucracy produces a destructive competition between ministries; a continuation of ponderous regulation, particularly in the telecommunications arena; and an inability to release entrepreneurial energies. For example, rather than find new ways to stimulate the growth of domestic content providers and software developers, the Japanese government has squandered energy by attempting to weaken copyright laws around the world to permit Japanese companies to expropriate more easily the works of foreign content and software creators.

Japan paid close attention to the early efforts of the Clinton administration in Washington to harness the new information infrastructure. In 1994, the Ministry of International Trade and Industry (MITI) published its "Program for Advanced Information Infrastructure."[17] Although the report mentioned in passing the leadership role of the private sector, it principally focused on the dissemination of the new digital technology into the public sector. It focused on the need for Japan to introduce advanced applications into five key areas of Japanese government: education, research and development, medical and welfare services, public administration, and libraries. Each section cited the U.S. example: the section on research, for instance, cited the U.S. High Performance Computing and Communications Act, the National Science Foundation's NSFNET, and the National Research and Education Network (NREN) and called for plans in Japan to introduce eleven supercomputers in 1994 into eight national organizations. Nowhere, however, was there mention of government action to stimulate private-sector research.

In addition to the five applications areas for government, the 1994 MITI report also discussed a number of policy areas that the government would need to address in order to promote the growth of digital technologies. These included providing better security, standardizing to promote interoperability, updating intellectual property laws, establishing multimedia centers, and improving the educational system to develop more programmers and software specialists. The MITI report touched very gingerly on the issue of telecommunications, since that was the province of MITI's principal rival in that area, the MPT.

The MPT also claims ownership of the information infrastructure and has focused on telecommunications regulation, research and development, and access. In 1985 Japan introduced competition into telecommunications, and further liberalization has followed. Unfortunately, Japan's complex telecommunications regulatory structure remains. Despite heavy lobbying by the Japanese computer industry, which has more influence at MITI, the MPT has not sufficiently loosened the reins. Thus, even though the MPT claims that telecommunications prices have dropped, they still remain higher than they would be with less regulation. The MPT's 1999 white paper did admit that Japanese city subscription charges for wired telephone lines and charges for digital leased circuits are higher than in other world cities.[18] Not only are Internet access charges high, but Japanese Internet service providers (ISPs) offer no flat-rate pricing. One big step the Japanese government could take to stimulate rapidly the development of new communications technologies would be to eliminate the MPT as a ministry. Such a dramatic action would not only be helpful to the development of the Net in Japan but would also be a strong signal of Japan's willingness to make the changes necessary for it to compete successfully in the twenty-first century.

The principal document guiding the Japanese government's policy efforts for cyberspace is MITI's paper, "Towards the Age of the Digital Economy: For Rapid Progress in the Japanese Economy and World Economic Growth in the 21st Century." This document is much more progressive in its acceptance of the primary role of the private sector. It says that issues relating to the digital economy "should basically be solved by technological means, as well as competition in the marketplace and the creation of new independent business practices in the private sector."[19] The paper then goes on to cover the major issue areas: legal framework, intellectual property, security, privacy, harmful content, participation by small and medium-sized business, education, and interoperability. In each, it stresses the role of the private sector, mentioning, for example, the Platform for Internet Content Selection (PICS) effort to develop a means of content filtering for children.

The Japanese government has taken positive steps to work with other countries and international organizations on the harmonization of electronic commerce rules in areas ranging from taxation to consumer protection. The MITI paper stresses the importance of both bilateral and multilateral efforts, and the government of Japan did sign a joint statement with the United States in 1998 on electronic commerce, promoting close international cooperation between the two countries. For example, both worked together at the WTO in 1998 and 1999 to assure that a duty-free environment for electronic commerce would remain in place.

The government has also paid attention to the policy views of the private sector. The Japanese Electronics Industry Development Association (JEIDA), under the leadership of the Fujitsu corporation, has been especially active through MITI. In particular, JEIDA has cooperated with its sister associations in the United States, Europe, and elsewhere to develop common positions on issues including trade, privacy, and intellectual property. In addition, the U.S.-Japan Business Council also produced a key document in July 1999, the "Joint Statement on Electronic Commerce," which deals with the full range of policy issues.

Japan also took an important organizational step by creating an advisory committee to the prime minister composed of key private-sector officials. Their advice on private-sector leadership has been sound. Japan's challenge for the future will be to create an entrepreneurial climate in the country that will foster the natural talent of Japan's bright young people. That would have implications for the nation above and beyond its efforts to harness the power of the Net.

The Philippines

Although other Asian nations have gotten more attention and perhaps earlier starts, the Philippines launched its own action plan in 1997 called "IT21: Action Agenda for the 21st Century."[20] Many of the ideas in "IT21" were derived from international sources, including help from the U.S. Agency for International Development, the United Nations Conference on International Trade Law (UNCITRAL), and others. "IT21" calls for four initiatives: the creation of a sound policy environment for electronic commerce, the enhancement of the telecommunications structure, the development of human resources through education and training, and the use of the technology by the government.

With regard to policy, "IT21" calls for the liberalization of foreign investments, the reform of intellectual property laws, ratification of the International Technology Agreement to eliminate tariffs on information-technology products, and the creation of "cyberparks," or high-technology industrial parks with economic incentives for investment. The Philippines already has five cyberparks, one of which, on the former site of the United States's Clark Air Force Base, houses a number of companies, including America Online. The Philippine legislature is at work on the policy issues and is in the process of passing a bill dealing with electronic signatures and contracts.

The Philippines is also working hard on education. The country is already second among Asian countries in terms of the number of facilities for teaching computer programming and other related courses. One result is that the Philippine software industry is a top exporter and has attracted investments by major global software companies, including Lotus, Oracle, Microsoft, and SAP. Software exports in 1997 amounted to $250 million. American and Japanese hardware manufacturers such as Seagate, Acer, and Fujitsu are also investing in the Philippines.[21] Another, unintended result is the training of programmers skillful enough to develop the "I love you" virus that caused worldwide damage in May 2000. The Philippines, where the virus originated, needs to modernize its legal code to deal with illegal hacking.

The Philippine government has also created a National Information Technology Council to coordinate government actions across agencies, and an Electronic Commerce Promotion Council. All in all, the Philippines provides a good example of how developing countries can use the Net to stimulate economic development. Says one Philippine expert, "Information technology offers renewed opportunities for developing countries, which can shift from exploitation of natural resources at the expense of the environment, to tapping its human resources."[22]

Malaysia

Distantly echoing the creation of ultra-modern Brasília by the Brazilian government in the 1960s, Malaysia has chosen a unique way to make its approach to cyberspace. The nation is attempting to create a cyber-region—the "Multimedia Super Corridor," or MSC—as a wedge into the future for the entire nation. The idea of the MSC has been attributed directly to Prime Minister Mahathir Mohammed and has its roots in "The Way Forward—Vision 2020," a paper developed by the prime minister's office and presented to the Malaysian Business Council in 1996.[23] "The Way Forward" expresses the hope that Malaysia will be a "fully developed country by the year 2020" but argues that Malaysia must go its own way. Although it recognizes that the development and application of technology is critical, the paper argues that the nation must deal at the same time with the challenges of preserving its culture and spirituality and deal with its ethnic and racial challenges. From this flows the notion that the information age must be exploited relentlessly for its economic potential but controlled at the outset so that it does not disrupt the social fabric.

Actually begun in 1997, the MSC is 50 kilometers long and 15 kilometers wide and flanked by two new cities: Putrajava is planned to be the government's new electronic administrative center, a key user of new applications developed in the MSC; Cyberjava will be the site for information technology companies investing in the region. A new multimedia university will be built to provide skilled workers, and the overall project is expected to employ 150,000 people.

To attract investors, the MSC offers high-technology companies tax-free status for ten years, tax exemptions for equipment, relaxed immigration rules for expatriates, and other economic incentives. In addition, in response to initial concerns by investors, the Malaysian government created a ten-point Multimedia Bill of Guarantees to apply within the corridor, providing for strong intellectual property protection, rights for corporate ownership, freedom from on-line censorship, and other concerns.[24] The government also agreed to develop a more comprehensive national framework for electronic commerce, and among the laws drafted or already passed are ones dealing with digital signatures, electronic contracts, computer crime, data protection, and electronic government.

The government has also identified seven application areas that investors would have to work on in order to qualify for economic incentives: electronic government, telemedicine, research and development, remote manufacturing, borderless marketing centers, multimedia funds transfer, and "smart" schooling. By 1998, the government had also added schools, universities, and company training facilities to the list of institutions that would qualify for MSC status.

Although the Asian financial crisis of the late 1990s slowed the development of the MSC, the government had received 176 applications from companies by early 1998 to locate in the MSC and had approved 103 of them. European companies made up the largest number of investors, followed by those from the United States and Japan. This test-bed approach to a nation's entry into cyberspace will be interesting to watch. If Malaysia can succeed in building an advanced infrastructure and attracting investment to create jobs, while at the same time preventing cyberspace from affecting other aspects of national life, other nations will attempt the same thing. But the genie of the Net, once let out, will be difficult to contain.

Singapore

Malaysia's neighbor Singapore presents another story. Singapore committed itself wholeheartedly to the digital age as early as any other country, developing and implementing a comprehensive national plan for building an electronic economy. But even as that plan has been implemented, the government has taken extraordinary measures to limit the power of its citizens to use the new technology, making Singapore a negative model for other Asian governments that seek to control their populations.

Singapore has had a National Computer Board to develop information policy since 1981 and was one of the first countries to recognize the tremendous economic potential of the information age. In March 1992, the board released its paper "IT2000—A Vision of an Intelligent Island."[25] The paper highlighted the fact that Singapore's past prosperity grew out of its being a transportation and communications hub in Asia. In the future, such hubs would be electronic, the paper pointed out, and Singapore would have to harness its human resources to maintain its position. Its goal: "In our vision . . . Singapore, the Intelligent Island, will be among the first countries in the world with an advanced nationwide information infrastructure."[26]

"IT2000" laid out five major thrusts for policy:

1. Developing a global hub: The paper's vision would "help turn Singapore into a highly efficient switching center for goods, services, capital, information, and people," attracting companies that wished to market products and services worldwide.[27]
2. Improving the quality of life: People would be able to use electronic media for government transactions and electronic commerce and to work more efficiently.
3. Boosting the economic engine: Information technology would help create jobs by developing high-value manufacturing, streamlining construction logistics, and increasing distribution efficiency.
4. Linking communities locally and globally: The new infrastructure could help link together all Singaporeans, including those living abroad.
5. Enhancing the potential of individuals: People would be able to use distance learning and training techniques to enhance their skills and to retrain. The physically handicapped would also benefit.

Singapore's early start had advantages and disadvantages. It harnessed the energies of the government long before most other governments had begun to think about the issue, but it did so at an early state of techno-logical development, when, for example, the World Wide Web had not yet been developed. Thus, although a great deal of money was spent to develop physical infrastructure, much was wasted on technologies that would become obsolete, such as Teletext. Nevertheless, Singapore's in-stitutions moved quickly to adopt the Internet. "Singapore was one of the first countries in Asia to adopt the Internet. The National University of Singapore was among the first in Asia to introduce Gopher servers in 1992, and the Worldwide Web in 1993."[28] By 2000, all 750,000 house-holds in Singapore are expected to be connected to the Net via broad-band coaxial or optical-fiber networks.

In addition to direct investments by the government under the "IT2000" plan, Singapore also made progress in Net policy areas. Singapore Tele-comm, the national telecommunications company, was privatized in 1993. Although it still maintains a monopoly in local wire line and interna-tional telephony, competition will be introduced beginning in 2002. Mo-bile telephony is competitive and there are several ISPs, though all are carefully regulated by the government.

In 1995, Singapore amended its laws to give legal status to computer-ized records. Other laws related to electronic commerce, including intel-lectual property, digital signatures, security, and privacy, are also being worked on by the government. Most interesting is the government's atti-tude toward content control. Another National Computer Board paper states, "Most countries are trying to maintain some form of content reg-ulation in the digital environment. They include the ASEAN [Association of Southeast Asian Nations] countries, China, Vietnam, the US with its embattled Communications Decency Act, and the EC countries."[29] In other words, the government has tried to make censorship of the Inter-net appear to be the national norm. In fact, Singapore has gone far be-yond what most democratic countries have done.

The government of Singapore and its ruling political party, the People's Action Party (PAP), have used the nation's Internal Security Act and other laws to control the traditional means of communications for years. As one observer notes, "Although the Internet represents a more difficult challenge for Singapore's control-minded officials, the government has embarked on an ambitious attempt to superimpose strict broadcasting censorship on the medium. Other authoritarian regimes in Asia have been inspired by this model of regulation."[30]

Singaporean authorities let it be known that they were monitoring the Internet as early as 1994, when they announced they had scanned ISP records and found a number of pornographic files. Since all of Singapore ISPs use the same backbone, and since there is a monopoly on telephone service, most Singaporeans believe the government monitors their Internet usage, and there is some evidence that it does.[31] In 1995, the government expressed growing concern about the use of the Internet to express antigovernment and antisocial views, and in 1996 it tightened control by giving the Singapore Broadcasting Authority the right to regulate and license Web sites. The government described this action an "an anti-pollution measure in cyberspace."[32]

The 1996 laws provide for registration and regulation of all ISPs; registration of Web sites dealing with politics, religion, and other sensitive items; and requirements for ISPs to prevent the transmission of "objectionable content and to provide to government detailed records about their users." Since the imposition of these new regulations there have been a number of instances of individuals being fined or having their Web sites closed down. Moreover, the policies have attracted attention from other authoritarian states, such as Vietnam and China, who have sent delegations to Singapore to learn about electronic censorship.

Can Singapore develop the economic and social benefits of cyberspace while still censoring and regulating it? As Garry Rodan, a professor at Murdoch University in Perth, Australia, says, "The Singapore model does not constitute a foolproof means of halting the advance of information. Moreover, the battle between control-minded authoritarians and those seeking to exploit the Internet for liberal and liberating purposes will continue. . . . However, against liberal expectations of the Internet as a force for the erosion of authoritarian states and the empowerment of individuals and civil society . . . such technology can also be harnessed by some states to consolidate a climate of fear and intimidation."[33]

China

The number of China's Internet users reached 1.175 million by July 1998—a mere one-tenth of a percent of China's 1.2 billion people, according to *Wired* magazine.[34] This represented a near-doubling of the number of users in just six months. Moreover, the number of Chinese companies connected on-line rose 64 percent in the same period, to 542,000. The Chinese government itself is a heavy Net user; government-backed sites such as 21 Dragon News Network and eastday.com.cn were launched in early 2000. One Chinese company—called "8848.net" after the height of Mount Everest in meters—was selling books, software, and consumer electronics at the rate of $1 million per month by the end of 1999. Run by a forty-six-year-old Chinese national, the company's biggest fear is the growing number of competitors. This explosion in usage did not happen by chance but is the result of both Chinese individual entrepreneurship and investments and government incentives to bring electronic commerce to China.

However, also in July 1998, China arrested and charged a young programmer with subversion, an offense punishable by ten years in prison or even death, for supplying a prodemocracy movement with a list of E-mail addresses. In January 1999 he received the "lighter" sentence of only two years in prison, and he was released early in September 1999. Thus, China faces the same dilemma as Singapore, but on a much greater scale.

China has moved aggressively for a number of years to modernize its telecommunications and computing infrastructure. For a nation with a telephone penetration rate of only 3.2 percent in 1995, this has been a formidable task. It is being achieved by massive government investments in wire line and wireless telephony, as well as by the introduction of limited competition. In addition to the Ministry of Post and Telecommunications, the Ministry of Electronics Industries now operates a competitive telephone provider and foreign companies such as Motorola are active in the equipment market. The growth rate of telephony has been running at 40 percent per year. The government has also worked hard to modernize laws in areas such as intellectual property to create a friendly environment for electronic commerce.

China has also invested heavily in the development of advanced networks that could be connected to the Internet. In the early 1990s, a number of academic and research networks were established, the most important of which is the China Education and Research Network (CERNET). From its beginnings in 1993, CERNET has grown toward meeting its objectives of becoming a national backbone network to connect more than a thousand Chinese universities and their 390,000 professors, as well as high schools and other educational and research entities. CERNET is located at Tsinghua University in the Zhongguancun district near Beijing. The region, which also includes Beijing University, has become a magnet for other research institutions and companies; the area now employs 15,000 researchers and is known as China's Silicon Valley.[35]

CERNET, along with hundreds of other local- and wide-area networks in China, is now connected to the Internet. As a result, all of the 390,000 professors, 15,000 researchers, and millions of university and high school students have access to outside information—potentially. Fearing the worst, on February 4, 1996, Xinhua, China's news agency, issued new Internet regulations.[36] These rules required all of China's networks to register with the police and required ISPs to connect to the Internet only through channels provided by the MPT. The regulations also banned organizations and individuals from Internet activities that violated laws related to state security, political content, and pornography. Later the law was extended to require registration for all Internet users.

In August 1996, China took a further step by blocking a wide variety of World Wide Web sites, including media from the United States and Taiwan, dissident sites dealing with Tibet, and sexually explicit sites such as *Playboy*'s. Echoing Singapore, Chinese government officials branded such sites as "spiritual pollution."[37] In another attempt to control the development of the Internet both financially and culturally, the Chinese government has drafted rules formally to bar foreign investment in Internet ventures in China—rules that would take effect in 2000. China's predicted entry into the WTO, however, may cause these rules to have an early demise. In early 2000, the Chinese government also announced that both foreign and Chinese companies would have to register the type of encryption software they use. It also bans foreign encryption products and requires that companies provide personal information about employees who use encryption. Since it is doubtful that either technical means or financial controls can really work and prevent people from free communication over the Internet (particularly the kinds of technical people using the Net in China), the only means left to the government is intimidation. That is obviously the purpose of the examples of arrest and prosecution for Internet offenses. In the long run, however, with millions of people online, both technical means of blockage and intimidation seem bound to fail. The Chinese Communists are right to fear the power of the Internet.

South Korea

"In 1998, in the midst of the International Monetary Fund regime to rescue economies after the Asian financial crisis when gross domestic product and industrial production shrank by 5.8% and 7.1% respectively, the volume of electronic commerce is estimated to have reached a figure exceeding twice the previous forecast. Recent projections routinely call for over 100% annual growth rate for years to come."[38] These remarkable facts, reported by a South Korean university professor at a WTO symposium on information technology, demonstrate the commitment of the government and industry in South Korea to exploit the commercial power of the Net.

South Korea's efforts to enter the digital age can be traced back to 1987, when the National Basic Information System Plan (NBIS) to promote the computer industry began, and to 1990, when the effort to deregulate telecommunications began. In 1994, mirroring the efforts of the Clinton administration in Washington, the government set up a Korean Information Infrastructure (KII) Policy Committee, chaired by the prime minister and run by the minister of economic planning, who also served as the vice chair of the committee. Officials from twenty ministries serve on the policy committee, which has four functions:

1. Deliberate on and coordinate KII policies and assist in implementing the KII vision;
2. Design the KII master plan and allocate funds;
3. Develop KII technology; and
4. Study related laws and regulation for revision.

The original idea of the policy committee was to use both government and private funding to build an advanced information network and to develop core applications such as electronic government services, remote medical care, and distance education. The South Korean government also created a KII Task Force, including not only government officials but experts from academia and industry. These officials made an extensive fact-finding trip to the United States, visiting the administration's national information infrastructure experts as well as numerous private companies and research institutes.

In 1996, South Korea's Ministry of Information and Communications brought out a more detailed plan to work with industry "to promote informatization in the country and bring information superhighway business to full scale."[39] Plans called for spending almost 70 billion Korean won on networks and applications.

South Korea's current vision for its information society is spelled out in "Cyber Korea 21," the government's 1999 vision for the digital age.[40] The aim of "Cyber Korea 21" is to create one million new jobs and $23.8 billion worth of new production in four years. Among the plan's key undertakings are

1. Upgrading telecommunications networks, using fiber optics, cable modems, and wireless local loop and satellite communications at a cost of $8.67 billion, mostly from private sources;
2. Targeting the entire population with a computer education program, ranging from basic literacy to advanced intensive classes. The plan calls for connecting every South Korean school to the Net;

3. Making legal revisions to intellectual property, taxation, encryption, and legal framework rules; and
4. Creating an electronic civil service and installing civil service kiosks to permit citizen transactions in areas involving real estate, motor vehicles, and education. By 1999, South Korea has already placed on the Internet more than 4,500 civil service procedures.

South Korea's approach appears to be working. By March 1999, about 3.7 million Koreans in a population of 45 million were using the Internet, and there were almost 200,000 hosts. Twenty-six domestic ISPs, of which 22 were commercial, linked South Koreans to the Internet. The total value of electronic commerce was estimated in 1998 at 46.5 billion won, and more than 250 Internet shopping malls had been established. Forecasts call for electronic commerce in South Korea to grow at 100 percent per year and to exceed 2 trillion won by 2003.[41]

The government is also moving ahead with policy changes. In January 1999, the South Korean parliament passed the Electronic Commerce Promotion Act, which went into effect in July 1999. The law provides a legal underpinning for electronic commerce. "The main point is that contracts signed electronically now have legal effect, and this will help make cyberspace more attractive for consumers," said one South Korean financial analyst.[42] South Korea also benefits to some extent because its *chaebol* structure of large, interlinked corporations lends itself to electronic commerce transactions among each *chaebol*'s units. The close integration of the *chaebol* leadership with the government also gives the government more say in the development of the Net and electronic commerce than in many other countries.

Although South Korea's approach has been successful to date, it faces some difficult challenges. The greatest of these is the role of the government and its tendency to want to control the Net in the traditional Korean way, while struggling to change and meet the contemporary need for private-sector control. For example, the Ministry of Information and Communications claims to have removed more than half of all telecommunications regulations, and it has made progress in deregulation. Nevertheless, the policies and rules for many areas such as interconnection, access, and pricing remain complex and murky. The South Korea Communications Commission (the national equivalent of the U.S. Federal Communications Commission) is not an independent body but exists as part of the ministry. South Korea is a signatory of the WTO Agreement on Basic Telecommunications, however, and is moving toward more liberalization and openness in telecommunications.

Thus, the development of the Net represents a great shift in South Korean government tradition. If South Korea can succeed in deregulating and letting the private sector move ahead, it will likely exceed the goals it had set for electronic commerce. Moreover, as one observer noted, "the KII plan represents an important departure from a well-established and successful tradition, and might be an example for future economic development initiatives in Asia."[43]

India

India is a country that may succeed in cyberspace despite its government's policies. The country that invented the concept of zero in the fifth century cannot seem to give up its nineteenth-century notions about socialism and the private sector. Long burdened with an archaic bureaucracy and notions of statism inherited from the British, India has been trying to reform its economy since the early 1990s. The process has been slow and difficult. For example, not only is basic telephone service still overwhelmingly a government monopoly, but the growth and modernization of the telephone system remains sluggish. India has one of the lowest teledensities in the world, lower than that of China, Pakistan, or Malaysia. Although the government has theoretically transferred telecommunications regulation to the Telecom Regulatory Authority of India (TRAI), the regulatory process remains complex and burdensome, with many ministries and government departments involved.

Worst of all, the poor business climate is driving the most talented Indians to the United States, where they are making an important contribution to the development of the Net. Today, many Silicon Valley startup ventures are run by Indians, many of whom are graduates of the prestigious Indian Institute of Technology in Bombay. Unlike for many other immigrants, the English language is not a problem for Indian researchers and software experts, and in the United States they find infinitely better business conditions, an instant infrastructure, and a higher standard of living.

There are some bright notes, however, in the development of the Net in India. For the advanced scientific sector, the government has provided important support that has laid the groundwork for a future national information infrastructure. The National Informatics Center (NIC) has established NICNET, a satellite-based network of 600 earth stations that connects government agencies at the central, state, and district levels. The Department of Electronics initiated the Educational and Research Network (ERNET) to provide connectivity for India's university and research community. A number of library networks have been established, and the network of India's Open University serves more than 500,000 students.

But India's greatest success has more to do with the private sector and the talents of individual Indians who remain in the country, than with the government. India's homegrown software industry employs more than 40,000 software engineers and a total of about 250,000 people, most of them producing software for export. India's software industry has been growing at over 40 percent per year and will bring in about $5.7 billion in revenue in 2000. India is expected to earn about $3.9 billion in software export earnings alone in 2000.[44] Almost two-thirds of India's software exports go to the United States, and almost one-quarter go to Europe. One estimate is that by 2010, India's software industry could earn almost $90 billion and employ more than two million people.

Part of this impressive revenue has been due to temporary demand for Y2K software services, but much has also been due to the skills of Indian software professionals and investors who are slowly weaning Indian software companies away from value-added services toward Indian-branded software products and more complex services. Indian-owned companies in the United States also form strong links with their compatriots back home. The Indian government's decision in 1998 to end the state monopoly in ISPs is also helping this trend, allowing Indian programmers to serve global clients without leaving Bangalore, Madras, or Hyderabad. Thus, Indian software can be delivered in three ways:

1. Offshore development through high-speed satellite links;
2. On-site services by international movement of people; and
3. Physical delivery by floppy disks, compact disks, etc.

For the future, India needs to develop some method of coordination among the many government ministries involved in its national information infrastructure effort. It also needs to move much more rapidly and substantively on eliminating government regulation in every sector, but particularly telecommunications. India did sign the International Technology Agreement, and its software export industry is partially dependent on national rules governing the movement of professionals across national borders. As two of India's leading students of the Internet point out, "For the NII to have its full impact upon the economy, a clear break with conventional ideas in India's telecom sector is called for."[45] For that matter, India needs a clean break with most of its past economic policies.

Australia

Australia is a country that was made for the digital age. It has a highly educated and literate population that is fluent in English and that has the disposable income to shop on-line. Combine those facts with a huge remote continent, far from the major commercial centers of the world, and with a population thinly spread across huge expanses of its continental land mass. The result is a nation with the third highest Internet usage in the world, after the United States and Finland.[46] Australians made 1.2 million on-line purchases in 1998, 64 percent of which were from overseas companies. More than 25 percent of Australians have Internet access—a growth rate of 65 percent from the previous year—and 63 percent of Australian businesses used electronic commerce in 1998.[47] Australia has more than 8,000 active business Web sites capable of secure electronic transactions.

All of this growth could have happened without government action, but in fact the Australian government has taken a strong position in support of the Net and has enacted appropriate measures to facilitate its growth. The National Office for the Information Economy has been set up, housed in the Ministry of Communications, Information Technology, and the Arts but reporting to the Ministerial Council for the Information Economy, a subcommittee of the Australian cabinet. Australia's overall policy principles making up its framework for the information economy were summed up in its joint statement with the United States on electronic commerce in 1998:

—The growth of electronic commerce will be led by the private sector;
—All Australians need to be able to access the information economy at sufficient bandwidth and affordable cost;
—Competitive market-based solutions to specific issues will promote optimal growth and benefits. Governments should avoid imposing unnecessary regulations. When necessary, governments should rely on a "light-touch" regulatory environment;
—Where the market alone will not solve problems, self-regulation gives maximum control and responsibility to the individual;
—Government approaches should be harmonized domestically and internationally; and
—Government should pursue excellence in the on-line delivery of its services.[48]

To achieve these objectives, Australia has pursued a number of legislative and regulatory changes. Telecommunications began to be deregulated seriously in July 1997, after the passage of a number of new telecommunications laws, including the Telecommunications Act of 1997, which eliminated any limit on the number of telecommunications carriers in the country. The law also set up a new independent regulatory body, the Australian Communications Authority (ACA), whose principal job is to regulate anticompetitive conduct in the new competitive telecommunications regime.[49] The ACA encourages self-regulation and has set up the Australian Communications Industry Forum to develop industry codes for issues ranging from technical standards to consumer issues.

One key area where the government has intervened is the area of the universal service obligation (USO). Given Australia's vast size and remote areas, "left to market forces, the difference between services in cities and those in regional and rural areas [would be] likely to widen" without government action.[50] The minister for communications, information technology, and the arts, Senator Richard Alston, is directing a number of efforts to achieve the USO, including possibly tendering out to private companies the USO, and funding a $250 million (Australian) regional telecommunications infrastructure initiative called "Networking the Nation." The ministry has also set up a "National Bandwidth Inquiry" to determine what needs to be done to assure that Australia will have the bandwidth to meet the future needs of the information economy.

Other efforts by the government include work on an electronic transactions bill based on the UNCITRAL approach, a national framework for authentication, so-called light-touch privacy legislation, and the development of on-line government services. Perhaps the most important area of government action, which may provide a model for others, is in consumer protection. Australia has moved vigorously to develop private-sector codes, with government help. A National Advisory Council on Consumer Affairs, consisting of representatives from business, consumer groups, and academia, developed in 1998 a set of twelve principles for consumer protection in the realm of electronic commerce that is now being used by the government to assist industry:

1. Consumers using electronic commerce are entitled to at least the same levels of protection as provided by the laws and practices that apply to existing forms of commerce;
2. Consumers should be able to establish the identity and location of businesses with whom they deal;
3. Consumers should have readily available clear and comprehensive information before and after any purchase of goods or services;

4. Sellers must state contract terms in clear, simple language;
5. Sellers should ensure they receive meaningful consent from consumers for a purchase of goods or services;
6. Consumers are entitled to receive clear information about the types of payments that will be accepted by the merchant or the payment provider;
7. Consumers are entitled to have their complaints and inquiries dealt with fairly and effectively;
8. Sellers should provide information to consumers about affordable and effective dispute resolution arrangements, where they are available;
9. Sellers must respect customer privacy;
10. Industry code administration bodies must closely monitor the application and effectiveness of their codes and be able to correct any deficiencies that are identified;
11. Each code operating body should strive to maintain and promote consumer confidence in the global marketplace; and
12. Governments should actively develop their consumer protection responsibilities.[51]

Finally, as a nation with critical international economic ties, Australia is aggressively pursuing its electronic commerce agenda with a number of other countries and at international organizations. In addition to its work with the United States, the government has been negotiating agreements with the European Union, Japan, New Zealand, and Canada. It is also very active in discussions at the Organization for Economic Cooperation and Development (OECD) and within the Asia-Pacific Economic Cooperation group, where it co-chairs the Electronic Commerce Task Force with Singapore.

EUROPE

Nuclear testing by the United States in the 1950s and 1960s set off a chain reaction in Europe that was decidedly non-nuclear. President Charles DeGaulle of France, concerned about American technological dominance, set in motion a series of government support measures for technology in France, including direct government support for research and development as well as strong commercial backing for French technological champions. Similar programs grew in other European countries, including Germany and the United Kingdom, and were eventually adopted at the European level by the European Union (EU). By the time the Internet emerged in the early 1990s, precedents and a structure already existed for how Europe might approach the new phenomenon. Although each of the individual European countries has developed its digital capacities at its own pace and within its own policy framework, an examination of European progress on the Net must begin with a look at EU policies.

The ten-nation European Community (EC) began its government approach to the information age in 1982 with a program called the European Strategic Program for Research and Development (ESPRIT). ESPRIT was a response to U.S. and Japanese leadership in semiconductors and computing and was originally suggested by a private advisory roundtable of European information-technology executives. It provided funding for a variety of technology partnerships among European companies, universities, and government agencies in areas such as microelectronics, computer networks, and application areas such as manufacturing, health care, and education. Over the next decade, ESPRIT was followed by a variety of similar research and development partnerships.

In the mid-1980s, the EC also took the first steps toward the liberalization and deregulation of European telecommunications, including the harmonization of standards and certification procedures for telecommunications services and equipment. An EC research and development program called RACE provided funding for research on advanced telecommunications infrastructure. The European Academic and Research Network was also inaugurated to provide interconnectivity for European university networks and to provide a connection to American universities. (Indeed, DeGaulle would have been pleased that much of the stimulus for these networking activities, as well as the invention of the World Wide Web, came from CERN, Europe's high-energy physics laboratory, which straddles the border between France and Switzerland.) In Brussels, DG XIII, the directorate responsible for telecommunications, emerged as a center of activity for many of these programs.

By 1994, with these programs established, the Internet and the idea of national information infrastructures had exploded onto the scene. Not to be outdone by the Americans, Martin Bangemann, European commissioner for telecommunications, research and development, and the internal market, grabbed the European lead and published a report in 1994 stressing the importance of the new information age to the future of Europe's economy. Turning away from concerns over the last decade that new technologies might eliminate jobs in Europe, the Bangemann report accepted that new computing and communications technologies could create jobs, provided the right actions were taken in education and other fields.

The EC acted quickly on the Bangemann report and presented a paper on the subject to the European Council meeting in Corfu in June 1994. The resulting document, "Europe's Way to the Information Society: An Action Plan," was adopted and published in July 1994.[52] The overall report stressed the need for further and faster liberalization of European economies and more harmonization of policies, but it also set a tone of concern: "The race is on at a global level, notably between the U.S. and Japan. Those countries which will adapt themselves most readily, will de facto set technological standards for those who follow."[53] The paper described four areas where coordinated action by Europe was needed:

1. Regulatory and legal framework: The paper called for more rapid liberalization of telecommunications, progress on standards and interoperability, lower telecommunications tariffs and financing of universal service, a study of copyright laws, rapid adoption of the European privacy directive, and development of rules for data security and encryption, among other things.
2. Networks, basic services, applications, and content: "The private sector will take the leading role in the implementation of the Information Society."[54] This was probably the single most important concept in the action plan, calling for private-sector investment, with some public help, in areas ranging from Internet Services Digital Network (ISDN) and automatic bank-teller services, along with both private- and public-sector applications. The notion of private-sector leadership was not yet fully embedded in European thinking, however, and an upcoming debate over standards would illustrate this. The paper also stressed the importance of European content.
3. Social, societal, and cultural aspects: The paper warned that although the information society held the promise of new jobs and promotion of Europe's "linguistic and cultural diversity," this could not be taken for granted. It recommended a variety of initiatives and studies in the fields of education, health, working conditions, and culture.
4. Promotion activities: Concerned about political support for all these endeavors, the paper expressed the need to raise the level of understanding among ordinary European citizens about the information society and proposed a wide series of media events and publications to educate people.

Following the publication of the action plan, Bangemann and the European Commission focused on two critical areas: standards and the functioning of the internal market. In the opening of its paper on standards, "Standardization and Global Information Society," the commission expressed its fear of U.S. dominance: "It is evident that the Information and Communications technology market is dominated by specifications from the USA." The paper argued that the traditional standards-setting process was not working, because of its slowness, thus permitting the development of proprietary systems, normally not European. The paper held out a large stick: "In order to safeguard the public interest, . . . the Community has to monitor developments in standardization. . . . Where public interests are at stake, the ultimate solution . . . consists of regulatory measures."[55] At about the same time, the European Telecommunications Standards Institute was considering procedures to expropriate technology embedded in standards. The U.S. government, committed to the idea that standards activity belongs principally to the private sector, resisted the European efforts, dragging its feet on cooperation on an international conference on the subject. Though the idea of government intervention in standards-making was weakening, the commission continued to attempt to use standards to gain access to technology until it became clear that it did not have strong support from European industry.

In 1996, the commission also published its paper on the impact of the information society on the internal market.[56] This paper pointed out that electronic services, by definition, take place at a distance, including distances involving border crossings. Since the types of services that could be provided electronically were all regulated in some way within the member nations, some kind of harmonization would be necessary. The paper pointed out that harmonization of some sort was urgent, since the individual governments were already at work on their own rules, which could become obstacles to the provision of electronic services within the internal market.

Other issues continued to percolate, and by 1997, the Clinton administration was at work on its "Framework for Electronic Commerce." Determined to beat the Americans, the European Commission published its major document, "A European Initiative in Electronic Commerce," in April 1997, three months ahead of the Clinton administration's report.[57] The "European Initiative" bore many similarities to its American counterpart, but it also contained subtle and not so subtle differences. For example, although the paper did state that the "expansion of electronic commerce would be market-driven" and that there should be "no regulation for regulation's sake,"[58] it did not stress the leadership role of the private sector to the extent that the U.S. document did. Thus, the EU left itself room for significant government involvement, as spelled out in the rest of the document.

On the other hand, the European document noted to a greater extent, the importance of obtaining global consensus on electronic commerce: With fourteen member states to deal with, the EU perhaps understood better the impact that the borderless Net would have on sovereignty: "Electronic commerce is inherently a global activity. . . . Any European action on electronic commerce therefore has to be compatible with . . . WTO commitments" and must "work through appropriate international for a . . . to establish a coherent global regulatory framework."[59] Fearful of U.S. dominance, the EU preferred to rely on international regimes such as the WTO to set the rules, lest the United States do it by default.

The European initiative contained four key elements and a long list of actions, some in progress, and some proposed. The first element was to promote technology and infrastructure. Noting that EU legislation called for establishing telecommunications liberalization and assuring full competition by January 1998, the paper said that European telecommunications prices were already lower. It also called for full implementation of the WTO Agreement on Basic Telecommunications and the International Technology Agreement, which would lower prices worldwide. The European Commission promised research and development funding through ESPRIT and through two new research and development programs designed to develop high-bandwidth networks and more user-friendly applications, including those that might encourage the use of electronic commerce by small and medium-sized enterprises and by government. Still concerned about standards, the commission stated that it would launch specific action programs on standardization projects, provoking business groups such as the American Chamber of Commerce in Brussels to object.[60]

The second element of the initiative sought to create a favorable regulatory framework for the development of the Net throughout the EU. The commission suggested four principles for a regulatory framework:

1. No regulation for regulation's sake;
2. Any regulation must be based on all Single Market freedoms (i.e., must conform to the obligations of the Treaty of Rome);
3. Any regulation must take account of business realities; and
4. Any regulation must meet general interest objectives effectively and efficiently.[61]

The regulatory section of the paper described the difficulties of regulating a virtual and borderless environment and suggested that without a sound legal and regulatory framework, electronic commerce would suffer. It called for work in the areas of electronic payment systems, data security, privacy, intellectual property, and taxation. It referred to work already in progress, such as the commission's privacy directive and the entry into force of the World Intellectual Property Organization copyright treaties, and to the need for new work in areas such as legal framework, digital signatures, and taxation. Particularly significant was the commission's rejection of a "bit tax" and its call for "tax neutrality" between physical and electronic commerce. The commission called for study of the impact of electronic commerce on the value-added taxes used throughout the EU member countries.

The third element of the initiative aimed to promote a favorable business environment. The commission referred to its three-year plan for a consumer policy (1996–98) and called for building consumer confidence and trust in electronic commerce. It recommended the widespread use of electronic commerce by public administrations; the encouragement of small and medium-sized businesses to use electronic commerce, and the use of business organizations such as local chambers of commerce to promote electronic business.

Finally, the fourth arm of the initiative was to work toward a global consensus on Net policy. The commission called for first developing a common European position on each of the key issues and then negotiating a global position bilaterally, regionally, and multilaterally, at an organization such as the OECD, UNCITRAL, or the U.N. Commission on Trade and Development (UNCTAD).

Since the publication of the initiative in 1997, the EU has moved ahead on its action program in each of the areas covered. A political storm over violent and pornographic material on the Internet led to a conference in Bonn on the content of global information networks later that year (this conference was discussed in Chapter 5). The EU also struggled over the issue of sovereignty in 1998 and 1999 as it developed a directive on consumer protection that found that providers of goods and services should be regulated in the country where they are established. The Commission staff said it would be impossible to design web sites to comply with every country's rules. Conversely, consumer groups argued that such a ruling would cause businesses to flee to countries with the least consumer protections. This issue remains unresolved.

The EU has also passed a Digital Signature Directive that must be ratified by individual governments. The directive is technology-neutral. By early 2000, many European observers felt that their continent still lagged behind the United States in Net use. Such figures as the Spanish industry minister, Josep Pique, German parliament member Friedbert Pflueger, and Bertelsmann chief executive Thomas Middelhoff all felt that government should get out of the way and let the private sector lead. At the EU European Commission's meeting in Lisbon in March 2000, the assembled presidents and prime ministers endorsed the commission's "eEurope" initiatives and endorsed passage of a legal framework for electronic commerce, further telecommunications liberalization and technology partnerships, and encouraged high-technology startups.

But the main thrust of new EU work focused on dealing with the international aspects of the Net. In particular, Bangemann led a call in 1998 for the creation of an "international charter" for electronic commerce that would govern activity worldwide. It was opposed by U.S. Secretary of Commerce William Daley, who said that such a charter "introduces top-down mandates for more government solutions—rather than letting industry and the market lead."[62] The debate ended with the formation of a private-sector-led "global business dialogue" organized by leading European and American high-technology companies to address Internet issues. In 1999, Commissioner Bangemann, who had done so much to promote the Net in Europe, resigned in a scandal along with all the other EU commissioners, concluding an important chapter in EU Net history.

The efforts of the EU have served citizens of its member states well, on the whole. By the end of 1998 there were 6.28 million Internet hosts in Europe, an average of 16.9 per thousand inhabitants. The number had grown 232 percent since 1995. Similarly, there were 2,790 ISPs on the continent, and the number was growing by 30 percent per year. The number of European households connected to the Internet doubled from 1998 to 1999, and Internet usage was predicted to hit 17 percent of all European households in 2000. Interestingly, the number of "teleworkers" in some European countries was quite high, making up 11.9 percent of the workforce in Sweden, 10 percent in Denmark, 9.3 percent in Ireland, and 4 percent in the United Kingdom.[63] These numbers begin to highlight the differences between European nations, despite the overall common policies. For example, in 1998, 10 percent of the United Kingdom population was on-line, compared to 5 percent in Germany and only 1 percent in France, although France had one of the fastest growth rates in 1999 and was beginning to catch up. To understand why, it is necessary to examine briefly the policies of individual European countries.

The United Kingdom

A study by the British Department of Trade and Industry in 1997 showed that among the major European countries, the United Kingdom led in Internet access for businesses and from home, as well as in the outlook for electronic commerce.[64] By 1999, seven million citizens, or 15 percent of the total population, were on-line, up from fewer than six million just six months earlier. This dramatic growth did not happen by accident.

In 1984, the United Kingdom enacted its Telecommunications Act, designed to promote competition and liberalization in the telecommunications sector. As a result, an independent regulator, the Office of Telecommunications (OFTEL), was created with the aim of promoting competition and lowering telecommunications rates. OFTEL has set July 2001 as the deadline for deregulating local telephone service. The act also attracted new investment in two new telecommunications infrastructures: BETnet provides high-speed domestic and international Internet connectivity, and SuperJANET is the United Kingdom's broadband academic and research network.

In October 1996, a select parliamentary committee published "Agenda for Action in the U.K.," a study of the potential impact of the Net on the country with recommendations for action.[65] The report found that the United Kingdom was in an excellent position to exploit its advanced telecommunications infrastructure to enter the digital age. It identified a series of issues that would need to be resolved, including data security and encryption, authentication and electronic signatures, illegal and "undesirable" material, consumer protection, and electronic payment systems. Interestingly, the report discussed in detail the role of the British government, but did not mention the need for private-sector leadership.

The report did point out the need for government to provide leadership by putting its own services on-line; Chapter 3 discussed how the United Kingdom has been a leader in on-line delivery of government services. The report also mentioned the need for a government committee or initiative to oversee the transition to the digital age. The Department of Trade's Information Society Initiative has been one important response. The government, with the partnership of the Federation of Electronic Industries, has also created a National Information Infrastructure (NII) Task Force to "enhance national competitiveness" by focusing on improved use of information and communications technologies. The NII Task Force has launched a number of initiatives with the Department of Trade and Industry, including a "Schools Online" program and a campaign to move small and medium-sized companies on-line.

The United Kingdom has also been a leader in the use of self-regulation to deal with objectionable content. Pressed by Scotland Yard, British ISPs, with the help of the Department of Trade and Industry and other industry groups, set up the Internet Watch Foundation (IWF) in 1996. Using a set of principles called the "R3 Safety Net" (R3 stands for rating, reporting, and responsibility), the IWF encourages Internet rating systems to permit voluntary filtering and also cooperates with the authorities to stop illegal material from being distributed via the Net. Several British laws dealing with obscenity, defamation, and sexual offenses have been updated to deal with the Net. Today the U.K. government has an "E-envoy," Alex Allan, to coordinate all government electronic commerce activities in four areas: deregulating the economy, educating people of all ages, using E-commerce in government, and measuring electronic commerce.

France

One observer has noted that French "high-tech Colbertism" may become a casualty of the free-wheeling Internet, and French *dirigism* may be being replaced by a pragmatic and nonideological policy.[66] One hopes this is true. Yet as late as 1999, a principal source of capital for technology startup ventures in France was the 900 million franc capital-risk fund run by the French Ministry of Economy, Finance, and Industry, whose minister said of France, "This is a capitalist country without capital or capitalists."[67]

France appeared to have gotten an early start on the electronic age with the national Minitel project in the mid-1980s. But this videotext system, an enhanced "yellow pages" directed by the state telephone monopoly, was quickly obsolete. France lagged in telecommunications deregulation until the imminent passage of the European directive on the subject helped push through the Telecommunications Act of 1996, liberalizing the sector. Although France Telecom had been moving away from direct government control since 1990, total privatization remains an issue today. Early in 1994, mindful of the Clinton administration's efforts and involved in Brussels as well, Prime Minister Edouard Balladur asked for a report on the role of the information society in France. The so-called Thery report, after its author, Gerard Thery, former director-general of telecommunications, warned that if France did not move quickly, the United States and Japan would take control of the "*chaine numerique*," the digital value chain, or key electronic commerce activities.[68]

The Thery report recommended the construction of a national high-speed network by one operator, France Telecom, which would not be burdened with "artificial competition." Universal service would be extended to multimedia services and public services would become electronic. Equipment would be supplied by national manufacturers. Every French household would be connected by 2015—a seemingly endless delay in the digital age. However, the French government never formally adopted the Thery plan, instead deciding to allow, for the time being, more private development of the new markets.

In August 1997, Prime Minister Lionel Jospin laid down a new digital marker for the French government in a key speech at the Universite de la Communication at Hourtin. In his speech, Jospin said that France's entry into the information society was decisive and that there was a firm need for government action. He laid out six priorities: improved education, French culture on the Internet, private initiatives for electronic commerce, stimulation of French information-technology products, electronic government services, and regulatory areas such as privacy.[69]

To implement the prime minister's speech, government departments provided their ideas to the prime minister's office, which, on January 16, 1998, presented the government's eighty-two-page action plan. Whereas the United States and other countries saw the private sector in the lead role, the French view was different: "France's entry into the information society represents an issue of decisive importance for our future.... That is why the government is offering the people of France a project and a political vision of information and communications technology founded on the ambition to create an integrated information society.... The State cannot do everything in this field. It is therefore essential that society itself takes the initiative, through the involvement of individual citizens, companies, local authorities and associations."[70] In other words, the Net in France is to be a government project based on a political vision, with those things the state cannot or does not wish to do left to the private sector.

The government's action plan expanded the six priorities the prime minister had identified earlier. First, it called for new information and communications technology tools in the education sector, involving extensive increases in technology in the schools over a three-year period and a major program to train teachers. Interestingly, it called for partnerships between schools and industry to help achieve this. By January 1999, the government reported that the creation of a support fund for technology, coming in part from the sales of France Telecom shares, had resulted in an increase in the number of secondary schools connected to the Internet from 40 percent to 85 percent in one year.[71]

Second, the plan laid out an ambitious cultural policy for new networks. This called for increased subsidies for the French cinema, press, publishing, and audiovisual industries to develop their digital potential. It also called for digitizing France's cultural heritage, creating multimedia centers around the country to "educate the public in information technology, with a cultural flavor," and promoting the French language in cyberspace. By 1999, 98 multimedia centers had been set up and a "French Language Fund for the Information Highway" had been created. These cultural initiatives represented a welcome turn away from cultural protectionism and toward the active promotion of French digital culture.

Third, the action plan portrayed information technology as a tool for modernizing public services. It called for providing on-line access to government data, migrating the Minitel system over to the Internet, permitting E-mail contact with government officials, and modernizing government in a variety of ways. By 1999, the government had made available on-line more than 300 forms covering more than 50 percent of the volume of government transactions and had placed numerous key documents, including the Official Journal (the government's official record), on-line.

Fourth, the plan called information technology an essential tool for companies. This section of the action plan covered electronic commerce, the area the government stated it would leave mainly to private-sector initiatives. Here, the government suggested a program of policy changes to facilitate electronic commerce in the areas of contract law, payment systems, taxation, consumer protection, and public services. It also stressed the need for international cooperation. Significantly, it stressed the strategic and defense role of information technology, as well. By 1999, it was apparent that much of the government's efforts in this area were devoted to the challenges of Y2K and the implementation of the EU's common currency, the euro.

Fifth, the plan sought to meet the challenges of industrial and technological innovation. It proposed investment and tax programs to stimulate new high-technology ventures, government funding for new research and development on advanced networks, continuing telecommunications deregulation to lower prices, and programs to promote French use of the Internet. By 1999, a capital risk fund of 900 million francs had been set up, an information society research and development program of 300 million francs was in place, and 260 million francs had been allocated to the National Network for Telecommunications Research.

Finally, the plan hoped to encourage the emergence of effective regulation for the new information networks. Noting that the "specific nature of the Internet makes it impossible to simply transpose existing regulation models,"[72] this section of the report called for self-regulation and the deregulation of encryption, which had previously been heavily controlled in France.

France has also begun to experiment with self-regulation after legislation designed to deal with the problem of objectionable and illegal content—the so-called Fillon amendment—was overturned by France's high court—much as the Communications Decency Act had been overturned by the U.S. Supreme Court. In place of this legislation, an industry-generated Internet Charter, developed by a public telephone and telegraph company working group, envisions a code of conduct dealing with a variety of issues, to be administered by France's association of ISPs. The country's organization of Internet users also plays a role in this self-regulation effort. In March 2000, in a move to promote electronic commerce, the French broadcasting authority CSA announced that Internet companies would be exempt from the ban on retail advertising on television. Part of the reason for relaxing the regulation was fear that foreign electronic-commerce companies were beginning to steal market share from traditional French retailers.

France is now heavily engaged in a number of international dialogues on the information society and has jointly signed with the United States a paper on the subject.[73] In the paper, France acknowledges the need for private-sector leadership in electronic commerce, which, of course, the French government views as only a subset of the information society. The paper also notes that the Internet can be used to "promote access" to cultural diversity. A French interministerial government committee on the information society, made up of representatives from more than twenty ministries and run out of the prime minister's office, coordinates the government's programs. Its last report cites progress, but also chastises some government departments for moving too slowly.[74]

Finland

Finland does not aspire to be an information society; it already is an information society. It aspires to be a "wireless information society," untethered by hard wiring. Today, Finland leads the world in Internet usage. It has the world's highest penetration of Internet hosts and the highest penetration of cellular telephones. As a result, half of the nation's banking and half of all securities trading is conducted on-line, and 26 percent of all bills are paid using cellular on-line connections. Finland is also the nation that makes the least use of currency and banknotes.[75]

This development came about in part because of the extraordinary success of one Finnish company: Nokia. As the *Wall Street Journal* pointed out, "Fueled by the booming high-technology sector, led by telecommunications equipment manufacturer Nokia Corporation, this small country's growth rate ranks second among European Union member states after Ireland."[76] But Nokia is not the only reason. In 1995, Finland's government, concerned about the negative economic impact of the loss of exports to Russia, looked for a new path to growth. The government published a landmark paper, "Finland Toward the Information Society: A National Strategy," which laid out a course of action.[77]

While the plan included many government actions, it also stressed the role of the private sector by aiming to create a "vibrant entrepreneurship in these areas."[78] The Finnish government set up an Information Society Advisory Board to oversee the plan, which stressed including all Finns in the information society, building an advanced national network, and promoting the growth of information-technology industries. The plan also called for extensive training and education for the population, which was highly literate to begin with. Interestingly, the plan also called for reaching out to Finland's Baltic neighbors.

Finland's plans have succeeded probably beyond the government's expectations. Today, everything from public services to education, airline and theater tickets, and health care services are on-line. Using hand-held wireless devices, Finns can work, play, and learn. "Digital Identity in Your Hand" is the new national slogan for the Finnish information society.

Estonia

In 1992, as it emerged from the old Soviet Union, Estonia had no telecommunications infrastructure, no financing or management structures, and no experience with networking. But it did have a shared language family with and geographic proximity to Finland. And today, Estonia is an Internet success story.

Almost 90 percent of government institutions have Web sites, adding a startling new transparency to government. There is an Internet host for every fifty-four Estonians, ranking the country just behind the United States and Finland in Internet host penetration. The country has 250,000 Internet users and 60 public access points, built by the government to provide universal access. With the country's more than 20 ISPs, Internet dial-up prices have been halved in two years.[79]

What has accounted for Estonian success? Estonians believe that the total lack of pre-existing technological infrastructure permitted them to build on the high technical literacy of the population to leap ahead into the latest technology. With a totally new government, the country had no existing and burdensome regulatory structure to deal with and quickly adopted a liberal economic environment that invited foreign investment. Foreign technical assistance also helped in a variety of ways. For example, the North Atlantic Treaty Organization sponsored a conference of the Central and Eastern European Networking Association in Tartu, Estonia, in May 1997. Led by the Estonian Educational and Research Network, the conference adopted the Tartu Declaration, which called attention to the importance of the information age to the people and nations of the region.[80] The declaration ratified the basic principles of liberalization of telecommunications, government–private sector partnerships in research and development, and universal access that were the foundations for building the Net in other countries. Today, Estonians are particularly proud that their parliament became the first in Europe to have live audio streaming of its proceedings on the Internet.

Spain

The Spanish government rewrote its penal code in 1995 to adapt it to the "needs of Spanish society for the 21st century."[81] The result deals with many of the legal framework issues surrounding the Net, including electronic fraud, theft and forgery, piracy, on-line pornography, and libel. Spain also revised its copyright law to conform with the EU's policies. Spain relies on self-regulation and filtering devices to deal with objectionable content.

To help jump-start Net use, a Spanish government support program called PISTA offers incentives to develop digital applications in areas such as public health, education, and tourism. Firms and local institutions such as hospitals and schools compete for funding.

Others

A few other European countries' developments are worth noting. Because of its past history, Germany has been aggressive in blocking Internet material and prosecuting those who violate laws prohibiting neo-Nazi and anti-Semitic materials, as well as child pornography. In addition to numerous charges brought by the public prosecutor, both the Bundestag and the Lander (the German states) have enacted legislation dealing with the responsibilities of ISPs. Germany has also been a leader in the EU discussions of the information society.

Ireland's economy is growing rapidly, in part propelled by the growth of computer and software services stimulated by low telecommunications rates. Policies favorable to foreign investment have also been helpful. Ireland has concluded a joint communiqué with the United States on electronic commerce that adopts most of the principles in the U.S. "Framework for Electronic Commerce."[82]

Hungary, too, has developed a software industry, building on its strengths of a well-educated population and an advanced infrastructure. In 1992, the Hungarian Academic and Research Network Association was launched, aimed at connecting all of Hungary's academic and research institutions and libraries. Today, well over 100,000 Hungarians are Internet users, and the government has begun a National Information Infrastructure Development Program supported by a number of government ministries.

THE MIDDLE EAST

The development and use of the Net in the Middle East is hampered by both the lack of a modern telecommunications infrastructure and a fear of the outside world in many countries. Nevertheless, digital technology also offers irresistible benefits to many groups within these countries— universities, businesses, and government agencies. In some cases, even the most traditional and conservative elements are experimenting with cyberspace. In Iran's main religious center in Qom, for example, clerics are putting on-line the full text and commentaries of all seven branches of Islamic law. As a result, the digital age is thriving in some countries and playing a quiet but sometimes subversive role in others.

Not surprisingly, Israel is the most wired country in the Middle East, with 600,000 people, or about 10 percent of the population, on-line at the beginning of 1999. In terms of the percentage of their populations that are on-line, the Gulf states of Qatar, the United Arab Emirates, and Kuwait are next, with between 2 and 3 percent, followed by Lebanon with just over 1 percent. In terms of absolute numbers, Egypt follows Israel with about 130,000 people on-line.[83] Iraq has no connection to the Internet, a situation that the government blames on the Western trade embargo against the country; in fact, it is due to the regime's fears of allowing the population access to news and other material from sources other than the government-controlled media.

Generally, Middle Eastern countries fall into two categories: those that have sought to develop and use digital technology and those who have purposely kept it at arm's length. Egypt is probably the best example of the former. Advanced networking in Egypt began in the 1980s, as Egyptian universities built the Egyptian University Network (EUN) to connect themselves to each other and to the European Academic and Research Network (EARN) of universities in Europe. This early work was helped with grants from IBM and from the United Nations Development Program. By the early 1990s, EUN connected such Egyptian institutions as the Center of Higher Education Research, the World Health Organization branch in Alexandria, the Medical Syndicate Union, and the National Telecommunications Union.

In the mid-1990s, the Egyptian government founded the Cabinet Information and Decision Support Center (IDSC) to develop advanced information technology for use by the government.[84] The IDSC's work resulted in Tradenet, an on-line network providing trade and commercial information, and RITNET and RITSEC, regional networking and software centers that connect Egypt to other countries in the region. These regional organizations are supported not only by the IDSC but also by the United Nations and the Arab Fund. Today, Egypt has an estimated fifty-five licensed ISPs and numerous Internet cafés in Cairo providing access for thousands of ordinary people. With literacy and education levels increasing, the Net has a bright future in Egypt. Says one key study, "Egypt's existing networks and network ties should provide a solid foundation for the continued growth of the Internet. . . . Relative to other Middle East nations, Egypt also has many social and business ties with the international community as well as an indigenous supply of software developers."[85] Egypt's key obstacles will be its low gross domestic product per capita and its traditionally over-regulated economy.

Israel is also a country whose economy has been traditionally over-regulated. Fortunately, Internet usage has grown despite this characteristic, doubling in the twelve months between 1997 and 1998 alone. This growth has been paralleled by the explosive growth in Israel's electronics and information-technology industries. These industries are expected to grow at a compound annual rate of 17 percent until 2005. In 1998, Israeli companies raised about $668 million in capital for high-technology companies and Israel had the highest concentration of startups outside Silicon Valley. Almost 3,500 Israeli companies were engaged in research and development in 1998.[86] As a result, much Israeli-developed information technology has been acquired by American firms, including America On-line, Lucent Technologies, General Electric, Bay Networks, and Eastman Kodak.

On the other hand, the Israeli government has been slow to take advantage of electronic commerce and the Internet for use in government applications. The government has established a Government Internet Committee in the Ministry of Finance to explore the use of the Internet by government. The Knesset (the Israeli parliament) has taken some actions to modernize Israeli copyright and freedom of information laws, but the government has not rushed to offer government services on-line. Says a recent report by the legal adviser to the Government Internet Committee, "Only a few government offices currently disseminate information over the Internet."[87] Israel can be a model for other countries, not only in the Middle East, but around the world, in terms of its ability to attract venture capital and to mimic the American experience, but the government will also have to learn to be more innovative itself.

Like Egypt and Israel, Iran is a country with a strong networking background. More than eighteen of its universities and research centers are linked by a network operated by the Institute for Theoretical Physics. Iran is also connected to European universities. But the government monitors Internet use closely and some clerics have opposed putting even religious texts on-line, arguing that such access would diminish their own power. The government attempts to filter Internet content, and following the 1999 student riots and the rise of the reform movement, it may crack down further on Internet use.

Saudi Arabia has also tried to balance the commercial benefits of the Net with its subversive democratic influence. The Saudi Council of Ministers established a permanent technical committee within the Ministry of Commerce to deal with the new information infrastructure. It identified six action items for the government, the first being "the formulation of strategies to ensure maximum benefit and safeguard against possible threats."[88] Other items on the committee's agenda include developing a legal framework, enhancement of telecommunications infrastructure, training, and guidelines for transfer of technology. In 1998, Saudi Arabia established thirty licenses for Internet service providers.

Fearing not only the exposure of their people to political information but also negative cultural influences ranging from pornography to secular material, Syria, and Libya severely restrict Internet use. In early 2000, Bashar al-Assad, heir apparent to the Syrian presidency, told Western reporters that he was beginning to promote wider use of the Internet and wireless networks. On the other hand, according to Human Rights

Watch, dissidents in Morocco and Algeria use the Internet as an open forum for their views. Over time, the closed societies of the Middle East will have to make the hard choice between openness and economic development, or the maintenance of closed society and perpetual economic backwardness. The Internet will be a primary indicator of which road they choose.

AFRICA

At first glance, Africa's entry into the information age would appear to be a pipe dream. As Jay Naidoo, South Africa's minister of posts, telecommunications, and broadcasting, has pointed out, a few months "before the dawn of the new millennium, we have 14 million telephones in Africa, less than you would find in New York or Tokyo."[89] That is only one telephone line for every two hundred people—and many of those are concentrated in urban South Africa, whose telephone system still evidences the legacy of apartheid. Moreover, the breakdown of civil society in countries like Rwanda and Sierra Leone makes any thought of Net development seem impossible.

Moreover, many African governments have not encouraged the growth of media in general, let alone the Internet. As one university professor in Cameroon notes, "since independence, the majority of Africans, who are mainly rural, have not had any meaningful access to the mass media: radio, television and the print media have been free and accessibly only in principle. Governments have seen and continue to see in information a weapon too powerful to be made accessible to the powerless masses."[90]

Fortunately, many educated young Africans are optimistic and reject both political and economic barriers. On the question of the lack of infrastructure, some see this as an advantage: "Africa's lack of infrastructure may be seen as a disadvantage. But on closer examination, this can be turned into an advantage. . . . African countries are not encumbered by extensive networks built on obsolete technology that will require an evolutionary process of replacement. The technological inertia is thus quite low. The push therefore should be for the cutting edge."[91]

With this kind of spirit, African ministers responsible for economic and social development and planning met in Addis Ababa in May 1995 under the auspices of the United Nations Economic Commission for Africa and passed a resolution, "Building Africa's Information Highway." This resolution called for a group of African technical experts to draw up a detailed plan for moving Africa into the information age within one year.

The group of experts did their work and presented the results—the African Information Society Initiative (AISI) to the ministers' conference the following year.[92] The AISI was endorsed by the Organization of African Unity Council of Ministers in Yaounde in July 1996.

The AISI envisioned that Africa could develop an information society by 2010 by focusing on a number of key areas:

—Creating value-added information networks for education, health, environment, trade, tourism, finance, commerce, and other areas;
—Creating a continent-wide information and communications networks allowing wide dissemination of information to individuals and businesses;
—Fostering a new generation of Africans by improving education systems and enhancing human resources with state-of-the-art technologies; and
—Allowing the inflow of new technologies and the export of intellectual products and services to the rest of the world.

The plan called on national governments to build elements of the plan into their national economic and social plans and programs, and to adopt a five-year implementation plan. Among the items for government consideration were liberalization of telecommunications and building a policy framework for electronic commerce, including intellectual property and digital signature laws. The AISI also identified efforts that would be of particular importance in Africa, such as improving food production with better information to provide crop-planting guidance, building tourism information systems, and preserving and communicating Africa's cultural heritage.

While the AISI started with good intentions and lofty aims, it lacked a key element: funding. Organizations such as the United Nations Development Program, the World Bank's InfoDev program, and the Canadian International Development Research Center have helped, but lack of funding has been a major hindrance. Additionally, privatization and liberalization of telecommunications is not popular in many countries, because of the loss of power and control it would bring for political elites and because of the short-term unemployment effects it would produce. Today, in most of sub-Saharan Africa, government is still the sole supplier of telecommunications. Prices remain high and services remain backward. There are, however, some signs of progress. Uganda has deregulated in some areas and allows some foreign investment in telecommunications.

Sudan has privatized telecommunications and Ghana is selling off 30 percent of Ghana Telephone to private investors.

According to two researchers at the University of Botswana, "Fourteen countries have achieved live Internet public access services: Algeria, Morocco, Tunisia, Egypt, Senegal, Ghana, Uganda, Kenya, Zimbabwe, Namibia, Mozambique, Mauritius and of course South Africa, which is among the top 20 countries in the world ranked by number of Internet nodes. . . . Full Internet access has now been achieved in Botswana, Lesotho and Namibia. Projects are under way for full Internet access in Burkina Faso, Eritrea, Cote d'Ivoire, Malawi and Swaziland."[93]

Whether or not Africa can achieve the goals of the AISI will depend on the organizational ability of the African states, the willingness of governments to allow the private sector to operate freely, and the help of international agencies. With its own more advanced infrastructure, South Africa is helping, not only by providing a model of activities in telecommunications in its own Reconstruction and Development Plan, but also in its regional leadership in southern Africa. South Africa's "Green Paper on Telecommunications Policy" identifies specific regional undertakings, such as telecommunications training and standards development, as well as the building of terrestrial networks, through which the country can begin to assist its neighbors along the information highway.[94]

CONCLUSIONS

In addition to the governments already have discussed, numerous others around the world are becoming involved. In Latin America, the private sector is moving quickly—much faster than government policy. Many Latin American companies partner with U.S. firms as Internet service providers, content providers, and E-retailers. In April 1998, the United States and Chile signed a Joint Statement on Electronic Commerce, adopting the principles of private-sector leadership and international cooperation and recommending policy on access, trade, government services, taxation, digital signatures, privacy, intellectual property, and consumer protection.[95] The United States signed a similar agreement with Colombia on May 17, 2000. In addition, the Free Trade Area of the Americas organization has been active in encouraging Internet development in Latin America; it will be discussed in the next chapter.

It would be difficult today to find a government that does not believe in the critical importance of the Net to its future. Perhaps Cuba and North Korea are examples, but even Cuba uses its government Web site for propaganda purposes. But in the pursuit of the digital grail, nations all face similar quandaries: How much power can and should governments give up to the private sector? Can the private sector be trusted to manage such an integral part of national life? Will the empowerment of their citizenry by the Internet weaken the hold of authoritarians and dictators? If they hold on to power by limiting use of the Net, will their countries fall further behind economically, politically, and strategically? How can governments change the policy framework around electronic commerce fast enough to keep up with change?

Yet another set of questions for governments to consider concerns the international environment in which all societies today operate. Can governments change their policies unilaterally or are they locked into an international framework? And are the international institutions adequate to deal with the issue? It is to the role of the international organizations that we now turn.

12

International Organizations and Programs

[W]hen we talk of the impact of the Internet or electronic commerce we are talking about . . . the rise of a new kind of global economic system—one that is creating the closest thing yet to a single, "borderless" world market.

—Renato Ruggiero[1]

[A]s there are no natural borders to cyberspace, the development of policies and solutions must, as much as possible, be a worldwide effort.

—Charlene Barshefsky[2]

Like the drafters of the United Nations Universal Declaration of Human Rights, the diplomats and economists who worked at Bretton Woods, at San Francisco, and at other international meetings in the early post–World War II period had no idea just how far-seeing they really were. Although their focus was on avoiding a repetition of the mistakes of the past—preventing another worldwide economic depression and war—by opening the world's borders to international trade and commerce, the work they did presciently prepared for the arrival of the twenty-first century. They spawned a broad series of agreements and institutions that facilitated open trade and investment and by so doing instituted rules that helped stabilize the global political and economic systems.

The formation of the General Agreement on Tariffs and Trade (GATT) began immediately to lower tariffs and eliminate nontariff barriers. The World Bank began to promote economic progress in developing countries. The Organization for Economic Cooperation and Development (OECD) began to coordinate economic policies of developed countries to promote growth. United Nations agencies such as the UN Development Program (UNDP) and the UN Conference on International Trade Law (UNCITRAL) began to assist in international trade and development efforts. In Europe, the European Coal and Steel Community eventually became the

European Union (EU), and the North Atlantic Treaty Organization provided the military and strategic backbone for economic cooperation. Of course, these efforts were impeded for decades because of the resistance from the communist bloc, but they still made important progress and then accelerated into more vigorous action after the death of the Soviet Union.

In addition to the more global and comprehensive agencies mentioned above, specialized and regional ones also grew in influence. The World Intellectual Property Organization (WIPO) became more important as trade in intellectual property grew, and the International Telecommunications Union (ITU) was active in promoting the growth of telephony worldwide. Moreover, regional organizations such as the Asia-Pacific Economic Cooperation group (APEC) and the Organization of American States (OAS) also became more crucial.

As the phenomena of the Net and electronic commerce began to grow in the mid-1990s, each of these organizations saw that it would need to play a role, and each wanted to. To some extent, there was a bit of diplomatic elbowing, as each international bureaucracy tried to carve out its own niche. Some efforts were duplicated and progress was sometimes slow, as these large and often cumbersome organizations tried to keep up with the torrid pace of technology. On the whole, however, they have made important progress, although the question remains as to whether the appropriate international institutional framework is yet in place to deal with international public policy related to the Net. This chapter provides a survey of the work being done by these organizations. Like Chapter 11, it is selective, covering only the most important agencies.

THE WORLD TRADE ORGANIZATION

The World Trade Organization (WTO) is the successor to GATT and was created by the Uruguay Round of GATT trade talks in January 1995. Today it has 134 members who account for the bulk of world trade and who use the WTO to make and enforce the international rules for trade in goods, services, and intellectual property.

The WTO is the forum for trade negotiations, the administrator of agreements, and the dispute-settlement mechanism. It also provides assistance in trade matters to developing countries. It came into being a few years after the stage had been set by GATT for its involvement in electronic commerce.

The Uruguay Round had lowered tariffs on information technology goods as part of a trend that had gone on for many years. But it still left in place a bewildering number of both significant and nuisance-value tariffs with a complex and unwieldy classification system. The Uruguay Round also resulted in an agreement that dealt with trade-related intellectual property issues (TRIPS), which drove the more rapid development of electronic commerce by providing copyright protection for software and integrated circuits—two areas where international piracy had become a growing problem. In the case of software, TRIPS provided that computer programs would be protected as literary works under the Berne Convention on copyrights, thus providing a safer and more predictable environment for international trade and investment in software.

Soon after its birth, the WTO concluded two other key agreements that would help accelerate electronic commerce. The first was the Ministerial Declaration on Trade in Information Technology Products, also know as the International Technology Agreement, or ITA, concluded at the Singapore conference of WTO members' ministers in December 1996. In the declaration, 29 countries agreed to reduce tariffs to zero on a list of information technology products by January 2000. Since the Singapore conference, a total of 48 countries representing more than 90 percent of world trade in information technology products (worth $600 billion per year) have signed on to the ITA, although some have asked for a delay in final implementation until 2005. As an ongoing effort, the WTO has been considering "ITA II," which involves an expansion of the original list of ITA products.

A second achievement for the new organization was the successful work of the Negotiating Group on Basic Telecommunications in February 1997. In the milestone agreement that this group produced, in the words of the WTO director-general, Renato Ruggiero, "69 countries representing 95 percent of the global market concluded a massive agreement to free telecommunications services—opening many markets which had up to till then been dominated by state-owned monopolies."[3] These talks had been quite difficult and had actually broken down early in 1996 when the United States walked out, charging that countries were not making sufficient commitments. The U.S. tough-minded strategy prevailed, however, when a more comprehensive and meaningful agreement with commitments from more countries was reached in 1998. As noted in Chapter 7, this Agreement on Basic Telecommunications provides for competition in telecommunications with nations and permits foreign investment. Its "reference paper" also commits nations to a series of principles, including such items as an independent telecommunications regulator and rights for interconnection to the public switched network. In many ways, it was one of the most far-reaching trade agreements ever, requiring countries to conform their systems of domestic regulation to international norms.

The conclusion of negotiations on the General Agreement on Trade in Services, especially as it affected banking and financial services such as insurance, was another important WTO cornerstone for electronic commerce. Clearly, the trade rules affecting all of the sectoral issues in services will have an important impact on the development of electronic commerce in these areas.

In 1998, the WTO turned its attention to more comprehensive cyberspace issues. The U.S. government, in particular, wanted to ensure that new duties were not imposed on electronic transactions as the number and value of them continued to grow. Since duties were not then applied to electronic transmissions, such as telephone calls or faxes, by any WTO member, the United States proposed that the WTO simply affirm the status quo. India and Pakistan, however, were concerned about accepting the proposal without further study and a compromise was agreed to: the May 20, 1998, "Declaration on Global Electronic Commerce." This declaration reaffirmed the importance of electronic commerce to the future of international trade and declared that "[m]embers will continue their current practice of not imposing customs duties on electronic transactions."[4] However, the ministers agreed to this as a "standstill," subject to the outcome of the WTO's electronic commerce work program.

The electronic commerce work program comprises a number of elements. For example, the various bodies and committees of the WTO are examining the impact of electronic commerce on their responsibilities and operations. In one case, the Council on Services is considering market access and nondiscriminatory treatment for providers of network, content, and information services, as well as conducting an examination of express package-delivery services. The Council on Trade in Goods is exploring how electronic commerce may facilitate customs transactions. The issue of not applying duties to electronic transactions will also be raised in the work program groups, along with the question of whether electronic transactions are goods, services, or constitute an altogether new category. For some countries, these last issues are important not only for trade reasons, but because of the precedent they set for taxation and other regulations. Japan has proposed that "digital products," however they are defined, receive the most liberal WTO treatment possible; the United States has agreed with the Japanese position.

For the future, the WTO will remain one of the most important international agencies—if not the most important one—for electronic commerce. Its agreements and directives are significant not only for the specific trade areas they cover, but also for the framework they create for other agreements in areas outside the organization's jurisdiction. As the U.S. trade representative, Charlene Barshefsky, has said, "As consumer protection regimes develop, governments should apply basic WTO principles like transparency and nondiscrimination, and ensure that their regulatory processes are fair and open to advice from businesses and civil society groups."[5]

THE ORGANIZATION FOR

ECONOMIC COOPERATION AND DEVELOPMENT

In 1961, it was clear that the Marshall Plan had worked so well in promoting democratic governments and economic growth in western Europe that it was decided to make permanent the Organization for European Economic Cooperation that had administered it. The new organization, the Organization for Economic Cooperation and Development, was expanded to include nations beyond the North Atlantic orbit, and today includes in its membership twenty-nine nations that together produce about two-thirds of the world's goods and services. Membership in the OECD requires a commitment to market economics and pluralistic democracy.

Like GATT and the WTO, the OECD has been helping to lay the groundwork for the role of the Net and electronic commerce in national economies and international trade for many years. For example, in the 1970s, the OECD concerned itself with the issue of the impact of information technology on employment. In 1980, the OECD adopted its "Guidelines Governing the Protection of Privacy and Transborder Data Flow of Personal Data." It followed this with the "Declaration on Transborder Data Flows" in 1985. These guidelines and declarations, although voluntary, provided the basis for national laws on privacy protection in many countries. The organization's work on issues such as international taxation and accounting standards has helped create the international financial framework within which electronic transactions will be able to take place. Other work has covered areas such as encryption and digital signatures, culture, employment and education, and the compilation of economic statistics.

The OECD is organized into departments, many of which take part in studies and reports involving cyberspace. Among the key departments are those in Economics; Statistics; Trade; Enterprises; Financial and Fiscal Matters; Science, Technology and Industry; and Social Policy. Its committees work on a variety of issues related to electronic commerce, but among the most important are taxation, consumer fraud and protection, privacy and security, and the impact of electronic commerce on jobs, education, and health. The OECD can bring its business and labor advisory committees together with government to deal with such complicated issues.

Specific OECD work on information infrastructures dates back to 1992, when the Committee on Information, Computer, and Communications Policy held a working session on the subject. The report prepared for that session was one of the first to compare government policies for the new national information infrastructures.[6] In 1992, the OECD also adopted international guidelines for protecting the security of information systems, and in 1994 it produced its report on electronic data interchange. In 1995, the OECD began work to develop a set of economic and statistical indicators to help government officials and others better measure the impact of the information revolution on national economies. Over the following years, the pace of activity on electronic commerce grew rapidly, and it continues full force today. Examining a few of the key initiatives in one year, 1997, gives some indication of the importance the OECD members attach to electronic commerce and the scope of the organization's work on the subject:

—In January 1997, the OECD published "Foreign Trade Aspects of Electronic Commerce," which surveyed the field and demonstrated the growing importance of electronic trade (E-trade). Today, the OECD's Trade Committee is looking at case study analysis of products and services involved in E-trade, in further developing E-trade statistics, and in educating developing countries about E-trade.

—In March 1997, the OECD Council adopted "Guidelines for Cryptography Policy," a nonbinding agreement outlining policy issues. Although the guidelines helped prepare a framework for understanding the issue, they have not resolved the major problem faced by the United States and other countries in finding the right balance between law enforcement, national security, civil liberties, and the role of the marketplace.

—In July 1997, the OECD held a conference in Paris on the issue of content on the Internet. The resulting publication, "Ad Hoc Meeting on Approaches to Content and Conduct on the Internet," vividly illustrates the clashes between nations as delegates debate the need to control content.[7] In its on-going work, the OECD is continuing to build an inventory of Internet content practices in different countries.

—In July 1997, the OECD released "Electronic Commerce: Opportunities and Challenges for Government," a report by a high-level group of business experts headed by John Sacher, the executive director of Marks and Spencer, the British retailer. Based on interviews with one hundred private- and public-sector decision-makers, the report covered areas such as security, taxation, competition, consumer protection, and the role of government.[8]

—In August 1997, the OECD published "Certification in the Electronic Environment," an analysis of the need for certification on an international level and some of the approaches that might be taken. Importantly, the paper helped establish the principle of technology neutrality for certification schemes.[9]

—In September 1997, the OECD published "Measuring Electronic Commerce," which defined the difficulties of measuring electronic transactions and proposed solutions. Drawing on both public and private statistics, the report also drew some early conclusions about the growth of both business-to-business and retail electronic commerce.[10]

—In November 1997, the OECD held its conference "Dismantling the Barriers to Global Electronic Commerce," in Turku, Finland, focusing on issues in finance and insurance, manufacturing, distribution and retail, transportation, and health care. The conference also dealt with the issues of privacy, security, consumer protection, taxation access and legal matters.

The year 1997 also saw the OECD active in other areas. It released its "Gateways to the Global Market: Consumers and Electronic Commerce," report, which resulted in the formation of a group to develop consumer protection guidelines for electronic transactions.[11] The Fiscal Affairs Committee also set up working groups to review the role of the OECD Model Tax Convention in the digital age and the issue of package delivery facilitation across national borders. Others efforts looked at universal service, Net-based job growth, "distant selling" techniques, and self-regulation.

Although much of the OECD's output is papers and documentation, its role is far more important than that of a publisher. The OECD creates a climate of opinion for governments and a reservoir of ideas that helps define laws and policy both within nations and at the international level. Thus, its work on international trade will help solidify opinion not only in Tokyo, Washington, Ottawa, and Brussels, but also at the WTO in Geneva. OECD opinion is also carefully studied and applied by non-members in the developing world.

In October 1998, the OECD held a ministerial conference on electronic commerce in Ottawa. The highlight was the presentation of a report prepared for the conference, titled "The Economic and Social Impact of Electronic Commerce" and prepared by the OECD staff with the help of the Canadian government and a group of private experts from a number of countries. From virtually every economic perspective—jobs, growth, productivity, international trade—the report painted a positive picture of electronic commerce. The report recommended continued study of the economic impact and other aspects of electronic commerce, but its principal value was in the tone it set.[12] The OECD clearly is the official international think tank for governments on the subject of cyberspace, and its future agenda makes clear that it will play a very influential role.

THE UNITED NATIONS COMMISSION ON
INTERNATIONAL TRADE LAW

Whereas the OECD helps harmonize economic and legal practices across its member nations, the United Nations Commission on International Trade Law has as its main mission the harmonization and unification of trade law for all the members of the United Nations. It also works to remove unnecessary obstacles to trade flows that arise from national differences in commercial law. Work by UNCITRAL over the years on projects such as its Convention on Contracts for the International Sales of Goods (1980) and its Legal Guide to Electronic Funds Transfers (1987) have helped make possible the existing international legal framework in which electronic commerce now operates, particularly in developing countries. UNCITRAL is particularly effective because it has been apolitical and its work is professional.

UNCITRAL has made two important and specific contributions to the international legal framework for cyberspace. The first is the Model Law on Electronic Commerce, which was adopted in 1996 and which helps set legal norms for electronic contracts and contract formation, for the definitions of valid writings, for the acceptability of electronic signatures, and for the admission of electronic evidence.[13] This model law was strongly supported by the United States and other industrial countries and was completed and adopted by the United Nations in only a few years—far faster than the norm.

UNCITRAL has also been working on uniform rules to deal with electronic signatures and certification authorities. After beginning its work based on the digital signature approach taken by the laws of Germany and state law in Utah using public key encryption, the UNCITRAL working group determined that an underlying principle of electronic signature ought to be technology neutrality. The draft convention that was considered at the UNCITRAL working group meeting in June 1998 contained "two principles that the U.S. delegation deems key to a successful legal framework . . . : party autonomy and technology neutrality,"[14] but there was no consensus for this approach, partly because some countries had already passed laws recognizing public key encryption systems, and partly because of simple uncertainty about how to proceed.

UNCITRAL prepared another draft to be considered at a working group meeting in Vienna in September 1999, which also called for "nondiscrimination" and a "technology neutral" approach,[15] but it was unclear whether the delegates would prefer to accept this language or to wait for further developments.

THE INTERNATIONAL TELECOMMUNICATIONS UNION

The International Telecommunications Union, founded in 1865, is a global organization of 188 nations and more than 500 private-sector members, mostly public and private telecommunications companies. Its principal purpose is the regulation, standardization, and coordination of international telecommunications, especially to make certain that national systems are technically compatible. In carrying out this mission, it has focused on technical standards for interconnection and on policy issues for developing countries, such as the provision of universal service. It was at the ITU Development Conference in Buenos Aires in 1994 that Vice President Al Gore first discussed the global information infrastructure.

Among the ITU's key efforts have been work on technical standards in areas including privacy, electronic banking, and system security and standards for the overall architecture of the global information infrastructure. The organization has also worked on the international provision of spectrum for wireless access through satellites and cellular systems. The ITU has also participated in Internet governance arrangements, and it works closely with the two international technical standards bodies, the International Standards Organization (ISO) and the International Electrotechnical Commission (IEC) on standards issues.

The ITU is also an international organization caught in the crossfire between the regulated and unregulated industries. On the one hand, ITU members and staff see themselves as firmly part of the new information infrastructure: "The ITU has been a pioneer in assisting its members and preparing for the forthcoming challenges arising form the convergence of technologies. . . . The ITU was the first multilateral forum to raise these issues."[16] On the other hand, much of the high-tech industry sees the ITU as an old-line regulatory body like the Federal Communications Commission that must be kept out of digital policy making. When the new ITU secretary-general, Yoshio Utsumi, addressed a gathering in Washington on June 9, 1999, he startled some of the high-technology executives in the audience when he suggested that the ITU would become involved in issues such as electronic signatures. Challenged by a senior executive of a large Internet company, he held his ground, and suggested that the Internet company, like its state-owned or -regulated telecommunications cousins, might soon become a member of the ITU. Clearly, the ITU has a role to play in the digital age, but it will need to update its procedures and shun its traditional regulatory approach.

THE WORLD INTELLECTUAL PROPERTY ORGANIZATION

The World Intellectual Property Organization may be the world's fastest-growing international organization. Its membership grew from 125 members in 1990 to more than 170 by 1999. The reason is spelled out by Kamil Idris, WIPO director-general, in his welcome to the organization's Web site: "[I]ntellectual property has moved into the mainstream of national economic and developmental planning" and "has emerged as a central issue in multilateral trade relations. . . . [I]n the new areas of protection of domain names, software code and the many other new digital technologies generated by the Internet, you can be sure that WIPO is there at the cutting edge."[17]

WIPO is one of the sixteen specialized United Nations agencies and is responsible for promoting the protection of intellectual property worldwide. It does this by administering sixteen treaties covering patents, copyrights, and other issues, as well as by helping resolve intellectual property rights disputes. WIPO also assists developing countries, and by charging fees to the private sector for its services, it raises almost 90 percent of its own budget.

As covered in Chapter 8, the 1996 Diplomatic Conference in Geneva that produced the new World Copyright Treaty and the World Performance and Phonograms Treaty may be WIPO's most important recent contribution to the Net's development. Both treaties help define the meaning of intellectual property in cyberspace and are in the process of being ratified by WIPO member nations. The United States ratified the treaties in 1998. Unfinished at the Geneva Diplomatic Conference was the issue of *sui generis* copyright protection for databases, and work continues on this issue.

WIPO has also been deeply involved in the creation of the new Internet domain-name system, particularly on the issues of protection of trademarks and in resolving disputes over top-level domains. WIPO's Arbitration and Mediation Center uses an on-line dispute-resolution mechanism that can resolve disputes, including those over domain names, quickly and inexpensively. WIPO is also working on a global on-line network and database that will make available patent, copyright, and trademark databases around the world and eventually provide for secure on-line filing of patents and trademarks. WIPO's work overlaps somewhat with that of the WTO and other organizations, but without serious consequence.

THE WORLD BANK

Since its founding in 1944, the World Bank had been extending loans and providing technical and policy assistance to developing countries to promote their economic growth and social development. Much of its financial resources helped build physical infrastructure such as transportation networks, water systems, electrification programs, and other public utilities. As a public utility, telecommunications was part of this effort, but only a small part, ranging between 1 and 2 percent of the bank's resources in the 1980s and early 1990s. Until 1985, the bank's telecommunications efforts were aimed at building the efficiency of the public telecommunications monopolies in developing nations. After 1985, to keep in tune with what was happening in telecommunications worldwide, the bank shifted to a policy of promoting competition and deregulation in telecommunications.

By 1994, with the new national information infrastructure initiatives under way in the United States, Europe, Japan, and Canada, the World Bank made a sharper break when it saw that future needs would lie not only in the development of physical infrastructure but in the development of information infrastructure as well. In a report to the bank's executive directors, the staff pointed out the phenomenon of convergence of informatics and telecommunications and recommended that the bank develop new strategies and programs to meet the needs of the information age.[18] The bank had some early experience in this area: in 1993, it had helped had helped the Turkish government develop strategies for an information-based economy. It had also helped Ghana introduce competition in telecommunications, and had helped Jordan assess its national information needs.

In 1995, the staff proposed a more organized approach with five objectives:

1. To accelerate growth and promote efficiency in telecommunications services;
2. To deploy the national information infrastructure and integrate it with the emerging global infrastructure;
3. To establish effective regulatory capacity;
4. To increase the role of the private sector in service provision; and
5. To promote the strategic use of information for economic growth and international competitiveness.[19]

The end result of the bank's deliberations was the creation of its Information for Development Program (InfoDev), using funding from fifteen member governments, the EU, the bank itself, and other private-sector organizations such as IBM and Motorola. Total funding in 1998 was $14.8 million, of which $8.5 million was diverted to assist developing countries prepare for Y2K.

InfoDev programs fall into four broad areas. First, they build consensus in developing countries on public policy issues ranging from telecommunications regulation to intellectual property through workshops and the use of networks to create virtual communities. Second, they assess national information infrastructure strategies for countries, including examining their public policy framework. Third, they help countries implement telecommunications reform and introduce competition. And fourth, they fund Net demonstration projects in a wide variety of areas.

By 1999, InfoDev was funding twenty-eight projects around the world and had completed twelve others. Among some of the key ones were the following:

—The African Empowerment Network in Information Technologies
—The Baltic Sea Information Society Project: Northwest Russia
—China's Industrial Pollution Projection System: New Information Tools
—Connectivity Information and Training Center for Internet: Cameroon
—Information Systems for Rural Development: Cajamarca, Peru
—Jamaica: Partnership for Technology in Basic Education

—Promotion and Development of Telematics in the Public Sector: United Nations Educational, Scientific, and Cultural Organization (UNESCO).

Besides UNESCO, InfoDev cooperates with other international organizations, including the ITU, the WTO, WIPO, and UNCITRAL. One of its most useful projects is the dissemination of best practices on issues and a tool kit that demonstrates the importance of Internet services to economic and social development. With assistance from InfoDev, the Inter-American Development Bank launched in 1997 its Informatics 2000 Initiative to foster electronic commerce in Latin America.

THE INTERNATIONAL LABOR ORGANIZATION

With human resources the key component of the Net, the International Labor Organization (ILO), founded in 1919, also plays a role. It helps develop understanding of labor-market changes resulting from the new information infrastructure, develops understanding of the impact of changes such as "teleworking," or telecommuting, on the workforce, and develops new training and education techniques. It also focuses on the protection of worker rights in the digital age. For example, the ILO developed a code of practice on the protection of worker privacy, which covers how personal data of employees is collected, stored, and used and the rights of employees.

Most importantly, a 1998 ILO report surveyed the overall impact of the information society on jobs and found that, although workers faced many challenges in the information age, including the loss of some jobs, new jobs were being created at a rapid pace: "[A] significant number of jobs should be created by new network operators resulting from the gradual opening up of markets to competition, as well as by providers of telecommunications services. . . . The new jobs created are appearing above all in . . . various activities linked with multimedia convergence and the information society."[20]

The ILO has also examined many of the issues surrounding work in the information society, including the extent of telecommuting and its implications for working conditions, compensation, health and safety, and collective bargaining. It has also published numerous studies on training and education.

THE ASIA-PACIFIC ECONOMIC COOPERATION GROUP

Of all the regional bodies involved in policy for the information age, and with the exception of the EU, which was covered in Chapter 11, the

Asia-Pacific Economic Cooperation group has probably achieved the most. Founded in 1989, APEC plays a key role in the dynamic Asia-Pacific region, whose entrepreneurship and vast distances make the Net and electronic commerce critical in member nations' economies. With eighteen member nations from both hemispheres, APEC is playing an important role in educating Asian governments on the need for a public policy framework with private-sector leadership. Much of Asia has never had such a framework. As Peter Lovelock, a scholar at the University of Hong Kong, has pointed out, "[I]n a worldwide trend towards privatization and liberalization, Asian states have distinctively managed to stay involved in the reform of the telecoms and information sectors. Nowhere else has the state attempted to maintain the control that it has in Asia, to manage the process of reform."[21]

Lovelock goes on to point out that there are great differences in approach in Asian countries, ranging from total state control in Vietnam to the private-sector approach used in the Philippines. Nevertheless, the overall effect of Asian government reluctance to let go was causing the region to remain "a step behind" in electronic commerce, as one news report put it.[22] Thus, business executives and others engaged in building the digital age in Asia took heart when the leaders of APEC, meeting in Vancouver in 1997, issued a declaration on electronic commerce: "We agree that electronic commerce is one of the most important technological breakthroughs of this decade. We direct ministers to undertake a work program on electronic commerce in the region, taking into account relevant activities of other fora, and to report to us in Kuala Lumpur. This initiative should recognize the leading role of the business sector and promote a predictable and consistent legal and regulatory environment that enables all APEC countries to reap the benefits of electronic commerce."[23]

This declaration was important not only for the recognition it gave to private-sector leadership but because it promised the kind of harmonization of policies in Asia that was being achieved among the states of the EU. Australia and Singapore were chosen to head jointly a task force to develop a work program and principles for electronic commerce. The task force developed an initial five-part work plan for APEC, focusing on education and research, economic and technical cooperation, expansion of infrastructure and Internet access, assistance to small and medium-sized businesses, and consumer/user confidence and trust. The work program that this task force developed produced a report at the APEC ministerial meeting in Kuala Lumpur in November 1998 and a "Blueprint for Action" issued by the ministers at the close of the meeting. In the

Asian environment, the blueprint was particularly important for its stress on the role of the private sector. It enunciated five key principles:

1. The business sector plays a leading role in developing electronic commerce;
2. The role of governments is to promote and facilitate electronic commerce by creating a predictable, transparent, and favorable legal and regulatory environment, promoting trust and confidence and becoming a leading-edge user;
3. Business and governments should cooperate to ensure affordable, accessible, and interoperable infrastructures;
4. Technology-neutral, competitive, market-based solutions—safeguarded by minimal regulation—should be favored; and
5. Government and business should cooperate to develop technologies and policies to address issues such as privacy, authentication and consumer protection.[24]

The ministers also set up an Electronic Commerce Steering Group, to be chaired by the United States and Thailand, to coordinate a wide-ranging work program. The steering group reported on its work the following year during APEC meetings in New Zealand. Among the items it reported on were the following:

—An APEC paper on electronic authentication had been produced and concluded that authentication legislation should be technology neutral.
—Work done in Taipei on "paperless trading" was examined as a potential model and suggested that national economies include paperless trading in their action plans.
—Economic work is proceeding to define better measurements for electronic commerce that could be adopted jointly to produce comparable data.
—A workshop on legal issues concluded that national judiciary systems would need to examine the issue to deal with issues such as jurisdiction and nexus. (A representative from UNCITRAL welcomed an APEC role into that organization's work on this subject.)
—Work on readiness for electronic commerce that had been done in the United States and Taiwan was welcomed as a tool for APEC countries to use to measure their own status.[25]

This last point about readiness was particularly important, since APEC was the first international organization to raise the subject of how to benchmark a nation's readiness. The issue of readiness was made even more critical because estimates of the number of people on-line in Asia and other data about electronic commerce in the region are often either unreliable or confusing. In addition, the 1999 electronic commerce meeting in New Zealand also reported on a number of other APEC initiatives in these areas, including some in training and education and for assistance to small and medium-sized enterprises.

Among the international organizations involved in cyberspace issues, APEC's approach has been one of the most important. For one thing, it is helping a region that might have easily taken the path toward increased government regulation. Although its work has not been a panacea for this problem, APEC has acted like the proverbial thumb on the scale, trying to correct a dangerous imbalance. APEC has also built the propositions of the digital age into all of its working groups, so that work on customs, telecommunications, and other issues all take into account the role of the Net. Finally, APEC has been innovative, breaking new ground in a number of areas such as the issue of readiness, to which we shall turn in the Conclusion.

THE ORGANIZATION OF AMERICAN STATES AND THE FREE TRADE AREA OF THE AMERICAS

In contrast to Asia, Latin America has seen much less activity on the public policy framework for the digital age. The Organization of American States and the Free Trade Area of the Americas (FTAA) have belatedly started to address this action deficit. At the ministerial meeting of the FTAA in March 1998, the ministers initiated a joint government–private sector committee of experts, headed by the Caribbean community (Caricom), to make recommendations to "increase and broaden the benefits to be derived from the electronic marketplace" in the region.[26]

At the OAS Second Summit of the Americas that took place a month later in Santiago, Chile, the governments present issued a comprehensive plan of action to deal with problems in the region. The plan included a large number of items dealing with the Net. It called for "supporting the evolution of the Global Information Infrastructure," "providing affordable access to the Internet," and building "community information service centers primarily to access the Internet and multimedia services." The document also called for governments to "foster private sector applications over electronic networks, including the Internet," and stressed education and health care, using health information systems and telemedicine. Finally, it called for member nations to implement the WTO Agreement on Basic Telecommunications.[27] This last point was particularly important, since many Latin American countries had been slow to deregulate telecommunications. In August 1999, for example, the OECD singled out Mexico as a country that needed to move faster to permit competition in telecommunications.

In November 1999, the Free Trade Area of the Americas (FTAA) Committee of Experts on Electronic Commerce issued a report containing more than 40 recommendations for member governments. Pointing out that 10 percent of the world's Internet use was expected to be in Latin America by 2005, the report acknowledged the leading role of the private sector. It recommended more telecommunications competition, enactment of legal frameworks for electronic commerce, and consumer and privacy protections.[28]

There is no question that Latin Americans want to use the Net as much as people elsewhere. In fact, the number of Latin Americans using the Internet was expected to grow from about seven million at the beginning of 2000 to sixteen million in 2002, a growth rate faster than that in the United States.[29] But national progress has been slow, and organizations such as the OAS and the FTAA can play a more important role in stimulating this growth in the future.

CONCLUSIONS

Numerous other international and regional organizations are, of course, involved in cyberspace. UN agencies such as the UN Conference on Trade and Development (UNCTAD) and UNDP are assisting developing countries, specialized institutions such as the ISO and the IEC are involved technically, and financial institutions such as the Bank for International Settlements are working on issues relating to the electronic transfer of funds. For those wishing a comprehensive but brief report on each of these, the OECD document "Report on International and Regional Bodies: Activities and Initiatives in Electronic Commerce," is an excellent source.[30]

On the whole, the international organizations should be given good grades for their performance to date on advancing the Net public policy issues and solutions. Given these organizations' reputation for slowness, this may be somewhat of a surprise. But the Net is compelling: its growth and its real and potential contributions to so many fields are no longer denied by anyone. Additionally, the international bureaucracies have noted, like everyone else, that future careers and personal prosperity lie in the direction of cyberspace, and thus they have been eager to get involved. The U.S. government has been an active and strong advocate and has provided a strong stimulus to action; the EU and Japan have also been especially active. So the normally plodding international organizations have sprung to action to facilitate progress on building a global information infrastrucure.

Can this progress continue? Many of the easiest issues to resolve have now been completed; the more difficult ones lie ahead. Agreeing that the private sector should lead the development of cyberspace was relatively simple compared to agreeing to an international legal framework or resolving serious extraterritorial issues such as privacy and content restrictions. Issues striking at national cultural and economic interests will not be easy to tackle. For now, however, there does not appear to be a compelling need for a new international organization or framework to deal with the issue. If the WTO, UNCITRAL, or the ITU become bogged down in the future, that need might arise. Today, however, the international arrangements that were put in place by leaders of an earlier generation appear adequate to prepare a new world for their grandchildren.

13

The Private Sector

[P]rivate entities . . . will be making many quasi-governmental decisions about technology that will shape our communications landscape and our world. . . . We must, however, be attentive to the power of this new code regulation. . . . Otherwise we'll be facing the prospect of the privatization of public policy."
—Andrew Shapiro, *The Control Revolution*[1]

As the new millennium opened, a race was on between the private sector and public opinion over control of the future of the Net. The private sector, led by groups of activists in the high-technology business community, was rushing to establish technological and organizational means to protect on-line consumers and other users of the Net from cyber-criminals, invasion of privacy, exposure to pornography, and other nasty content. The public, however, was not yet convinced that the private sector could succeed. A national poll done by NBC News and the *Wall Street Journal* in June 1999 found that 38 percent of Americans rated the "Internet pornography and privacy issues" the second most important social and cultural issue with which they were concerned. Only youth violence scored higher.[2]

Moreover, 60 percent of the public said they were in favor of new laws "regulating sexually explicit Internet content." Ira Magaziner, who had been the chief architect of the Clinton administration's electronic commerce policy, also said in 1999, "The next two to three years will be crucial in determining whether the Internet remains a free medium or whether it becomes an area that governments can't resist regulating."[3] In fact, the U.S. government had issued numerous warnings that if the private sector did not move quickly or forcefully enough to deal with Internet issues, that it would step in. The administration's seminal document on the subject, "A Framework for Electronic Commerce," carefully addressing directly the question of private-sector self-regulation and government action. The first three principles stressed the need for govern-

368

ment restraint but also left the door open to government intervention, if it became necessary:

[G]overnments should encourage industry self-regulation wherever appropriate and support the efforts of private sector organizations to develop mechanisms to facilitate the successful operations of the Internet. . . . Where government action or intergovernmental agreements are necessary, on taxation for example, private sector participation should be a formal part of the policy making process. . . .

[G]overnments should refrain from imposing new and unnecessary regulations, bureaucratic procedures, or taxes and tariffs on commercial activities that take place via the Internet.

In some areas, government agreements may prove necessary to facilitate electronic commerce and protect consumers.[4]

On the issues of privacy and consumer protection, the principle of private-sector leadership was hedged even further:

The Administration considers data protection critically important. We believe that private efforts of industry working in cooperation with consumer groups are preferable to government regulation, but if effective privacy protection cannot be provided in this way, we will reevaluate this policy. . . .

[C]onsumers must have confidence that the goods and services offered are fairly represented, that they will get what they pay for, and that recourse or redress will be available if they do not. This is an area where government action is appropriate.[5]

Thus, the administration seemed to be offering the private sector a good deal. "Go ahead and run the Net," it seemed to be saying, "but protect users from a variety of nuisances, outrages, and criminal acts. If you fail to do that," however, they implied, "you will take the political heat and the public will demand government regulation which we will deliver."

How did a Democratic administration come to espouse a policy with such a powerful role for the private sector—a policy that might have been denounced strongly by congressional Democrats if it had been proposed by a Republican administration? There were a number of key reasons, not the least among them that the high-technology companies played a central and effective role in the policy's development. To understand the role of the private sector, it is important to understand why and how this happened, and which private-sector organizations were involved. By the mid-1990s, high-technology lobbying had become skillful, and industry used a wide variety of means to achieve its ends. It found in the White House a receptive Clinton administration.

First, President Bill Clinton and Vice President Al Gore came into office as "New Democrats," and the new administration's eagerness to see issues in a different, "third" way was by no means restricted to the Net. Welfare reform and budget discipline were far more important indicators of the change taking place in the Democratic Party. Second, the campaign in 1992 had focused heavily on the importance of technology. Many of the ambitious, bright people who had worked on the issue were brought into the new administration, such as Tom Kalil and Mike Nelson at the White House, and David Barram and Kent Hughes in the Commerce Department. Barram, for example, had come from Apple Computer; Hughes had been president of the Council on Competitiveness, the organization of business leaders, university presidents, and labor union officials who had come together to push an agenda for advancing American global competitiveness. The group advocated a new emphasis on high-technology cooperation between business, government, and universities.

The administration even tried to recruit John Rollwagen, then chairman of Cray Research, as deputy secretary of commerce. But he served only a few months as the designate for that position and then withdrew. Nevertheless, many of the people the administration did bring in had worked with the high-technology community in their previous positions in the private sector or with trade associations or in Congress, and they understood the new industry. They had an important mentor in the form of Gore, for whom Nelson had worked on Capitol Hill and who also, as we have seen, had a strong interest in technology and especially computing and telecommunications.

Politically, it was also "cool" to be associated with the Net and its proponents, who were seen by many as proof that "baby boomers," nerds, and former hippies could succeed both as technology freaks and as economically successful businesspeople. They contrasted nicely with the old-fashioned businesspeople who seemed to have supported the Republicans for years—traditional, older, grey-suited white men. Thus, at Clinton's first State of the Union address, Hillary Rodham Clinton sat very publicly next to John Sculley, at that time president of Apple Computer and seen as something of an iconoclast. (Unfortunately, Sculley, no hippie but a former Pepsi-Cola marketing executive, was soon out of that job.)

The banal matter of political contributions also played a role in the administration's attention to the Net. In the new high-tech industries, where many newly wealthy entrepreneurs and executives had more liberal political leanings than their heavy industry forebears, the new Democrats saw a breakthrough opportunity for fund raising and political support. This was particularly important in the unregulated areas of computing and software: unlike regulated industries, such as telecommunications, which contributed heavily to political campaigns, especially to members on the telecommunications subcommittees in Congress, high-tech executives had little immediate motivation to make contributions. Whereas AT&T, for example, had given millions over the years in political contributions, IBM (actually a patriarch of the industry) did not even have a political action committee. An administration with an especially strong interest in raising money had spotted some potentially deep pockets.

Finally, and most important, was the substance. Key members of the administration, including the president himself, recognized the critical importance of the new technology for the future of the U.S. economy and wanted to use the government to exploit it and help it grow as rapidly as possible. They had not come to this understanding accidentally. In fact, the high-tech community had mounted an aggressive campaign to shape the administration's policy from the beginning, which is itself an important statement on the role of the private sector.

As the Clinton administration came into office in January 1993, it was greeted by a document called "Perspectives on the National Information Infrastructure," published by the Computer Systems Policy Project, or CSPP. The CSPP had been founded in 1989 by the chief executive officers of the computer systems companies. In 1993, it had thirteen members and was chaired by Sculley. Ken Kay, a technology-savvy lobbyist, was the CSPP's executive director. The group had originally been formed to counter moves of the semiconductor industry to place trade sanctions on Japanese semiconductor manufacturers—who also supplied the computer industry. The computer companies feared the higher prices for their chips that would result from sanctions. (It is indicative of the dramatic change in the industry that by the end of 1999, six of the original thirteen CSPP member companies would either no longer exist or would have left the computer business. By then the CSPP would have three new members—Dell Computers, Cisco Systems, and ironically one of its earlier semiconductor antagonists, Intel. Only one of the founding executives had survived the six intervening years—Scott McNealy of Sun Microsystems.)

The CSPP document was widely read within the administration and it helped form policy. In particular, it defined the new digital technologies; illustrated their importance in pivotal areas such as health care, education, and manufacturing; and laid out an agenda for action that largely became administration policy. Most significantly, it said that "the development and deployment of the infrastructure must be led by the private sector, guided by the forces of a free and open market." The document went on to state that "the federal government can accelerate its implementation by acting as a catalyst and a coordinator." It recommended an action plan that would include funding for research and development, application pilot projects, a coordinating council in the government, and public education efforts.[6] In one form or another, the administration adopted this agenda.

The CSPP further shaped the direction of Net policy with a series of key papers and through meetings with the president, the vice president, other officials of the administration, and to a lesser extent, key congressional leaders. In 1994, when interoperability had become a major issue for the emerging Net, with threats of government intervention to set standards, the CSPP published "Perspectives on the National Information Infrastructure: Ensuring Interoperability."[7] This paper defined the issue clearly in terms of the critical interfaces built into the infrastructure and set the stage for the American National Standards Institute (ANSI) Information Infrastructure Standards Panel (IISP), discussed in Chapter 7. At the urging of CSPP members and other companies, the IISP took over the role of identifying and helping resolve critical interface standards issues, thus warding off government action and keeping the private sector in control of standards. IBM and AT&T were particularly active in the IISP's formation. Larry Wills, a senior IBM executive, was chairman of ANSI, and Chick Hayden, a retiring IBM executive, became the IISP's director. Woody Kerkeslager, an AT&T vice president and CSPP activist, was also instrumental in setting the IISP up.

In 1995, as the issue of the national information infrastructure became internationalized, the CSPP published "Perspectives on the Global Information Infrastructure."[8] This document helped establish the principle of private-sector leadership in the global arena and set an agenda for international action that included eliminating tariff and nontariff barriers, providing protection for intellectual property, and eliminating restrictive export controls. Other papers on issues such as security and competition followed, and in 1997, CSPP published its paper "The Benefits of Global Electronic Commerce."[9] With live case studies to illuminate the impact of electronic commerce in areas such as government services, health care, retailing, and financial services, the document sought to buttress the administration's "Framework" document. The paper also laid out the CSPP's policy agenda on security and encryption, tax neutrality, access and competition, and legal framework. Continued meetings between the chief executive officers who made up the CSPP and senior government officials and congressional leaders kept the CSPP agenda moving.

But the CSPP was not the only private-sector group shaping the policy agenda in Washington and other capitals. The Information Technology Industry Council (ITIC) is a broader organization of high-tech companies that includes not only the U.S. computer makers but more than twenty-five companies such as Lucent Technologies, Xerox, Eastman Kodak, and the U.S. subsidiaries of Sony and Hitachi. The ITIC has been extremely active in helping the administration, Congress, and agencies such as the Federal Communications Commission formulate policy. Much of its lobbying skill is derived from its members (most with experienced lobbyists on staff) and from Rhett Dawson, the ITIC's president, an able former Reagan White House official with a strong background on Capitol Hill.

In the 1995–96 period alone, the ITIC published more than thirty-five policy documents dealing with Net issues, including telecommunications regulation, encryption, the International Technology Agreement, and intellectual property. Some of these documents were testimonies before the Federal Communications Commission on advanced services, interconnection, access, safeguards, and spectrum issues; others were congressional testimony on the International Technology Agreement, in the negotiation of which the ITIC played a leadership role. As one observer put it, if the CSPP was the strategic nuclear force of the computer industry, then the ITIC was the marines, the infantry, and the armored brigades. By 1999, ITIC was publishing a "High-Tech Voting Guide," rating members of the House and Senate on how they voted in the 106th Congress on high-technology issues.

Its lobbying and its policy positions also swayed agencies such as the office of the U.S. Trade Representative, as well as Congress. For example, the ITIC successfully led the International Technology Agreement Coalition, jointly with the American Electronics Association, by gathering broad support in the administration and in Congress, and just as important, overseas.

In fact, one of the ITIC's greatest contributions has been to the international aspects of Net issues. At an early stage in the global debate, the ITIC led an effort at the International Information Industry Congress (IIIC), a loose coalition of high-technology associations from the United States, Europe, Canada, Japan, Australia, New Zealand, and Brazil, among other countries, to do internationally what the CSPP had done in the United States: define the agenda. The result was a paper, "Common Views Paper on GII," which declared that "[t]he private sector and the competitive marketplace must be the driving force," for the global information infrastructure (GII).[10] Coming to terms on many of the issues in the paper, including interoperability and intellectual property, was quite difficult, and the drafting session in Tokyo was unruly at times. But the ITIC's leadership persisted, and agreement was reached. The paper's views had a major influence on the governments preparing for the meeting of the ministers of the G-7 group of advanced industrialized nations in Brussels in February 1995.

The IIIC capitalized on its successful beginnings by producing just prior to the ministerial meeting a new and more detailed paper. This paper dealt with six issues: interoperability, privacy, intellectual property rights, universal access, access to research and development and new applications, and market access. The overall message was private-sector leadership, open markets, deregulation, and competition.[11] Senior executives from the key IIIC member countries were present in Brussels, including Michael Spindler, the CEO of Apple. They helped ensure that the ministerial declaration that resulted from the meeting met their objectives. It did. The IIIC has gone on to publish other key papers on privacy, security, international trade, telecommunications, and other electronic commerce issues. Its transnational lobbying in Geneva during key negotiating periods had a major impact on the outcome of the World Trade Organization's Agreement on Basic Telecommunications. Moreover, the U.S. members, such as Digital Equipment, helped keep the support of members of Congress back in Washington, such as Representative Edward Markey of Massachusetts (where Digital was based at the time), who at one point threatened to oppose the agreement.

In addition to the IIIC, other international business organizations have been used by the high-technology industry to influence policy. The U.S. Council for International Business and the Organization for Economic Cooperation and Development's Business-Industry Advisory Committee (BIAC) have been deeply involved in the broad issue of electronic commerce as well as in specific policy issues such as the International Technology Agreement (ITA) and telecommunications deregulation. The Transatlantic Business Dialogue, which later grew into the Global Business Dialogue, has been another key forum for dealing with issues such as encryption, legal framework, and copyright issues. Its work has had a strong influence on the views of the European Commission in Brussels, in particular.

In Washington, other high-technology trade associations have also played a role in defining Net policy. The American Electronics Association, headed by Bill Archey, was originally a California-based group and consisted of many smaller companies as well as the big players. It has played an especially strong role on trade, export controls, and the ITA. It also published a key paper documenting the economic impact of the new technologies on state economies. The Business Software Alliance, an association of the powerhouse software companies, including Microsoft, Novell, Lotus, Intel, and IBM, has been especially active on copyright and encryption policy; the leading chief executive officers of its members lobby together in Washington.

The Electronics Industry Association, representing a broad spectrum of high-technology industry but especially the consumer electronics segment, played an important role on many issues including export controls, the ITA, and taxation. It is now headed by Dave McCurdy, a former member of Congress from Oklahoma with a strong interest in technology. It is a measure of the new importance of high-tech lobbying that Representative Tom DeLay of Texas, the Republican whip, tried to stop McCurdy's appointment because he wanted a Republican in the job.

A related organization, the Telephone Industry Association, represented the telephone-equipment manufacturers, and other organizations represented the cable television companies, telecommunications carriers, and newspaper and magazine publishers. The Communications and Computer Industry Association (CCIA), headed by Ed Black, represented a broad group of telecommunications, software, and computer companies and was especially active in the Microsoft antitrust case, advocating the company's breakup. Even the Motion Picture Association of America was engaged on issues related to content such as copyright protection, standards, and content regulation.

Organizations of high-tech professionals have also been active in discussing Net policy issues. For example, the Association for Computing Machinery (ACM), which has more than eighty thousand members, has been active nationally and locally on such issues as access, copyright, encryption, privacy, free speech, and research funding. The ACM lobbied state legislators on the issue of the Uniform Computer Information Transactions Act, calling for more protection for software users.

In addition to standard lobbying activities, however, high-tech companies decided that more education for government officials and members of Congress was needed on the new issues. They achieved this in a variety of ways. A group of companies including AT&T, IBM, Microsoft, and Apple started Highway One, a demonstration center in downtown Washington, D.C., to show off their new applications in areas such as education and health care. IBM itself built a mock-up of a small town in a downtown building, including a school, a courthouse, a town hall, and other government buildings to demonstrate how the Net was changing government services. IBM invited to the center not only U.S. government officials but many foreign government officials passing through Washington.

These companies had also learned the importance of producing thoughtful and credible ideas backed by facts and so sponsored a number of "think tank" activities. Take, for example, the Information Technology Association of America (ITAA), a large association of about 11,000 companies engaged in fields from telecommunications to computer services to software, whose president has been politically well connected to the Clinton administration and is a pioneer in the study of the labor and employment effects of electronic commerce. The ITAA, together with James Clark, the founder of Netscape, started the Global Internet Project (GIP), whose purpose was to remove barriers to Internet growth by producing thoughtful papers and educating government officials. The GIP's 1998 paper, "The Opportunity and the Challenge," developed an interesting policy architecture for the Internet, defining six policy levels: infrastructure, governance, security, privacy, content, and commerce. The paper endorsed the Clinton administration's approach and urged industry to continue efforts for self-regulation in areas such as privacy, content, and business practices.[12]

Another educational policy effort was the formation of the Global Information Infrastructure Commission (GIIC) at the Center for Strategic and International Studies in Washington. The GIIC was founded by a group of senior information industry officials from a number of countries, including Carlo di Benedetti of Olivetti. It convened a seminal meeting in Brussels in conjunction with the G-7 ministerial meeting in February 1995 that helped create the policy climate worldwide for the GII. It continues to produce a variety of papers and reports.

Another key academic effort—perhaps the key university initiative—is the Harvard Information Infrastructure Project (HIIP). Begun in 1989, the HIIP is a joint project of the John F. Kennedy School of Government, the Harvard Law School, the Belfer Center for Science and International Affairs, and the Center for Business and Government. It is supported by a number of prominent high-technology companies, as well as by a number of government agencies. Its driving force has been Lewis Branscomb, the Aetna Professor in Public and Corporate Management at Harvard, and formerly head of the National Bureau of Standards and vice president and chief scientist of IBM. The HIIP has been an invaluable national resource, producing numerous books and publications access, standards, research and development, and international Net policy issues. It also maintains the most extensive Web site on the subject of Internet policy issues. Its halls have attracted a number of high-level officials: Deborah Hurley, its current director, formerly worked for the Organization for Economic Cooperation and Development; her predecessor, Brian Kahin, served in the White House Office of Science and Technology Policy after leaving HIIP.

High-technology companies have also supported other think tank activities on policy issues. In 1998, the Brookings Institution and the Cato Institute held a business-sponsored conference on digital age policy. The book produced from that conference recommended that "policymakers should let markets rather than governments address any problems associated with digital technology. . . . Government decision making is slow, whether at the legislative level (where competing interest groups play tugs of war) or at the regulatory level (where rulemaking must be preceded by analysis and accompanied by a notice and comment procedure.) By the time the government acts, the nature of the problem . . . is likely to change radically."[13] Thus, the notion of private-sector control of the Net was again ratified, this time by two important Washington think tanks, one usually associated with the left, the other usually far to the right of the political spectrum.

Industry also provided official policy guidance, through a number of key advisory committees. The National Information Infrastructure Advisory Committee, which was discussed in Chapter 10, was one important but temporary such mechanism. Another more permanent one, discussed in Chapter 9, is the President's Information Technology Advisory Committee, which provided high-level advice on research and development. In the trade area, the Advisory Committee on Trade Policy and Negotiations is a group of senior executives who advise the U.S. Trade Representative on trade policy. Although it covers the entire range of trade issues, its inclusion of a number of high-technology executives such as Louis Gerstner from IBM has ensured that issues such as the ITA remain near the top of the list.

Another important advisory body is the State Department's Advisory Committee on International Communications and Information Policy (ACICIP). Its members, who include more than thirty officials from a wide variety of telecommunications, computing, content, and other industries, as well as a few scholars, meet regularly with senior government officials to discuss issues ranging from security and encryption, to consumer protection and privacy, to telecommunications deregulation. The

ACICIP has also been helpful in educating State Department officials about technical aspects of the Net.

Finally, high-technology industry has also had a great impact on Net policy through the normal lobbying operations of individual companies. Despite the view commonly expressed in the press that the high-technology companies did not have a significant Washington presence until the Microsoft case woke them up, many companies had long maintained a significant Washington presence. Their sophisticated operations included the use of trade associations, think tanks, and advisory committees, as we have already seen in this chapter, but many of the key players also fielded experienced full-time lobbyists. AT&T, for example, had long had one of the largest of all Washington offices. For many years, it had skillfully used its contract for supplying special telecommunications services to the White House and other agencies as a route to gain access to senior officials. One of AT&T's key Washington executives, Jack Gertz, was even in President John Kennedy's motorcade in Dallas in 1963, for example.

IBM had been offering sophisticated information technology education to government officials since the early 1970s, and in 1975 established a large Washington office to cover a wide range of issues. Although the company made no political contributions, it had not needed to; its advice was widely sought and its presence in so many congressional districts gave it all the access it needed. Among other high-technology companies with sophisticated Washington offices were Apple Computer, Compaq, Hewlett-Packard, Motorola, Xerox, and Eastman Kodak. Many of these used their own technology to offer their policy positions. IBM, MCI, and America Online all offered Web pages containing their positions on a variety of Net public policy issues.

On the issue of political contributions, however, the industry tended to split between those who were regulated and those who were not. In 1998, for example, the list of the top ten corporate contributors included four regulated telecommunications companies—AT&T, Ameritech, Bell South, and SBC—but no computer or software companies. In the years from 1996 to 1998, the long-distance, local, and cellular telephone companies spent an average of about $75 million per year on political contributions. By contrast, the computer and software companies spent $19.9 million in 1996.[14]

In July 1997, John Doerr, a California venture capitalist, and Jim Barksdale formed a new organization, Technology Network, "a bipartisan coalition aimed at giving high technology companies a more significant voice in politics."[15] With a budget of $2 million, the group said it intended to fund candidates and political causes that benefited high technology. In the minds of some, this was a brand-new activity for high-technology companies. The organization was begun too late to have any impact on the initial basic policy framework for the Net, but it brought a number of new companies into the fray, such as Intuit, Cisco Systems, and Marimba, and it would later become active on specific issues.

Thus, the private sector has used a wide variety of sophisticated political tools to help define the policy agenda for the Net and for electronic commerce. Governments had already accepted the notion of private-sector leadership and had enacted a number of laws favorable to industry. Having wrested control of the Net from government, the private sector needed to meet its new responsibilities for self-regulation in areas such as privacy and content regulation. If it could not, its broader control would begin to erode as the public demanded government regulation.

PRIVACY

By mid-2000, the jury was still out on whether industry was doing enough to protect the on-line privacy of Internet users. Although the private sector had made much progress since the Clinton administration had set out its self-regulation challenge in July 1997, the critics were not mollified. For example, in the spring of 1999, the Georgetown University business school released the results of a study of on-line privacy practices. The Federal Trade Commission (FTC) had found that in the preceding year, only 14 percent of commercial Web sites informed consumers of their privacy practices and allowed them to opt out; a number of high-technology companies had commissioned the Georgetown study to see if this number had improved at all since then.

The study found that it had improved. It showed that two-thirds of the Web's most popular sites (accounting for 99 percent of the Web's traffic) posted a privacy policy. Of these, 87 percent explained how they collected and used data; 77 percent offered consumers a choice as to how their information was used; 40 percent offered consumers access to their data; and 49 percent offered a way to contact the company. Said FTC Chairman Robert Pitofsky of the results, "If the raw numbers are any indication, self-regulation is working." The critics, however, were not convinced: Marc Rotenberg, executive director of the Electronic Privacy Information Center, said "For us, it was never about posting privacy policies. That's setting a very low bar." Rotenberg went on to say his group prefers laws to protect on-line privacy.[16]

The government, however, was becoming convinced that the companies were making enough progress to avoid broad new laws, at least for the time being. In a report to Congress in July 1999, the FTC said there had been a substantial improvement in how the business community was implementing FTC privacy policies: "The commission believes that legislation to address online privacy is not appropriate at this time. . . . The present challenge is to educate those companies which still do not understand the importance of consumer privacy. . . . Industry must work together with government and consumer groups to educate consumers about privacy protection on the Internet."[17]

In fact, companies had used the intervening years to make progress in the area of on-line privacy in a number of areas. These included individual company on-line privacy policies, technological advances to protect privacy, the development of industry privacy codes, and the development and use of specific organizations to create, monitor, and enforce privacy practices.

Company Privacy Policies

As the Georgetown study showed, most companies now publish privacy policies on their Web sites. Typical is Hewlett Packard's, which covers awareness, tells consumers what the company collects and how that information is used, gives consumers the choice of opting out, and offers access to consumer records. Hewlett Packard also informs consumers that it participates in broader programs, such as the Better Business Bureau's BBB Online privacy program, and complies with their standards.

Other companies offer similar privacy information. Eastman Kodak offers a description of how it uses "cookies" to enhance customer service, but informs consumers they can set their browsers to reject them, if they wish. Apple, AT&T, and America Online offer more information about children's on-line privacy and how they protect it. Bell Atlantic offers its ten privacy principles with detailed information, for example, on how its employees are trained to safeguard information.

Some companies have gone beyond posting information on their own Web sites and have announced that they will not buy advertising on Web sites that don't post privacy policies. Microsoft, IBM, and Walt Disney are among the companies taking this stand; Disney goes a step further, also refusing to sell advertising to companies without a privacy policy. Steve Wadsworth, president of Disney's Internet Group, said that although the policy might have a short-term negative effect on advertising revenues, he believes the long-term impact on consumer confidence will be positive and will more than make up for any lost revenue.[18]

Moreover, as electronic commerce began to thrive among traditional companies, they joined with their high-technology counterparts on promoting privacy initiatives. In May 2000, Proctor and Gamble's chief executive, Durk Jager, and his IBM counterpart, Louis Gerstner, announced the they would jointly lead a Privacy Leadership Initiative to invest more than $3 million in new privacy technologies.

Technology

As public concerns about privacy have risen, new technological means to protect it have been developed and used by companies, government agencies, and other institutions. Some of these innovations have been aimed specifically at protecting personal privacy. Others were developed to protect the security and confidentiality of business, government, or other institutional information, but they protect personal privacy as well. Technology that protects personal privacy includes provisions for anonymity and the Platform for Privacy Preferences; the double-duty technologies that protect institutional as well as personal information include firewalls, software security, and cryptography.

Firewalls. Firewalls are complex filters that use hardware and software to keep intruders out of private networks. Simple firewalls may simply examine packets of information to check their password or other information; more complex ones may include authentication and encryption services, as well. An efficient firewall for the network of a hospital or health maintenance organization, for example, will prevent unauthorized people from examining patient records in their systems. Not surprisingly, a large commercial market has developed for firewalls.

Software Security. A variety of techniques to protect security are built into operating systems and network-management software. These include not only passwords and authentication but also refusing entry after a certain number of incorrect password attempts, automatic shutdown of systems or workstations when not in use, or the building of enclaves of security within a network. Thus, personnel files within an intranet may be much more secure than other files on the same network.

Cryptography. Advanced versions of cryptography (discussed in Chapter 7) are used to protect the privacy and security of both stored files and transmissions of information. For example, the Secure Socket Layer is a commercial encryption system for electronic commerce that authenticates, protects confidentiality, and assures the integrity of data. It and even more advanced systems are commonly used in electronic commerce transactions.

Anonymity. A variety of techniques have been developed to permit Internet users to remain anonymous. One technique in wide use is the use of anonymous "remailer" services, which remove the original sender's name and address from a message before it is sent and substitute another. For return mail, the process is simply reversed. Another technique is the anonymity provided to users of Internet newsgroups, where standard software protocols such as the Simple Mail Transfer Protocol assure the user's anonymity. Other anonymity tools include anonymous payment mechanisms, such as DigiCash or NetBill; pseudonymizers, such as the Lucent Personalized Web Assistant, which assigns an alias to users; and advanced database technology, which can permit data warehouses to respect privacy rules.

Platform for Privacy Preferences. Perhaps the most comprehensive technological tool for protecting personal privacy is the Platform for Privacy Preferences (P3P). Supported by business and university researchers, P3P was developed by the World Wide Web Consortium at the Massachusetts Institute of Technology (MIT). Its developers call it a "privacy assistant." Basically, it provides a framework of specifications so that users of the Net can express their privacy preferences and make sure that Web sites they visit have practices that fall within the range of their preferences. This matching of the user's privacy preferences with a Web site's is done automatically.

For example, if a user prefers to deal only with Web sites that do not share or use customers' personal data with others, P3P automatically scans the Web site's privacy practices to make certain it complies. If the Web site's policies match the user's, the user is connected. If the site's practices do include selling or sharing data, or if the site has no privacy policy at all, the user will be informed of that fact before being connected and has the choice of going ahead or browsing elsewhere.

The use of P3P should prompt more on-line businesses and other services to adopt privacy policies quickly. Without them, they may cut themselves off from many customers. However, P3P does not protect the user from businesses, government agencies, or other institutions that either lie about their policies or otherwise fail to abide by them. That is the province of industry self-regulation and legal rules.

Industry Codes of Conduct and Enforcement

As discussed in Chapter 5, a number of industries have developed their own privacy principles or codes of conduct. One of the earliest was the Direct Marketing Association (DMA), whose members' use of mail and telephone solicitation had created numerous political storms. More recently, the DMA moved to require its members to follow a set of consumer privacy protection practices that apply to mail, telephone, and on-line marketing; refusal to adhere to these practices results in expulsion from the organization. Given that it has about 4,500 members, including financial institutions, retailers, publishers, manufacturers, and nonprofit institutions in the United States and other countries, the DMA's action was significant. Praise came from FTC Chairman Pitofsky: "I commend the DMA's ongoing efforts to educate and build consumer trust in how responsible marketing should take place."[19] DMA action, however, was unlikely to stanch broader criticism of direct-marketing practices in general.

Since the completion of privacy codes and practices by the ITIC and the American Bankers Association (discussed in Chapter 5), numerous other trade associations have taken action. For example, the Association of National Advertisers surveyed all of its members and notified those without privacy practices displayed on their Web sites; it also helped develop children's on-line privacy guidelines for its members.

The United States Council for International Business developed a "Privacy Diagnostic" tool for members and has also held privacy workshops for members. One of the more important developments is the work by the American Institute of Certified Public Accountants (AICPA), whose CPA Webtrust seal was discussed in Chapter 5. In March 1999, the AICPA added a system of binding third-party arbitration to their seal program, thereby adding a significant enforcement mechanism.

Another important organization working to enhance privacy on the Net is TRUSTe, a nonprofit organization whose seal on a Web site guarantees consumers that the site abides by TRUSTe's privacy principles, which include the fair information practices recommended by the FTC and the Department of Commerce. TRUSTe was inaugurated in 1997 with support from the Electronic Freedom Foundation and a number of high-technology and media companies. It now has hundreds of members and is used by all the major Internet portal sites such as Yahoo, Excite, and Lycos. One of TRUSTe's interesting features is that it publishes on its Web site the results of the more important complaints that it investigates. These "Watchdog Reports" let the public see some of the more interesting issues that may affect many users.

Finally, the most comprehensive attempt at industry self-regulation has been the Online Privacy Alliance. By 1998, it was obvious that although programs of individual companies and industry associations were critically important, it was also necessary to have a broad umbrella group to represent as large a chunk of industry as possible. Such a group could thus communicate with more authority to the public, Congress, and others about the state of self-regulation. The result was the Online Privacy Alliance, which currently includes more than eighty global corporations and associations representing thousands of businesses. The alliance's membership covers a variety of industries including advertising, banking, insurance, financial services, marketing, manufacturing, retailing, and travel and publishing, in addition to telecommunications, computers, software, consumer electronics, semiconductors, and other high-technology fields.

Over this broad spectrum, the alliance has, in its own words, "created guidelines for privacy policies, a special policy on the collection of individually identifiable information from children and a framework for enforcement that gives policy teeth."[20] In particular, its Web site offers to on-line organizations a framework for "Effective Enforcement for Self Regulation." The framework defines the characteristics that a privacy seal program should have, including ubiquity, comprehensiveness, accessibility, affordability, integrity, and depth. The site also defines the requirements for a credible and practical verification and monitoring system and standards for consumer complaint resolution. For example, the requirements provide that the revocation of a seal for privacy violations should be a matter of public record. Tough requirements like this are designed both to protect privacy and to convince legislators and government officials that new laws and regulations are not needed.

In fact, one of the alliance's major activities has been to inform government officials and members of Congress about the actions taken. In May 1999, for example, Christine Varney, a former FTC commissioner representing the alliance, told a congressional subcommittee about the progress business had made in self-enforcement: "Consumers now have to take the initiative and use the tools available. . . . They must remember on the digital street, as on Main Street, to think before sharing personal information." She added that, although no broad new legislation was needed, "government should keep the spotlight on this issue by prosecuting the bad actors."[21] One year later, Varney continued to hold to this position and told the FTC that it was wrong to have concluded that there was a need for legislation.

Varney's verdict on the self-regulation of privacy seems to be on target. The private sector has indeed made great advances in moving to protect the personal information of on-line consumers. Agreements on principles, advances in technology, and the organization of self-regulatory tools and enforcement mechanisms were accomplished in only a few years—a faster pace than government could have achieved through a legislative and regulatory process. On the other hand, many organizations still do not "get it," and serious violations of privacy continue. Some, like the state government sales of information, will be resolved in the courts. Instances involving violations of law may be prosecuted by the FTC or by other jurisdictions.

The jury is still out on whether the private sector can regulate itself in such a critical area, or whether the government should step in, as governments have in others countries. The situation is similar in the area of content regulation.

CONTENT

In the early days of the computer industry, programmers used the expression "garbage in, garbage out," meaning that the output of a computer operation was dependent on the quality of the information it received. The problem of dealing with on-line content today is the same. Societies that produce and tolerate vast amounts of pornographic, obscene, violent, and hateful material will face the consequences of producing it, no matter how much Net technology advances to rate and filter it. Unfortunately, the United States is such a society. Trying to filter out objectionable content on the Net is like trying to regulate relative humidity under the ocean.

In her book *Mayhem,* the author Sissela Bok asks, "Is it alarmist or merely sensible to ask what happens to the souls of children nurtured, as in no past society, on images of rape, torture, bombings and massacre that are channeled into their homes from infancy?"[22] The FTC's Robert Pitofsky gave his answer: "I believe . . . that by desensitizing young people to the consequences of violence, by making violence seem commonplace and ordinary, by a cumulative celebration of the effectiveness of violence, we make violent behavior more likely to occur."[23]

The motion picture, recording, television, and video-game industries deny this, of course, and cite their First Amendment rights. Their defense might be more believable if they were nonprofit institutions and not earning huge profits—and huge compensation packages for their executives—by exploiting children. Their claims might also be more credible if advertisers were not enriching them by paying huge sums for advertising they clearly expect to change the purchasing behavior of viewers. Any parent who observes their children as they grow up can see how they learn fundamentally from imitation and by mimicking adult behavior, including the behavior of fictional characters in films and on television. Studies of the link between media exposure and child violence, such as the one ordered by President Clinton in the summer of 1999 following the Littleton, Colorado, high-school shootings, are interesting and may help focus public opinion, but they are really not needed to prove the point.

The content industries also cite in their defense the rating systems they have developed. Of course, one wonders, if they believe their products to be harmless, why they developed ratings at all, if not simply to mollify public opinion with minimalist action. Nevertheless, the Motion Picture Association of America, the Entertainment Software Rating Board, the Interactive Digital Software Association, the Recording Industry of America, the National Association of Broadcasters, and the National Cable Television Association have all developed systems to rate their products, as well as codes to control the content of advertising they accept. In the case of the television industry, the V-chip requirements in television sets help parents filter material, at least for younger children. Unfortunately, this technology works only in the child's own home, and even then allows the broadcasting of offensive material.

Yet these measures are likely to be ineffective in the face of a flood of harmful content. Theater, video store, record shop, and software store owners rarely enforce the rating systems; they sell material to all comers. Parents are confused by different rating systems and defeated by peer pressure. Into this emotional setting has come the Net and the easy access it provides to harmful content. In this arena, however, unlike in the privacy arena, the private sector itself is central to the problem. The creation of violent, obscene, and hateful content is often at the very heart of such businesses, not a byproduct of them. Although much of the public concern has focused narrowly on professional pornographers and on the Web sites of hate groups, they are just the tip of the harmful content iceberg. Parents are rightly concerned with the impact of all such content on their children, not to mention the debasement of society as a whole. They have let politicians at the state and federal levels know of their concerns and the result has been the legislation discussed in Chapter 5 dealing with content regulation, some of which overreached the Constitution.

As for the private sector in the high-technology area, holding back the flood of objectionable content on the Internet has been a more difficult task than dealing with privacy. Perhaps it is an impossible one. Nevertheless, some progress has been made, especially in the technological means to permit parents to control content.

Filtering software has been in use for some time. CyberPatrol, Cybersitter, Cyber Snoop, I-Guard, Net Nanny, SafeSurf, SurfWatch, WinWatch, and Kinder Guard are just a few of the commercial products that are now available to parents. Software filters generally work by blocking access to sites that have been negatively reviewed by the staffs of the companies that produce them, or sites containing certain words or that are very near a blocked site. The market for these products is growing rapidly.

According to the *Washington Post*, a poll taken by the Annenberg Public Policy Center in June 1999 showed that 32 percent of American parents with home Internet connections now use such programs.[24] CyberPatrol reported that its sales jumped 50 percent in the months after the Littleton shootings, and federal legislation could require the use of filters in schools and libraries. Nevertheless, such filters are not a panacea. For one thing, it is difficult to rate sites. CyberPatrol alone has a list of 100,000 banned sites, rated by category. Its reviewers add up to 1,200 new banned sites per week, as many change names and others are added. The reviewers even have difficulty finding sordid sites. Some pornographic sites use key "index" words like "teen" and other seemingly harmless words to snare innocent Internet searchers. Hate groups use certain words to lead people to their sites. English words are sometimes confused with innocent foreign words, and sometimes it is difficult to distinguish a legitimate health site, for example, from a pornographic one.

To help deal with the difficulties involved in filtering, the private sector has developed a number of tools. Perhaps the most important is the Platform for Internet Content Selection (PICS) developed by the World Wide Web Consortium at MIT (the same group that developed the P3P privacy software). PICS is not a rating system but a common technical standard for encoding ratings of any type that works with any filtering software. It is rating and content-neutral and neutral as to the choice of filtering software. The PICS standard is supported by all of the major software-filtering vendors and by all of the major Internet service providers. PICS also maintains a service Web site containing technical information for those who wish to adopt the standard.

The Recreational Software Advisory Council (RSAC) has developed a standard rating system for video games and Web sites. RSAC on the Internet, or RSACi, can be easily understood by parents and set either at the browser level or in a blocking program such as CyberPatrol. It uses PICS as its technical standard and rates four categories for restriction: violence, nudity, sex, and language. Each of these is rated from 0 to 4, characterizing the content, for example in the case of sex, from innocent kissing to explicit sexual acts or sex crimes. SafeSurf is another rating system like RSACi that uses PICS technology. Both RSACi and SafeSurf publish their rating processes so that anyone can use them.

The emergence of PICS and common rating systems like RSACi have improved the ability of the private sector to self-regulate in the area of content. They have made filtering simpler and more efficient for producers of content, for software developers, for Internet service providers, and for parents, teachers, and others who wish to protect children or others from objectionable material. Since both technologies are flexible, they also have international application: non-U.S. businesses and entities can also make use of them. There are more than a thousand RSACi-rated sites in the United Kingdom alone, and many others in Asia and Australia.

Nevertheless, problems still remain. Among them is the issue of education. As pointed out in Chapter 5, the Interactive Services Association published its guide for parents and teachers, "Child Safety on the Information Highway," as early as 1994. Other groups such as the Center for Media Education and the National Center for Missing and Exploited Children have also developed educational programs. Local groups including Boy Scout troops, boys' and girls' clubs, parent-teacher associations, and others have done the same. Yet many parents still do not understand how to use filtering and other techniques to protect their children. To address this issue, in August 1999, a group of high-technology companies inaugurated GetNetWise, an Internet service to educate families on how to have "educational, entertaining, and safe online experiences."[25] Get-NetWise's "Online Safety Guide" was written by a number of childhood education specialists, and the organization's advisory board includes representatives of the American Library Association, the Children's Partnership, the National Urban League, and the Center for Democracy and Technology.

Another approach is to use the Net actively to fight Web sites promoting hate and hate groups. For example, the Nizkor Project (www.Nizkor. org) is a site designed to expose neo-Nazi and Holocaust-denial sites and to counter them with accurate information. Another site, Hatewatch (www.hatewatch.org), sorts hate sites by category and exposes them. Citizens of Colorado developed a site called Coloradans United Against

Hatred (www.cuah.org), "a virtual community designed to fight hate in Colorado."[26]

Will private-sector self-regulation of content work? It is probably too early to tell. The RSAC's president, Dianne Martin, says, "The process of content screening and selection will continue to be highly unstable for the near future. One must remember that it is only within the past year that many of these standards and services became available to users of the Internet."[27] Stephen Balkam, the executive director of the RSAC, holds the same view of the role of government pressure in the content area that Varney of the Online Privacy Alliance expressed in the privacy area. Says Balkam,

[I]t is the role of government to reflect the legitimate concerns of the public. . . . If this means that legislators embarrass, criticize or even humiliate an industry into recognizing its shortcomings . . . then so be it. If it means that through legitimate pressure, Congress can persuade an industry to take action itself or suffer the consequences, then that seems like a perfectly reasonable role. . . .

With the right framework, checks and balances, oversight and controls, self-regulation is by far a more attractive road to take than central government mandate. But self-regulation is a tough road and it takes time, money and resources to make it work.[28]

In the end, the regulation of content on the Net does not belong to government. Nor does the issue of regulation of content on the Net fall solely to the high-technology industries of the digital age; rather, it is the responsibility of those who produce all of our society's content: filmmakers, musicians, writers, publishers, and broadcasters. If they want to avoid government censorship, ultimately they will have to act responsibly. If they continue to produce the ocean of violent, prurient, and hateful material they have been turning out in recent years, we will all drown—not only those of us who are on-line. Perhaps they should heed the advice of Dr. Seuss in his book *Oh, the Places You'll Go:*

You'll look up and down streets.
Look 'em over with care.
About some you will say, "I
Don't choose to go there."
With your head full of brains
And your shoes full of feet,
You're too smart to go down any
Not-so-good street.

Conclusion: Lessons for the Future

Our mirror reflection is a virtual image of ourselves, a fleeting collection of photons bouncing off a silvery surface at the speed of light and igniting neural activity in billions of cells in our eyes, optic nerves, and brains. Our reflection is an accurate image of how we look. But we perceive it in an exaggerated way. It seems to magnify and call attention to every physical defect—every skin blemish, clothing stain, and out-of-place strand of hair. The ephemeral image in the mirror seems to us more real and more compelling in some ways than our physical selves.

The Net has a similar effect. Cyberspace is no more than a virtual extension of the physical world that we have created, and yet it seems like more. Issues that have festered and bothered us for decades—privacy and media content, for example—suddenly seem more threatening and more urgent. Social issues such as educational reform or the cost and quality of health care become more compelling. International issues such as legal jurisdiction or the right to tax income become more pressing and fill government agendas. The Net creates an immediacy that forces us to deal with matters like these more directly.

The Net is also revolutionary. It is changing our institutions, as we have seen. The changes are not trivial; they are important enough to require great changes in learning, work, commerce, and governance. But the Net is not the only nor even the most important revolution with which we have dealt in our long history. Humanity's old shifts from stone to bronze to iron; the inventions of agriculture, paper and printing; the Industrial Revolution and the taming of electricity and the coming of the gasoline-powered automobile all changed past societies irrevocably. These advances had good effects—and bad. The Net is yet another incoming wave that we must jump, but it is faster, broader, and deeper than those that hit us earlier. We do not have centuries, decades, or even many

390

years to build the right framework to negotiate it. We have at most a few years to shape it to our own desires before it evolves organically, creating interests both benign and harmful that will be difficult to change.

In the meantime, there are a variety of observations we can make and conclusions we can draw about the Net in the public policy arena. Perhaps most important is the conclusion that despite its intellectual complexity, the speed of its development, and its global reach, the Net is indeed subject to national policies and governments are in fact coming to grips with it. Borders can play a role in defining the Net, despite its borderless nature. Policy making for the Net has been successful in some areas, and has so far failed in others. But in most areas incremental progress has been made to one extent or another, both within nations and internationally.

The same can be said of the new private-sector role. Government ownership and regulation are in retreat around the world, and for the most part, the Net is in private hands. Moreover, self-regulation is beginning to show signs of improvement in some areas, as in the protection of privacy, while working less well in others, such as protecting children from inappropriate content. In still other areas, such as protecting consumers from on-line criminals, it is clear that the government must step in forcefully. No one can predict whether or not the private sector will police itself sufficiently in cyberspace. If it succeeds, within democratic frameworks, we will have a new model for governance. If it fails, the government will need to intervene once again, reinvigorated for a regulatory role by outraged citizens. We will have lost an important chance to test a new, possibly more democratic method of governance for the twenty-first century.

It is also clear that we badly need further leaps of the imagination in policy making. So far, the policy makers have been timid, too influenced by existing interest groups and too bound by the past—unlike the technologists who thrive by abandoning the past. In some public policy areas, such as telecommunications regulation, we should totally abandon our traditional regulatory approach. We have to stop building on nineteenth-century regulatory policy and examine the problems we face as if we were beginning anew. Sometimes, radical change fails. But the technologies we have at hand are so different from those that existed when our regulatory schemes for telecommunications and broadcasting began that we owe it to ourselves to try a sharp break with the past.

Finally, it is also clear that the United States will continue to lead the Net's development—its technologies, its applications, and its legal and regulatory framework. The happy confluence of basic twenty-first-century

American values—free expression of ideas; openness to change; the free flow of technology, ideas, products, people and capital; respect for private property, diversity, and the work ethic—provides the rich broth for the rapid evolution of the Net in the United States. In turn, the Net's diffusion around the world enhances American economic, political, and cultural power. The global impact of the Net on rising living standards and the advance of democratic values in many countries is in the U.S. interest. Important transitional nations, such as China and India, can only benefit themselves by promoting the free and open use of the Net.

Of course, not all of the Net's effects will be positive or transforming. The worst dictatorships, such as those in North Korea, Cuba, and Iraq, will close off the lives of their citizens from the Net. Such regimes will be tempted to strike out at the Net with cyber-warfare and could cause serious disruptions. Drug dealers, international criminal gangs, and terrorists will also attempt to both use and attack the Net. Citizens in countries such as Sierra Leone or Rwanda, which have seen the total breakdown of civil society, will be basically untouched.

Nevertheless, the Net is on the side of history. Those who try to stop it to repress their people will weaken their nations and fall further into irrelevance. Those who attack it will stimulate new countermeasures to protect it. If we can develop new ways to provide wider access, even the poorest and most remote of the world's inhabitants can see some benefit.

Toward that end, there are a number of conclusions and specific suggestions to be drawn from the preceding chapters. In particular, there are specific activities that governments and the private sector could engage in that would enhance the Net's ability to improve people's lives.

DIGITAL MEASUREMENTS AND STATISTICS

We need better measurements of the Net and its economic and social effects. All sound policies begin with sound data. *Nations need to agree both internally and internationally on standardizing the measurements of the digital economy.* Not only are measurements of the Net and electronic commerce important in and of themselves, they are also crucial to determining the broader economic changes in productivity, employment, growth, and trade spurred by the Net. According to two top economists at the U.S. Bureau of the Census, John Haltiwanger and Ron Jarmin, "[t]here is widespread belief that significant changes to the U.S. statistical system are needed if we are to track the growth and impact of the digital economy."[1] Haltiwanger and Jarmin believe that new measurements should complement existing measurements and leverage existing data resources, but they do recommend new standard measurements in five areas:

1. Physical and software infrastructure, including investments in computers, telecommunications, software, networks, traffic, and depreciation;
2. E-commerce, including measures of business-to-business commerce, digital vs. nondigital goods and services, and transactions vs. no transactions (e.g., customer service responses, information requests);
3. Firm and industry structure, including location, industry, size and organizational structure of businesses, change in input mix (i.e., capital, labor, inventories) and relationships with other businesses (outsourcing);
4. Demographic and worker characteristics, including occupations, skills, education, age, and gender; and
5. Price behavior, including price deflators, price differentials, and price dispersion across producers.

The United States took an important step on March 2, 2000, when for the first time, the Department of Commerce reported on on-line retail sales for the 1999 holiday period and promised to begin reporting business-to-business statistics in 2001. These types of data need to be standardized and measured not only within the United States, but internationally as well. The Organization for Economic Cooperation and Development and perhaps other international organizations that include developing countries need to take the lead in securing international agreement on measurements and providing assistance to countries in adopting them. In addition to these purely economic measurements, we should standardize measurements of the Net's social impact, as well, in particular the "digital divide," or the differences in on-line access and usage between different groups both within and between nations.

NET READINESS

Nations and states do not have comparable and reliable methods of understanding their readiness to use the Net. Just as important as measuring the impact of information technology and the Net on our economies is measuring the readiness of nations, states, and localities for electronic commerce and the other uses of the Net. *Regions should be able to understand their readiness, both in absolute terms and in relation to each other.* The results of such understanding should allow nations, regions, or communities to invest their resources better to plan for the future and to be competitive. A number of formats have been developed to accomplish this. The first of these was developed by the Computer Systems Policy Project (CSPP) in 1998 and produces a grid ranking four stages of readiness against a variety of capabilities and activities. Stage One of readiness indicates that the physical infrastructure for full use of the Net is not yet fully deployed. Stage Two occurs when the basic infrastructure is in place and businesses and governments start to use it, principally for internal transactions. Stage Three is when most citizens have access at home, work, or school and when businesses and governments include on-line transactions in their basic operations. Stage Four is full broadband deployment of the infrastructure and advanced competitive usage in all sectors of society.²

The CSPP guide measures readiness against these four stages in six broad areas:

1. Infrastructure capabilities, including available local backbone for telephone, cable, broadcast, and wireless services, as well as the presence of local Internet service providers (ISPs) with sufficient capacities and reliability;
2. Access to critical services, including the availability and affordability of a range of quality services for small-business, residential, and large-business users, and a good choice for all users between competitive services;
3. Citizens on-line, including access for citizens at home, at work, at school, and at public access points such as public libraries;
4. Business on-line, including a large number of businesses with registered domain names and full-service Web sites, as well as the widespread use of networks for use in most internal business functions and for retail and business-to-business transactions;
5. Government on-line, including the use of government Web sites for on-line government transactions and for internal government operations—procurement, accounting, personnel, etc.; and
6. Plans for community growth, including plans to remove legislative and regulatory barriers, the building of community on-line resources, and the full use of the Net in school curriculum and operations.

The CSPP guide is available on the Web at *www.cspp.org* for communities and other jurisdictions that wish to use it.

Another readiness guide that is geared more toward national use is one created by the Asia-Pacific Economic Cooperation group's steering group on electronic commerce. This tool was developed for the use of Asia-Pacific countries and measures six areas of readiness:

1. Basic infrastructure and technology, including telecommunications, cable, broadcast and Internet access;
2. Access to necessary services, including ISP availability, penetration, competition, pricing, and usage;
3. Current level and type of use of the Internet, including business, government, and other institutions;
4. Promotion and facilitation activities, including initiatives to raise public awareness and to promote use among small and medium-sized businesses and the disabled;
5. Skills and human resources, including the use of the Net in schools and other educational institutions; and
6. Positioning for the digital economy, including policies on taxation, legal framework, electronic signatures, copyright, content, and privacy.[3]

The newest such guide was produced by the Center for International Development at Harvard University and is called "Readiness for the Networked World: A Guide for Developing Countries."[4] This guide builds on the Computer Systems Policy Project guide, focusing on developing-country issues such as wireless communications and education. It would be useful for an international agency such as the UN Development Program to publish an annual report on worldwide Net readiness.

SECTORAL ISSUES

Governments have not paid the same organized attention to public policy issues involving the Net and its impact on specific sectors as they have to generic issues such as privacy and taxation. Together, the readiness tools discussed above are very comprehensive, but both miss one important area that should be added—the readiness of individual sector public policy frameworks in specific areas of economic and social life. Among the most important are banking and insurance regulation, health care administration and regulation, government services, educational accreditation and licensing, securities trading regulation, and retail consumer protection.

Governments at both the national and state levels need to assess each of these areas individually and develop a plan to deal with each of the issues raised, working jointly with the private sector. All in all, the use of measurements and readiness tools such as those discussed above would not only guide government officials themselves, but would help educate a public that badly needs to understand the role of the Net in their national or local economy.

GOVERNMENT ORGANIZATION AND STRATEGY

As we have seen, governments have not yet reorganized to deal with the public policy challenges of the Net. For the most part, in fact, the Net is causing governments to reorganize as government services move on-line: the traditional government bureaucracy flattens and individual civil servants become more professional. But as for organizing for the public policy side specifically, although there is no need for large new government bureaucracies to deal with Net issues, *governments do need to think about making permanent the temporary interagency committees (such as the Information Infrastructure Task Force in the United States) they have set up.* Public interest is fleeting and individual politicians change, so some permanence is needed to help anchor policy.

The best model is a small office headed by an official who reports to the president or prime minister with support from a permanent interdepartmental committee representing the departments most concerned. In the United States, this would include the White House staff; the departments of Commerce, Treasury, State, Defense, Justice, Education, and Health and Human Services; the office of the U.S. Trade Representative; and the National Science Foundation. The office would also work with Congress and the independent agencies, such as the Federal Trade Commission.

Legislative bodies also need to examine their own committee structures to determine if they need improvement. For example, in the United States, the commerce committees may need a new subcommittee with a specific charter to examine Net issues rather than "telecommunications" issues. Such subcommittees would have to be wary of jurisdictional boundaries, but they would also provide a powerful "bully pulpit" to allow the emergence of a congressional spokesperson on this subject. A new subcommittee would also supplant the more informal and unofficial Internet Caucus that has begun to give the issue visibility in Congress. The states also need to examine their capacities to deal with the Net; perhaps the National Governors Association task force could recommend a common solution.

Individual government departments also need to look at their objectives, strategies, and organization in light of the Net's impact. For example, the foreign policy community, including the Departments of State and Defense, as well as foreign and defense ministries in other key countries should be asking a number of questions:

—Do we really understand the challenges the Net poses and are our objectives in line with the new realities? For example, if the global digital divide is widening the gap between rich and poor nations, how are we addressing that? Do new threats arise and are our priorities correct in addressing them?

—Is the correct international organization structure in place? Is it sufficient to oversee the global reach of the Net? Can it deal with the nonstate actors that the Net is empowering?

—As we seek to spread democracy around the world, are we taking full advantage of the possibilities of the Net? Just as old media such as radio (Voice of America and Radio Free Europe) were used during the Cold War, are we taking full advantage of the Net?

EDUCATION AND THE WORKFORCE

Nations must do more to prepare their citizens, especially their young people, to join the new, highly skilled workforce. The Net provides a remarkable opportunity to provide employment opportunities for the citizens of all nations. Not only are high-technology jobs plentiful and growing, but they are also far more lucrative than other jobs. But the opportunity is accompanied by a daunting challenge: How can nations produce a workforce in large enough numbers to meet the need?

As we have seen, the shortage of high-technology workers is a major barrier to the growth of the Net in many countries. Moreover, lower-skilled jobs in both factories and offices will continue to be displaced by information technology and automation tools. Demographic changes in many countries will further affect workers and national workforces. For example, in many industrial countries, the workforce and the population are growing older. In others, the workforce is expanding to include women and other groups that have been excluded or untapped in the past. Immigration patterns also play a role in the changing workforce.

Thus, although education reform and lifelong training are important answers, they are not the only ones. Carol D'Amico, co-author of *Workforce 2020*, has suggested five strategies for the U.S. government, based on all of these factors:

1. Analyze immigration policies and their effect on high-skilled jobs. Can nations find ways to increase the number of skilled immigrants in ways that are politically acceptable? For example, should the United States grant automatic citizenship to anyone earning an American Ph.D. in science, engineering, or mathematics?

2. Examine social security policies and their effect on participation in the workforce by older workers. Should older skilled workers continue to be discouraged from working by social security rules that cut their benefits if they earn too much?

3. Stimulate strategies to improve education. Despite years of effort at educational reform in the United States, student performance is still poor. We need to try harder.

4. Develop a user-friendly labor-market information system. We need community-based systems to help workers find jobs and training, using partnerships between local government, labor unions, and businesses.

5. Use organizations to draw into the labor force former welfare recipients, former military personnel, and the unemployed. The private sector must become more engaged on seeking workers in previously untapped quarters.[5]

Governments should also make maximum use of the Net itself in all of these tasks. It should not only be a central tool in the reform of elementary and secondary education, but can be used as a global resource in keeping education professionals, economists, government officials, and the public everywhere up to date on what works and what does not.

REGULATION AND COMPETITION

The mantras of telecommunications liberalization, deregulation, and privatization have been accepted almost everywhere, yet they are being effectively accomplished in a manner consistent with technological progress almost nowhere. That is not to say that many countries, including the United States, have not made enormous progress toward these goals. But most countries are inching toward them with small, incremental steps, when some, at least, could be kicking the ball over the goal line. The reasons proffered for the slow progress to date include the need to deal with incumbent monopolies and to make a phased transition to competition.

The legal issues now, with incremental liberalization, seem to have reached the zenith of complexity; could they be any worse if we abandoned regulation and let the competition laws govern the telecommunications and broadcasting industries? Aren't we confident enough about the pace of technology to believe that it can outrun monopoly behavior? Haven't we enough faith in our courts to trust that they will deal with cases of illegal business conduct that hinders free competition? Many commentators have noted, for example, that the new competition issue that technology raises is the "lock in" often achieved by the early dominance of a standard enshrining the intellectual property of one company. Yet no one seriously proposes regulation of, for example, the software industry—a "Federal Software Commission." We expect the antitrust laws to deal with the situation—as they are in the Microsoft case. It is time to think the same way about telecommunications. *Governments should start with a clean slate, set a date for the abandonment of their telecommunications regulatory systems, and let those responsible for competition laws monitor the results.*

UNIVERSAL ACCESS: PUBLIC AND PRIVATE PARTNERSHIPS

In an unregulated world, the old concept of subsidized and regulated universal service cannot work. *Most important, price decreases due to intense competition and rapid innovation will play the biggest role in providing access for everyone.* And yet government cannot totally abandon responsibility for at least creating an equal playing field so everyone has a fair chance at participation in the digital age. How can they accomplish universal access without regulation? The best answer is to work with the private sector, which also has a vested interest in universal access. Market expansion has always been a goal of the private sector, but it is particularly so in the case of the Net, since its value rises exponentially with the number of people connected to it.

Therefore, *governments should use public funds to assist with Net connections to schools, hospitals, libraries, and other public institutions.* However, these funds should come from general revenues, not from special taxes on the very services government is trying to stimulate (e.g., advanced telecommunications services), and they should be publicly debated, not passed in the dead of night. The public should be informed and no one should be surprised. The funding should not go to subsidize any industry, but should flow directly to the users.

The private sector should participate in these programs, not only as suppliers but as donators of equipment, software, and most importantly, know-how. People in high-technology careers are doing well in our society. They also tend to be thoughtful and are already volunteering in great numbers in schools and community programs. They can do more, and their companies can provide critical support with time off and financial assistance. We should set a national goal of 100 percent access and participation for young people and use both government funding and the private-sector spirit of volunteerism to achieve it.

PRIVACY

Nowhere has public concern about the Net been greater than in the area of privacy. Concerns about the invasion of personal privacy are deep, they exist globally, and they differ in the type of concern from country to country. While some regions such as the European Union have turned to regulation for the solution, the United States, at least for the time being, is inclined to see if industry can police itself. To date, the record is moderately good, and the private sector has made a great deal of progress, both technological and organizational, with business changing its operations to protect the privacy of its customers and employees.

The problem is that business still has not done enough, particularly in the area of enforcement, prompting the Federal Trade Commission in early 2000 to call for national legislation. Therefore, *businesses must do more to provide the best assurances for privacy.* It must do more not only because it has to deal with the privacy issue, but also because privacy is a kind of test case. If the private sector can successfully meet the privacy challenge, it will have demonstrated that it can take the lead in dealing with Net issues. If it fails, and the public loses confidence in its ability to provide leadership, it could lose more than just the privacy wars. It could see backsliding in many other areas of regulation and the return of more government control and even ownership in some countries. As the business community—particularly high-technology businesses—deals with privacy and considers the investment of resources in ensuring it, business leaders must take in this broader point of view.

CONTENT

If high-technology industry has to met the challenge of protecting privacy as a kind of litmus test for private-sector control of the Net, then the media and content industries must do more to meet the challenge of objectionable content. Perhaps the producers of films, the broadcasters, and the recorders of music will argue that they are not responsible for the existence of child pornography or neo-Nazi material. But just as police departments and community groups have jointly learned that neighborhoods full of trash, broken windows, and profanity breed muggings, rapes, and murders, so too do the soft pornography and violence of films, television shows, and songs create a culture that is then able to tolerate much worse. A kind of cultural Grisham's law operates in which bad content drives out the good.

High-technology industry should continue to develop filtering techniques, educational materials, and other tools to help parents deal with content on the Net, but in the end, the content producers need to behave responsibly. They themselves are the greatest threat to the First Amendment, because if they do not change the overall direction and tone of our film, music, broadcasting, and publishing industries, public outrage will eventually result in government censorship. Perhaps government could push the content industry in the right direction by withholding government support in areas such as global copyright enforcement and piracy protection for the film and recording industries, until content providers begin to act more responsibly.

INTERNATIONAL ORGANIZATIONS

International organizations need to continue and even intensify their work on taxation, standards, legal frameworks, intellectual property, encryption, and other issues. Although there does not appear to be an immediate or pressing need for a new international organization to deal with these areas, such a need may arise in the future. Progress has been slow or difficult on two issues in particular: the broad legal framework and consumer protection. Governments should begin to consider how they will deal with these areas if faster progress is not made, or if there is backsliding on other issues.

A FINAL WORD

Undoubtedly, the digital age will surprise us. New issues and crises will appear. Issues that are now divisive will melt away and historians will wonder what the fuss was about. Of one thing we can be sure: The digital age will not be the last revolutionary wave to challenge humanity. The Net changes our institutions, but it does not change us, ourselves, our individual beings. The revolution within ourselves awaits the next great wave of technology—in genetics and biology—which will be made possible largely by the very advances in information technology and advanced computing that created the Internet.

The new sciences of nanotechnology, genetic engineering, and robotics will combine the advanced computing and communications networking technologies of the Net with those of molecular biology, genetics, and neuroscience, perhaps finally to duplicate human intelligence or even sentience. Machines that are self-aware and that can replicate themselves or other bio-machine entities have been the staple of science fiction writers for a century. But they may be closer to reality than we think.

In a controversial article in *Wired* magazine in April 2000, Bill Joy, co-founder and chief scientist of Sun Microsystems, made the case that scientists will be capable of producing such entities within the next few decades.[6] He argued that they could be superior to *homo sapiens* from an evolutionary standpoint and could replace us. Joy proposed a new Pugwash conference series at which scientists and policy-makers could meet to forge an understanding of these developments, much as the original Pugwash conferences helped deal with the threat from nuclear weapons by bringing together nuclear scientists and arms-control experts from around the world.

I agree. Such a series of high-level conferences could cover both the more timely issues that Net technology has raised as well as the longer-term and more profound issues of the ultimate direction in which this still-new technology is headed. One thing is clear: The next wave of scientific advance will bring public policy dilemmas that will make today's Net controversies seem like the last whimpers of doves before a summer thunderstorm.

Notes

Preface

[1] Daniel Patrick Moynihan, *Pandaemonium: Ethnicity in International Politics* (New York: Oxford University Press, 1993).

[2] Daniel Bell, *The Coming of Post-Industrial Society* (New York: Basic Books, 1973).

Chapter 1

[1] Ithiel de Sola Pool, *Technologies without Boundaries* (Cambridge, Mass: Harvard University Press, 1990).

[2] Richard John, *Spreading the News: The American Postal System from Franklin to Morse* (Cambridge, Mass.: Harvard University Press, 1995).

[3] Daniel Bell, *The Coming of Post-Industrial Society* (New York: Basic Books, 1973), p. 3.

[4] Fritz Machlup, *The Production and Distribution of Knowledge in the United States* (Princeton: Princeton University Press, 1962).

[5] Marc Porat, "The Information Economy: Definition and Measurement," U.S. Department of Commerce, 1977.

[6] Internet Society on-line history at *www.pbs.org/internet/timeline/index.html.*

[7] As reproduced at www.cs.columbia.edu/~hgs/Internet/definition.html.

[8] Al Gore, Speech to ITU ministerial meeting, Buenos Aires, March 21, 1994, copy of speech obtained from the Office of the Vice President.

[9] "The Emerging Digital Economy II," U.S. Department of Commerce, Washington, D.C., June 1999.

[10] Information Technology Association of America Action Plan, available at *www. itaa.org/actionplan.*

[11] "Bridging the Gap: Information Technology Skills for a New Millennium," ITAA report available at www.itaa.org/workforce/studies.

[12] William Gibson, *Neuromancer* (New York: Ace Books, 1984).

[13] "The Emerging Digital Economy," U.S. Department of Commerce, Washington, D.C., April 1998.

[14] "The Emerging Digital Economy II," p. 5.

[15] Figure from Forrester Research, Inc., as reported in "The Click Here Economy," *Business Week,* June 22, 1998, p. 62.

[16] "The Emerging Digital Economy II," p. 5.

[17] Michael Dertouzos, *What Will Be* (New York: HarperCollins, 1997).

[18] "The Emerging Digital Economy," p. 4.

[19] Computer Systems Policy Project, Global Electronic Commerce paper, Washington D.C., 1997, available at www.cspp.org.

[20] Shop.org, Boston Consulting Group, quoted in "Clicks and Mortar," William M. Bulkeley, *Wall Street Journal*, July 17, 2000, p. R-4.

[21] The Emerging Digital Economy II, p. 16.

[22] Ibid., p. 38.

[23] Ibid.

Chapter 2

[1] Regis McKenna, *Real Time: Preparing for the Age of the Never Satisfied Customer* (Cambridge, Mass.: Harvard Business School Press, 1999), p. 3.

[2] Diane Coyle, *The Weightless World*, (Cambridge, Mass, MIT Press, 1997).

[3] "Ministerial Declaration," European Ministerial Conference on Global Information Networks, Bonn, July 6–8, 1997, p. 2, available from the European Commission, Brussels.

[4] Brian Kahin and Charles Nesson, eds., *Borders in Cyberspace* (Cambridge, Mass.: MIT Press, 1997).

[5] "The Emerging Digital Economy," U.S. Department of Commerce, Washington, D.C., April 1998.

[6] Robert Solow, "We'd Better Watch Out," *New York Times Book Review*, July 12, 1987, p. 6.

[7] Solow, "We'd Better Watch Out"; Steven Roach, "America's Technology Dilemma: A Profile of the Information Economy," *Morgan Stanley Economic Newsletter*, April 22, 1987, p. 2.

[8] Erik Brynjolfsson and Lorin Hitt, "Beyond the Productivity Paradox," Communications of the Association for Computing Machinery, August 1998.

[9] Daniel Sichel, *The Computer Revolution: An Economic Perspective* (Washington, D.C.: Brookings Institution Press, 1997).

[10] Alan Greenspan, testimony before the Committee on the Budget, United States Senate, January 21, 1997, available at www.federalreserve.gov.

[11] Lee W. McKnight and Joseph P. Bailey, "An Introduction to Internet Economics, in McKnight and Bailey, eds., *Internet Economics* (Cambridge, Mass.: MIT Press, 1997), p. 4.

[12] "The Economic and Social Impact of Electronic Commerce: Preliminary Findings and Research Agenda," OECD Directorate for Science, Technology, and Industry, August 1998, p. 19.

[13] "The Emerging Digital Economy II," U.S. Department of Commerce, Washington, D.C., June 1999.

[14] Marshall McLuhan, *Understanding Media: The Extensions of Man* (New York: McGraw-Hill, 1964), p. 8.

[15] Ibid., p. 61.

[16] Robert O. Keohane and Joseph S. Nye, Jr., "Power and Interdependence in the Information Age," *Foreign Affairs*, September/October 1998, pp. 81–94.

[17] Jack Weatherford, *History of Money* (New York: Crown Publishers, 1997).

Chapter 3

[1] "Reducing Uncertainty in Our Health Care," IBM Living in the Information Society Series, 1997, available at www.ibm.com/ibm/publicaffairs.

[2] Sharon Machlis, "Web links cancer patients to drug trials," CNN Interactive, October 14, 1998, available at www.cnn.com.

[3] Michael Dertouzos, *What Will Be* (New York: HarperCollins, 1997), pp. 13–14.

[4] Linda Harris, *Health and the New Media* (New York: Lawrence Erlbaum Associates, 1995).

[5] National Center for Education Statistics, U.S. Department of Education, available at www.nces.ed.gov.

[6] U.S. National Commission on Excellence in Education, "A Nation at Risk: The Imperative for Educational Reform" Washington, D.C., 1983.

[7] U.S. Office of Technology Assessment, "Teachers and Technology: Making the Connection," Washington, D.C., April 1995.

[8] President Bill Clinton, "State of the Union Address, " January 23, 1996, available at www.whitehouse.gov.

[9] National Center for Education Statistics, "Digest of Education Statistics: 1997," available at www.nces.ed.gov/edstats/index.

[10] Willard Daggett and David Nohara, "Technology in Education: Excellence vs. Equity," International Center for Leadership in Education, Schenectady, N.Y., 1997.

[11] Donald P. Ely, *Trends in Educational Technology* (New York: Syracuse University Press, 1996), p. 37.

[12] As quoted in "Education Boost for Net Learning," BBB Online Network, November 6, 1998, p. 1, available at www.bbc.co.uk/hi/english/education.

[13] Pamela Mendels, "U.S. Program Wires Remote Native American Reservations," *New York Times*, May 6, 1998, available at www.nyt.com/search/daily/bl...7362+15+wAAA_education.

[14] Eileen Cotton, *The Online Classroom: Teaching with the Internet* (Bloomington, Ind.: EDINFO Press, 1998).

[15] Peter Harris, "A Teacher's Place," available at www.pluto.njcc.com/~harris.

[16] Henry A. Spille, David Stewart, and Eugene Sullivan, *External Degrees in the Information Age* (Phoenix, Ariz.: Oryx, 1997).

[17] Donald Tapscott, *The Digital Economy* (New York: McGraw-Hill, 1996), pp. 198–99.

[18] "Participation in Adult Education," National Center for Education Statistics, U.S. Department of Education, Washington, D.C., 1996.

[19] "Higher Education: The Lessons of Experience," International Bank for Reconstruction and Development, Washington, D.C., 1994.

[20] Richard Judy and Carol D'Amico, *Workforce 2020: Work and Workers in the Twenty-First Century* (Indianapolis, Ind.: Hudson Institute, 1997), p. 140.

[21] Jeri Clausing, "Costa Rica to Try Online Elections," New York Times on the Web, October 22, 1997.

[22] David Osborne and Ted Gaebler, *Reinventing Government* (New York: Addison-Wesley, 1992).

[23] "Government.direct: A Prospectus for Electronic Delivery of Government Services," London, November 1996, section 9.2, available from greenpaper@citu.gov.uk.

[24] David Norfolk, "Power in the Wrong Hands," *IBM Police and Justice* (a publication of IBM United Kingdom), London, 1998.

[25] "Government.direct," section 9.9.

[26] "Reengineering through Information Technology: NPR Recommendations," available at www.npr.gov/library/annrpt/vp-rpt96/appendix/infotech.

[27] President William J. Clinton, "Memorandum for the Heads of Executive Departments and Agencies on Electronic Government," White House, December 17, 1999, p. 1, available at www.pub.whitehouse.gov.

[28] Robert Pear, "Government to Use Vast Database to Track Deadbeat Parents," New York Times On the Web, September 22, 1997.

[29] "The Digital State: How State Governments Are Using Digital Technology," Progress and Freedom Foundation, Washington, D.C., August 1997, p. 3.

Chapter 4

[1] Bill Gates, *The Road Ahead* (New York: Penguin, 1995), p. 206.

[2] Jack Weatherford, *A History of Money* (New York: Crown, 1997).

[3] "The Future of Money," Thomas A. Bass, Wired, www.wired.com/wired/archive/4.10/wriston.

[4] Greg Ip, "Credit Crunches Aren't What They Used to Be," *Wall Street Journal*, October 7, 1998, p. A18.

[5] Derek Leebaert, *The Future of the Electronic Marketplace* (Cambridge, Mass.: MIT Press, 1998), p. 103.

[6] John Authers, "Citigroup Targets Web-Site Sales," *Financial Times* on-line, www.ft.com, November 16, 1998.

[7] Frank Byrt, "Mortgage Refinancings Go High-Tech," *Wall Street Journal*, November 17, 1998, p. 8.

[8] Ibid.

[9] Wayne Arnold, "Asian Banks Trailing in Technology, Look to West," *Wall Street Journal*, October 19, 1998, p. A23.

[10] Michael K. Evans, "Trading on the Internet," *Industry Week*, December 18, 1997, p. 140.

[11] Jean Gora, "The Internet and Online Services," LOMA (an international association of insurance companies), New York, 1995, p. 2.

[12] Francis Cairncross, *The Death of Distance: How the Communications Revolution Will Change Our Lives* (Cambridge, Mass.: Harvard Business School Press, 1997), p. 122.

[13] Leslie Walker, "Internet Retail Sales Rising Sharply," *Washington Post*, November 18, 1998, p. C11.

[14] "Internet Shopping: An Ernst and Young Special Report," January 1998, p. 6.

[15] George Anders, "Internet Advertising, Just Like Its Medium, Is Pushing Boundaries," *Wall Street Journal*, November 30, 1998, pp. A1, A6.

[16] "Internet Shopping," p. 25.

[17] Quoted in Leebaert, *The Future of the Electronic Marketplace*, p. 64.

[18] "Challenges: Plugged into the IT Revolution," FT.com (*Financial Times*), October 13, 1998, available at *www.ft.com/hippocampus/qa467e*.

[19] "How Network Computing Is Changing Industrial Processes," IBM Living in the Information Society series, available at www.ibm.com/ibm/publicaffairs.

[20] John Zysman and Andrew Schwartz, "Reunifying Europe in an Emerging World Economy: Economic Heterogeneity, New Industrial Option and Political Choices," paper delivered at the Berkeley Roundtable on the International Economy, University of California, Berkeley, March 29, 1998, p. 4.

[21] Haig Simonian, "Case Study: U.S. Carmakers," *Financial Times*, November 3, 1998, available on FT.com, www.ft.com/hippocampus/qbba96.

[22] Timothy J. Sturgeon, "Does Manufacturing Still Matter? The Organizational Delinking of Production from Innovation," paper presented at the International Conference on New Product Development and Production Networks, Berlin, March 20–22, 1997, p. 5.

[23] Richard B. Schmitt, "More People Consult the Firm of Cyber, Web and Dot-Com," *Wall Street Journal*, August 2, 1999, p. B1.

Chapter 5

[1] Alan F. Westin, *Privacy and Freedom* (New York: Atheneum, 1967), pp. 23–25.

[2] President William J. Clinton and Vice President Al Gore, "A Framework for Global Electronic Commerce," White House, July 1, 1997, available at www.whitehouse.gov.

[3] Westin, *Privacy and Freedom*, p. 27.

[4] Ibid.

[5] Ibid. p. 338.

[6] Cited in ibid., p. 299.

[7] United States Department of Health, Education, and Welfare, *Records, Computers, and the Rights of Citizens: Report of the Secretary's Advisory Committee on Automated Personal Data Systems* (Washington, D.C.: U.S. Government Printing Office, 1973).

[8] "Guidelines on the Protection of Privacy and Transborder Flows of Personal Information," Organization for Economic Cooperation and Development, Paris, September 23, 1980.

[9] H. Jeff Smith, *Managing Privacy: Information Technology and Corporate America* (Research Triangle Park: University of North Carolina Press, 1994), p. 10.

[10] Westin, *Privacy and Freedom*, p. 338.

[11] Nina Bernstein, "Lives on File: Privacy Devalued in Information Economy," New York Times On the Web, June 12, 1997.

[12] Clinton and Gore, "A Framework for Global Electronic Commerce," p. 11.

[13] Ibid., p. 18.

[14] "Public Workshop on Consumer Privacy on the Global Information Infrastructure," Federal Trade Commission, available at www.ftc.gov/privacy.

[15] David Madine, testimony before the Subcommittee on Courts and Intellectual Property, House Judiciary Committee, United State House of Representatives, March 26, 1998, p. 2.

[16] Ibid., p. 8.

[17] "Privacy Principles for U.S. Financial Institutions," American Bankers Association, Washington, D.C., 1997.

[18] "The Protection of Personal Data in Electronic Commerce," Information Technology Industry Council, Washington, D.C., December 1997, p. 1.

[19] "Principles on Notice and Choice Procedures for Online Information Collection and Distribution by Online Operators," Interactive Services Association, Silver Spring, Md., 1997.

[20] "Common Views Paper: Electronic Commerce," International Information Industry Congress, Frankfurt, Germany, September 1999.

[21] "Gore Calls for 'Electronic Bill of Rights'; Urges Passage of Laws Bolstering Privacy," *Electronic Commerce and Law Report,* Bureau of National Affairs, Washington, D.C., August 5, 1998, p. 985.

[22] "Commerce Secretary Criticizes Industry over Absence of Enforcement in Privacy Plan," *Electronic Commerce and Law Report,* Bureau of National Affairs, Washington, D.C., July 1, 1998, p. 847.

[23] "FTC Sets End-of-Year Deadline for Effective Industry Self-Regulation," *Electronic Commerce and Law Report,* Bureau of National Affairs, Washington, D.C., July 29, 1998, p. 953.

[24] Ibid.

[25] Online Privacy Alliance Mission Statement, *www.privacyalliance.org/mission*, July 1998.

[26] Heinz Zourek, "Information Privacy: An Example of Necessary Regulation for the European Community's Internal Market," speech at Harvard University, April 1997, p. 5.

[27] Noah Schachtman, "EU Privacy Law Is Awkward for U.S.," *Wired News, www. wired.com/news/business*, October 23, 1998.

[28] Simon Lazarus and Brett Kappel, "Protecting Privacy from Prying Eyes," *Legal Times,* May 1998, p. 14.

[29] William J. Drake, "Conclusions," in William J. Drake, ed., *The New Information Infrastructure: Strategies for U.S. Policy* (New York: Twentieth Century Fund Press, 1995), p. 357.

[30] Michael Laris, "Internet Police on the Prowl in China: Free Flow of Ideas Worries Leaders," *Washington Post,* October 24, 1998, p. A12.

[31] "Action for Change: IT Policy Plan 1997–98," Ministry of Research and Technology, Danish State Information Service, Copenhagen, November 1997, p. 8.

[32] "French Court Holds Service Provider Partly Liable in Nude-Photos Privacy Case," *Electronic Commerce and Law Report,* Bureau of National Affairs, Washington, D.C., July 15, 1998, p. 896.

[33] New York Times News Service, "Canada Tries to Bar Pro-Nazi View on Internet," *Washington Post,* August 1, 1998, p. 9.

[34] Mark Landler, "Bringing China on Line (With Official Blessing)," *New York Times,* October 20, 1998, p. B1.

[35] Don Tapscott, *Growing Up Digital: The Rise of the Net Generation* (New York: McGraw-Hill, 1998), pp. 244–45.

[36] *Janet Reno, Attorney General of the United States, et al. v. American Civil Liberties Union et al.,* 117 S.Ct. 2329 (1997).

[37] "A Framework for Global Electronic Commerce," p. 15.

[38] Ibid., p. 24.

[39] "Global Information Networks," declaration issued at the meeting of the Council of Ministers, European Union, in Bonn, Germany, July 8, 1997, p. 3.

[40] Ibid., p. 4.

[41] Ibid., p. 8.

[42] "U.S.-Japan Joint Statement on Electronic Commerce," Washington, D.C., May 15, 1998, pp. 2–3, available at www.ecommerce.gov.usjapan.

[43] "Towards the Age of the Digital Economy: For Rapid Progress in the Japanese Economy and World Economic Growth in the 21st Century," Ministry of International Trade and Industry, Government of Japan, Tokyo, April 1997, p. 20.

[44] "Child Safety on the Information Superhighway," Interactive Services Association/National Center for Missing and Exploited Children, Arlington, Va., 1994.

[45] "Internet Content and Youth Protection," Internet Communications Roundtable Resolution, Surrey, United Kingdom, December 1996.

[46] "Regardless of Frontiers: Protecting the Human Right to Freedom of Expression on the Global Internet," Global Internet Liberty Campaign, Washington, D.C., September 1998, p. 43.

[47] Ibid., p. 35.

[48] President William J. Clinton, speech, Anaheim, California, July 8, 1999, available at www.whitehouse.gov.

[49] Sir Donald Maitland, chair, "Report of the Independent Commission for Worldwide Telecommunications Development," International Telecommunications Union, Geneva, December 1984.

[50] "World Telecommunication Development Report 1998: Universal Access," International Telecommunications Union, Geneva, Switzerland, March 1998.

[51] Ibid, Box 4.1.

[52] "Falling Through the Net II: New Data on the Digital Divide," National Telecommunications and Information Administration, U.S. Department of Commerce, Washington, D.C., 1997.

[53] "Statement on Universal Access to Basic Communication and Information Service," transmitted by Secretary-General Kofi Annan to the UN General Assembly, New York, December 1997.

[54] "World Telecommunication Development Report," Appendices A-8, A-80.

[55] Dean Takahashi, "Likelihood of Weak Sales by PC Makers in 1st Quarter Helps Depress PC Stocks," *Wall Street Journal,* March 24, 1999, p. A3.

[56] "The National Information Infrastructure: Agenda for Action," U.S. Department of Commerce, September 1994, available at www.sunsite.unc.edu/nii.

[57] "Common Ground: Report of the U.S. National Information Infrastructure Advisory Council" (Washington, D.C.: U.S. Government Printing Office, March 1995).

[58] Conference Committee Report, House Report 104-458, Telecommunications Act of 1996.

[59] Christopher DeMuth, "The Strange Case of the E-Rate," American Enterprise Institute for Public Policy Research, Washington, D.C., August 1998.

[60] A Michael Noll, "The Costs of Competition: FCC Telecommunications Orders of 1997," *Telecommunications Policy* 22, no. 1 (1998), p. 55.

[61] Lawrence Gasman, "Universal Service: The New Telecommunications and Entitlements and Taxes," Policy Analysis series, Cato Institute, June 25, 1998, p. 3.

[62] Herbert Dordick, "The Social Consequences of Liberalization and Corporate Control in Telecommunications," in Drake, ed., *The New Information Infrastructure*, p. 156.

[63] Trevor Haywood, *Info Rich—Info Poor* (London: Bowker Saur, 1995), p. 77.

[64] "The Economic and Social Impact of Electronic Commerce: Preliminary Findings and Research Agenda," OECD Directorate for Science, Technology, and Industry, Committee for Information, Computer and Communications Policy, Ottawa, Ont., June 1998, p. 17.

[65] Michael Dertouzos, *What Will Be* (New York: HarperCollins, 1997), p. 324.

[66] "Internet Helps Stem Human Rights Abuses," CNN Interactive, www.cnn.com, June 16, 1999.

[67] John Pomfret, "Free Speech Is Flourishing Online," *Washington Post,* June 23, 1999, p. 18.

Chapter 6

[1] Alan Greenspan, "The American Economy in a World Context," speech at the Thirty-fifth Annual Conference on Bank Structure and Competition, Federal Reserve Bank of Chicago, Chicago, May 6, 1999, available at www.bog.frb.fed.us.

[2] J. Bradford De Long, "What 'New' Economy?" *Wilson Quarterly,* Autumn 1998, p. 20.

[3] Daniel E. Sichel, *The Computer Revolution: An Economic Perspective* (Washington, D.C.: Brookings Institution Press, 1997), p. 3.

[4] George Anders and Scott Thurm, "The Rocket under the Tech Boom: Big Spending by Basic Industries," *Wall Street Journal,* March 30, 1999, p. A1.

[5] Padmanabhan Srinagesh, "Internet Cost Structures and Interconnection Agreements," in Lee W. McKnight and Joseph P. Bailey, eds., *Internet Economics* (Cambridge, Mass.: MIT Press, 1997), p. 122.

[6] Donald S. Allen, "Where's the Productivity Growth (from the Information Technology Revolution)?" *Federal Reserve Bank of St. Louis Review,* March–April 1997, pp. 15–26.

[7] Ibid., p. 18.

[8] Erik Brynjolfsson and Loren Hitt, "Beyond the Productivity Paradox: Computers are the Catalyst for Bigger Changes," Communications of the Association for Computing Machinery, August 1998, p. 3.

[9] Ibid., p. 1.

[10] "The Emerging Digital Economy II," U.S. Department of Commerce, Washington, D.C., June 1999, pp. 15–31.

11 "The Economic and Social Impacts of Electronic Commerce," prepared for the OECD Ministerial Conference on Electronic Commerce, Ottawa, October 7–9, 1998, OECD Publications Service, Paris, pp. 11–13.

12 Greenspan, "The American Economy in a World Context."

13 Paul Romer, "The Outlook: Corporate Caveat: Dell or Be Delled," *Wall Street Journal,* May 10, 1999, p. 1.

14 Arthur J. Cordell, T. Ran Ide, Luc Soete, and Karin Kamp, *The New Wealth of Nations: Taxing Cyberspace* (Toronto: Between the Lines Press, 1997), p. 88.

15 "Disappearing Taxes: The Tap Runs Dry," *Economist,* May 31, 1997, p. 21.

16 Cordell et al., *The New Wealth of Nations,* p. 56.

17 "Selected Tax Policy Implications of Global Electronic Commerce," U.S. Department of the Treasury, Office of Tax Policy, November 1996, pp. 27–28.

18 Organization for Economic Cooperation and Development Model Tax Convention, Article 5.

19 Ned Maguire and Alan Levenson, "International Tax Issues in Electronic Commerce," Deloitte and Touche, New York, 1997, p. 17.

20 "Selected Tax Policy Implications," p. 29.

21 Ibid., p. 33.

22 Ibid., p. 39.

23 "Living in the Information Society: Taxation of the Internet," IBM Corporation, 1998, p. 6, available at www.ibm.com/ibm/publicaffairs.

24 Tim W. Ferguson, "Web Grab," *Forbes,* March 9, 1998, p. 125.

25 Ken Griffen, Paula D. Ladd, and Roy Whitehead, Jr., "Taxation of Internet Commerce," *CPA Journal,* January 1998, p. 44.

26 President William J. Clinton and Vice President Al Gore, "A Framework for Global Electronic Commerce," White House, July 1, 1997, p. 7, available at www.whitehouse.gov.

27 "Ministerial Declaration," European Ministerial Conference on Global Information Networks, Bonn, July 6–8, 1997, p. 4, available from the European Commission, Brussels.

28 Andre Vallerand, Chairman, "Electronic Commerce and Canada's Tax Administration: A Report to the Minister of National Revenue from the Minister's Advisory Committee on Electronic Commerce," Ottawa, April 1998.

29 Donald J. Johnston, speech at the *Wall Street Journal Europe* Fifth Annual CEO Summit, "Europe's New Digital Economy," London, September 8, 1998.

30 Quoted in Neil Winton, "Internet Tax Dodge Is Subtext of Global Conference," Yahoo! Technology News, October 7, 1998, p. 2, www.dailynews.yahoo.com/headlines/wr/story.

31 "CSPP Policy Agenda: Tax Neutrality," Computer Systems Policy Project, Washington, D.C., November 1997.

32 "Taxation of Electronic Commerce," International Information Industry Congress, Berlin, October 1998.

33 Renato Ruggiero, "A Borderless World," address to the ministerial conference of the OECD, Ottawa, Ontario, October 7, 1998.

34 United States Trade Representative comments on WTO Initiative on Global Electronic Commerce, Washington, D.C., May 20, 1998

35 Bruce Stokes, "Trade Friction in Cyberspace," *National Journal,* July 11, 1998, p. 1634.

36 "Statement of Thomas A. Ehrgood, Jr., International Trade Counsel, Digital Equipment Corporation, on behalf of the Information Technology Agreement Coalition," Subcommittee on Trade, House Ways and Means Committee, September 11, 1996, pp. 2–3.

[37] "Developing a Global Information Society: Industry Recommendations to the G-7 Meeting in Johannesburg," International Information Industry Congress, Frankfurt, May 6, 1996.

[38] William J. Clinton, "Memorandum for the Heads of Executive Departments and Agencies," White House, Washington, D.C., July 1, 1997, available at www.whitehouse.gov.

[39] U.S. Trade Representative, "Global Electronic Commerce: Proposal by the United States," General Council, World Trade Organization, Geneva, February 19, 1998, available from the Office of the U.S. Trade Representative, Washington, D.C.

[40] "Presentation by U.S. Ambassador Rita Hayes to the WTO General Council," Geneva, February 19, 1998, p. 6, available from the Office of the U.S. Trade Representative, Washington, D.C.

[41] "Declaration on Global Electronic Commerce," Ministerial Conference of the World Trade Organization, Geneva, May 20, 1998.

[42] "Electronic Commerce Covered by WTO Pact," Bureau of National Affairs, *Electronic Commerce and Law Report,* July 22, 1998, p. 927.

[43] Stephen Byers, speech to Social Market Foundation, London, February 28, 2000.

[44] Robert Pitofsky, "Antitrust Analysis in High-Tech Industries: A Nineteenth-century Discipline Addresses Twenty-first-century Problems," speech to the American Bar Association Antitrust Workshop, Scottsdale, Arizona, February 25, 1999.

Chapter 7

[1] Peter Huber, *Law and Disorder in Cyberspace: Abolish the FCC and Let Common Law Rule the Telecosm* (New York: Oxford University Press, 1997), p. 8.

[2] W. Russell Neuman, Lee McKnight, and Richard Jay Solomon, *The Gordian Knot: Political Gridlock on the Information Highway* (Cambridge: MIT Press, 1997), p. 160.

[3] "The Federalist, No. 62," in Jacob E. Cooke, ed., *The Federalist* (Middletown, Conn.: Wesleyan University Press, 1961), p. 421.

[4] Leslie D. Simon, ed., *Business Information Systems* (New York: American Telephone and Telegraph Company, 1996), p. 8.

[5] Henry Geller, "Reforming the U.S. Telecommunications Policymaking Process," in William J. Drake, ed., *The New Information Infrastructure: Strategies for U.S. Policy* (New York: Twentieth Century Fund Press, 1995), p. 125.

[6] Eli Noam, "Beyond Telecommunications Liberalization," in Drake, ed., *The New Information Infrastructure,* p. 41.

[7] Elizabeth Wasserman, "In Washington, the Phone Wars Rage and the Net Seeks Cover: As the Telecomm Act of 1996 Crumbles, the FCC and Kennard Face a Daunting Challenge," *Industry Standard,* August 24, 1998, p. 1.

[8] Neuman, McKnight, and Solomon, *The Gordian Knot,* p. xiii.

[9] Noam, "Beyond Telecommunications Liberalization," p. 32.

[10] Don Cruickshank, remarks at conference on "The Digital Economy in International Perspective: Common Construction or Regional Rivalry," Willard Hotel, Washington, D.C., May 27, 1999.

[11] Ben Petrazzini, "Global Telecom Talks: A Trillion Dollar Deal," Institute for International Economics, Washington, D.C., June 1996, p. 15.

[12] Cynthia Beltz, "Global Telecommunications Rules: The Race with Technology," *Issues in Science and Technology,* Spring 1997, p. 64.

[13] "Statement of Ambassador Charlene Barshefsky: Basic Telecom Negotiations," Office of the U.S. Trade Representative, Washington, D.C., February 15, 1997, p. 3.

[14] "Global Telecommunications to the Year 2000: The Impact on Corporate IT Strategies and Applications," *Economist* Intelligence Unit, London, 1996, p. 9.

[15] "Digital Tornado: The Internet and Telecommunications Policy," Federal Communications Commission, Office of Plans and Policy, Washington, D.C., March 1997, pp. ii–iii, 27–28.

[16] "Comments of the Internet Access Coalition Before the Federal Communications Commission," CC Docket No. 96-263, Washington, D.C., March 24, 1997, p. i.

[17] Letter from Representative Christopher Cox and Senator John McCain to William E. Kennard, FCC Chairman, March 18, 1999, copy provided to author.

[18] Geller, "Reforming the U.S. Telecommunications Policymaking Process," p. 126.

[19] Noam, "Beyond Telecommunications Liberalization," p. 49.

[20] "Precluding Regulation of Internet and Other Advanced Information Services—Containment Policy," Telecommunications Policy Backgrounder, Progress and Freedom Foundation, Washington, D.C., August 1997, p. 4.

[21] Huber, *Law and Disorder in Cyberspace*, p. 8.

[22] Jenna Greene, "Rewiring the FCC," *Legal Times,* May 15, 2000, pp. 1, 16.

[23] Frances Cairncross, *The Death of Distance: How the Communications Revolution Will Change Our Lives* (Cambridge, Mass.: Harvard Business School Press, 1997), pp. 156–57.

[24] "Report of the President's Commission on Critical Infrastructure Protection," Executive Office of the President, Washington, D.C., October 13, 1997, p. 7, available at www.pccip.gov.

[25] Ibid., p. A24.

[26] "The Clinton Administration's Policy on Critical Infrastructure Protection: Presidential Decision Directive 63," The White House, Washington, D.C., May 22, 1998, p. 2.

[27] "Report of the President's Commission on Critical Infrastructure Protection," p. 45.

[28] "Final Report of the Defense Science Board Task Force on Globalization and Security," Office of the Undersecretary of Defense for Acquisition and Technology, Washington, D.C., December 1999.

[29] "The Electronic Frontier: The Challenge of Unlawful Conduct Involving the Use of the Internet," Interagency Working Group on Unlawful Conduct on the Internet, Washington, D.C., March 2000, available at *www.usdoj.gov/criminal/cybercrime/unlawful.*

[30] Solveig Singleton, "Encryption Policy for the 21st Century: A Future without Government-Prescribed Key Recovery," Policy Analysis, Cato Institute, Washington, D.C., November 19, 1999, p. 7.

[31] Thomas Parenty, testimony before the Subcommittee on Courts and Intellectual Property of the U.S. House Judiciary Committee, March 4, 1999, p. 7.

[32] Paul Johnson, *A History of the Modern World: From 1917 to the 1980s* (London: Weidenfeld and Nicolson, 1983), pp. 397–400.

[33] Barbara A. McNamara, statement for the record before the Subcommittee on Courts and Intellectual Property of the U.S. House Judiciary Committee, March 4, 1999, pp. 4–5.

[34] Ronald D. Lee, statement before the Subcommittee on Courts and Intellectual Property of the U.S. House Judiciary Committee, March 4, 1999, pp. 2–3.

[35] Ed Gillespie, testimony before the House Subcommittee on Courts and Intellectual Property of the U.S. House Judiciary Committee, March 4, 1999, p. 6.

[36] Henry B. Wolfe, "The Myth of Superiority of American Encryption Products," Cato Institute, Washington, D.C., November 12, 1998, p. 3.

[37] Gillespie testimony, p. 4.

[38] Alan B. Davidson, testimony before the Subcommittee on Courts and Intellectual Property of the U.S. House Judiciary Committee, March 4, 1999, p. 5.

[39] Kenneth Dam et al., *Cryptography's Role in Securing the Information Society* (Washington, D.C.: National Academy Press, 1996), p. 3.

[40] Steven Levy, "Courting A Crypto Win," *Newsweek*, May 17, 1999, p. 85.

[41] "Encryption and Free Speech" (editorial), *Washington Post*, May 10, 1999, p. 24.

[42] Louis Freeh, "Encryption and Electronic Surveillance," speech before the Citizen's Crime Commission of New York, New York City, October 1, 1999.

[43] Lewis M. Branscomb and Brian Kahin, "Standards Processes and Objectives for the National Information Infrastructure," essay in *Standards Policy for Information Infrastructure*, Brian Kahin and Janet Abbate (Cambridge, Mass.: MIT Press, 1995), pp. 3–4.

[44] Internet Engineering Task Force Web site, at www.ietf.org.

[45] "Perspectives on the National Information Infrastructure: Ensuring Interoperability," Computer Systems Policy Project, Washington, D.C., February 1994, p. 5.

[46] Derek Leebaert, *Technology 2001: The Future of Computing and Communications* (Cambridge, Mass.: MIT Press, 1991), pp. 158–59.

[47] Branscomb and Kahin, *Standards Policy*, p. 17.

Chapter 8

[1] "Uniform Computer Information Transactions Act," draft legislation for approval at the National Conference of Commissioners on Uniform State Laws, Denver, Colo., July 23–30, 1999, p. 13.

[2] Ibid.

[3] President William J. Clinton and Vice President Al Gore, "A Framework for Global Electronic Commerce," White House, July 1, 1997, p. 11, available at www.whitehouse.gov.

[4] "CSPP Policy Agenda: Legal Framework," Computer Systems Policy Project, Washington, D.C., November 1997, p. 3.

[5] "Enabling E-Signature Laws Gain Popularity, Study Finds, NCCUSL Rejects Presumptions," *Electronic Commerce and Law Report*, Bureau of National Affairs, Washington, D.C., July 22, 1998, p. 915.

[6] Albert Gidari, John Morgan, and Perkins Cole, "Survey of Electronic and Digital Signature Legislative Initiatives in the United States," Internet Law and Policy Forum, September 12, 1997.

[7] "California Digital Signatures Regulations," California Administrative Code, Title 2, Section 22004, "Provisions for Adding New Technologies to the List of Acceptable Technologies."

[8] Amelia Boss, quoted in the Report to the House of Delegates of the Sections on Business Law, International Law and Practice, and Science and Technology, American Bar Association August 1977, p. 5.

[9] "Uniform Computer Information Transactions Act," p. 14.

[10] Ibid.

[11] Dan Greenwood, testimony before the Senate Commerce, Science, and Transportation Committee, July 15, 1998, quoted in *Electronic Commerce and Law Report* 3, no. 28 (July 22, 1998), p. 923.

[12] Theodore S. Barassi, "International Developments in Digital Signature Legislation," CertCo, New York, July 7, 1997, p. 9.

[13] "Background Report to the APEC Blueprint for Action on Electronic Commerce," APEC, Singapore, 1998.

[14] "Proposal for a European Parliament and Council Directive on a Common Framework for Electronic Signatures," European Commission, Brussels, May 13, 1998, p. 5.

[15] "A Global Action Plan for Business with Government toward Electronic Commerce," OECD, Toronto, October 1999, p. 14.

[16] Robert Pitofsky, opening remarks at workshop on "Consumer Protection in the Global Electronic Market," Washington, D.C., June 8, 1999, available at www.ftc.gov/hearings.

[17] Esther Dyson, *Release 2.0* (New York: Broadway Books, 1997), p. 133.

[18] Neil Kleinman, "Don't Fence Me In: Copyright, Property, and Technology," in Lance Strate and Ronald Jacobson, eds., *Communication and Cyberspace* (New York: Hampton Press, 1996), p. 60.

[19] Mike Godwin, *Cyber Rights: Defending Free Speech in the Digital Age* (New York: Random House, 1998), p. 163.

[20] Jack Valenti, speech at Summer Internet World, Chicago, July 16, 1998, available at www.mpaa.org/jack.

[21] "Forecasting a Robust Future: An Economic Study of the U.S. Software Industry," Business Software Alliance, Washington, D.C., June 16, 1999.

[22] Pamela Samuelson, "The Digital Rights War," *Wilson Quarterly*, Autumn 1998, p. 53.

[23] Dyson, *Release 2.0*, p. 142.

Chapter 9

[1] "Information Technology Research: Investing in Our Future," report of the President's Information Technology Advisory Committee, Washington, D.C., February 24, 1999, available at www.ccic.gov/ac/report.

[2] Bush quotation available at www.physics.uiuc.edu/general_info_vbush.html.

[3] Allen Bromley, "U.S. Technology Policy," Office of Science and Technology Policy, Executive Office of the President, Washington, D.C., September 26, 1990.

[4] Brian Kahin, *Building Information Infrastructure: Issues in the Development of the National Research and Education Network* (New York: McGraw-Hill, 1992), p. 11.

[5] "Perspectives on the National Information Infrastructure: CSPP's Vision and Recommendations for Action," Computer Systems Policy Project, Washington, D.C., January 12, 1993, p. 3.

[6] "The Information Infrastructure: Reaching Society's Goals," report of the Information Infrastructure Task Force Committee on Applications and Technology, National Institute of Standards and Technology, Washington, D.C., 1994, p. 2.

[7] President William J. Clinton, "Memorandum for the Heads of Executive Departments and Agencies: Electronic Commerce," White House, July 1, 1997, p. 5, available at www.whitehouse.gov.

[8] "Endless Frontier, Limited Resources: U.S. R&D Policy for Competitiveness," Council on Competitiveness, Washington, D.C., April 1996, p. 3.

[9] Ibid., p. 5.

[10] John. T. Gibbons, testimony before the Subcommittee on Science, Technology and Space of the Senate Committee on Commerce, Science, and Transportation, November 4, 1997, p. 3.

[11] "Information Technology Research," p. 1.

[12] Ibid., p. 8.

[13] Ibid., p. 9.

[14] "The Networking and Information Technology Research and Development Act: Background and Need for Legislation," House Science Committee, Washington, D.C., May 1999, p. 1.

Chapter 10

[1] President William J. Clinton and Vice President Al Gore, "A Framework for Global Electronic Commerce," White House, July 1, 1997, p. 3, available at www. whitehouse.gov.

[2] Seymour Martin Lipset, "Still the Exceptional Nation?" *Wilson Quarterly,* Winter 2000, p. 31.

[3] Quoted in Steve Lohr, "Welcome to the Internet, the First Global Colony," *New York Times,* January 9, 2000, sec. 4, p. 1.

[4] The National Information Infrastructure: Agenda for Action," White House, Washington, D.C., September 15, 1993.

[5] National Institute of Standards and Technology, *Putting the Information Infrastructure to Work* (Washington, D.C.: U.S. Government Printing Office, 1994); *The Information Infrastructure: Reaching Society's Goals* (Washington, D.C.: U.S. Government Printing Office, 1995).

[6] "First Annual Report," U.S. Working Group on Electronic Commerce, Department of Commerce, Washington, D.C., November 1998, p. iii.

[7] Juliana Gruenwald, "Congress Haltingly Begins Writing the Book on Internet Regulation," *CQ Weekly,* October 17, 1998, p. 2817.

[8] National Telecommunications and Information Administration, "Falling through the Net: New Data on the Digital Divide" (Washington, D.C.: Department of Commerce, 1998).

[9] Gruenwald, "Congress Haltingly Begins Writing the Book," p. 2817.

[10] Jeri Clausing, "State Legislatures Across the U.S. Plan to Take Up Internet Issues," *New York Times,* January 24, 1999, p. 15.

[11] Jim Geringer, speech to the Governing Conference on Managing Technology, Seattle, March 30, 1999, available at www.nga.org.

[12] National Governor's Association Information Technology Task Force home page, www.nga.org/InfoTech/index.asp.

Chapter 11

[1] Lionel Jospin, "Preparing France's Entry into the Information Society," speech at Universite de la Communication at Hourtin, France, August 25, 1997, p. 5, available at www.premier-ministre.gouv.fr/GB/INFO/HOURT.

[2] Marc Raboy, "Cultural Sovereignty, Public Participation, and Democratization of the Public Sphere: The Canadian Debate on the New Information Infrastructure," in Brian Kahin and Ernest Wilkson, eds., *National Information Infrastructure Initiatives: Vision and Policy Design* (Cambridge, Mass: MIT Press, 1997), p. 190.

[3] Michel Dupuy, speech at G-7 ministerial meeting on the global information infrastructure, February 26, 1995, quoted in Raboy, "Cultural Sovereignty," pp. 203–4.

[4] John Manley, speech at G-7 ministerial meeting on the global information infrastructure, February 26, 1995, quoted in Rabov, "Cultural Sovereignty," p. 205.

[5] "Connection, Community, Content: The Challenge of the Information Highway," final report of the Information Highway Advisory Council, Ottawa, September 27, 1995, Chapter 8, p. 1.

[6] "Convergence Policy Statement," Government of Canada, Ottawa, August 6, 1996.

[7] Ibid., p. 4.

[8] Ibid.

[9] Stan Skrzeszewski and Maureen Cubberley, *Future Knowledge: The Report: A Public Policy Framework for the Information Highway* (Ottawa: Canada's Coalition for Public Information, 1995).

[10] "Electronic Commerce and Canada's Tax Administration," Ministry of National Revenue, Government of Canada, Ottawa, September 1998, p. 5.

[11] "Preparing Canada for a Digital World: Final Report of the Information Highway Advisory Council," Industry Canada, Ottawa, October 8, 1997, Chapter 9, p. 3.

[12] Ibid., p. 5.

[13] "Communications in Japan," white paper, Ministry of Posts and Telecommunications, Tokyo, May 1999, Chapter 1, p. 1.

[14] "The Emerging Digital Economy II," U.S. Department of Commerce, Washington, D.C., June 1999, p. 6.

[15] "Emerging Markets, Emerging Technologies," The Global Scenarios Series of papers, Intellibridge Corporation, Washington, D.C., June 2000, p. 12.

[16] Joel West, Jason Dedrick, and Kenneth Kraemer, "Back to the Future: Japan's NII Plans," in Kahin and Wilkson, eds., *National Information Infrastructure Initiatives,* p. 100.

[17] "Program for Advanced Information Infrastructure," Ministry of International Trade and Industry, Government of Japan, Tokyo, May 1994.

[18] "Communications in Japan," p. 6.

[19] "Towards the Age of the Digital Economy: For Rapid Progress in the Japanese Economy and World Economic Growth in the 21st Century," Ministry of International Trade and Industry, Government of Japan, Tokyo, May 1997, p. 3.

[20] "IT21 Philippines: Action Agenda for the 21st Century," National Information Technology Council, Government of the Philippines, October 1997.

[21] Claro V. Parlade, "The Philippine IT Plan: Prospects and Problems," paper presented at the WTO Information Technology Symposium, Geneva, July 16, 1999.

[22] Ibid., p. 10.

[23] Prime Minister Dr. Mahatir Mohamed, "The Way Forward—Vision 2020," Prime Ministers Office, Government of Malaysia, Kuala Lumpur, 1996.

[24] "The Multimedia Super Corridor: Malaysia's Blueprint into the 21st Century," www.asiapages.com.sg/direct/text/super.

[25] "IT2000—A Vision of an Intelligent Island," National Computer Board, Government of Singapore, 1992.

[26] Ibid., p. 1.

[27] Ibid.

[28] Poh-Kam Wong, "Implementing the NII Vision: Singapore's Experience and Future Challenges," in Kahin and Wilkson, eds., *National Information Infrastructure Initiatives,* p. 45.

[29] "IT Policy and Legal Framework," National Computer Board, Government of Singapore, *www.ncb.gov.sg/nii,* p. 6.

[30] Garry Rodan, "The Internet and Political Control in Singapore," *Political Science Quarterly,* Spring 1998, p. 65.

[31] Ibid., p. 78.

[32] Ibid., p. 80.

[33] Ibid, p. 88–89.

[34] "China's Internet Explosion," *Wired* News Online, July 13, 1998, www.wired.com/news/politics/story/14099.

[35] D. LaMont Johnson and Leping Lu, "China and the Internet: Global Questions About a Global Information Infrastructure," *Computers in the Schools,* Vol. 12 (Binghamton, N.Y: Haworth Press, 1996), p. 6.

[36] John H. Taylor III, "The Internet in China: Embarking on the Information Superhighway with One Hand on the Wheel and the Other Hand on the Plug," *Dickinson Journal of International Law* 15, no. 3 (Spring 1997), p. 633.

[37] Ibid., p. 635.

[38] S. H. Kyong, "The State of the Digital Economy in Korea," paper presented at the WTO Information Technology Symposium, Geneva, July 1999, p. 1.

[39] "The Korea Basic Plan on Informatization Promotion," National Computerization Agency, Ministry of Information and Communications, Republic of Korea, January 1996, p. 1.

[40] "Cyber Korea 21: Korea's Vision for a Knowledge-Based Information Society," Ministry of Information and Communication, Republic of Korea, March 1999.

[41] Kyong, "The State of the Digital Economy in Korea," p. 2.

[42] "South Korea's New Law to Boost E-Commerce Firms," Reuter's Asia, January 13, 1998, available at www.asia.internet.com/Reuters/1999.

[43] Kuk-Hwan Jeong and John Leslie King, "Korea's National Information Infrastructure: Vision and Issues," in Kahin and Wilkson, eds., *National Information Infrastructure Initiatives,* p. 144.

[44] Dewang Mehta, "Non-Tariff Trade Barriers in I.T. Trade: Experience of India," speech at the WTO Information Technology Symposium, Geneva, July 16, 1999.

[45] Ajay Shah and Shuvam Misra, "Designing India's National Information Infrastructure," *Economic and Political Weekly* (New Delhi), November 8, 1997, p. 2880.

[46] Paul Twomey, "Electronic Commerce: Back to Basics," speech to Internet Service Providers' Convention, April 19, 1999, p. 1.

[47] Paul Twomey, "The Government Vision: Strategic Framework of the Information Economy," speech to the *Economist* Intelligence Unit Forum, July 2, 1999, available at www.noie.gov.au/speech/twomey/eiu.

[48] "Australia–United States Joint Statement on Electronic Commerce," November 13, 1998, available at www.doc.gov/ecommerce/AUfinal.

[49] "The New Australian Telecommunications Regulatory Environment," Australian Communications Authority, www.aca.gov.au/authority/overview.

[50] Twomey, "Electronic Commerce: Back to Basics," p. 6.

[51] "Consumer Protection in Electronic Commerce: Principles and Key Issues," National Advisory Council on Consumer Affairs, Federal Ministry for Customs and Consumer Affairs, Government of Australia, April 1998.

[52] "Europe's Way to the Information Society: An Action Plan," Commission of the European Communities, Brussels, July 19, 1994.

[53] Ibid., p. 2.

[54] Ibid., p. 6.

[55] "Standardization and the Global Information Society," communication from the Commission to the Council and the Parliament, European Commission, Brussels, July 24, 1996, p. 7.

[56] "Regulatory Transparency in the Internal Market for Information Society Services," Communication to the European Parliament, the Council of the European Union, and the Economic and Social Committee, European Commission, Brussels, July 24, 1996.

[57] "A European Initiative in Electronic Commerce," Communication to the European Parliament, the Council, the Economic and Social Committee, and the Committee of the Regions, European Commission, Brussels, April 12, 1997.

[58] Ibid., pp. 1, 14.

[59] Ibid., pp. 7, 20.

[60] "EU Committee Position Paper on the Communication from the Commission on a European Initiative in Electronic Commerce," American Chamber of Commerce, Brussels, August 28, 1997.

[61] Ibid., p. 15.

[62] "Business Leaders to Propose Charter to Address Problems of Internet Regulation," *Electronic Commerce and Law Report,* Bureau of National Affairs, July 1, 1998, p. 849.

[63] "Basic Indicators," Information Society Project Office, Commission of the European Community, Brussels, January 1, 1999.

[64] "Moving into the Information Society: An International Benchmarking Study," Department of Trade and Industry, Government of the United Kingdom, London, July 1997.

[65] "Agenda for Action in the United Kingdom," Stationery Office, Parliament, London, October 24, 1996.

[66] Thierry Vedel, "Information Superhighway Policy in France: The End of High Tech Colbertism?" in Kahin and Wilkson, eds., *National Information Infrastructure Initiatives,* p. 307.

[67] Julie Pitta, "Laissez-faire Not Spoken Here," *Forbes,* December 1, 1997, p. 58.

[68] Anders Henten, Knud Skouby, and Morten Falch, "European Planning for an Information Society," *Telematics and Informatics Journal* (London) 13, nos. 2–3 (Summer 1996), pp. 177–90.

[69] Jospin, "Preparing France's Entry into the Information Society."

[70] "Preparing France's Entry into the Inform@tion Society: Government Action Programme," Prime's Minister's Office, Government of France, Paris, January 16, 1998, pp. 4–5.

[71] "French Government Action Programme for the Information Society: Appraisal of the State of Progress after One Year," Interministerial Committee on the Information Society, Government of France, Paris, January 19, 1999.

[72] Ibid., p. 58.

[73] "French-American Background Paper on the Challenges of the Information Society and the Digital Economy," Office of the U.S. Trade Representative, Washington, D.C., November 1998.

[74] Interministerial Committee on the Information Society (CISI), "Appraisal of State of Progress after One Year," January 19, 1999, available at www.internet.gouv.fr/english.

[75] Erkki Ormala (director of technology policy for the Nokia Corporation), remarks at conference on "The Digital Economy in International Perspective," Washington, D.C., May 27, 1999.

[76] "Why Economic Health Gives the Finns Fits," *Wall Street Journal,* July 26, 1999, p. 1.

[77] "Finland Towards the Information Society: A National Strategy," Ministry of Finance, Government of Finland, Helsinki, January 18, 1995.

[78] Ibid., p. 3.

[79] Linnar Viik, "Information Society Indicators in Practice: Estonian Achievements," presentation at WTO Information Technology Symposium, Geneva, July 16, 1999.

[80] "CEENet Tartu Declaration," Tartu, Estonia, May 31, 1997.

[81] Omar Perez, "Regulation vs. Autoregulation: Internet Legislation in Spain," Woodrow Wilson International Center for Scholars, Washington, D.C., August 1999.

[82] "Joint U.S.-Ireland Communiqué on Electronic Commerce," Governments of Ireland and the United States, September 4, 1998, available from the Office of the U.S. Trade Representative.

[83] Howard Schneider, "In a Spin over the Web: Cautious Arab States Confront Challenges of Unleashing Internet," *Washington Post,* July 26, 1999, p. A13.

[84] Tarek Kamel and Nashwas Abdel-Baki, "Introducing Internet to Egypt: Experiences and Challenges," paper presented at the Institute of Electrical and Electronic Engineers' Global Data Networking Conference, Cairo, December 12–15, 1993.

[85] C. B. Gabbard and G. S. Park, "The Information Revolution in the Arab World: Commercial, Cultural and Political Dimensions: The Middle East Meets the Internet," RAND Corporation, Santa Monica, Calif., 1996, p. 21.

[86] Hanan Aschsaf, "Contribution of the IT Industry to Economic Development: The Israel Perspective," paper presented at the WTO Information Technology Symposium, Geneva, July 16, 1999.

[87] Brian Negin, "Legal Issues: Law and the Internet in Government," Government Information Committee, Ministry of Finance, State of Israel, Jerusalem, June 26, 1997.

[88] "The Jiddah IT Forum on E-Commerce Report," October 2–3, 1999, Harvard Information Infrastructure Program and John F. Kennedy School of Government, Harvard University, Cambridge, Mass., p. 2.

[89] Jay Naidoo, Remarks at OECD Ministerial Conference on Electronic Commerce, Ottawa, October 9, 1998, p. 3.

[90] Francis B. Nyamnjoh, "Africa and the Information Superhighway: Silent Majorities in Search of a Footpath," *Africa Media Review* 10, no. 2 (1996), p. 13.

[91] S. Yunkap Kwankam and N. Ntomambang Ningo, "Information Technology in Africa: A Proactive Approach and the Prospects of Leapfrogging Decades in the Development Process," University of Yaounde, Cameroon, 1997, available at www.twinic.net/inet97/B7.

[92] "Building Africa's Information Highway: Africa's Information Society Initiative," Economic Commission for Africa, United Nations, Addis Ababa, March 16, 1996.

[93] Amos P.N. Thapisa and Elizabeth Birabwa, "Mapping Africa's Initiative at Building an Information and Communications Infrastructure," *Internet Research: Electronic Networking Applications and Policy* (London) 6, no. 1 (1998), p. 51.

[94] "Green Paper on Telecommunications Policy," Ministry of Posts, Telecommunications, and Broadcasting, Government of South Africa, Saxonwold, September 1995, p. 37.

[95] "Joint Statement on Electronic Commerce by the governments of the United States and Chile," Santiago de Chile, April 17, 1998, available from the Office of the U.S. Trade Representative, Washington, D.C.

Chapter 12

[1] Renato Ruggiero, "Building the Framework for a Global Electronic Marketplace," address to the Ninth International Information Industry Congress (IIIC), Berlin, September 17, 1999, p. 2, available at www.wto.org/wto/speeches/berlin2.

[2] Charlene Barshefsky, "Electronic Commerce: Trade Policy in a Borderless World," address to the Woodrow Wilson International Center for Scholars, Washington, D.C., July 29, 1999, p. 2.

[3] Renato Ruggiero, "A Borderless World," address to the OECD ministerial conference, Ottawa, October 7, 1998, p. 2, available at www.wto.org/wto/speeches/ott.

[4] "Declaration on Global Electronic Commerce," WTO Ministerial Meeting, Geneva, May 20, 1998, p. 1.

[5] Barshefsky, "Electronic Commerce," p. 6.

[6] "Information Technology Policies: Organizational Structure in Member Countries," OECD, Paris, 1995.

[7] "Ad Hoc Meeting on Approaches to Content and Conduct on the Internet," Directorate for Science, Technology, and Industry, Committee for Information, Computer, and Communications Policy, OECD, Paris, July 1–2, 1997.

[8] "Electronic Commerce: Opportunities and Challenges for Government," report of the High-Level Group of Private Sector Experts on Electronic Commerce, OECD, Paris, July 1997.

[9] "Certification in the Electronic Environment," report of the Group of Experts on Security, Privacy, and Intellectual Property Protection in the Global Information Infrastructure, OECD, Paris, August 22, 1997.

[10] "Measuring Electronic Commerce," Directorate for Science, Technology, and Industry, Committee for Information, Computer, and Communications Policy, OECD, Paris, September 1997.

[11] "Gateways to the Global Market: Consumers and Electronic Commerce," OECD, Paris, March 1997.

[12] "The Economic and Social Impacts of Electronic Commerce: Preliminary Findings and Research Agenda," report prepared for the OECD Ministerial Conference on Electronic Commerce, Ottawa (Paris: OECD, October 1998).

[13] "UNCITRAL Model Law on Electronic Commerce," UNCITRAL, United Nations, New York, 1996.

[14] "UNCITRAL Digital Signature Rules Progress; U.S. Proposed Interim International Accord," *Electronic Commerce and Law Report,* Bureau of National Affairs, Washington D.C., June 10, 1998, p. 745.

[15] "Draft Uniform Rules for Electronic Signatures," UNCITRAL, Working Group on Electronic Commerce, 35th Session, Vienna, September 6–17, 1999, p. 12.

[16] Pekka Tarjanne, "The Need of International Standards for Technology Development to Serve the Information Society," speech at the International Distributed Conference, Lisbon, Sepember 28, 1998, p. 3, available at www.itu.int/plwen-cgi.

[17] "Message from Dr. Kamil Idris, Director General of WIPO," WIPO Web site, www.wipo.org.

[18] "Telecommunications Sector: Background and Bank Group Issues," presentation to executive directors at the Joint World Bank/IFC Seminar, Washington, D.C., February 16, 1994.

[19] "Harnessing Information for Development: A Proposal for a World Bank Group Strategy," Telecommunications and Informatics Sector, World Bank, Washington, D.C., 1995.

[20] "Structural and Regulatory Changes and Globalization in Postal and Telecommunications Services: The Human Resources Dimension," ILO, Geneva, April 1998, p. 2.

[21] Peter Lovelock, "Is There an Asian Model of Information Infrastructure Development?" *Pacific Review* 11, no. 1 (1998), p. 79.

[22] "Asia Behind the Curve in Internet Revolution," Reuters News Service, New Delhi, September 9, 1999.

[23] "APEC Leaders Declaration," Vancouver, Canada, November 25, 1997, p. 1, available at www.ecommerce.gov/apec.

[24] "APEC Blueprint for Action," APEC ministerial meeting, Kuala Lumpur, November 14–15, 1998.

[25] "Co-Chair's Report: First Meeting of the Electronic Commerce Steering Group," APEC, Auckland, New Zealand, June 27–28, 1999.

[26] "Ministerial Declaration of San Jose," FTAA, San José, Costa Rica, March 19, 1998, p. 1, available at www.ecommerce.gov/minister.

[27] "Plan of Action II," Summit of the Americas, OAS, Santiago, Chile, April 18–19, 1998, p. 1, available at www.ecommerce.gov/OAS.

[28] "Report with Recommendations to Ministers," Joint Committee of Experts on Electronic Commerce, Free Trade Area of the Americas, November 10, 1999, available at www.ftaa-alca.org.

²⁹ Pamela Druckerman, "Investors Rush South of the Cyberborder," *Wall Street Journal,* July 26, 1999, p. 22.

³⁰ "Report on International and Regional Bodies: Activities and Initiatives in Electronic Commerce," Directorate for Science, Technology, and Industry, Steering Committee for the Preparation of the Ottawa Ministerial Conference, October 7–9, 1998 (Paris: OECD, 1998).

Chapter 13

¹ Andrew L. Shapiro, *The Control Revolution: How the Internet Is Putting Individuals in Charge and Changing the World We Know* (New York: PublicAffairs, 1999), p. 229.

² "American Opinion: Issues Have Few Easy Solutions," *Wall Street Journal,* June 24, 1999, p. A15.

³ James Niccolai, "Government Circles in on the Net," CNN Interactive, www.cnn.com, January 13, 1999, p. 1.

⁴ President William J. Clinton and Vice President Al Gore, "A Framework for Global Electronic Commerce," United States Government, July 1, 1997, p. 4, available at www.whitehouse.gov.

⁵ Ibid., pp. 18, 25.

⁶ "Perspectives on the National Information Infrastructure: CSPP's Vision and Recommendations for Action," CSPP, Washington, D.C., January 12, 1993, p. 17.

⁷ "Perspectives on the National Information Infrastructure: Ensuring Interoperability," CSPP, Washington, D.C., February 1994.

⁸ "Perspectives on the Global Information Infrastructure," CSPP, Washington, D.C., February 1995.

⁹ "The Benefits of Global Electronic Commerce," CSPP, Washington, D.C., November 1997.

¹⁰ "Common Views Paper on GII," IIIC meeting in Tokyo, September 1994, p. 3, available from IIIC, Frankfurt.

¹¹ "Global Information Infrastructure: Industry Recommendations to the G-7 Meeting in Brussels," IIIC, Brussels, January 27, 1995.

¹² "The Opportunity and the Challenge to Sustain Rapid Internet Growth: A Policy Architecture for the Internet," Global Internet Project, ITAA, Arlington, Va., June 1998.

¹³ Robert E. Litan and William A. Niskanen, *Going Digital* (Washington, D.C.: Brookings Institution Press and the Cato Institute, 1998), p. 7.

¹⁴ Federal Election Commission reports, 1996–98, available at www.fec.gov/finance/ftpdet.

¹⁵ Ashley Craddock, "Blazing the Trail to the New Economy," *Wired* News, July 9, 1997, p. 128.

¹⁶ John Simons, "New Internet Privacy Laws Appear Less Likely with Release of New Survey," *Wall Street Journal,* April 23, 1999, p. 6.

¹⁷ "Self-Regulation and Online Privacy: A Report to Congress," Federal Trade Commission, Washington, D.C., July 13, 1999, quoted in Jerry Guidera, "FTC to Monitor How Net Firms Police Privacy," *Wall Street Journal,* July 13, 1999, p. 9A.

¹⁸ "Disney and Infoseek Initiative Privacy Policy on Go Network Portal," *Wall Street Journal,* June 30, 1999, p. B9.

¹⁹ Stephen Altobelli, "Direct Marketers Make Industry-Wide Commitment: 'Privacy Promise to American Consumers' to Build Trust," *DMA Headline News* (New York), July 7, 1999, p. 1.

[20] Online Privacy Alliance Website, www.privacyalliance.org.

[21] Christine Varney, testimony before the Subcommittee on Courts and Intellectual Property, House Judiciary Committee, May 27, 1999, available at www.privacyalliance.org.

[22] Sissela Bok, *Mayhem: Violence as Public Entertainment* (Reading, Mass.: Addison Wesley Longman, 1998), p. 3.

[23] Robert Pitofsky, "The Influence of Violent Entertainment Material on Kids: What Is to Be Done?" remarks to the meeting of the National Association of Attorneys General, Nashville, June 25, 1999, pp. 1–2, available at www.ftc.gov.

[24] John Schwartz, "It's a Dirty Job: Web Childproofers Keep Surfing Through Muck," *Washington Post,* June 23, 1999, p. A1.

[25] GetNetWise Web site, www.getnetwise.org/aboutGNW.

[26] Kenneth S. Stern, "Hate and the Internet," American Jewish Committee, New York, 1999, p. 44.

[27] C. Dianne Martin and Joseph M. Reagle, Jr., "An Alternative to Government Regulation and Censorship: Content Advisory Systems for the Internet," RSAC and WC3, George Washington University and Massachusetts Institute of Technology, p. 9, available at www.rsac.org.

[28] Stephen Balkam, "Content Rating for the Internet and Recreational Software," submission to the National Telecommunications and Information Administration report on self-regulation, p. 7, available at www.rsac.org.

Conclusion

[1] John Haltiwanger and Ron Jarmin, "Measuring the Digital Economy," Center for Economic Studies, U.S. Bureau of the Census, paper presented at Digital Economy Conference of the U.S. Department of Commerce, Washington, D.C., May 25–26, 1999, p. 1.

[2] "Ready? Set? Go! The CSPP Guide to Global Electronic Commerce Readiness," Computer Systems Policy Project, Washington, D.C., July 1998.

[3] "APEC Electronic Commerce: Readiness Assessment Tool," APEC Steering Group on Electronic Commerce, Auckland, June 1999.

[4] "Readiness for the Networked World: A Guide for Developing Countries," Center for International Development, Harvard University, Cambridge, Mass., available at www.readiness.org.

[5] Carol D'Amico, "Understanding the Digital Economy: Workforce Implications," paper presented at the Digital Economy Conference of the U.S. Department of Commerce, Washington, D.C., May 25–26, 1999.

[6] Bill Joy, "Why the Future Doesn't Need Us," *Wired,* April 2000, pp. 238–62.

Selected Bibliography

Adams, James. 1998. *The Next World War: Computers Are the Weapons and the Front Line Is Everywhere.* New York: Simon and Schuster.

Agre, Philip, and Marc Rotenberg. 1998. *Technology and Privacy: The New Landscape.* Cambridge, Mass.: MIT Press.

Ahiya, V. 1996. *Service Commerce on the Internet.* New York: A. P. Professional.

Alexander, Michael. 1997. *Net Security: Your Digital Doberman.* Research Triangle Park, N.C.: Ventana.

Arquilla, John, and David Ronfeldt, eds. 1997. *In Athena's Camp: Preparing for Conflict in the Information Age.* Santa Monica, Calif.: RAND Corporation.

Baumgardner, Gerald D. 1997. *Implementing the Internet into Higher Education.* East Rockaway, N.Y.: Cummings and Hathany.

Bell, Daniel. 1973. *The Coming of Post-Industrial Society.* New York: Basic Books.

Bender, David L., et al. 1998. *The Information Revolution: Opposing Viewpoints.* San Diego: Greenhaven.

Berleur, Jacques. 1994. *The Information Society: Evolving Landscapes.* New York: Springer-Verlag.

Bermant, Charles. 1995. *Information Technology: New Direction for the 21st Century.* Charleston, S.C.: Computer Technology Research Corporation.

Bittner, John R. 1994. *Law and Regulation of Electronic Media.* Englewood Cliffs, N.J.: Prentice-Hall.

Branscomb, Anne W. 1986. *Toward a Law of Global Communications Networks.* New York: Longman.

Branscomb, Lewis M. 1993. *Empowering Technology: Implementing a U.S. Strategy.* Cambridge: MIT Press.

Branscomb, Lewis M., and Brian Kahin. 1995. *Standards Policy for Information Infrastructure.* Cambridge, Mass.: MIT Press.

Branscomb, Lewis M., and James H. Keller. 1996. *Converging Infrastructures: Intelligent Transportation and the National Information Infrastructure.* Cambridge, Mass.: MIT Press.

———. 1998. *Investing in Innovation: Creating a Research and Innovation Policy That Works.* Cambridge, Mass.: MIT Press.

Brin, David. 1998. *The Transparent Society: Will Technology Force Us to Choose between Privacy and Freedom?* Reading, Mass.: Addison-Wesley.

Brockman, John. 1996. *Digerati: Encounters with Cyberspace Elite.* San Francisco: Hardwired.

Brown, Geoffrey. 1990. *The Information Game: Ethical Issues in a Microchip World.* Atlantic Heights, N.J.: Humanities.

Cairncross, Frances. 1997. *The Death of Distance: How the Communications Revolution Will Change Our Lives.* Cambridge, Mass.: Harvard Business School Press.

Carnoy, Martin, et al. 1993. *The New Global Economy in the Info Age.* University Park: Pennsylvania State University Press.

Cavazos, Edward A., and Gavino Morin. 1994. *Cyberspace and the Law.* Cambridge, Mass.: MIT Press.

Collins, Betty A., et al. 1996. *Children and Computers in School.* Mahwah, N.J.: Lawrence Erlbaum.

Cordell, Arthur, et al. 1997. *The New Wealth of Nations: Taxing Cyberspace.* Toronto: Between the Lines.

Cotton, Eileen. 1998. *The Online Classroom: Teaching with the Internet.* Burlington, Ind.: EDINFO.

Coyle, Diane. 1998. *The Weightless World: Strategies for Managing the Digital Economy.* Cambridge, Mass.: MIT Press.

Cronin, Mary J. 1997. *Banking and Finance on the Internet.* New York: Van Nostrand Reinhold.

Daggett, Willard, and David Newsome. 1997. *Technology in Education: Excellence vs. Equity.* Schenectady, N.Y.: International Center for Leadership in Education.

Dam, Kenneth, et al. 1996. *Cryptography's Role in Securing the Information Society.* Washington, D.C.: National Academy Press.

Defining the Internet Opportunity: Online Business Opportunities in the U.S. 1995. Sebastopol, Calif.: O'Reilly and Associates/Trish Information Services.

Dern, Daniel P. 1994. *The Internet Guide for New Users.* New York: McGraw-Hill.

Dertouzos, Michael. 1997. *What Will Be.* New York: HarperCollins.

Dyson, Esther. 1997. *Release 2.0: A Design for Living in the Digital Age.* New York: Broadway.

Etzioni, Amitai. 1999. *The Limits of Privacy.* New York: Basic Books.

Garfinkel, Simson. 1997. *Web Security and Commerce.* Sebastopol, Calif.: O'Reilly and Associates.

Gates, Bill. 1996. *The Road Ahead.* New York: Penguin.

Ghosh, Anup. 1998. *E-Commerce Security.* New York: Wiley.

Godwin, Mike. 1998. *Cyber Rights: Defending Free Speech in the Digital Age.* New York: Random House.

Gompert, David C. 1998. *Right Makes Might: Freedom and Power in the Information Age.* New York: Foreign Policy Association.

Gora, Jean Crooks. 1995. *The Internet and Online Services.* Atlanta: LOMA, Research Division.

Gurak, Laura. 1997. *Persuasion and Privacy in Cyberspace.* New Haven: Yale University Press.

Harris, Linda M. 1995. *Health and the New Media.* Mahwah, N.J.: Lawrence Erlbaum Associates.

Harris, Michael, and Stan Hannan. 1993. *Into the Future: The Foundation of Library and Information Service in the Post-Industrial Era.* Greenwich, Conn.: Ablex.

Haywood, Trevor. 1995. *Info Rich–Info Poor.* London: Bowker Sour.

Hirschfeld, Rafael. 1997. *Financial Cryptography.* Berlin: Springer.

Huber, Peter. 1997. *Law and Disorder in Cyberspace: Abolish the FCC and Let Common Law Rule the Telecosm.* New York: Oxford University Press.

Hudson, Heather. 1997. *Global Connections: International Telecommunications Infrastructure and Policy.* New York: Van Nostrand Reinhold.

Jamison, Brian, et al. 1997. *Electronic Selling.* New York: McGraw-Hill.

John, Richard. 1995. *Spreading the News: The American Postal System from Franklin to Morse.* Cambridge, Mass.: Harvard University Press.

Jones, Glenn R. 1997. *Cyberschools: An Education Renaissance.* Englewood, Colo.: Jones Digital Century.

Judy, Richard W., and Carol D'Amico. 1997. *Workforce 2020: Work and Workers in the 21st Century.* Indianapolis: Hudson Institute.

Kahin, Brian, and Janet Abbate, eds. 1995. *Standards Policy for Information Infrastructure.* Cambridge, Mass.: MIT Press.

Kahin, Brian, and James Keller, eds. 1995. *Public Access to the Internet.* Cambridge, Mass.: MIT Press.

———. 1997. *Coordinating the Internet.* Cambridge, Mass.: MIT Press.

Kahin, Brian, and Charles Nesson, eds. 1997. *Borders in Cyberspace.* Cambridge, Mass.: MIT Press.

Kalakota, Ravi, et al. 1997. *Readings in Electronic Commerce.* New York: Addison-Wesley.

Kalakota, Ravi, and Andrew B. Whinston. 1996. *Frontiers of Electronic Commerce.* New York: Addison-Wesley.

Katz, Raul Luciano. 1988. *The Information Society: An International Perspective.* New York: Praeger.

Keen, Peter, and Craig Balance. 1997. *Online Profits: A Manager's Guide to Electronic Commerce.* Cambridge, Mass.: Harvard Business School Press.

Kizza, Joseph. 1998. *Civilizing the Internet: Global Concerns and Efforts toward Regulation.* Jefferson, N.C.: McFarland.

———. 1998. *Ethical and Social Issues in the Information Age.* New York: Springer-Verlag.

Leebaert, Derek. 1991. *Technology 2001: The Future of Computing and Communications:* Cambridge, Mass.: MIT Press.

———. 1998. *The Future of the Electronic Marketplace.* Cambridge, Mass.: MIT Press.

Leer, Anne, ed. 1999. *Masters of the Wired World.* London: Financial Times/Pitman.

Levinson, Paul. 1997. *The Soft Edge: A Natural History of the Information Revolution.* New York: Routledge.

Loader, Brian. D. 1997. *The Governance of Cyberspace.* New York: Routledge.

Lucky, Robert W. 1989. *Silicon Dreams: Information, Man, and Machine.* London: St. Martin's.

Ludlow, Peter. 1996. *High Noon on the Electronic Frontier.* Cambridge, Mass.: MIT Press.

Luke, Timothy W. 1989. *Screens of Power.* Urbana: University of Illinois Press.

Lund, Leonard, and Cathleen Wild. 1993. *Ten Years after a Nation at Risk.* New York: Conference Board.

Lynch, Daniel C., and Leslie Lundquist. 1996. *Digital Money: The New Era of Internet Commerce.* New York: Wiley.

Lyon, David, and Elia Zureik, eds. 1996. *Computers, Surveillance, and Privacy.* Minneapolis: University of Minnesota Press.

MacKie-Mason, Jeffrey K., and David Waterman. 1998. *Telephony, the Internet, and the Media.* Mahwah, N.J.: Lawrence Erlbaum.

Martin, William J. 1995. *The Global Information Society*. Aldershot, U.K.: Aslib Gower.

McClure, Charles R., et al. 1994. *Libraries and the Internet/NREN*. Westport, Conn.: Mecklermedia.

McKenna, Regis. 1999. *Real Time: Preparing for the Age of the Never Satisfied Customer*. Cambridge, Mass.: Harvard Business School Press.

McKnight, Lee W., and Joseph P. Bailey, eds. 1997. *Internet Economics*. Cambridge, Mass.: MIT Press.

McLuhan, Marshall. 1964. *Understanding Media*. New York: McGraw-Hill.

Miller, Steven E. 1996. *Civilizing Cyberspace*. New York: Addison-Wesley.

Mulgan, Geoff. 1998. *Connexity: How to Live in a Connected World*. Cambridge, Mass.: Harvard Business School Press.

Negroponte, Nicholas. 1995. *Being Digital*. New York: Knopf.

Osborne, David, and Ted Gaebler. 1992. *Reinventing Government*. New York: Addison-Wesley.

Perelman, Michael. 1998. *Class Warfare in the Information Age*. London: St. Martin's.

Porter, Alan, and William Read. 1998. *The Information Revolution: Current and Future*. Greenwich, Conn.: Ablex.

Porter, James E. 1998. *Rhetorical Ethics and Internet Worked Writing*. Greenwich, Conn.: Ablex.

Radlow, James. 1995. *Computers and the Information Society*. Danvers, Mass.: Boyd and Frasier.

Scheinent, J. R., and L. Lieuroun. 1987. *Complexing Visions, Complexing Realities: Social Aspects of the Information Society*. Greenwich, Conn.: Ablex.

Schwartau, Winn. 1994. *Information Warfare*. New York: Thunders Mouth.

Scott, Allen John. 1993. *Technopolis*. Berkeley: University of California Press.

Shapiro, Andrew L. 1999. *The Control Revolution*. New York: Public Affairs.

Shapiro, Carl, and Hal Varian. 1999. *Information Rules: A Strategic Guide to the Network Economy*. Cambridge, Mass.: Harvard Business School Press.

Smith, Richard E. 1997. *Internet Cryptography*. New York: Addison-Wesley.

de Sola Pool, Ithiel. 1990. *Technologies without Boundaries*. Cambridge, Mass.: Harvard University Press.

Spar, Deborah. *Cyberrules: Problems and Prospects for Online Commerce*. Cambridge, Mass.: Harvard University Press.

Spille, Henry A., et al. 1997. *External Degrees in the Information Age.* Phoenix, Ariz.: Oryx.

Splichal, Slavko, Andrew Calabrese, and Colin Sparks. 1994. *Information and Civil Society.* West Lafayette, Ind.: Purdue University Press.

Stoll, Clifford. 1995. *Silicon Snake Oil.* New York: Doubleday.

Strate, Lance, Ronald Jacobson, and Stephanie Gibson, eds. 1996. *Communication and Cyberspace.* Cresskill, N.J.: Hampton.

Tapscott, Don. 1996. *The Digital Economy.* New York: McGraw-Hill.

———. 1998. *Growing Up Digital: The Rise of the Net Generation.* New York: McGraw-Hill.

Wayner, Peter. 1997. *Digital Cash: Commerce on the Net.* Boston: A. P. Professional.

Westin, Alan. 1967. *Privacy and Freedom.* New York: Atheneum.

Whittle, David B. 1997. *Cyberspace: The Human Dimension.* New York: W. H. Freeman.

Williams, Frederick. 1988. *Measuring the Information Society.* Newbury Park, Calif.: Sage.

Wilson, Ernest J. 1998. *Globalization, Information Technology, and Conflict in the Second and Third Worlds.* New York: Rockefeller Brothers Fund.

Wresch, William. 1998. *Disconnected: Haves and Have Nots in the Info Age.* New Brunswick, N.J.: Rutgers University Press.

Zaleski, Jeffrey P. 1997. *The Soul of Cyberspace.* San Francisco: HarperEdge.

About the Author

Leslie David Simon is Senior Policy Scholar at the Woodrow Wilson International Center for Scholars. Simon retired from the IBM Corporation in 1998 after serving as IBM's director of public affairs in Washington, D.C.; as vice president, external affairs for IBM Europe in Paris; and as vice president, communications, for IBM United States in New York.

Simon is a member of the Department of State's Advisory Committee on International Communications and Information Policy and has lectured at the National Defense University in Washington. He has testified on electronic commerce issues before the International Trade Commission and other government bodies and has served as a private-sector adviser to the U.S. Trade Representative, participating in the World Trade Organization Geneva negotiations on the Agreement on Basic Telecommunications in 1997.

Simon has also been chair of the Global Electronic Commerce Committee of the Information Technology Industry Council, co-chair of the International Information Industry Congress, and president of the Conference Board's Council of Public Affairs Executives.

Simon holds degrees from the University of Rochester and New York University and attended the University of Exeter in the United Kingdom. He and his wife, Ruth, divide their time between Boca Raton, Florida, and Washington, D.C. They have three sons and three grandchildren.

Index

431